NELSON'S
BAND of BROTHERS

ADMIRAL LORD NELSON K.B. and the VICTORY of the NILE.

In which the French Fleet consisting of 17 Sail, commanded by Admiral Brueys, were destroyed or taken, excepting 2 Ships of the Line and 2 Frigates.

"O GOD! thy Arm was here;
"And not to us, but to thy Arm alone
"Ascribe we all."

This PORTRAIT of Admiral Lord Nelson, and VIEW of

The Situation of the ENGLISH and FRENCH FLEETS, in the above memorable Engagement at the awful Moment of The French Admiral's Ship's tremendous Explosion Are zealously Inscribed to J.J. ANGERSTEIN Esq. And the Gentlemen who have so humanely, strenuously, successfully exerted themselves for the relief of the Widows & Orphans of those Seamen who bravely fell on the above occasion.

By George Riley

NELSON'S BAND OF BROTHERS

LIVES AND MEMORIALS

PETER HORE

Seaforth
PUBLISHING
In Association with the 1805 Club

Copyright © Peter Hore, 2015

First published in Great Britain in 2015 by
Seaforth Publishing
An imprint of Pen & Sword Books Ltd
47 Church Street, Barnsley
South Yorkshire S70 2AS

www.seaforthpublishing.com
Email info@seaforthpublishing.com

British Library Cataloguing in Publication Data
A catalogue record for this book is available
from the British Library

ISBN 978 1 84832 779 5

Designed by David Rose
Printed by Printworks Global Ltd,
London/Hong Kong

✦ Contents ✦

The Campaign of Trafalgar

Map of Memorials

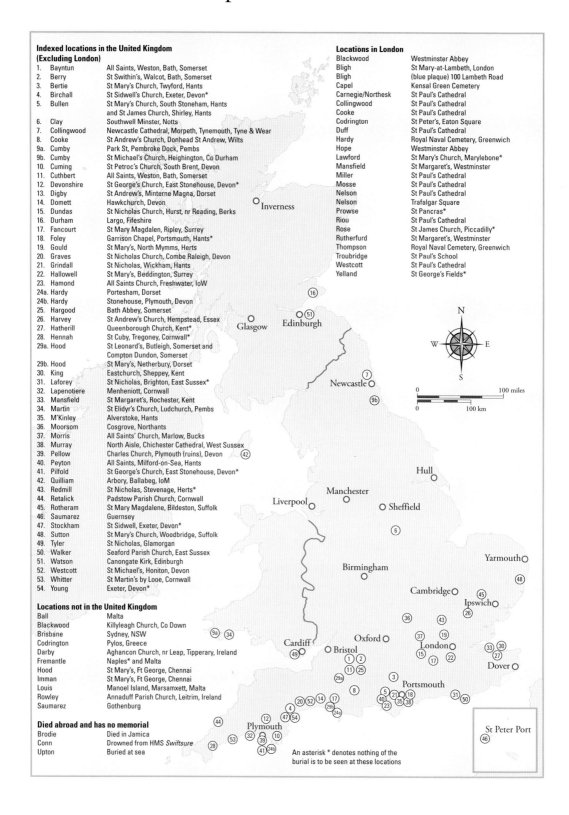

Indexed locations in the United Kingdom (Excluding London)

1. Bayntun — All Saints, Weston, Bath, Somerset
2. Berry — St Swithin's, Walcot, Bath, Somerset
3. Bertie — St Mary's Church, Twyford, Hants
4. Birchall — St Sidwell's Church, Exeter, Devon*
5. Bullen — St Mary's Church, South Stoneham, Hants and St James Church, Shirley, Hants
6. Clay — Southwell Minster, Notts
7. Collingwood — Newcastle Cathedral, Morpeth, Tynemouth, Tyne & Wear
8. Cooke — St Andrew's Church, Donhead St Andrew, Wilts
9a. Cumby — Park St, Pembroke Dock, Pembs
9b. Cumby — St Michael's Church, Heighington, Co Durham
10. Cuming — St Petroc's Church, South Brent, Devon
11. Cuthbert — All Saints, Weston, Bath, Somerset
12. Devonshire — St George's Church, East Stonehouse, Devon*
13. Digby — St Andrew's, Minterne Magna, Dorset
14. Domett — Hawkchurch, Devon
15. Dundas — St Nicholas Church, Hurst, nr Reading, Berks
16. Durham — Largo, Fifeshire
17. Fancourt — St Mary Magdalen, Ripley, Surrey
18. Foley — Garrison Chapel, Portsmouth, Hants*
19. Gould — St Mary's, North Mymms, Herts
20. Graves — St Nicholas Church, Combe Raleigh, Devon
21. Grindall — St Nicholas, Wickham, Hants
22. Hallowell — St Mary's, Beddington, Surrey
23. Hamond — All Saints Church, Freshwater, IoW
24a. Hardy — Portesham, Dorset
24b. Hardy — Stonehouse, Plymouth, Devon
25. Hargood — Bath Abbey, Somerset
26. Harvey — St Andrew's Church, Hempstead, Essex
27. Hatherill — Queenborough Church, Kent*
28. Hennah — St Cuby, Tregoney, Cornwall*
29a. Hood — St Leonard's, Butleigh, Somerset and Compton Dundon, Somerset
29b. Hood — St Mary's, Netherbury, Dorset
30. King — Eastchurch, Sheppey, Kent
31. Laforey — St Nicholas, Brighton, East Sussex*
32. Lapenotiere — Menheniott, Cornwall
33. Mansfield — St Margaret's, Rochester, Kent
34. Martin — St Elidyr's Church, Ludchurch, Pembs
35. M'Kinley — Alverstoke, Hants
36. Moorsom — Cosgrove, Northants
37. Morris — All Saints' Church, Marlow, Bucks
38. Murray — North Aisle, Chichester Cathedral, West Sussex
39. Pellow — Charles Church, Plymouth (ruins), Devon
40. Peyton — All Saints, Milford-on-Sea, Hants
41. Pilfold — St George's Church, East Stonehouse, Devon*
42. Quilliam — Arbory, Ballabeg, IoM
43. Redmill — St Nicholas, Stevenage, Herts*
44. Retalick — Padstow Parish Church, Cornwall
45. Rotheram — St Mary Magdalene, Bildeston, Suffolk
46. Saumarez — Guernsey
47. Stockham — St Sidwell, Exeter, Devon*
48. Sutton — St Mary's Church, Woodbridge, Suffolk
49. Tyler — St Nicholas, Glamorgan
50. Walker — Seaford Parish Church, East Sussex
51. Watson — Canongate Kirk, Edinburgh
52. Westcott — St Michael's, Honiton, Devon
53. Whitter — St Martin's by Looe, Cornwall
54. Young — Exeter, Devon*

Locations not in the United Kingdom

Ball — Malta
Blackwood — Killyleagh Church, Co Down
Brisbane — Sydney, NSW
Codrington — Pylos, Greece
Darby — Aghancon Church, nr Leap, Tipperary, Ireland
Fremantle — Naples* and Malta
Hood — St Mary's, Ft George, Chennai
Imman — St Mary's, Ft George, Chennai
Louis — Manoel Island, Marsamxett, Malta
Rowley — Annaduff Parish Church, Leitrim, Ireland
Saumarez — Gothenburg

Died abroad and has no memorial

Brodie — Died in Jamaica
Conn — Drowned from HMS *Swiftsure*
Upton — Buried at sea

Locations in London

Blackwood — Westminster Abbey
Bligh — St Mary-at-Lambeth, London
Bligh — (blue plaque) 100 Lambeth Road
Capel — Kensal Green Cemetery
Carnegie/Northesk — St Paul's Cathedral
Collingwood — St Paul's Cathedral
Cooke — St Paul's Cathedral
Codrington — St Peter's, Eaton Square
Duff — St Paul's Cathedral
Hardy — Royal Naval Cemetery, Greenwich
Hope — Westminster Abbey
Lawford — St Mary's Church, Marylebone*
Mansfield — St Margaret's, Westminster
Miller — St Paul's Cathedral
Mosse — St Paul's Cathedral
Nelson — St Paul's Cathedral
Nelson — Trafalgar Square
Prowse — St Pancras*
Riou — St Paul's Cathedral
Rose — St James Church, Piccadilly*
Rutherfurd — St Margaret's, Westminster
Thompson — Royal Naval Cemetery, Greenwich
Troubridge — St Paul's School
Westcott — St Paul's Cathedral
Yelland — St George's Fields*

An asterisk * denotes nothing of the burial is to be seen at these locations

Foreword

As president of the 1805 Club I welcome the opportunity to write the foreword to a new edition of *Nelson's Band of Brothers* whose illustrations have been sponsored by the club. The club has grown steadily in academic credibility since the bicentenary of the Battle of Trafalgar in 2005. The club's flagship is its annual publication, the *Trafalgar Chronicle*, to which experts and enthusiasts each year contribute their eclectic and quintessential knowledge of the age of sail and in particular of the Georgian Navy. In this vein and following on from the publication in 2005 of *Nelson's Trafalgar Captains*, the club is pleased to support the publication of *Nelson's Band of Brothers*.

This new volume comprehensively covers all those officers who commanded ships or squadrons of the fleets which fought under Nelson's tactical control at his three great sea battles. Under the editorship of Captain Peter Hore, *Nelson's Band of Brothers* has been an international effort, featuring contributors from Canada, Britain, Germany, Gibraltar, Malta, Spain, Sweden and the USA. Included among the contributors are both established subject-authors and novice writers who have researched their subjects, and uniquely for a volume of this sort, some ten contributors are descendants of men who fought under Nelson. Many of the subjects have entries in the *Oxford Dictionary of National Biography*, and size alone has prevented there being entries in this volume on all the brothers in detail comparable to the *Oxford DNB*. Nevertheless the opportunity has been taken to correct historical inaccuracies, and the contributors have tried to emphasise the incidents and the displays of character which at once unified, distinguished and separated Nelson's Band of Brothers one from another.

I congratulate the editor and the contributors on the publication of this volume in 2015, which also marks the bicentenary victory of sea power at the end of the Great War 1792–1815 and heralded in the Pax Britannica which endured for the next century.

Jonathon Band
Admiral
President of the 1805 Club

✦ Nelson and the Band of Brothers ✦

Vice-Admiral Lord Nelson was exceptional, not just for his strategic thinking and tactical flair, but for his leadership. He possessed the gift of drawing out the best from people. He trusted them and they in return resolved not to let him down. The appeal of this 'affectionate, fascinating little fellow', his personal charm and charisma, combined with some of the faults of ordinary men, which paradoxically made him more accessible, was irresistible. Nelson was deified after his death in battle, his name became synonymous with the success of the Royal Navy, and two hundred years later he remains one of the most famous of all Britons. While hundreds of books have been written about him, there is comparatively little about most of his contemporaries, and yet it would be a mistake to isolate him from the system which was the Royal Navy, the most sophisticated administrative enterprise and largest industrial complex in the world.

It was never 'Nelson's Navy': it produced him and he became its most prodigious chieftain. Nelson was the first to recognise that his astounding achievements at sea and in battle were only possible through the part played by his officers and men and especially his fellow captains, the Band of Brothers whom he 'had the happiness to command'. They formed an elite, so much so that when Lord Barham, First Lord of the Admiralty in 1805, invited Nelson to choose his captains, Nelson is alleged to have replied, 'Choose yourself, my lord. The same spirit actuates the whole profession; you cannot choose wrong.'

The phrase 'band of brothers' comes, of course, from the King's speech on the night before Agincourt in William Shakespeare's *Henry V*. Specifically Nelson used it to refer to those captains who had fought under his command at the Battle of the Nile (before that they were known as 'the fire-eaters'), but Nelson at other times used similar expressions. For example, after the Battle of Copenhagen he told the Duke of Clarence, 'It was my good fortune to command such a very distin-

guish'd set of fine fellows'. And off Cadiz in 1805 he referred to 'the best-disposed fleet of friends'. Even Admiral Lord St Vincent, not known for hyperbole in his prose, wrote about the 'elite of the Navy of England', and of Nelson's 'gallant train of heroes'. Each time they were, of course, referring to a specific group of people in the context of a battle, but they were able to do so because there was a community of men who, though from different backgrounds, shared similar experiences, motivation and aims. Consequently, in this volume I have no qualms in taking *Nelson's Band of Brothers* to encompass all those admirals, captains, commanders and lieutenants who fought under Nelson's tactical command at his three great battles.

The defining words 'tactical command' have been carefully chosen, because that excludes Hyde Parker's squadron which did not participate in the fighting on 2 April 1801, and it does not include Thomas Louis's squadron, Pulteney Malcolm's *Donegal* or Peter Parker's *Weazel*, who, though part of Nelson's operations off Cadiz until days before the Battle of Trafalgar, did not take part in the fighting on 21 October 1805.

Studies of the Band of Brothers have been attempted before, and it is apposite to consider whether there is anything new to learn. Amongst other works are Fitchett (1911), Fraser (1913), perhaps most successfully Kennedy (1951) and most recently Heathcote (2005), but the present volume is the first to attempt to record the lives of all of the Band of Brothers. The task has not been easy. In some cases the details are masked by decades of accepted story-telling or lost in the fine grain of history. Indeed, only a very few years ago it was acceptable for a writer to allege that not a great deal of information survived about one of the band's professional life, or about another that very few of details of his life and career were known for certain. These statements need to be re-examined now that the encyclopaedic works of Pam and Derek Ayshford, Patrick Marioné and Rif Winfield are available.

However, all too distressingly, writers often repeat each other and students copy a supposed authority without questioning its source, accuracy or inspiration. Two examples of this will be cited. Works about John Quilliam say he was press-ganged in Castletown harbour in 1794 and posit a story of a man of humble background rising despite the odds to the quarterdeck: yet Quilliam had already been two years at sea in *Lion*, under his patron Sir Erasmus Gower, on Macartney's embassy to China, and there is no break in his service or in Gower's patronage. Stripped of myth, a different Quilliam peers out from the pages of history. In a second example, ever since a mistake occurred in Steel's *Navy List* in 1801, every source gives William Bolton, a kinsman of Nelson, as the captain of *Arrow* at the Battle of Copenhagen, yet it is beyond dispute that the captain of *Arrow*, who signed the logbook and the ship's muster-book from February 1801 onwards, was Thomas Brodie. Only careful research can correct errors or fill gaps in our knowledge and fortunately this volume has been blessed with a company of energetic, determined and enthusiastic volunteers who have adopted several of the Band of Brothers.

The Band of Brothers were not special – not special in the sense that they had been specially chosen for the task at hand – and the eighty officers whose lives are summarised here are a small sample of the thousands of officers who served in the Royal Navy during the Great War of 1792–1815. At the Battle of the Nile, Nelson had under him some of the most battle-hardened and experienced officers and at their core a group, Hood, Saumarez and Troubridge who were the fire-eaters. They had been chosen by St Vincent at Lisbon, who sent the better officers and the better ships he had available to reinforce Nelson in the Mediterranean. At Copenhagen, Nelson was given command of a squadron chosen for no other reason than that they were the shallower-draught ships that could enter the King's Deep off the city. At Trafalgar Nelson commanded a fleet which was still being assembled when the battle took place, and others, Louis's squadron, had been detached on other

tasks essential to Nelson's operational plan. So the story of Nelson demurring from Barham's invitation to choose his officers may be apocryphal, but it rings true.

Some writers have mistakenly concluded that their subjects either went to sea at an impossibly young age or crossed from the lower deck to the quarterdeck. When in *Persuasion* (1817) Jane Austen has Sir Walter Elliot describe the Navy as 'the means of bringing persons of obscure birth into undue distinction, and raising men to honours which their parents and grandparents never dreamt of', she was enjoying a jest at the expense of her brothers Charles and Francis, and the acquaintances she had made through them, who were indeed rising in the Navy. She was referring to men whose rise within the officer class of the Navy was reflected by their rise within the class of gentlemen as a whole. There are no cases in this volume of anyone rising from the lower deck to cross onto the quarterdeck (though in some cases the sons of warrant officers did).

Each case needs to be examined closely. The supposed example of John Quilliam, already mentioned, can easily be disproved as he enjoyed the patronage of Sir Erasmus Gower from 1792 to 1798: the successive ranks he held were AB,

VICTORS OF THE NILE

'The victors of the Nile': a popular
engraving in which the original Band
of Brothers are commemorated, though
as Nelson said 'Victory is not a name
strong enough for such a scene'. Few
engravings are as handsomely coloured
as this one.

were sometimes more young
gentlemen than were allowed
as midshipmen in a ship and
the surplus served as AB, but
it is unlikely that Quilliam or
Lapenotiere, or anyone else,
changed messes as they alter-
nated ranks.

Cases of boys sent to sea
extremely young are rare and
exceptional. The orphaned
George M'Kinley was ap-
prenticed at sea aged eight as
an act of charity, and Henry Bayntun may have gone
to sea aged nine as a way of
avoiding the dangers of living ashore in Algiers. However, many boys were placed
on ship's books as admiral's,
captain's and even chaplain's
servants or as volunteers,
for the purposes of acquiring notional sea time, while
they remained at home or
at school. A score of others
who were borne in ships
before their teens proba-
bly never left home: the
practice was like putting a

quartermaster's mate, master's mate, acting lieutenant, master's mate, midshipman, acting lieutenant, and, at last in 1798, lieutenant, but he
always remained on the quarterdeck. In another
case, John Richards Lapenotiere served as gentleman volunteer, midshipman, AB, master's mate,
and midshipman before taking his examination
for lieutenant, when he produced the journal
which he had kept as an AB. Quite simply, there

child's name down for a good school. The majority of the brothers first went to sea in their teens,
usually aged about thirteen.

Less than one-fifth of this sample had any sec-
ondary education such as would be recognised in
the twenty-first century. Francis Laforey attended
Trinity College, Cambridge and went to sea aged
seventeen, and William Rutherfurd is alleged to
have attended Edinburgh University before going

to sea aged thirteen. William Carnegie (later Earl of Northesk) briefly attended Eton College and Edward Codrington went to Harrow for a pair of years. Eight others attended the nation's ancient grammar schools or its public schools, and a few attended the Royal Naval Academy in Portsmouth, and in these cases their entry into the Navy was delayed until they were fifteen or more. All the rest must have received their education at home, in village schools and at sea.

It is easy to understand that when schooled at sea they learned seamanship and the complex mathematics needed for navigation and possibly a language, and most had good handwriting. Maybe it was navigational reckoning, illustrating their journals (they could nearly all draw well), and keeping decklogs which trained their minds, but some other process was at work too. Nelson could quote Shakespeare, James Saumarez was versed in the Classics, and Collingwood (though he only enjoyed two years at the Royal Grammar School in Newcastle) wrote peerless prose. Some importance was placed on languages, and, for example, Nelson and Alexander Ball studied in France (James Saumarez studied in England, as

French was his mother tongue).

On completion of sea service of six years, a midshipman could present himself to be examined for lieutenant: sea service was carefully calculated, to the day, in the Navy Office and amounted to 2,184 days. The candidate also had to present a certificate that he was older than twenty years. Patrick Marioné has shown that since many young officers entered the Navy younger than fourteen, their six years' sea service were completed when they were between seventeen and nineteen. However, a study of certificates of sea service show that most presented themselves for examination within weeks of completing the required six years. To do so many, maybe more than 50 per cent, produced false certificates of age showing them to be twenty or more years old. Overseas, the commander-in-chief of a fleet or station had greater freedom to appoint acting lieutenants, commanders and captains, but on return home candidates for lieutenant still had to pass in London. So, more than a third were

Nelson lies in the crypt of St Paul's with monuments beside him to Captain John Cooke of the *Billy Ruffian* and *Mars'* Captain George Duff who also fell at the Battle of Trafalgar.

lieutenants by the time they were twenty; another third did not become lieutenants until they were in their mid- to late twenties, and the average age on promotion was twenty-two.

Thereafter talent and opportunity played a much greater role in promotion to commander and to captain. For the average officer it was ten years from promotion to lieutenant to being made post captain at about thirty-two, though even the precocious Nelson, who was twenty-one and had spent just two years as lieutenant, was beaten (in this sample) by Thomas Bladen Capel, Graham Eden Hamond, and Richard King who had noble birth or political influence or were the sons of senior officers. Hamond (1779–1862) was also the last of all the Band of Brothers to die. For the record, the earliest born was Robert Devereux Fancourt (1742–1826).

Patronage was also important to promotion and careers. A study of the returns of officers' services at The National Archives at Kew reveals the extraordinary extent to which an officer's career was governed by patronage. It was usual for a young man having won a position at sea to follow his captain from ship to ship until he was promoted to lieutenant or commander. It was also usual for an officer in mid-career to form a close professional relationship with a senior officer and stay with him for a number of years. For example, the Dorset-born Thomas Masterman Hardy's patrons from 1781 to 1793 were his father's neighbour Francis Roberts and other Dorset men (and this was a favour which he returned to Roberts's grandsons); then from 1796 onwards Hardy's career was intimately involved with Nelson's. There are so many similar cases amongst the eighty or so in this sample of officers that the custom must have been the rule rather than the exception. The effect of patronage was magnified by the great naval dynasties like the Graveses, the Hoods and the Parkers. Others like Constantine John Phipps was not only one of young Nelson's patrons but patron to William Pryce Cumby, Thomas Graves and Robert Moorsom. Nelson himself favoured young men from Norfolk.

There were two factors which had the capability to unify or to divide: these were religion and prize-money. The Band of Brothers were predominantly Protestants and some of them supported the 'blue lights' or Evangelical movement which had been growing in strength in the Navy since the American War; Jonas Rose was presumably the only Catholic (the Test Act which was still force); and several of the Band of Brothers were Freemasons (the Royal Naval Lodge was founded in 1739, the symbology of the Nile medal was redolent of Masonry, and Nelson was admitted to the Ancient Order of Gregorians in 1801). Prize-money was an obsession: the Brothers competed for cruises when they might earn prize-money and they sued each other in courts over their shares. Some officers, like John Cooke and Henry Digby, made themselves fabulously wealthy through prize-money (though Cooke did not live to enjoy his fortune), and others like Richard Retalick and John Stockham, for want of prize-money, left their widows in poverty.

The largest single caucus amongst the Brothers came from established Scottish families with military or naval or noble backgrounds. Of the others, 4 came from North America (all born before Independence), 5 from Ireland, 2 each from Wales and the Isle of Man, one from Guernsey and all the rest from England. In proportion to the size of their populations, Scotland and England provided a roughly equal number of Brothers (10 and 55 respectively), whilst Wales and Ireland provided a rather lower proportion (2 and 5). Notably, a quarter of the English officers, like their men, came from just two counties, Devon and Cornwall (16). A significant group (7) came from the hinterland of two ports, Newcastle upon Tyne and Whitby in the north-east of England. A very important minority of officers, as is discussed in an essay at the end of this volume, hailed from North America.

It is more difficult to be categorical about the social origins of the Brothers. Two dozen of the Brothers came from naval families. The younger sons of the nobility and scions of minor nobility provided a dozen, another dozen were sons of landed gentry, and half a dozen were sons of parsons, in an age when the cloth was less a calling and more a profession for gentlemen. All the rest were the sons of ship-owners, farmers, merchants, and tradesmen including a maltster, an oilman and two bakers.

The years 1775 to 1815 were an era of near continuous warfare, with only brief and partial pauses in the years 1783–1792 and in 1802, and the Band of Brothers were well-tempered in battle. The principal wars and battles mentioned in this volume are:

1775–1783 The American Revolutionary War, the American War of Independence, or simply, as it was known at the time, the American War.

1780 The Moonlight Battle, also sometimes called the Battle of Cape St Vincent.

1781 The Battle of the Chesapeake, or Battle of the Capes, a crucial naval battle in the American War.

1782 The Battle of the Saintes, a four-day battle in April when Rodney broke the French line.

1790 The Spanish Armament or Nootka Crisis, when Britain armed itself for war over the arrest, by the Spanish, of British ships in the Nootka Sound on the west coast of North America. (Its significance is that many officers' careers – but not Nelson's! – which had languished during the years of peace were boosted when large numbers of ships were rapidly commissioned.).

1792–1815 The French Revolutionary and Napoleonic Wars, or simply the French War. Also referred to as the Great War.

1794 The Battle of the Glorious First of June: the British won tactically but a much-needed grain convoy from America arrived in France. Both sides proclaimed victory.

1797 Battle of Cape St Vincent.

1798 Battle of the Nile, sometimes called the Battle of Aboukir Bay.

1801 Battle of Copenhagen (there was another Battle of Copenhagen in 1807).

1802 The Peace of Amiens, a temporary lull in the French War.

1805 The Battle of Trafalgar.

Finally, a mention must be made of the Royal Marines, whose own glorious history is entwined with their parent service, the Royal Navy. No officers of the Royal Marines have entries in this volume, because none were in tactical command of ships at Nelson's three great battles, but they can never be forgotten. There were, for example, 84 officers and 2,783 marines at Trafalgar, and because they served largely on the upper deck and in the rigging, they suffered a higher rate of casualties than the seamen. Captain Charles Adair was shot on the quarterdeck of *Victory* within a few minutes of Nelson, and Sergeant James Secker helped carry the dying Nelson below; and Lieutenant James Atcherley accepted the surrender of *Bucentaure* and took Admiral Pierre-Charles Villeneuve into custody. For the Royal Marines, these were commonplace actions in their long history of exceptional service.

All told, the Brothers were an eclectic and diverse group of men, but as is shown here, it was that great leader of men, Nelson, who took what officers he was given to command, touched them with his magic, and forged them into a unique, irresistible Band of Brothers.

PETER HORE

Collingwood House
Menorca
October 2014

THE
BATTLE
OF THE
NILE

Detail from Robert Dodd's painting 'The Blowing up of the
French Flagship *Orient* at the Battle of the Nile 1 August 1798'.

✦ Introduction ✧

By 1798 France controlled Northern Italy, the Low Countries and the Rhineland, and of the European powers which had been allied against France in five years of revolutionary war, only Britain remained in arms against the French. In the Mediterranean, France was allied to Spain, and for two years the British had felt obliged to vacate all their bases in the Mediterranean, except Gibraltar. St Vincent had withdrawn the Mediterranean Fleet to the Tagus, where Portugal was Britain's last continental ally.

However, by May 1798 Nelson was a rear-admiral and was newly restored to health after his wounding at Santa Cruz de Tenerife in the previous year. St Vincent now felt able to send a small force back to the Mediterranean and in May he sent Nelson in *Vanguard* (Captain Edward Berry), *Alexander* (Captain Alexander Ball), and *Orion* (Captain Sir James Saumarez) and two frigates and a sloop. By the end of the month Nelson had learned that an expedition under Bonaparte was about to depart from Toulon but he knew not its destination. When his squadron reached the Îles d'Hyères, they were struck by a storm and *Vanguard* dismasted, only being saved by the extraordinary exertions and seamanship of Alexander Ball. Meanwhile Bonaparte had sailed: on 19 May he was off Genoa, on the 23rd Corsica, on the 30th the Strait of Bonifacio, gathering reinforcements as he went, and on 9 June he was off Malta which soon fell to him.

Nelson completed repairs to *Vanguard* and was off Toulon on 31 May, but the horse had bolted. On 7 June Nelson's fleet received substantial reinforcements but his pursuit was frustrated by light airs. He concentrated his search between Naples and Sicily and did not pass through the Straits of Messina until 20 June. That day Nelson wrote to assure the Grand Master of Malta that he was sailing towards Malta 'with a full determination to prevent your island from falling into the hands of the common Enemy'. Two days later he learned that the French had already taken and garrisoned Malta and sailed again, destination unknown.

Nelson worried that Egypt was Bonaparte's destination and renewed his pursuit to the east. The fleets were so close that on the night of 21/22 June his signal guns were heard in the French flagship, *Orient*, and in the early hours of 22 June, south of Sicily, *Defence* sighted sails to the east-south-east. An hour later Nelson received intelligence from a neutral ship that the French had sailed from Malta, and *Culloden* reported that the strange sail were east by north. At 6.46am *Leander* signalled, 'Strange ships are frigates' but Nelson replied, 'Call in chasing ships'. He must have had doubts for at 7pm, while the strange sail were in sight, he summoned on board 'those Captains in whom I place great confidence [Saumarez, Troubridge, Ball and Darby]'. His council decided that Alexandria was the French destination, and Nelson set course hoping 'to arrive time enough to frustrate their plans'. At 8.29 *Leander* repeated that the strange sail were frigates, but Nelson was determined that nothing would now deter him from keeping his fleet together and pressing on to Egypt. The exchange of messages by flag was read and repeated by several ships in the fleet, but one can only guess at the incredulity which this caused when Nelson decided to ignore the largest ships which he had seen since starting his Mediterranean chase.

The frigates were, of course, the outlying ships of Bonaparte's fleet, and Nelson had missed a chance to change the course of history.

On 28 June Nelson arrived off Alexandria, saw that the harbour was empty of French ships, and sent the little *Mutine* in for news. Offshore Nelson, in a paroxysm of anxiety, waited a day before sailing first north-east towards Syria and then west towards the central Mediterranean. Nelson had arrived – and left on the 29th – in such 'time enough' that he had arrived before the French.

The next day at 1pm a French lieutenant from the frigate *Junon* landed at Alexandria and so, while Nelson sailed northwards, Bonaparte was able to land on 1 July 1798 in Egypt unopposed and thus to threaten India (as was believed by Nelson and in London). After disembarking troops, Brueys, the French admiral took his fleet to Aboukir Bay, some twenty miles north-east of Alexandria, there to await developments.

Eventually a lonely, enervated and frustrated Nelson reached Syracuse on 19 July from where he wrote to Sir William Hamilton in Naples that he was as ignorant of the enemy 'as I was twenty-seven days ago'. On the same day he wrote to Lady Nelson (this was before his great infatuation with Emma Hamilton), 'We have been off Malta, to Alexandria in Egypt, Syria, into Asia and are returned here without success … I yet live in hopes of meeting these fellows: but it would have been my delight to have tried Bonaparte on a wind.' His use of the past tense perhaps reveals his dawning sense of having failed.

After watering at the Fountain of Arethusa, on 23 July Nelson wrote, 'No frigates! – to which has been and may again be attributed the loss of the French fleet.' Meanwhile on 21 July Alexandria was visited by two British frigates, *Seahorse* and *Terpsichore*, who seeing French flags flying ashore, sailing westwards to warn Nelson: somewhere in the eastern Mediterranean even they missed him.

Nelson's next dispatch, to St Vincent, was on 3 August after the Battle of the Nile. On 1 August *Swiftsure* and *Alexander* reached Alexandria and also saw French flags flying, but no enemy fleet. There was despondency throughout Nelson's ships until in mid-afternoon the French were sighted at anchor in Aboukir Bay, in line of battle, flanked by shoals and smaller vessels and protected by guns and mortars on land, 'but nothing could withstand the Squadron your Lordship did me the honour to place under my command'.

However strong Brueys' position, despite the imminent sunset, and lacking

charts, Nelson attacked at once. Thomas Foley in *Goliath* led the way on the inshore of the French ships and soon their van was doubled and defeated, and in a fierce night-time action all but two ships and two frigates were taken.

When St Vincent read the news he wrote enthusiastically to Nelson: 'God be praised! and you and your gallant band rewarded by a grateful country! for the greatest achievement the history of the world can produce.' To London he wrote of 'the almost incredible and stupendous victory … which Rear-Admiral Sir Horatio Nelson and his gallant train of heroes has under the blessing of God obtained over the Toulon squadron'.

No one asked what might have happened to the course of the war or to world history if, either on 22 June or a week later, Nelson had 'tried Bonaparte on a wind'. Instead, to the Lord Mayor of London Nelson sent a captured sword with the message that 'Britannia still rules the Waves': the Lord Mayor responded with the freedom of the City and a fine sword commemorating the victory.
PETER HORE

The Panorama was built in Leicester Square, London in the 1790s and this is the flyer for a show entitled *A Short Account of Lord Nelson's Defeat of the French at the Nile.*

❖ BALL ❖

Alexander John Ball (1757–1809) was born at Stonehouse Manor, Stroud, Gloucestershire, the great-grandson of Marshe Dickinson, lawyer, MP, and Lord Mayor of London in 1756–7. Young Ball was educated at the King's School, Gloucester. In the 1700s the Ball family was impoverished by a disastrous series of court cases fought over land and property, and when Ball's father died suddenly and intestate, administration of the Stonehouse estates was granted to one of the creditors. So, aged thirteen, young Ball was shipped off to the Royal Naval Academy at Portsmouth, and in 1772–3 he served in *Pearl* (32) and then *Nautilus* (16), starting in both ships rated 'able' and later midshipman. In February 1774 Ball joined *Preston* (50) where he met and befriended Midshipman Cuthbert Collingwood.

In the American War Ball served in *Egmont* (74, Captain John Elphinstone), at the Battle of Ushant on 7 July 1778 and the following day he transferred to *Magnificent* (74) where he was made lieutenant. His next ship was *Atalanta* (14) on the North America station, where in May 1780 he moved into the captured Spanish frigate *Santa Monica* (32). 1781

saw Ball gain Admiral Rodney's patronage and he moved with him to *Sandwich* (98), *Gibraltar* (80) and *Formidable* (90). In the aftermath of the Battle of the Saintes he was made commander of *Germaine* (16), and, on 20 March 1783, Ball was made post-captain at the age of twenty-six.

In the peace which followed, Ball travelled to France where he incurred the wrath – or envy – of one Horatio Nelson who, in a letter to his patron Captain William Locker, noted the presence of Captain Ball and another captain in St-Omer: 'Two noble captains are here, Ball and Shepherd. They wear fine epaulettes for which I think them great coxcombs. They have not visited me and I shall not, be assured, court their acquaintance.'

In 1785 Ball married Mary Smith at St James's, Piccadilly, and their son was christened William Keith, possibly a compliment to the Elphinstones, at St Alfege's, Greenwich, three years later.

Ball had command of *Nemesis* (28) during the Spanish Armament, and unlike some for whom the armament only meant temporary employment, over the next few years Ball held other commands. In early 1798 Ball in *Alexander* (74) was put under command of newly-promoted Rear-Admiral Nelson, whose welcome was not warm: 'What,' said the admiral, 'Are you come to have your bones broken?' The suave Ball replied that he certainly had no wish to have his bones broken, unless his duty to his King and Country required such a sacrifice, and then they should not be spared.

On 8 May Nelson, Ball, and Saumarez sailed from Gibraltar, but on the 20th Nelson's flagship *Vanguard* was dismasted and left foundering in a storm. Ball took her in tow and when they reached Sardinia, Nelson lost no time in going on board *Alexander* to embrace Ball and exclaim, 'A friend in need is a friend indeed!' and from that moment a very firm friendship commenced. A somewhat chastened Nelson wrote to Fanny his wife:

'Figure to yourself this proud, conceited man, when the sun rose on Monday morning, his Ship dismasted, his Fleet dispersed, and himself in such distress, that the meanest Frigate out of France would have been a very unwelcome guest. But it

LEFT: In 1810 the Maltese people built a monument in Ball's memory and as testament of their love and respect.

BELOW: The monument to Ball in the Lower Barrakka Gardens as it appears today.

has pleased Almighty God to bring us into a safe Port … I ought not to call what happened to the *Vanguard* by the cold name of accident; I believe firmly that it was the Almighty's goodness to check my consummate vanity. I hope it has made me a better officer, as I feel confident it has made me a better man.'

Nelson soon discovered the injustice he had done to Ball's character and abilities; he wrote numerous letters to Ball, and in the weeks which followed Ball became one of Nelson's closest advisers.

On 1 August 1798 Nelson sent Ball to look into Alexandria where he reported that the French flag was flying. So, when the French fleet was seen in Aboukir Bay and Nelson signalled his ships to form line of battle as convenient, *Alexander* was towards the rear end of the British line. Entering the bay, Ball made directly for a position from where he could rake the stern of the French flagship *Orient*, and it was *Alexander*'s shots which started the fire that caused the Frenchman to explode. When Ball realised that the fire on the Frenchman was out of control, he cut his anchor cable and drifted down onto another French target, *Tonnant*, and when he thought that *Orient* would drift down on him, he cut his remaining anchor cable. Even so, when *Orient* did blow up, burning timbers fell on and around *Alexander*, starting small fires and obliging Ball to cut away some of his sails. *Alexander* drifted for about two hours while Ball put his ship in

order and then he recommenced the fight against three French ships to the south, where at sunrise he was still in action. Surprisingly *Alexander*'s casualties were just 1 officer and 13 seamen killed, while Ball and 3 other officers, 48 seamen and 5 marines were wounded.

Six weeks later, when some of the victorious British ships arrived at Naples, Ball, in common with some other officers, fell under the spell of Lady Hamilton.

In October 1798 Ball was ordered to take over the blockade of Malta from Portuguese allies, with the object of ousting the French garrison, a blockade which would last many months and seal Ball's future. Ball endeared himself to the Maltese, and in February 1799 the Maltese legislature elected Ball their president and commander-in-chief: he was now 'at liberty to go ashore to act as commander-in-chief of all the Maltese people and all such seamen and marines on the island of Malta'. The king of Naples conferred on him the title of Governor of Malta, and in May 1800, Tsar Paul, as Grand Master, made Ball an Honorary Commander of the Order of St John of Jerusalem. For her part in aiding the Maltese, Lady Hamilton became Dame Petit Croix of the order.

The siege of the French ensconced in Valletta might not have lasted so long had the besieging forces been united, but British generals lobbied against Ball, while the British, Neapolitan and Russian governments argued about whose flag was to fly when the French were defeated. At the end of the siege, Ball, who was now strongly identified with the Maltese people, was denied a role in negotiating the surrender of the French garrison, a political blunder as the Maltese, who had asked for British help which they had received through the intervention of Ball, lost faith in their protectors.

Instead, in May 1801 Ball was appointed to an administrative post as Commissioner of the Navy in Gibraltar. From the Baltic in June, Nelson wrote to console him: 'My dear, invaluable friend … believe me, my heart entertains the very warmest affection for you … but as I trust the war is at an end, you must take your flag when it comes to you, for who is to command our fleets in a future war? … I pity the poor Maltese; they have sustained an irreparable loss in your friendly counsel and an able director in their public concerns; you were truly their father.'

By December 1801 Ball was reunited at home with his family after four years' absence. However, in May 1802, Ball returned to Malta as His Majesty's Plenipotentiary to the Order of St John of Jerusalem, charged with overseeing the evacuation of British forces under the terms of the Peace of Amiens. When the peace faltered, Ball procrastinated; perhaps he knew that Bonaparte had said that he would rather see the British in possession of a Parisian suburb than in Grand Harbour, Malta.

Almost as soon as Ball arrived back at Malta he acquired enemies who accused him of maladministration and engaged him in a bitter disagreement. They were spurred on by one William Eton, who had set his sights on Ball's position, and Vincenzo Borg, who had been an ally during the siege. Together Ball and Borg had stirred Malta into the arms of Great Britain, yet for some reason relations between these two pioneers in early Maltese statehood ended in feud.

In May 1804 Ball appointed as his private secretary, and then as Public Secretary, the poet Samuel Taylor Coleridge, who described Ball as 'a truly great man'.

In October 1805 Ball heard that he was promoted to rear-admiral, a pleasure tarnished by news of Trafalgar and of the death of Nelson. As the news spread through the Mediterranean, Ball wrote on 25 November to the British Minister at Naples:

> Before this reaches you, you will probably have heard of the greatest Victory gained over the Combined Fleets of France and Spain by Lord Nelson that ever adorned the British Navy … Our joy upon so glorious an event [is] deeply clouded by the irreparable loss of the Hero who has by his brilliant Action exceeded his former exploits and crowned his career with immortal Fame. I have not only to lament the death of our dear Nelson, as a public loss, but to feel it as an invaluable and sincere friend to whom I was under the greatest obligations.

Ball lived simply, which Lord Byron discovered in 1809 when he landed on Malta on his continental tour. Byron was rattled at not being given a personal welcome and a gun salute by Ball, described Lady Mary as being 'rather stiff', and remarked 'dinner [was] all in one course, with lectures on temperance and commendation of our abstinence'.

Rear-Admiral Sir Alexander John Ball died after a short illness on 25 October 1809 at the palace of San Anton. After a lying in state, he was buried with great pomp on 31 October.

LIAM GAUCI

→ CUTHBERT ←

Robert Cuthbert (1755–1821) was baptised in Chelsworth, Suffolk, on 17 September 1755, the son of John Cuthbert, a maltster, and he entered the Navy rated 'able' in *Invincible* (74, Captain Hyde Parker) on 7 January 1777.

Having spent a year in *Invincible* in the Channel and at Gibraltar, at some point being rated midshipman, he transferred in February 1778 to *Minerva* (32). He served in *Minerva* off the African coast and in the Caribbean until in August 1778 she was captured by the French *Concorde* (32). Cuthbert was exchanged or freed in 1779, travelling from Jamaica to England in *Blast* (16) and then back to the Caribbean in *Salamander* (8, Commander Seymour Finch). His next ship was *Thunderer* (74) and in April 1780 Cuthbert joined *Sandwich* (90), flagship of Rear-Admiral George Rodney, later Lord Rodney. Cuthbert served in *Sandwich* for nine months in 1780 and 1781, being rated 'able' for seven months and midshipman for the last two; he was present at Rodney's two actions against the French fleet under de Guichen in April and May 1780.

He must have impressed Rodney since, 'by Order of Adml. Rodney', he was appointed fifth lieutenant in *Montagu* (74, Captain George Bowen),

and there he saw action in Admiral Graves's battle with de Grasse off the Chesapeake on 5 September 1781 and again under Rodney at the Saintes in April 1782. In July 1782, again as a result of Rodney's direct order, he was appointed lieutenant in *Lively* (12, Lieutenant Michael Stanhope). *Lively* was captured late in 1782 by American prisoners she was carrying; they sailed her to Havana and Cuthbert was freed.

Cuthbert returned to England in 1783 and became unemployed. During the Nootka Sound crisis in 1790, Cuthbert served as 'able' or midshipman in *Juno* (32, Captain Samuel Hood), *Iris* (32, Captain Thomas Wells) and *Assistance* (50, Captain Lord Cranstoun). He was clearly difficult to place because, though he had served temporarily as a lieutenant during the American War, he had not amassed the six years' sea time necessary for a lieutenant's commission. When the crisis was over, Cuthbert was unemployed again.

The start of the French war saw him still only rated 'able' in the store ship *Camel,* Captain Benjamin Hallowell, and midshipman in *Mentor* (10) and *Sandwich* (90, Captain James Mosse). At last, having accumulated his six years' sea time, Cuthbert was examined and passed for lieutenant on 8 October 1793, and appointed to *Thorn* (14, Commander Edward Foote) in the North Sea and Caribbean until March 1796.

The names of his commanding officers are given here because they show that, though Cuthbert served with some famous and succesful officers, and had caught Rodney's eye, he enjoyed little 'interest' and acquired no patron. His appointment in March 1796 to *Majestic* (74) under Captain George Westcott seems to have been at random.

Majestic sailed to the Caribbean and back before joining the Channel Fleet on the blockade of Brest late in 1796. At Plymouth in early 1797, the Majestics joined the Great Mutiny but order was soon restored and she put to sea in May, returning to the Channel blockade until late 1797 when she sailed south to join Lord St Vincent's fleet off Cadiz. In May 1798, *Majestic* was sent into the Mediterranean to reinforce Nelson's fleet,

Detail of Cuthbert's Nile sword and dirk.

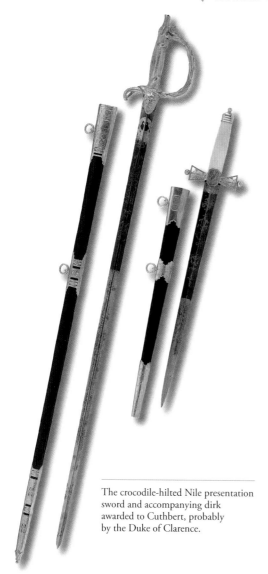

The crocodile-hilted Nile presentation sword and accompanying dirk awarded to Cuthbert, probably by the Duke of Clarence.

where as the Battle of the Nile began, Cuthbert was *Majestic*'s first lieutenant.

As the action in Aboukir Bay began, Westcott identified *Tonnant* (80) as his target and bore down upon her; he intended to engage *Tonnant*'s starboard side with *Majestic*'s starboard battery but the anchor failed to stop his way and he overshot, entangling his mizzen rigging with the jib-boom of the next French ship, *Heureux* (74). Westcott was shot in the throat by a French marksman and died almost at once, command of the ship thus devolving upon Cuthbert.

In the dark and smoke, *Majestic* was entangled with an enemy and her guns could not easily be

brought to bear, but *Heureux*'s jib-boom broke, *Majestic* drifted alongside and commenced a gun-to-gun and yard-to-yard duel. In the confusion Cuthbert finally anchored between *Heureux*'s stern and the bow of the next ship in the line, *Mercure* (74). So devastatingly did Cuthbert rake his two opponents that they both cut their cables and drifted inshore. Cuthbert now warped *Majestic* towards the port quarter of *Tonnant*, a ship much more heavily armed than his own, and engaged her at very close range with his starboard guns, his port guns continuing to fire on the now grounded *Heureux* and *Mercure*.

The consequences of the victory at the Nile for Cuthbert were swift and gratifying: Nelson wrote saying,

> In consequence of your gallant conduct in fighting His Majesty's Ship *Majestic* after the death of the brave Captain Westcott you are required and directed to take command of her, until his Lordship's, the Commander in Chief's, pleasure is known.

Further, Nelson wrote to St Vincent, his commander-in-chief Mediterranean,

> I have the honor to enclose a copy of the order by which Lieutenant Cuthbert commands the *Majestic*, so highly honorable to him, and in addition, every Officer in the Squadron, he served so gloriously in, proclaims his conduct to have been equally judicious and intrepid, after the fall of his gallant Captain: I therefore

have Encouraged him to hope your Lordship will recommend him to the Board for the rank of Post-captain.

Cuthbert's commission as a post-captain was dated 28 November 1798 and he remained in command of *Majestic* until 21 March 1799.

However, thereafter he was unemployed until January 1801 when he was given command of his former ship, *Montagu*, which by 1801 was old and rotten. On 15 February 1801, in heavy weather off Portugal, she lost her main and mizzen masts and her fore topmast, which reduced her to a wallowing hulk in danger of capsize. Skilfully Cuthbert brought her into the Tagus to refit. There followed another period in unemployment until Cuthbert was given a last appointment, *Orion*, where he remained until July 1802.

On 7 July 1803, at St George's, Hanover Square, he married Elizabeth Willock of Bedford Square, London. Captain Robert Cuthbert died at Bath in 1821 and was buried at the parish church of Weston.

STEPHEN WOOD

→ DARBY ←

Henry D'Esterre Darby (1749 – 1823) has the distinction of having been born in the most haunted castle in Ireland, Leap Castle in Tipperary.

Darby went to sea aged thirteen but took fourteen years to become a lieutenant, albeit in *Britannia* (100), flagship of his uncle Sir George Darby, who was commander-in-chief of the Channel Fleet 1779–82 at a time of great crisis for Britain. This suggests that, despite his uncle's patronage, he was not altogether gifted. Nevertheless his uncle ensured that Darby was given command of *Infernal* (8) on an expedition to take the Cape of Good Hope from the Dutch, but in an inconclusive battle in the Cape Verde islands, the Battle of Porto Praya, on 16 April 1781, Darby was clumsy enough to be captured by the French. Even though *Infernal* was soon abandoned, Darby and his crew were taken away as prisoners. He does not appear to have escaped this indignity until the end of the war, when, nevertheless, he was made post-captain, though at the relatively late age of thirty-four. He spent the next ten years of the peace ashore.

However, when war was renewed he was given in quick succession *Amphitrite* (28), *Pomona* (28) and *Adamant* (50), escorting convoys to and from the Mediterranean and the West Indies. In late 1796 he was given his most famous command, *Bellerophon* (74). His appointment was marked by a piece of singular good fortune: he was supposed to dine with Israel Pellew in his ship *Amphion* on the evening, 22 September 1796, when she blew up, but Darby was delayed by business with the port admiral and had just stepped into his boat when he heard the explosion.

Bellerophon was at the blockade of Cadiz in 1797, before she was detached to join Nelson in the Mediterranean, and the hunt for Bonaparte and the French fleet. When, on 22 June, the British and French fleets passed within a few miles of each other, and Nelson called a council of war of four of his most senior and valued captains, Darby was included with Ball, Saumarez, and Troubridge, though by some accounts he contributed least to the discussion.

It is not clear what Darby intended to do during the Battle of the Nile itself as he sailed down the outside of the French line – he may have intended to exchange broadsides with *Franklin* (74) or to rake *Orient* (120) – but at 7pm whether by bad luck or bad seamanship he anchored by the stern alongside the three-decker, which with her heavier armament towered over *Bellerophon*. With the advantage of height, French marines were able to pick off their targets and Darby was one of the first to fall, hit on the head and rendered unconscious. At 8pm *Bellerophon*'s mizzen mast fell and as *Orient* began to burn, *Bellerophon* suffered yet more casualties. Her log records: 'At 9, observing our antagonist on fire on the middle gun deck, cut the stern cable and wore clear of her by loosing the spritsail – shortly, the fore mast went over the larboard bow. Employed clearing the wreck and putting out the fire which had caught in several places of the ship.'

Darby had recovered and resumed command as *Bellerophon* drifted out of action, and was about a mile away when 'At 10 *L'Orient* blew up. Got up jury sails on the stumps of the masts, the winds favouring us enabled us to clear the French fleet.' *Bellerophon* was fortunate, for in the darkness Hallowell in *Swiftsure* passed a dismasted ship leaving the line of battle, but declined to open fire. It took the rest of the night to clear away the wreckage and begin to repair the hull, but by 4am sufficient cable had been spliced together for her to drop anchor. At dawn *Bellerophon* was discovered about six miles away, mastless, but with an ensign flying from the stump of her mainmast. Her casualties were 49 killed and 148 wounded. Nelson wrote: 'My Dear Darby, I grieve for your heavy loss of Brave fellows, but look at our glorious Victory. We will give you every assistance as soon as you join us, till then God Bless You. Ever yours faithfully, Horatio Nelson.' He too had been wounded in the head and added: 'We shall both I trust soon get well.'

Darby returned to England in the spring of 1800 and commanded the new-built *Spencer* (74), and was part of Robert Calder's fleet when he was sent in search of a French fleet which was thought to have gone to the West Indies in 1801. He took part in the Battles of Algeciras Bay (thirty men killed and wounded) and of the Gut in July 1801. He flew his commodore's pennant briefly in the West Indies in 1802, but after his promotion to rear-admiral in 1804 he did not go to sea again.

Admiral Sir Henry D'Esterre Darby died on 30 March 1823 at Leap Castle.

PETER HORE

❧ FOLEY ❧

Thomas Foley (1757–1833) was the second son of John Foley of Ridgeway, from an old-established Pembrokeshire land-owning family. His uncle Thomas Foley was a captain in the Royal Navy and had taken part in Anson's circumnavigation.

In 1770 Foley entered the Navy as midshipman in *Otter* (14), serving in her for three years on the Newfoundland station. In 1774 he was transferred to *Antelope* (54), flagship of Rear-Admiral Clark Gayton, commander-in-chief of the Jamaica station. During the first years of the War of American Independence Foley frequently transferred to smaller vessels operating against American privateers. In spring 1778 he returned to Britain, where he was promoted lieutenant and appointed to *America* (64, Captain Lord Longford) and took part under Admiral Augustus Keppel in the Battle of Ushant on 27 July 1778.

In October 1779 Foley was appointed to *Prince George* (98), flagship of Rear-Admiral Robert Digby on the Channel station, in which one of the midshipmen was the future King William IV. Thomas Byam Martin, a contemporary naval officer, remarked, if the prince had not had the 'infinite good fortune' to meet Foley and Richard Keats, another of Nelson's future captains, 'his youthful spirits and propensities might not have been checked with such good judgement'.

In 1780 *Prince George* joined Rodney's fleet, destined for the Leeward Islands. En route Rodney was to relieve Gibraltar, then under siege by the Spanish. Thus Foley took part in the capture of a Spanish convoy off Cape Finisterre on 8 January 1780, and the defeat of a Spanish squadron under Lángara in the Moonlight Battle on 16 January, followed by the relief of Gibraltar. In the West Indies, *Prince George* was present in the attempted relief of St Kitts and the Battle of the Saintes in April 1782.

After serving as acting captain of *Warwick* (50) Foley was promoted commander in December 1782 in the armed ship *Britannia* and then *Atalanta* (14) and *Racehorse* (16), seeing service off New York, in the Bay of Fundy and at Quebec.

Foley was made post-captain on 21 September 1790, but was unemployed for three years until he was appointed captain of *St George* (98), flagship of Rear-Admiral John Gell. On the way to join the Mediterranean Fleet, Gell's squadron captured two prizes, the French privateer *Général Dumourier* and a richly laden Spanish vessel. With his share of the prize-money Foley purchased the estate of Abermarlais Park, near Llangadog in southern Wales.

Foley was present in Admiral Hood's pursuit of the French Fleet into the Gulf of Jouan in June 1794, and when Gell was replaced by Rear-Admiral Sir Hyde Parker, Foley remained as the new admiral's flag captain. In March and July 1796 he took part in two indecisive actions against the French fleet under Rear-Admiral William Hotham, the successor of Lord Hood, who had returned to Britain on account of his bad health.

In March 1796 Foley followed Parker to his new flagship *Britannia* (100), where he re-mained as flag captain of Vice-Admiral Charles Thompson, when he replaced Parker as second-in-command to Admiral Sir John Jervis. Foley therefore played a prominent part in the Battle of Cape St Vincent on 14 February 1797, for which he was awarded the gold medal. Shortly after the battle Foley was ordered by Jervis, to change command with Captain Sir Charles Knowles of *Goliath* (74), according to Jervis, 'an imbecile, totally incompetent'. Foley, considered by Jervis as one of his ablest captains, soon restored discipline in *Goliath*. Midshipman George Elliot recorded: 'We were all obedience and respect for our captain. His kindness only increased as years rolled up.'

In July 1797 Foley took part in an attack on Cadiz when, despite heavy fire from the shore batteries, *Goliath* and *Terpsichore* (32) were successful in saving the bomb vessel *Thunderer* from a sortie by a flotilla of Spanish gunboats.

Betsey Wynne, the future wife of Captain Thomas Fremantle, who made Foley's acquaintance during this time, described him in her diary as: 'A man between thirty and forty and seems very good natured'. Foley was over six feet tall and since his once brown hair was already turning grey, Betsey called him 'the old gentleman'. Foley spoke very loudly and behaved in a bluff manner; nevertheless, according to Betsey Fremantle, he kept 'an excellent good table', his ship being 'a little town – you get all your desires in it'. His day was very regular; he had breakfast at eight, dinner at half past two, supper at nine and went to bed at ten o'clock. Betsey rejected his suit in favour of Thomas Fremantle.

In May 1798 *Goliath* was detached to the Mediterranean to reinforce Nelson in his search for Bonaparte's expedition to Egypt. When Nelson finally found the French fleet moored in Aboukir Bay, he decided to attack immediately, despite the fall of night. Since Foley was the sole captain in possession of a reliable chart of the Egyptian coast, his *Goliath* led the British line into battle.

Encouraged by Nelson to use his own initiative, Foley decided to attack the French on the landward side, thus doubling the enemy line, in the correct assumption that the French had only their seaward guns ready for action. His first, devastating broadside hit the leading French two-decker *Guerrier* (74). Then, within ten minutes, *Goliath* dismasted *Conquerant* (74). When the French frigate *Sérieuse* opened fire on his ship, Foley angrily ordered, 'Sink that brute', and a broadside sent her to the bottom. With several British ships following Foley's example, the enemy line was engaged from both sides, and only two of thirteen French ships of the line escaped surrender or destruction. In a battle of annihilation Nelson had regained British naval supremacy in the Mediterranean.

Foley continued in *Goliath* in the Mediterranean until the end of 1799, when he was appointed captain of *Elephant* (74), on blockade duty off Brest and Lorient, before joining the newly formed Baltic fleet commanded by Admiral Sir Hyde Parker. Since Foley's ship was lighter and thus drew less water than his own flagship, *St George*, Nelson, Parker's second-in-command, transferred his flag to the *Elephant* before entering the Baltic. The night before the Battle of Copenhagen, Foley assisted Nelson in composing the order of battle, writing down detailed instructions for the individual ships.

On the morning of 2 April 1801, Foley skilfully manoeuvred *Elephant* in the shallow waters of the King's Deep, to anchor opposite the Danish flagship *Dannebrog* (62). When Parker gave his famous signal of retreat, Nelson, determined to ignore the order, turned to Foley, remarking: 'You know, Foley, I only have one eye – I have the right to be blind sometimes.' Later Nelson praised Foley's 'advice on many and important occasions during the battle'.

On 31 July 1802 Foley married Lady Lucy Anne Fitzgerald, the youngest daughter of the Duke of Leinster, but they had no children. The Foleys' main residence was their estate at Abermarlais, but during their visits to London they met Nelson, who remained a close friend.

In 1803, after the short interlude of the peace of Amiens, Nelson asked Foley to serve with him,

but he had to refuse due to poor health. On 28 April 1808 Foley was promoted rear-admiral, but remained ashore until March 1811, when he was appointed commander-in-chief of the Downs, an appointment he held until the peace of 1815.

In 1814 Foley refused to telegraph what proved to be a fake message of Napoleon's death to London. Thus he unwittingly baffled a scheme to manipulate the London stock exchange, in which another naval officer, Lord Cochrane, was accused of complicity and dismissed dishonourably from the Royal Navy.

After the peace Foley retired to Abermarlais. Promotion and honours continued to accrue and in 1830 Admiral Sir Thomas Foley was appointed commander-in-chief at Portsmouth, where he died in 1833. He was buried in the Garrison Chapel there, in a coffin made from the oak of the *Elephant*, saved when she was broken up in 1830.
JANN DE WITT

✦ GOULD ✦

Davidge Gould (1758–1847) was born at Bridgwater, Somerset, the son of the Reverend Richard Gould: he was distantly related to the authors Henry and Sarah Fielding, and the naturalist William Gould.

Gould joined the Navy in 1772 as a volunteer in *Alarm* (32) on the Mediterranean and North American coasts. He was rated midshipman in *Winchelsea* (32) and remained on Mediterranean station for three years. In 1775 he joined *Phoenix* (36, Captain Hyde Parker) and returned to North America, seeing hard service in the American Revolutionary War. Few frigates were more busily employed than *Phoenix,* when Gould was engaged in attacks on shore batteries and cutting out operations and in boat actions on the Hudson River, including on 12 July 1776 passing the defences of the city and bombarding it for two hours. *Phoenix* was also at the reduction of Georgia, and after three years she was ordered back to England for repairs, arriving in early spring 1779, when Gould, having passed for lieutenant, was promoted on 7 May 1779 and appointed to the *Ulysses* (44, Captain Thomas Dumaresq), bound for Jamaica.

Shortly after arriving on station, *Ulysses* was caught in a severe hurricane, in which she lost all her lower masts, and was obliged to throw all the lower-deck guns overboard. After arrival at Port Royal, Dumaresq exchanged into *Bristol* (50), the ship being under orders for England, taking Gould with him. Gould next volunteered his services to Sir George Rodney, about to sail to the West Indies, and was appointed a supernumerary lieutenant in *Conqueror* (74): *Conqueror* was in the van division at the breaking of the line at the Battle of the Saintes on 12 April 1782,

In the round of promotions after the battle Gould was appointed first lieutenant in Rodney's flagship *Formidable* (74, Captain Sir Charles Douglas), receiving further rapid promotion on 13 June 1782 to commander of the sloop *Pacahunter* [sic]. It is unlikely he took command of her other than for the records: the sloop was much decayed and very soon was sold out of the service. Gould was charged to carry dispatches to England in a packet.

His first active sea-going command was the sloop *Pylades* (18), the former Dutch privateer *Hercules.* For thirteen months he cruised against smugglers in the Western Approaches. He gained

What contemporaries thought important: '… served in the first American war … present at Rodney's victory over Count de Grasse … commanded ships at the sieges of Bastia and Calvi in Lord Hotham's action and the *Audacious* at the memorable Battle of the Nile … The last surviving captain of this great victory' – no mention of Nelson.

more useful experience in ship handling during the same service in the newly built brig-sloop *Ferret* (12) in the Mediterranean during 1785.

At the age of twenty-seven Gould's long naval apprenticeship seemed to be at an end when he was appointed to *Salisbury* (50) under the orders of Vice-Admiral Mark Milbanke, but she sailed to her station, Newfoundland, before Gould joined her. Suddenly, he found himself on half pay.

Unexpectedly, he achieved post rank on 23 March 1789 and was given *Brune* (32) with orders for Jamaica. *Brune* was a French frigate built in 1754 and had been taken as a prize in 1762; after thirty-five years' service she was worn out and after a few months in the West Indies Gould was recalled. Instead he was given *Cyclops* (28) with a complement of 200 officers and men and proceeded to the Mediterranean, joining Nelson at the reduction of Corsica in 1794.

After Corsica Gould was appointed to *Bedford* (74) in which on 14 March 1795 he was involved in a confused and unsatisfactory victory over two French ships *Ça Ira* (80) and *Censeur* (74) when *Bedford*, an extremely bad sailer, suffered severely in her masts and rigging from the stern chasers of *Ça Ira*. She had nine killed and seventeen wounded, including her first lieutenant, who was struck on the head whilst in conversation with Gould. Nelson was not impressed, writing to William Locker, 'You will have heard of our brush with the French Fleet, a Battle it cannot be called, as the Enemy would not give us an opportunity of closing with them; if they had, I have no doubt, from the zeal and gallantry endeavoured to be [shown] by each individual Captain, one excepted, but we should have obtained a most glorious conquest.'

Bedford was also present on 13 July at the Battle of Hyères when the Toulon fleet attempted a sortie, though it is doubtful if *Bedford* even fired her guns. The highlight of the action came when the French *Alcide* took fire in her foretop and shortly after detonated. British boats saved 300 of her complement but many more were lost. *Bedford* was now considered scarcely seaworthy and was ordered to England.

Gould exchanged into *Audacious* (74), joining Lord St Vincent off Cadiz in July 1797 and was selected to form part of the squadron detached to reinforce Nelson in the Mediterranean.

There are frequent glimpses of Gould in the vast Nelson literature but he remains a somewhat shadowy figure, and unfortunately at the Battle of the Nile he appears to have stepped into the limelight for the wrong reasons.

The Battle of the Nile was fought at night, when at the best of times anchoring can be a test of seamanship. Done under fire, anchoring by the stern needed luck as well as skill and ships ended up in places different to that planned. Gould followed *Goliath* (74) and *Zealous* (74) down the lee side of the French line; both ships had poured their broadsides into *Guerrier* and *Conquérant*, while *Theseus* had done likewise in passing on the seaward side. Gould arrived fifteen minutes later and, while passing *Guerrier*, fired three broadsides into her claiming to have brought her mainmast down. Gould then anchored *Audacious* between *Guerrier* and *Conquérant* when both ships were already beaten. Signal midshipman George Elliot of *Goliath*, the second son of Nelson's friend Lord Minto, regarded this in his memories of the Nile as a 'useless berth between the first and second ships of the enemy's line, both of them being utterly beaten and dismasted'. Then, when the battle was not yet half over, Gould wrote a hasty note of congratulations to Nelson. He had done his duty as he conceived it, and at light cost to *Audacious* with just one dead and seventeen wounded. The note made him unpopular with the Nile captains for it appeared that he was taking the credit for *Conquérant* striking. Nor did he reposition *Audacious* during the action, saying *Goliath* was in the way even after she (*Goliath*) had moved down along the line to engage others of the French fleet.

The following morning Gould was busy rigging jury-masts in *Conquérant* and it needed more than one signal from the flagship to make him slip and, with *Zealous,* pursue two escaping French ships.

As an administrator Gould maintained good order and discipline in all of his commands, with a firm shipboard routine for cleanliness, and recognised the value and the needs of the ordinary sailor. He wrote in his orders that in his ship:

The men are never to go into their hammocks with their wet clothes on, nor sleep anywhere without their clothes on, as there was nothing more prejudicial to their health – a seaman in the King's service is too much consequence to his country to be allowed to risk his life by such means as saving himself a little trouble.

In these same orders he set minimum standards for the kit of his men: 'Each should have a blue jacket, a waistcoat or undergarment (preferably white), a pair of shoes and a Dutch cap or round hat marked with his name and available to be worn for inspection.' Two days, Monday and Friday, were set aside for washing clothes and inspections by divisional officers were on a Saturday. James Ralfe describes Gould 'as calm and serene amidst dangers, brave and animated in battle, and was at all times the friend of his officers and crew'.

Oliver Warner wrote about the 'the easy going attitude assumed by Captain Gould of the *Audacious*' and, as a fighting officer, judged: 'he was a cheerful, kindly man, brave enough no doubt, but without imagination, or sense of what was happening in the action as a whole'.

After the Nile he was engaged in the blockades of Malta and Genoa and returned to England at the end of 1800. In the spring of 1801 he was appointed to *Majestic* (74) attached to the Channel Fleet. In early 1802 *Majestic* was ordered to the West Indies, but after a few months Gould went on half pay until 1803 before being appointed to *Windsor Castle* (98). He was very soon after obliged to resign the command due to ill health brought on by fatigue and anxiety.

Gould left no account of his impressions of the Nile, and having gained his place in naval history he rested on his laurels. He received his due share of plaudits and promotion but he was not employed again. As perhaps the least distinguished and least popular of the Nile captains, a letter from Nelson to Thomas Troubridge sums up Gould: 'If the enemy come out I have no fears but I shall send you a good account of them, for more Zeal and attention with good humour I never saw exceeded, it is like the Nile fleet without Davidge Gould.'

When Gould married, at the age of forty-five, Harriet Willes, the eldest daughter of an archdeacon, a somewhat spiteful Troubridge wrote to Nelson on 28 December 1803: 'Davidge Gould has taken to himself a wife & I believe, & hope, left off the sea.'

Admiral Sir Davidge Gould died childless on 23 April 1847 at the age of eighty-nine.

KEN FLEMMING

✧ HALLOWELL ✦

Benjamin Hallowell (1761–1834) was this officer's name throughout his naval career, but when he inherited the estate of Beddington Park near Sutton in Surrey, a condition was that he should add Carew to his name.

He was born in Boston, Massachusetts, to a long-established family of merchants and shipbuilders. His father, also Benjamin, was in command of *King George,* built and maintained by the colony of Massachusetts to protect its coasts from Louisbourg-based privateers during the Seven Years War, and he formed many personal connections which would later prove useful to his son. He was also awarded large land grants in what is now the province of Nova Scotia.

After the war Hallowell senior became Commissioner of the American Board of Customs, a controversial appointment at a time when colonial discontent with British rule was mounting. Seen as supporters of the imperial connection, the Hallowell family were unpopular and, aged seven, young Benjamin was sent to school in England. When revolution broke out in 1776 numerous Loyalist refugees arrived in England via Halifax, including the Hallowells; formerly well-off, they were now in financial difficulties, and when Benjamin was

months in *Victory* (100), Hallowell gained his first command, the sloop *Scorpion* (16) in which under Commodore John Inglefield in *Medusa* he made two voyages to the slave forts in Sierra Leone and the Gold Coast, in disease-ridden West Africa.

Renewed war brought Hallowell command of the storeship *Camel* (26) in which he joined Hood's squadron at the Siege of Toulon, where Hood made him post-captain of *Robust* (74) and he played an important part in the evacuation of troops and civilians before the port fell to the Republicans. When Captain Elphinstone (later Lord Keith) re-assumed command of *Robust*, Hallowell briefly commanded the ex-French *Courageux* (74) until Captain Waldegrave returned after a temporary absence. Waldegrave was due to leave the station shortly, and it was understood that Hallowell would succeed him, but in the meantime he was without a ship.

British forces now attempted to conquer Corsica, and at the Siege of Bastia Hallowell commanded the boats of the inshore blockade. Bastia having fallen, the British lay siege to Calvi. With Hallowell as his second-in-command, Nelson landed with 250 seamen and guns of the fleet to augment the Army's siege artillery. The two took alternating twelve-hour shifts on the batteries, which were constantly under return fire from the fortress. Nelson reported, 'Hallowell and I are always on the batteries with them, and our jacks don't mind it. Hallowell, who is a very good, worthy man, and myself, feel equal to the duty here.' Later, a shell bursting in front of the parapet threw up a shower of gravel, striking Nelson in the face and leading to the loss of sight in one eye. Hallowell too suffered and shortly before the city fell on 1 August 1793 he succumbed to the malaria which would plague him throughout the rest of his days.

expelled from school, he was entered as a midshipman in *Sandwich* (90) in 1777 under the patronage of Samuel Hood (1724–1816).

Hood saw that Hallowell was frequently lent into smaller vessels combating French privateers in the Channel, until 1778 when Hallowell was accepted as a midshipman in *Asia* (64, Captain George Vandeput), in which he was mentored by Wilfred Collingwood, brother of Cuthbert Collingwood. Having escorted a convoy of East Indiamen to Bombay, *Asia* stayed on the station where Hallowell passed for lieutenant.

On return, he was rated 'able' in *Fortunée* (40) for passage to Antigua, where in July 1778 he joined now Rear-Admiral Samuel Hood's flagship *Barfleur* (98). Hood's squadron sailed to New York and in August Hallowell was appointed fifth and acting lieutenant of *Alcide* (74), and on 5 September he participated in the Battle of the Chesapeake.

When Hood returned to the West Indies, Hallowell transferred to *Alfred* (74), which suffered heavy casualties at the Battle of the Saintes in 1782; by now Hallowell was a full lieutenant.

With the end of the American War, Hallowell stayed in the West Indies in the brig-sloop *Falcon* (14) which co-operated with Nelson, in *Boreas*, in the attempt to stamp out illegal trade between the new United States and the British Caribbean islands.

In October 1787 Samuel Hood took Hallowell aboard his flagship, *Barfleur*. Later, after a few

Still awaiting his appointment to *Courageux*, Hallowell became captain of *Lowestoffe* (32). In an engagement off Genoa his ship was becalmed under the fire of a French 74 and unable to reply; Hallowell ordered the ship's company to take shelter below while he remained on the quarterdeck with the officer of the watch and the helmsman.

Finally, Hallowell took command of *Courageux* on 19 June 1795, taking part in the 1796 blockade of Toulon under the command of Sir John Jervis. Jervis later commented, 'How highly I think of the three captains … Troubridge, Hood and Hallowell, who will achieve very important services to their King and Country.'

However, on 11 December 1796 a furious storm struck the ships moored off Gibraltar. *Courageux* dragged her two anchors until Hallowell dropped a third. At this point he was summoned to *Britannia* to be a member of a court-martial. Observing that his ship was still in difficulties Hallowell requested to be excused, but his request was denied. In his absence the first lieutenant unmoored ship and tried to ride out the storm in the Straits, but she grounded at the base of Apes Hill on the African coast, and

439 of the ship's company of 610 were drowned. At his court-martial Hallowell was honourably acquitted, but he had lost all his personal possessions and the opportunity to play a major role in future operations. Admiral Jervis commented to the Admiralty, 'At any time the loss of such a ship to his Majesty, so manned and so commanded, would have been very great, but in the present circumstances of my force, compared with that of the enemy, it is beyond all calculation.'

Next Hallowell embarked as a volunteer in Jervis's flagship *Victory*. Thus he was on the quarterdeck on the morning of 14 February 1797 when the ships of Admiral Langara's Spanish fleet appeared over the horizon, the flag captain reporting their growing number. Tiring of this, Jervis forbade further reports, saying that he would fight them whatever their strength. At this the combative Hallowell clapped his admiral on the back, exclaiming: 'That's right, Sir John, and we'll give them a damned good licking too.' The onlookers were aghast, but Jervis made no comment.

'The Nile' is the only external reference to Hallowell's origins or achievements.

After the victory, in which Nelson so distinguished himself, the soon-to-be Earl of St Vincent entrusted to Hallowell his duplicate dispatches to the Admiralty. For reward he was given command of *Lively* (32) and rejoined the fleet off Cadiz. Nelson placed *Minerve* (38, Captain George Cockburn) under his command, with orders to cruise off the Canary Islands where treasure ships often called. Nelson commented, 'I long to see poor Cockburn and Hallowell enrich themselves.'

In October 1797 Hallowell took command of *Swiftsure* (74) and joined Nelson's inshore squadron in the Cadiz blockade, where minor actions were frequent. The next year he was ordered into the Mediterranean to reinforce Nelson, and thus Hallowell took part in Nelson's frustrating search for Napoleon's Egyptian invading force, and in his decisive victory at the Nile. Hallowell engaged the 120-gun French flagship *Orient,* and *Swiftsure* amazingly escaped major damage when her enemy blew up. The next day part of *Orient*'s giant mainmast was recovered and from it Hallowell had his carpenter fashion a coffin which he presented to his friend and commander. Nelson was delighted, for some time carrying it in his cabin, and was eventually buried in it.

Hallowell served on shore directing artillery fire during the recapture of Naples from the French. *Swiftsure* was still in the Mediterranean when Admiral Keith succeeded Nelson in late 1799, and Hallowell took an active part in the preparations for landing General Abercromby's army to attack the French in Egypt.

While escorting a small convoy to England Hallowell received intelligence that Admiral Ganteaume's squadron of four ships of the line and one frigate was at sea. Abandoning the convoy, Hallowell steered for Malta to warn and reinforce Admiral Warrender's squadron, but on 19 June 1801 he was intercepted by Ganteaume and forced to surrender after a long engagement against odds. He was imprisoned in Toulon until 24 July, when he was paroled and then court-martialled for the loss of *Swiftsure*. The court acquitted him, instead commending him both for his decision to abandon the convoy and for his tactics during the engagement.

During the Peace of Amiens Hallowell commanded *Argo* (44) on another mission to the West Africa Company's possessions in Sierra Leone, which had not lived up to its intended purpose of providing a home for freed slaves. Hallowell penned a scathing report to the Board of Trade which led to Sierra Leone becoming a crown colony.

He was in the West Indies when war again broke out, and led a landing force of seamen and marines in the capture of St Lucia in June 1803. On patrol in the Channel approaches, *Argo* later captured the privateer *Oiseau*, and subsequently played a key role in a secret British intervention in Egypt. The mission having failed, he was ordered to return home, and carried gifts from Nelson to Lady Hamilton. On Nelson's orders he embarked specie at Lisbon, a very lucrative opportunity for a captain, and another instance of Nelson's continuing friendship.

Argo having paid off, Hallowell took command of *Tigre* (80). The former First Lord of the Admiralty, Earl Spencer, confided his son Robert to Hallowell's care as a first-class volunteer, an honour testifying to Hallowell's reputation. The need to report regularly to the boy's parents would grow into a correspondence in which professional matters formed an increasing part. Sailing on 3 September 1804, *Tigre* joined Nelson's fleet in the Mediterranean and accompanied him on the fruitless chase of Villeneuve's force to the West Indies and back.

Hallowell was present in *Victory* when Nelson outlined his plan for attacking the combined French and Spanish fleets blockaded at Cadiz. However, *Tigre* was in Admiral Louis's squadron which Nelson detached to replenish at Gibraltar, and thus he took no part in the Battle of Trafalgar. By chance *Swiftsure*, which he had had to surrender, was recaptured by the British.

At this time Hallowell was forced to bring charges against one of his officers, who responded by demanding a court-martial of Hallowell himself: Hallowell was honourably acquitted for the third time while the officer was dismissed the service. In *Tigre*, Hallowell served in the Mediterranean under Admiral Viscount Cuthbert Collingwood, enforcing the vital but largely uneventful blockade of the French and Italian coasts. The one serious action saw *Tigre* leading a force which intercepted a French coastal convoy and forced two ships of the line to run aground and be burned.

The only break in this demanding service came when *Tigre* returned for a short time to England. Hallowell was entrusted with a secret reconnaissance of the mouth of the Scheldt to determine if it could be blocked to prevent the egress of several enemy ships then building in the river. Having personally supervised the soundings under fire he reported that blocking was impossible, a conclusion that led to the abortive British landings of 1809.

In 1811 Hallowell was promoted rear-admiral, initially hoisting his flag in *Royal George* (100) and, in the early spring of 1812, in *Malta* (84), when another of Earl Spencer's sons was a volunteer under Hallowell's tutelage. The role of Hallowell's squadron was to support a British-Spanish army operating on the east coast of Spain to relieve pressure on Wellington's main force in the centre of the country.

Under Hallowell's direction, on 29 May 1813, General Sir John Murray's 16,000-strong army was embarked in transports at Alicante, and on 3 June successfully landed to undertake the Siege of Tarragona. With his long experience of land warfare Hallowell assumed an active role ashore and was infuriated when Murray broke up the siege on illusory reports of the approach of a French relieving force, and an argument between Hallowell and Murray's chief of staff General Donkin resulted in a challenge being given and accepted.

With the campaign in eastern Spain winding down, in early 1814 some allied troops were transferred to Italy. Escorting the convoy, Hallowell unexpectedly encountered the frigate *Undaunted*, which signalled, 'I have got the Emperor Napoleon on board, going to the Isle of Elba.' Naval strength was rapidly reduced, and Hallowell became senior officer in the Mediterranean. Presciently, he observed, 'Bonaparte is not idle in Elba, and if he is not watched he will give us the slip from that island … it is impossible to be too much on our guard with such a fellow.'

Unexpectedly, in November 1814 Hallowell was recalled to England to be a witness at General Murray's court-martial for his actions at Tarragona. In the absence of Spanish witnesses Murray was convicted on one minor count only and escaped with a reprimand. Immediately afterwards both Donkin and Hallowell were visited by an emissary from the Prince Regent, absolutely forbidding them to proceed with their duel.

In time of peace very few admirals were employed. Hallowell however received two appointments: first, commander-in-chief in Ireland in 1815–18, and secondly, commander-in-chief at the Nore 1821–24 where on 23 May 1823 he witnessed the launch of paddle-wheeler *Comet*, one of the Royal Navy's first steam vessels.

On 17 February 1800 he had married Ann Inglefield in the Garrison Church at Gibraltar; her father, John Inglefield, had been Hallowell's commander on his West African patrols. Of their nine children, two sons joined the Navy but retired early. Hallowell was knighted in 1815 and in 1833, when he was the last survivor of the captains at the Nile, he was asked in confidence if he would accept the further honour of a baronetcy. Hallowell declined, fearing that his reprobate second son would disgrace the title.

Admiral Sir Benjamin Hallowell Carew died at Beddington Park where his coffin lies in the crypt of St Mary's Church. As Loyalists, Hallowell's father and sister received large land grants in and near York, now Toronto, and Hallowell senior died there. The village of Boylston, Nova Scotia, is named after Hallowell's mother's family. A cape on Baffin Island and a mountain in British Columbia both bear the Hallowell name, as does the Ontario township after which the Second World War frigate HMCS *Hallowell* was named.

BRYAN ELSON

➤ HARDY ➤

Thomas Masterman Hardy (1769–1839) was born at Kingston Russell, near Long Bredy, Dorset, where his grandparents were tenants, the third son of ten children of Joseph and Nanny Hardy. His parents moved to Portesham, pronounced 'Possum' in Dorset dialect, but also appropriate for young Thomas, meaning in Latin 'I can'.

Weymouth is but four miles from Portesham and just to the south of the village is Chesil Bank and the Fleet lagoon. It is said that when Thomas and his brothers were offered ponies, he wanted a wooden one, meaning a small boat.

Surprisingly he did not attend Hardye's School in Dorchester, a grammar school founded by a distant relative, but went instead to Crewkerne just over the border in Somerset, where his stay was not long. In 1781 he was rated captain's servant in the brig *Helena* (14) commanded by a neighbour and a

A plaque on the house in then-fashionable Durnford Street, Stonehouse, in Plymouth where Hardy once lived.

friend of the family, Francis Roberts (1748–94). Roberts indulged young Hardy by allowing him to bring his dog, Bounce. (Bounce seems to have been a favourite name for seadogs: Collingwood also had a dog called Bounce, and many years later Hardy had another Bounce at Greenwich.)

Roberts became Hardy's sea-daddy, arranging for him to return to school, keeping him on the ships' books, sending him away to gain experience in the merchant navy, and seeing that in 1790 yet another eminent Dorset sailor, Captain Alexander Hood (1758–98), took him as a midshipman into *Hebe* (36).

In 1793 he sailed for the Mediterranean in *Amphitrite* (24, Captain Anthony Hunt), where he passed for lieutenant and was transferred to *Meleager* (32, Captain George Cockburn), part of a squadron off the coast of Genoa under Nelson's command.

In 1796 he moved with Cockburn to be first lieutenant of *Minerve* (40), Commodore Nelson's flagship, which was saved by Hardy in a courageous act of defiance. On 19 December 1796 *Minerve* and her consort, *Blanche* (32), fought two Spanish frigates and captured *Santa Sabina* (40) commanded by Don Jacobo Stuart. Hardy commanded the prize crew, and the three ships continued towards Gibraltar, but ran into a larger Spanish squadron. Hardy hoisted the British ensign prominently over the Spanish colours and drew off the Spaniards, fighting *Santa Sabina* until she was dismasted and captured, thus allowing Nelson to escape. Hardy became a prisoner of war for six weeks but was exchanged for Stuart, and rejoined *Minerve* at Gibraltar in February 1797.

Within days Nelson and Cockburn were being chased by a superior Spanish fleet and Cockburn had ordered more sail when a man fell from aloft into the water. Hardy in a boat was searching for the man when Nelson exclaimed, 'By God, I'll not lose Hardy, back that mizzen topsail!' This confused the Spanish who checked their own progress, allowing Hardy time to return to *Minerve*.

Hardy assured his future at Santa Cruz de Tenerife on 28 May 1797 when he commanded boats

In 2014 the Nelson Society planted an oak to commemorate the appointment of Hardy as governor of Greenwich hospital: his body is entombed in the mausoleum beyond the sapling.

from *Minerve* and *Lively* to cut out the French *Mutine* (18). When he was promoted to command *Mutine*, she became the wooden pony which he had wanted since he was a boy. He would be present at all of Nelson's major fleet actions.

In May 1798 Hardy wrote to his brother Joseph, 'We are bound to Naples under the command of Sir Horatio Nelson and you may expect to hear of something handsome being done very soon by his squadron which at present is small but I believe will consist of eighteen sail of the line. I hope Sir Horatio will have it in his power to do something.'

Sir Horatio did do something: he annihilated the French fleet in Aboukir Bay.

Mutine did not participate directly in the battle but came to the assistance of *Culloden*, which had run aground, and afterwards, when Nelson sent Edward Berry home with dispatches, Hardy was promoted to captain of Nelson's flagship, *Vanguard* (74).

That year *Vanguard* carried King Ferdinand IV, his Queen, the British ambassador Sir William Hamilton and his wife Emma from Naples to safety in Sicily. Hardy did not approve of Emma, who had tried to intervene on behalf of a boat's crew; he had the crew flogged twice, once for the original

offence and again for petitioning the lady. When Nelson transferred his flag to *Foudroyant* in 1799 he took Hardy with him.

After a year ashore Hardy commissioned *San Josef* (114) and when it became clear that she drew too much for operations in the Baltic, shifted to *St George* (98) as Nelson's flag captain. On the eve of the Battle of Copenhagen Hardy sounded with a pole around the anchored Danish fleet, but he took no part in the fighting on 2 April 1801, which he described as 'the most daring attack that has been attempted this war (the Nile not accepted) … the more I see of his Lordship the more I admire his great Character for I think on this occasion his Political management <u>was if possible</u> greater than his Bravery'.

After the failure of the Peace of Amiens and the renewal of hostilities, the fear of a French invasion was very real to contemporaries. On Blackdown Hill, north of Portesham, where a monument to Hardy now stands, was a warning beacon, one of a chain, which William Boyt of Possum was paid to maintain. Hardy asked Joseph to remind other landowners, the Welds of Lulworth Castle who had a beacon on Flowers Barrow and the Bankes

Memorial for Hardy on the wall of the mausoleum at Greenwich where he is entombed.

of Kingston Lacy who had a beacon on Badbury Rings, to maintain theirs.

At Trafalgar Hardy made several attempts to reduce the risk to his chief's life. First he urged Nelson to shift his flag into one of the frigates, which Nelson refused; then he asked Nelson not to wear the decorations which would single him out as a target but Nelson quipped that it was too late and, as he had won them in battle, he would wear them in battle; and, finally, Hardy asked Nelson to allow *Temeraire* to take her designated station ahead of *Victory* in the order of battle, which Nelson at first agreed to, but as she drew level, he called for her to resume her station astern of the flagship. Then, as Hardy paced the quarterdeck with Nelson in the thick of battle, and when a splinter took the buckle from his shoe, Nelson smiled at him, 'This is too warm work to last, Hardy.' A few minutes later Nelson fell, crying, 'Hardy, I believe they have done it at last … my back bone is shot through.'

Nevertheless, after the battle, Hardy wrote to his brother-in-law John Manfield with news that would make William Boyt redundant: 'We have on the 21st just obtained a most glorious Victory over the combined fleets, but it has cost the Country a life that no money can replace and for whose death I shall forever mourn.' This letter was amongst others which John Lapenotiere, in his race to London with Collingwood's dispatches, left at Bridport. Another from Hardy was to his old friends, the Roberts family, reassuring them that their boy, Richard Francis Roberts whom he had promoted to midshipman on the eve of battle, was safe. Thus the bells of St Mary's, Burton Bradstock, were the first bells in England to ring out with the news of Trafalgar: indeed the 'bells rang till several of the ropes broke'.

Hardy was created a baronet and took command of *Triumph* (74) in which he served on the North America station until 1809. At Halifax he formed an alliance with a new chief, Vice-Admiral Sir George Berkeley (whose orders led to the *Chesapeake–Leopard* affair), and married one of Berkeley's spirited daughters, Anne Louisa, who was twenty years younger than he. When, after the

Marquis of Buckingham had made inappropriate advances to her, Hardy met Buckingham at the theatre he called him a scoundrel and challenged him to a duel. Whether shots were exchanged is unclear, but when the authorities were informed, Hardy told his brother, 'I was taken into custody by the Peace officers … and bound over to keep the Peace.'

Meanwhile, when Berkeley was appointed commander-in-chief at Lisbon in 1809, Hardy became his flag captain in *Barfleur* (98) and was made a commodore in the Portuguese Navy in 1811. Between them they brought order to the supply system for Wellington's army in the Peninsula War, used seamen and marines to man coastal defences, thus freeing soldiers for Wellington, and also formed a squadron of river gunboats on the Tagus to harry the French.

In 1812 Hardy returned to North America in *Ramillies* (74). There, on 25 June 1813, commanding a squadron off New London, Connecticut, he captured an American privateer. The crew, before escaping in boats, declared her to be carrying provisions, but she was laden with gunpowder and, expecting her to be taken alongside *Ramillies*, they had set a clockwork fuze. However, Hardy had ordered the privateer to berth on another prize, where she blew up, killing Lieutenant John Geddes and ten seamen.

Next, Hardy was commodore on the South America station, where, while President James Monroe was formulating his doctrine which opposed European colonisation or interference in the Americas, Hardy's ships oversaw the achievement of independence by several South American states.

Hardy was promoted to rear-admiral in 1825. He had one last diplomatic service to perform when in *Wellesley* (74) he convoyed a 4,000-strong British expeditionary force to Lisbon to quell a revolt against the Portuguese regency. He last flew his flag at sea while commanding an experimental squadron, hauling it down on 20 October 1827.

In 1830 Hardy joined the Admiralty Board as First Naval Lord under Sir James Graham, where he encouraged Sir William Symonds to look at ways to improve the sailing performance of ships and took an interest in the introduction of steam, but was less interested in politics, writing to his brother, 'Thank God I was not returned [as Member of Parliament] for Weymouth, I have nothing to do with politics.' By 1833 he was beginning to be worried by the economies being pursued by Graham and wished to leave the Admiralty. He was also feeling the effects of age and in June 1833 wrote, 'You can see by my handwriting that my hands begin to fail me and as I cannot dress myself I'm obliged to bring a servant with me.'

Hardy was appointed Governor of the Royal Hospital at Greenwich to succeed Sir Richard Keats, an appointment William IV only consented to if Hardy would agree, if asked, to command a fleet on the high seas. After Hardy's appointment there were several royal visits to Greenwich: King William and Queen Adelaide liked to celebrate naval battles by attending Sunday morning service in the chapel. They first came in 1834 to celebrate Howe's victory on the Glorious First of June, arriving by river in the royal barges. There were return visits too: in October 1835 William visited Greenwich to celebrate the Battle of Camperdown and later that day Hardy dined at St James's Palace, 'Where I had to make a speech which annoyed me more than fighting the battle.' King William placed a bust of Keats and promised Hardy that he would do the same for him. When the King died in 1837, his Queen sent Admiral Hardy a lock of his hair as a token of the esteem in which King William held him.

The Hardys were guests at the coronation of Queen Victoria in 1838, but mostly Hardy devoted himself to improving the care of the pensioners at Greenwich. He put them into trousers instead of breeches and he also abolished the hated yellow coat with red sleeves that pensioners found drunk had been obliged to wear. A visitor who had served under Hardy on the South American station overheard a pensioner say, 'There goes our Good Old Governor, God Bless Him. We honour the very ground he walks on.' He also ensured that Tom Allen, Nelson's body servant, passed his last years in comfort at Greenwich and had a plaque put on his grave, 'To the memory of Thomas Allen, faithful servant of Lord Nelson, born at Burnham Thorpe, in the County of Norfolk 1764 and died at The Royal Hospital 23rd November 1838.'

Hardy saw steam power as the future, yet in 1836 when the London Bridge to Greenwich railway opened and Lady Hardy booked a party to travel there and back, Hardy declined, saying he would not go at any price – and never did. When Lady Hardy heard that *Victory*, then more than seventy years old, was to be broken up, she is reputed to have said 'Thomas, you simply cannot let this happen.' Hardy received many honours in his life, but he said his proudest moment was to be elected an Elder Brother of Trinity House.

Vice-Admiral Sir Thomas Masterman Hardy, Bt, GCB, died in office in 1839 and was interred in the mausoleum at Greenwich. In 1849 Lady Hardy presented a portrait of him to Greenwich Hospital, which in now in the National Maritime Museum.

ELIZABETH BAKER AND GENEVIEVE ST GEORGE

✦ HOOD ✦

Samuel Hood (1762–1814) was born in Kingsland, Netherbury, Dorset. His brothers were Lieutenant Arthur Hood (born 1753, lost from the sloop *Pomona* during a hurricane in 1775 in

RIGHT: Samuel Hood's monument high on a hill near Butleigh, Somerset.

ABOVE: The Chelengk: Hood wrote to Nelson just after the Nile that a hat covered with diamonds was being prepared for him as a gift by the Grand Vizier.

Arthur, Alexander and Samuel's father was a purser in the Navy who had retired to farm in Dorset, and entrusted his three sons to their older cousins' care and patronage. Aged fourteen, the youngest of this clan, Samuel Hood, joined cousin Samuel's *Courageux* (74).

From that moment until his death thirty-eight years later, he spent only three years not on active service. At sea, 'He was devoted to his profession, for he was never happy out of it, and he … appeared to me to like sea life par excellence.' Indeed, he so relished being at sea that in 1806 he declined a seat on the Board of Admiralty, stating that his 'greatest ambition has always been for active service at sea'.

The future Admiral of the Fleet Sir Thomas Byam Martin, who served as third lieutenant in *Juno* (32) under Hood's command, wrote in 1791, 'If the salvation of the Kingdom had rested on this single ship, she could not have been more constantly at sea … blow high, blow low … peace offered no temptation to be there.' Byam Martin also described Hood as 'very absent … and silent for hours on deck', and when at his table 'reserved to a distressing degree', apparently 'absorbed in thought about his ship'.

Even when he was not on active service between 1783 and 1785, his enquiring mind and keenness to improve his knowledge of navigation, geography, shipbuilding, fortification and the customs and cultures of other countries led him to live in France. Unlike Nelson, Hood mastered French and he could also speak Spanish – which he used to great effect in extracting the remnants of Nelson's people from the failed attempt on Santa Cruz de Tenerife.

Sailors were pleased to serve with him: they told how in 1791 he defied a violent Caribbean storm to lead a boat crew in rescuing three men from a wreck. He leapt into the barge being used to undertake the rescue amidst massive breakers saying, 'I never gave an order in my life, which I was not ready to undertake and execute myself.'

Renowned for his own stern discipline, Lord St Vincent was impressed with how Hood turned the

the West Indies), and Captain Alexander Hood (1758–98) a veteran of James Cook's second voyage in *Resolution*, who fell in a famous single-ship action between his ship *Mars* (74) and the French *Hercule* (74).

Their cousins were two admirals, Samuel Hood, 1st Viscount Hood (1724–1816), veteran of the Battles of the Chesapeake and the Saintes and the Siege of Toulon, and Alexander Hood, 1st Viscount Bridport (1726–1814), also a veteran of the American War of Independence and the blockade of Brest. It is said that Samuel and Alexander were attracted to the Navy when Captain (later Admiral) Thomas Smith's coach broke down near Butleigh, Somerset, and he was given hospitality by the local vicar whose sons were fascinated by his tales of derring-do.

The Hood memorial dominates the family chapel at St Leonard's, Butleigh, Somerset. There is a fourth memorial in St Mary's, Chennai (Madras).

surly ship's company of *Zealous* into an effective one. Hood also concerned himself with the education of his midshipmen and with their welfare, for example, writing to his cousin, Alexander Hood, about one of his midshipmen, 'The mother is in a fair way of spoiling [him] by giving him Money and Clothes without my knowledge and which I am sorry to say he does not manage as he ought, and it would be good if your lordship would write to Mrs Harrison not to send him anything but through me'.

Hood's ability as a seaman, strategist and tactician included his understanding of the importance of effective combined operations with the Army. His first involvement with the Army was in Corsica in 1794, and when he was in the Caribbean in 1803–4, together with troops commanded by Lieutenant General Grinfield (in 1803) and Major General Green (in 1804), St Lucia, Tobago, Demerara, Essequibo, Berbice and Surinam were all overwhelmed. These combined operations provided Hood with valuable experience which he put to excellent effect in a masterful evacuation of Sir John Moore's Peninsular army from Corunna in the winter of 1808–9.

Hood was renowned for his quick but calm thinking. A remarkable instance of this is when commanding *Juno* (32), he combined brilliant ship-handling with rapid, intelligent action to escape being captured in Toulon harbour on the

night of 9 January 1794. Under cousin Alexander, now Lord Hood and commander-in-chief of the Mediterranean fleet, Hood had been dispatched to the Adriatic to convoy merchant shipping. On his return in January 1794 he entered Toulon believing it to be still in Anglo-Spanish control. Before Hood realised his predicament *Juno* grounded on a shoal and she was boarded by French officers, but using boats and a kedge anchor, and with a fortunate wind shift, he quickly got *Juno* out to sea and safety.

Commanding *Zealous* (74) at the Battle of the Nile, Hood saw the greater picture from start to finish. As they approached Aboukir Bay, he was hailed by Nelson in *Vanguard* as to the depth of water around the French fleet. Lieutenant William Webley serving in *Zealous* reported Nelson as

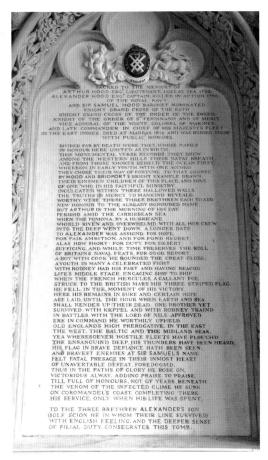

The memorial to the three Hood brothers tells Samuel's history in verse.

replying in the affirmative to Hood's offer to sound and lead, taking off his hat to him. Hood, replied by taking off his own hat, accidentally dropped it into the sea whereupon Hood exclaimed, 'Never mind Webley! There it goes for luck!'

Towards the end of the battle it was *Zealous*, having overcome the French *Guerrier* (74) and engaged a number of others, which began to pursue two undamaged French ships of the line as they got under way. Captain Edward Berry recalled, 'Captain Hood … handsomely endeavoured to prevent their escape: but as there was no other Ship in a condition to support the *Zealous*, she was recalled.'

Hood was also an adept diplomat, a quality Nelson admired. In 1793 Lord Hood had sent him to negotiate between Turkish forces and the French in the Aegean. After the Nile, Nelson trusted him to work with Turkish and Russian forces in a blockade of Alexandria. It was from Alexandria in September 1798 that Hood wrote to Nelson informing him of an impending gift, a 'Hat set with diamonds, indeed they say covered, is preparing for you as a present from the Grand Vizier.'

One of Hood's astonishing feats was in 1804 while he was Commodore of the Leeward Islands. He used *Centaur* (74, Captain Murray Maxwell) to haul two 18-pounder guns to the top of Diamond Rock (a 450ft pinnacle rising sheer out of the sea off Martinique). He recognised the strategic importance of achieving what was considered to be impossible; devised a way of doing it through the use of skilful boat-handling and use of cables strung between the top of the rock and *Centaur's* mainmast; inspired his seamen to achieve it; and annoyed the French in Port Royale and Bonaparte in Paris.

Later, he did something similar at Madras, when he saw a party of men struggling to place a heavy cornerstone and he 'used a crowbar and small iron pin as a fulcrum to lever [it] into place … When the operation was completed, he … called out to the grinning party but with infinite good humour, "There! You hay-making, tinkering, tailoring fellows, that's the way to move a stone – when you know how!"'

In the Caribbean in 1804 Hood met and married Mary MacKenzie, daughter of the Governor of Barbados, Lord Seaforth, a man whose advanced ideas about the abolition of slavery created many enemies among the planters. Mary was a character in her own right. She toured India when Hood became Governor of Madras and was the first British woman to shoot a tiger. She and Hood had no children, but Mary remarried in 1817 after his death and mothered six children and founded her own naval dynasty. When her father died in 1815 she inherited all the Seaforth estates, becoming chief of the clan MacKenzie. Sir Walter Scott admired her for 'the spirit of the chieftainess in every drop of her blood'. In 1862 her coffin was followed for twenty miles by pipers and mourners to Fortrose cathedral, Cromarty.

Other examples of Hood's steadfast pursuit of the enemy include his fight in *Venerable* (74) against the French *Formidable* (80) at the Second Battle of Algeciras; the capture of four French frigates in September 1805 when Hood had his right elbow shattered by a musket ball requiring the arm to be amputated; and the chase and destruction of the Russian *Sevelod* (50) in the Baltic in 1808. However, when George III heard about Hood's loss of his right arm, he remarked that 'he would sooner the French kept their frigates and Hood his arm.' For capturing *Sevelod*, the King of Sweden awarded Hood the Grand Cross of the Order of the Sword.

Another of Hood's qualities which endeared him to Jervis was the prudent, honest and upright manner in which he handled resources generally, but financial ones in particular. His last appointment, in 1811, was as Governor of Madras where he reorganised and restructured affairs to make them more effective and economical, achieving a 30 per cent reduction in the costs of running the East Indies command.

From humble beginnings, Vice-Admiral Sir Samuel Hood, 1st Baronet, died at Madras on Christmas Eve 1814, after a short bout of fever.

STEPHEN TREGIDGO

❧ LOUIS ❦

Thomas Louis (1759–1807) was a good, hard-working sea officer, but it is an indication of the calibre of Nelson's Band of Brothers that this statement has implications of ordinariness.

Louis always addressed his father as 'père' but John Louis (1720–1815) was secretive about his origins: however, the family hold that John was born in the Tuileries Palace and received his name and a small pension from the French royal family. In 1749 John Louis married a widow, Elizabeth Atkinson, and settled at Alphington Cross outside Exeter, where he taught dancing and music. He also gave lessons 'once a week, at two guineas per year' at Ottery St Mary Grammar School. Later portraits of Thomas show a likeness with Louis XV that may have been a painterly device.

Louis's career opened quietly: from 1769 to 1771 he served in the sloop *Fly* (18) under the Yorkshireman Captain Mitchell Graham, and then from 1771 to 1775 in *Southampton* (32), *Orpheus* (32) and *Kent* (74) under the Scots Captain John MacBride, a veteran of the Seven Years War. After brief service in *Martin* (14, Captain William Parker), off Newfoundland, Louis returned to his first patron, Graham, in *Thetis* (32), and then rejoined MacBride in the French-built *Bienfaisant* (64) where he was made lieutenant in July 1777.

Louis's first fleet action was the indecisive and controversial Battle of Ushant in 1778.

So far Louis's naval career was uneventful but he was evidently a practical seaman and MacBride took him as first lieutenant of *Bienfaisant*. On 8 January 1780 Admiral Rodney commanded a supply convoy bound for the besieged Gibraltar when his faster, copper-clad ships captured a Spanish convoy off Cape Finisterre protected by the *Guipuzcoana* (64). While Rodney snapped up the rich convoy and its smaller escorts, *Bienfaisant* engaged *Guipuzcoana* at close quarters from dawn to noon, and, when she hauled down her colours, Louis was sent across to take possession. Eight days later Rodney spotted the sails of the Spanish Commodore Juan de Lángara's fleet. The ensuing chase and night-time battle in a howling gale and a tumbling sea became known as the Moonlight Battle. *Bienfaisant* first engaged *Santo Domingo* (70) which blew up early in the evening; though showered with debris, Louis was unharmed. *Bienfaisant* then took Lángara's flagship *Fénix* (80) which surrendered about two in the morning, when Louis was appointed as her prize-master. When *Fénix* struck her flag, *Bienfaisant* had smallpox on board, so MacBride unusually did not take prisoners aboard, in order to protect them from the disease, on the undertaking of the Spanish officers that they would act as prisoners of war. Louis's tact and skill as prize captain actually earned him the assistance of the Spanish in getting the badly damaged and renamed *Phoenix* into Gibraltar in foul weather, and praise from MacBride in a letter to Rodney. Lángara would subsequently serve as an ally of the British at the Siege of Toulon.

Louis took *Phoenix* to England, but rejoined the *Bienfaisant* in time for the capture of a large French privateer *Comte d'Artois* (60), of which he was again made prize-master. Coincidentally, in the following month (September), *Bienfaisant* also took another French privateer, named *Comtesse d'Artois*.

In 1781 Louis went with MacBride to *Artois* (40), a French prize, and on 9 April he was promoted commander and appointed to a small armed vessel *Mackworth*, convoying the Milford–

Plymouth trade. Fifteen months later Louis was appointed to the impress service at Sligo and Cork (still under MacBride) where he raised 5,000 Irishmen for the Navy.

At the end of the war with America he was promoted captain, but spent the next ten years of peace on half pay. On 15 July 1784 he married Jacquetta Belfield, daughter of Samuel Belfield of Stoke Gabriel on the Dart, a wealthy Devon landowner. Thomas and Jacquetta had three daughters and four sons, of whom the eldest, Sir John Louis, 2nd Baronet, died an admiral in 1863 having gone to sea with his father in 1793, and the third son fought in the Royal Horse Artillery at Waterloo.

When war resumed in 1793 Louis was recalled; he took command of *Cumberland* (74), which he was able to man fully from volunteers, being held in high esteem by local Devon seamen, and a year later transferred to *Minotaur* (74), as flag captain to his friend, now Vice-Admiral MacBride. Prior to joining the Mediterranean Fleet in 1796 he escorted a convoy to the West Indies and back, during which his attentive conduct nearly cost him the customary 'compensation' from the merchant captains. They all thought he was their friend and were reluctant to insult him with a gratuity, though fortunately for Louis they overcame their qualms.

In 1798 Louis joined Nelson's squadron at the Nile, where *Minotaur* followed Nelson's flagship *Vanguard* (74) into battle, anchoring opposite the French *Aquilon* (74), which in the smoke and confusion was unengaged and was battering Nelson's flagship. Berry asked if he should shift *Vanguard*, but Nelson's reply was, 'No, it is all right, Louis will be here.' After a two-hour duel the Frenchman surrendered to Louis. By this time Nelson had been wounded and expected soon to pass away. He called Louis to his presence and said, 'Farewell dear Louis, I shall never forget the obligation I am under to you for your brave and generous conduct; and now, whatever may become of me, my mind is at peace.'

In 1799 *Minotaur*'s marines and seamen were in action under Commodore Troubridge in *Culloden* (74) in the liberation of Civita Vecchia from the French. Louis gained a unique distinction in

September when he was rowed up the Tiber by bluejackets to hoist British colours over the Capitoline Hill, and for several weeks he was the governor of Rome. The King of Naples gave him the Order of St Ferdinand, and Louis kept a papal flag which he used to show off in Devon.

Louis met Lord Keith when, after the accidental burning of his flagship, Keith shifted his flag into *Minotaur*, and, under Keith, Louis took part in the amphibious operations in Egypt in 1801, when they blockaded Alexandria and a major invasion by British, under General Ralph Abercromby, and Ottoman armies finally expelled the French from Egypt. Unfortunately for Abercromby, he found himself fatally wounded and died aboard ship a week later. Louis returned home the following year at the Peace of Amiens.

When the brief peace ended in 1803, Louis was given *Conqueror* (74) until, on St George's Day 1804, he hoisted his flag, blue at the mizzen, in the 'horrible old' *Leopard* (50) with Francis Austen, brother of the author Jane, as his flag captain. Louis commanded the fleet of small vessels watching Boulogne, where Napoleon's invasion fleet was collecting.

Louis had served under Nelson several times and now in 1805 Nelson asked for Louis as his second-in-command in the Mediterranean. Louis and Austen in *Canopus* (80), the former French *Franklin* taken at Aboukir, took part in the famous chase of the Franco-Spanish fleet to the West Indies and back.

When Nelson returned to take command of the fleet off Cadiz in September, Louis reprised his command of the inshore squadron. Then on 2 October Louis, to his dismay, was ordered to Gibraltar and Tetuan, with six ships, to replenish and collect stores for the fleet. 'You are sending us away,' he protested, 'The enemy will come out, and we shall have no share in the battle.' Nelson replied, 'I look upon *Canopus* as my right hand, and I send you first to insure your being here to help to beat them.' The next day, Louis learned from a Swedish ship that troops were embarking in the ships in Cadiz and so he returned to Nelson, only to have his orders repeated, perhaps with some irritation and insistence. Later these orders were reinforced when Louis received written instructions from Nelson to escort a merchant fleet, carrying a large sum of cash, past the Spanish ships at Cartagena.

Blackwood, when he saw the Franco-Spanish fleet coming out, sent the sloop *Weasel* to find Louis and warn him, which she did on 22 October. Then on 26 October, *Weasel* signalled to Louis, 'Enemy defeated, but our fleet off Cadiz in want of assistance.' But against contrary winds Louis and his squadron could not rejoin the fleet until 30 October. These episodes illustrate the good and bad in Louis: Nelson seems to have realised he was good at obeying orders, poor in using his initiative, and he exploited this aspect of Louis's character.

That winter *Canopus* sailed with Vice-Admiral Sir John Duckworth to the West Indies, where, in a grudge match for those officers who had missed Trafalgar, they annihilated a French squadron at the Battle of St Domingo in February 1806; all five French ships of the line were captured or destroyed after a general action lasting about an hour and a half, in which the total British 'butcher's bill' was 74 dead and 264 wounded (of which *Canopus* suffered 8 and 22 respectively). Louis was created a baronet in March and awarded a second gold medal, together with an inscribed vase worth £300 and the thanks of Parliament.

Next, in November 1806, Louis in *Canopus* reconnoitred the defences of the Dardanelles, and three months later he led Duckworth's squadron up the straits and, a few days later, down again, having sustained huge damage from the massive Turkish stone shot. Nevertheless, Louis earned praise for his gallantry and cool judgement. The squadron then sailed for Alexandria, where Louis was left in command, but while he was there he died, on 17 May 1807, of an unidentified disease caught in the West Indies the year before.

Rear-Admiral Sir Thomas Louis's body was taken to Malta, where, much mourned, he was interred on 8 June.

PETER TURNER

↣ MILLER ↢

Ralph Willett Miller (1762–99) was born in New York on 24 January 1762, into a colonial society that had been British for 150 years. His mother, Maria Willett, was descended from the first English mayor of New York, Thomas Willett (1605–74), and for the Millers, the Declaration of Independence in 1776 was a call to treason, not to reason, and it drove them into exile. Their property was confiscated, but they kept their honour and some capital. With their son and two daughters they left America and went to England where Ralph was sent to the Royal Naval Academy in Portsmouth.

Miller went to sea in 1778 in *Ardent* (64), flagship of Rear-Admiral James Gambier, who employed him in boats against the American rebels. Unlike Nelson, who ended up in a hellish Nicaraguan jungle, Miller had a good war, even though he was wounded three times. He was one of those plucky lads with heart-breaking courage, the kind that is likely to get himself killed because he is always volunteering for dangerous missions.

He passed for lieutenant in 1781 and joined *Terrible* (74) in time to fight in the Battle of the Chesapeake. As General George Washington had understood early on, naval superiority was 'the basis upon which every hope of success must ultimately depend. French seapower tipped the balance, resulting in the surrender of British forces at Yorktown.

Miller's ship was so badly damaged off Cape Henry that she was set alight and abandoned. He was appointed to the new *Fortitude* (74), but the war was over. The former colonies became the United States of America.

After ten years of peace, Miller went back to sea in 1793 in *Windsor Castle* (98). He was thirty-one years old, a married man with two young daughters, having married Anne 'Nancy' Witchell, daughter of his former headmaster at the Royal Naval Academy. From sea he wrote vividly detailed letters to his father about the new war's events and horrors. To his adored wife he wrote of his love for her and for their little girls: 'Kiss them a thousand times for me.'

Windsor Castle was the flagship of Vice-Admiral Phipps Cosby, third in command of the Mediterranean Fleet under Lord Hood. In August 1793 Toulon surrendered to Hood who, as Nelson put it, got possession of the French fleet 'without firing a shot'. The problem was keeping it, which proved to be impossible as soon as Captain Napoleon Bonaparte appeared in the field. On the night of 17 December 1793 his artillery opened fire, and his troops easily routed the French royalists. Hood had no choice but to destroy twenty French sail of the line and the arsenal. Miller volunteered for what was described as a dangerous and 'very severe service' under the command of Sir Sidney Smith.

Miller boarded a 74 and lit a fire that leapt out of control. As he scrambled down the side to escape the smoke, he fell and nearly drowned for the second time that night. And what was he to do about the towering *Sans Culottes* (120)? Absurd to try to board her, but Miller thought about it! 'We found it was totally impracticable and, full of mortification, gave it up.' Nelson and others were dissatisfied with Smith's results, but Miller was commended for a job well done. He had long awaited promotion and told his father he now had hopes of enough interest to make it happen. 'At all events I shall enjoy the noble reward of knowing that I have done essential good to my country, which I have served with all my heart and all my soul.' All he got was a transfer to Lord Hood's flagship, as *Victory*'s third lieutenant.

'Heart and soul' – that was Ralph Miller, whatever he undertook, whether it was helping to eject the French from Corsica, or trying against impossible odds (once again) to burn a French fleet securely anchored in Gourjean Bay, or supporting Austrian land forces trying to hold back the swarming French. By 1796 the war was three years old and going wrong for the Allies. After eighteen years' service, Miller was at last a post-captain, in command of the newly captured frigate *Mignonne* (32).

His cool courage under fire inspired subordinates and impressed his superiors. Nelson, who met him on Corsica, wanted him for his flag captain, in *Captain* (74). Miller, who in his portrait looks nothing like a cynical combat veteran, had been in the service long enough to know that it could be a thankless job – 'nobody generally has less influence with an Admiral than his Captain'.

As it happened, Nelson did thank his flag captain on 14 February 1797, when 'the invincible Fifteen', as Lady Parker called them, took on twenty-seven Spanish ships. The Battle of Cape St Vincent might have ended differently but for Nelson's unexpected tactics, when he ordered Miller to wear out of the line to cut off the Spanish van. Miller, sword in hand, was in the act of jumping into the *San Nicolas* (80) when Nelson ordered him back, relegating him to the job of sending across more and more men as the commodore boarded first *San Nicolas* and then *San Josef* (120). Nelson thanked Miller and made amends by giving him one of two surrendered Spanish swords, as well as his own topaz and diamond ring. Miller does not say much about Nelson in his letters, but he stayed with him when Jervis asked them to transfer into the mutinous *Theseus* (74).

In the summer of 1797 Admiral Nelson commanded a squadron sent to annoy Cadiz. Morale in the *Theseus* had so improved under his and Miller's leadership that an anonymous note of thanks from the crew was found on the quarter-deck. On the night of 3 July the Admiral and Miller were out with boats filled with armed seamen. Miller had all he could do to get his men to stay together. 'I was … ordering and exhorting loudly all the boats to follow me to the Enemy, but sorry I am to say that few obeyed.' In the darkness he fell in with a Spanish gunboat, at point-blank range. 'They fired their pistols in our Faces and then threw them, and even billets of wood, and a Tin pot at us. I had the good fortune to shoot the Commanding Officer of her.'

After a second night attack on 5 July, it all seemed more trouble than it was worth. The crew of the *Theseus* did not perform to Miller's satisfaction: they cut tows, dropped anchor too soon, and got lost. 'However, by great exertions and the strongest language I soon repaired the evil.' Only one man from the *Theseus* was killed and, as often happens, he was one of the good ones. 'I lost a fine young man, the Strokesman of my boat, who received a grape shot through his head.' As soon as the attack broke off, 'I had two 18 pound shot tied to the body, and when ready to bury it I made the crew lay their oars across, and each, by my example, uttering an emphatic "God bless him" we committed his remains to the deep, few have prayers equally sincere said over them – the observations of some of my people gave me an opportunity of inculcating the necessity of Religion, morality and sobriety without seeming to intend it.'

Miller and his men wearily regained the *Theseus* at breakfast time the next morning. 'Gave orders for my poor fellows to have their hammocks down, set them to their breakfasts and then went to bed myself … I took some tea and bread and butter in bed, then returning thanks to the Almighty Father whose providence had preserved me, full of thoughts of my beloved Nancy and my children and completely satisfied with the part I had acted, I resigned myself to the downy arms of Sleep.'

On 6 July 1797 Betsey Fremantle recorded the last word about the Cadiz operation in her diary: 'Admiral Nelson, Captains Miller, Martin and Foley dined with us. The Admiral [Jervis] wrote that this bombardment must be given over, Thank God, it was sacrificing men for nothing.'

The necessity for greater sacrifice soon came. Within ten days Nelson had assembled a picked squadron to attack and take the Spanish town of Santa Cruz de Tenerife. He had with him three ships of the line, a fourth-rate, three frigates and the *Fox* cutter – a considerable force. They were intended for an ambitious amphibious operation, a complicated surprise attack that would require near-perfect timing and some luck. Nelson meant to capture the town and a rumoured treasure ship. If mutiny were still in the air, the possibility of prize-money would not go amiss. According to Betsey Fremantle, the crew of the *Theseus* was still unruly, 'the most tiresome noisy mutinous people in the world, they annoyed me amazingly, and Fremantle still more'.

Nelson made three attempts on Tenerife, in all of which Miller played a prominent part. Through inaccurate intelligence and failure to reconnoitre, a surprise dawn attack on 21 July failed and instead fatally alerted the Spanish to their danger.

On 23 July Miller landed near the town and 'made a forced march or rather scramble up a tremendous hill without a path and full of rocks and loose stones; when we got to the Top excessively fatigued … [t]ired as we were, we gave three cheers to encourage and direct our friends that were following us.' It was no use. 'Hunger, thirst, fatigue and sickness, Enemies too powerful for the bravest men, imperiously forced us … About half an hour before sunset … to withdraw.' Always looking for a way to save a bad situation, Miller stopped halfway down, at a point where he thought he might be able to establish 'a very good reconnoitring post' but 'it was becoming so dark that my eyes, at best not strong, would soon be scarce able to discover where I could set my foot with safety'. He caught up with two men and followed them down, whereupon he was so grateful that he gave them 'a new crown I had in my pocket'. By 8pm he was back on the *Seahorse*, where he 'drank three cups of tea as fast as possible, one after another and ate some bread and butter, which except three mouthfuls of Tongue just on leaving the hill and a few grapes, was all I had eaten since I had left the ship. I could have had plenty but did not chuse to eat while my people were starving.'

Nelson refused to give up and on the night of 24 July he personally led the assault. Before launching the men from the *Theseus*, Miller inspected them and 'saw that all were perfectly sober and said a few words of encouragement to them, and cautioned against straggling, plundering or injuring any person not found in arms'.

In the chaos of that night, Miller met Captains Thomas Troubridge and Samuel Hood, and other officers, near dawn, in the town centre. But where was Nelson? The consensus was that he must be dead. It was clear that they must get themselves 'out of a very serious scrape, for we found ourselves with 350 men, ill calculated for shore service, almost without ammunition and totally destitute of provisions and water, in a considerable town entirely strange to us, with as many thousands in arms against us as we counted hundreds, and crowds coming in, We had every reason to fear the Admiral, Capns Bowen, Fremantle and Thompson killed … and we had a report that the *Fox*, with our corps of reserve and supplies of ammunition, was sunk … that the boats being all lost we were cut off from the possibility of receiving more men from the ships.'

The solution was sheer bravado and bluff: the British threatened to burn down the town unless they were allowed to re-embark. The Spaniards were disinclined to risk a counter-attack. Miller, Troubridge and Hood 'went as Gentlemen to pay our respects to the Governor from whom we had received an invitation to dine which it was impossible to accept … He offered us every sort of refreshment, but we took only some iced lemonade and cakes, and most welcome it was to us, as we were parched with heat and thirst, and the dirt on our wet clothes had form'd a perfect crust.' How extraordinary to take lemonade and cake, in a filthy uniform, with the governor of the enemy stronghold you have just failed to capture. 'The very genteel respectable old man,' as Miller de-

scribes him, succoured the English wounded and quickly packed them off the island.

When he later wrote about the assault, Miller was not happy with the conduct of many seamen who had refused to follow his lead during the desperate attempt to force the citadel. Forgivingly he wrote that he was 'not surprised' that 'men unassisted by the high sense of honour, and that rational courage which causes officers to prefer death to shame, should [have] as a body behaved indifferently through the night.' There were those, he added, who conducted themselves with 'great intrepidity'.

The expedition ended in grief for those who were killed and for the amputation that might end Nelson's career. He returned to England with Fremantle in the *Seahorse*, both nursed by Betsey Fremantle, who was herself ill with morning sickness. Captain Miller remained in command of *Theseus*, in which he returned to the blockade of Cadiz.

When Nelson returned to the Mediterranean in *Vanguard* in April 1798 the Earl of St Vincent, gave him the most important detached command of his career. His orders were to find and destroy the French fleet whose purpose was to convoy an army commanded by Bonaparte. Wherever it was going, Nelson and his fourteen 74s, including Miller in *Theseus*, were ordered to intercept it. The French were found in Aboukir Bay.

In a letter to his wife Miller described the attack of 1–2 August 1798. He wanted her to feel like an eyewitness and to imagine the battle 'raging in all magnificent, awful, and horrific grandeur'. Miller had requested 'the honour of leading the Fleet into Battle', but Nelson ordered the *Theseus* to follow *Zealous* and *Goliath* as they ran down the anchored French line.

Miller's account explains why British gunnery was deadly. 'In running along the Enemy's line … I observed their shot sweep just over us, and knowing well that at such a moment Frenchmen would not have coolness enough to change their elevation, I closed them suddenly, and, running under the arch of their shot, reserved my fire … until I had the *Guerrier*'s masts in a line …

We then opened with such effect, that a second breath could not be drawn before her main and mizzen mast were also gone.' This happened 'precisely at sun-set', read Nancy Miller in her husband's meticulous description of British gunnery ripping apart French ships, until just before midnight, when the French flagship *Orient* (120) blew up. The crew of the *Theseus* began to cheer, but Miller stopped them, although he admitted that 'my heart scarce felt a pang for their fate.' He had seen 'numerous and horrid atrocities' committed by Bonaparte's army at Toulon five years before, and did not pity the seamen of republican France, which he called an 'unprincipled and blood-thirsty Nation'.

Theseus sustained heavy damage to masts and rigging, and more than eighty large shot had hit the hull. It was astonishing that they counted no more than six men killed and thirty-one wounded. After so many men from the *Theseus* were drowned when the *Fox* sank at Santa Cruz, Miller felt that 'Providence, in its goodness' had spared them. When in daylight the battle was over, it was safe to stand down and take in the enormity of victory. Miller personally thanked his officers and ship's company 'for their gallantry and good conduct'. The crew of *Theseus*, previously mutinous, had proved themselves in battle on the great day.

The Band of Brothers quickly became the Egyptian Club and pledged a sum for a sword to give Nelson. The admiral himself gave his former flag captain the greatest reward of all: leave to go home. Miller was overjoyed that Nelson, unasked, had thought of it, and had said 'that after so many services to the public I owed it to myself to pursue my own happiness'.

Miller left with a group of prizes bound for England, but at Gibraltar was sent back to the Levant to join Sir Sidney Smith, who had asked for him. Bonaparte still had an army with which to attempt more conquests, and Miller's help was needed at Acre.

There Miller began the hazardous practice of picking up unexploded French ordnance, which was then modified and fired back at the enemy.

Paid for by his companions in victory, Miller is crowned with the laurels of the Battles of St Vincent and the Nile.

According to his first lieutenant, on 14 May 1799 'twenty 36-pounder howitzer shells and fifty 18-pounder shells had been got up and prepared for service by Captain Miller's order'. At 9.30am the ammunition on deck exploded, engulfing *Theseus* in flames. Among the twenty-nine dead was the ship's captain. He was thirty-seven years old.

In his will Miller left everything he had to his wife and two daughters. The heirlooms of his house were few but priceless: '[T]he Gold Medal sent me by my Sovereign in consequence of the defeat of the Spanish Fleet, on the 14th February, 1797, the Spanish sword taken that day, the Ring given me by Commodore Nelson on the occasion, and my own sword, which thank Heaven! has never been drawn in a private quarrel.'

Captain Ralph Willett Miller, American-born but British by choice, died in the service of his King and was forever mourned by his fellow captains at Aboukir, who commissioned a monument to his memory in St Paul's Cathedral.

SUSAN K SMITH

→ PEYTON ←

John Goodwin Gregory Peyton (1752–1809) was born at Wakehurst, Ardingly, Sussex, one of at least five generations of Peytons who served in the Royal Navy; his grandfather, father and brother also became admirals. His family's naval history is extensive but his own service is obscure, and though there are several sightings of him in the years before the Nile, some authors have conflated the Peytons.

Most probably he was entered on the books of his father's ship, the former French East Indiaman *Belleisle* (64) in 1766. He was made lieutenant in 1772, and, still under his father, saw the opening moves of the American War, and the Moonlight Battle in 1780 in *Cumberland* (74). By March 1782 he was in command of *Kite* (12), when he took the privateer *Fantasque* off Dunkirk. His commission as post-captain is dated the day his next command, *Carnatic* (74), was launched at Deptford, 21 January 1783. Two more commands followed, *Seahorse* (38) and *Ceres* (32) before he took up his most famous ship, *Defence* (74).

Peyton travelled in the same coach as Fanny Nelson, before joining Nelson in *Vanguard* for passage out to the Mediterranean, Nelson writing to his wife on 1 April 1798: 'A Captain Peyton, a fellow-traveller of yours, is a passenger with me, [who] is going to the *Defence*.' The voyage gave Nelson the opportunity to assess Peyton's charac-

In the eighteenth and nineteenth century portraits of couples were frequent, but in the twentieth century museum curators would only accept for their collections the male halves of these pairs, and thus man and wife were divorced in death. However, the portraits of John and Susanna Peyton have survived, in private hands, across the centuries.

ter and may explain why, despite Peyton's fifteen years' seniority, he was not summoned to the flagship to be consulted during the chase to the east in search of Bonaparte's fleet.

His ship's company in *Defence* had one of the longest sick lists in Nelson's fleet, suffering from intermittent fevers and sore throats, besides the scurvy and ulcers which were commonplace. *Defence* herself, nearly thirty years old, was worn out and needed a refit, and Peyton himself fell ill. He wrote to Nelson on 3 July 1798: 'The rapid decline of my health and bodily strength is such to place me in the most uncomfortable situation in looking to the long continuance of the hot weather that must take place. I feel but too strongly its operation on my constitution will make it very unjustifiable in retaining a situation I shall not be equal to.'

Notwithstanding the wretched condition of her captain, crew and the carcase of *Defence*, at the Battle of the Nile, Peyton commanded his ship with good sense and courage and she acquitted herself well. At 7pm she commenced a slow and terrible duel with *Peuple Souverain* which lasted three hours before her opponent was completely dismasted. *Defence* lost her fore-topmast over the side but a few minutes later, Peyton veered out his sheet anchor in order to engage *Franklin*. Warner wrote of Peyton's action. 'Not a moment was lost; not a break for recovery. It is no wonder that the Band of Brothers were invincible.'

Nelson's original dispatches and three bags of the fleet's mail were lost when the vessel carrying them was captured, and few first-hand accounts of the battle have survived, so Peyton's second letter describing the aftermath of the battle is unique:

Defence off the Nile

August 13th 1798

My ever Dear Love

I wrote you by the *Leander* who sailed from hence the 6th instant with the Admirals dispatches since which we have been busily employed refitting our own ships & prizes. Tomorrow we shall sail & make the best of our way to Gibraltar or Lisbon – & I should hope ultimately to England – at any rate my own Dear Susan, we shall be better situated to hear from each other – no small comfort to both parties – I have my fears you will hear of our action through France before the *Leander* can probably arrive in England & that in consequence you as well as many others will be kept for some time in a state of anxiety. The more I think of our victory, & its consequences the more I am gratified – & if Bonaparte should fail in his expedition – which we here flatter ourselves he may – I believe peace not very far distant … The 3 frigates, *Alcmene* & *Emerald* & *Bonne Citoyenne* that have been looking for us these two months are now coming in – truly mortified they must be – in not meeting us until after the action. I hope to have John to dine with me. I think the Captains will get two thousand pounds perhaps more if our prizes all get to England. The *Emerald* has just passed us & gone to endeavour to free one of the prizes that is aground so that I fear I shall not see John. I must send this to Capt. Capel who leaves us this afternoon …

Believe me ever your faithful affectionate husband

John Peyton

P.S. I find myself a stouter man since the action, another such would make me a fine young fellow. God bless you.

The reference to John is to his nephew John Strutt Peyton, a midshipman in the frigate *Emerald*.

Peyton had married a widow, Susanna Gurnell, in 1793. When he retired in 1800 he bought the house and extensive grounds of Priestlands, Lymington, which is now a school. Rear-Admiral John Peyton died on 2 August 1809; unfortunately the memorial to him in All Saints Church, Milford-on Sea, is in a sad state of repair.

KEN FLEMMING

Peyton's memorial has not survived so well, but the Milford on Sea Historical Record Society, in conjunction with the 1805 Club, hopes to restore it in All Saints' Church, Milford on Sea.

→ SAUMAREZ ←

Aged ten, James Saumarez was put on the books of *Solebay* spending the years in England to improve his English. In 1770 he joined the frigate *Montreal* sailing for the eastern Mediterranean where British merchant shipping needed protection during the Turkish-Russian war. He later served in *Winchelsea* (32) and *Levant* (28), returning to England in 1775.

He passed for lieutenant in 1778 and joined Sir Peter Parker's flagship, *Bristol* (50), which sailed for America with troop reinforcements for Cornwallis during the American War of Independence: he turned down the offer of an Army commission as aide-de-camp to the general.

Saumarez's first taste of action was at the Siege of Charleston in 1776, when he saw several of his gun crew killed as well as a fellow midshipman, to whom he was talking, having his head carried off by a cannonball. He was commended for his courage and initiative and, promoted to lieutenant,

James de Saumarez (1757–1836) was the third son of Matthew Saumarez, a retired naval surgeon in St Peter Port, Guernsey, an island five by seven miles with a population in the 1800s of around 20,000, where the Saumarez family go back to at least the thirteenth century.

Henry de Sausmarez (the spelling has changed over the centuries) invented a device for measuring distance at sea, which was submitted to Sir Isaac Newton, who referred it to Trinity House because he 'had no experience in sea affairs, nor ever was at sea'. Henry also published a chart of the Channel Islands in 1727 making a particular reference to the dangers of the Casquets. Two of James's uncles, Philip and Thomas, served under Anson on the 1740–44 circumnavigation when the Spanish treasure galleon *Nuestra Señora de Covadonga* was captured. As captain of *Nottingham* (60) Philip took the French ship *Mars* (64) in 1746 but was killed the following year at the Second Battle of Finisterre: there is a monument to him in Westminster Abbey. In 1758 Thomas, in *Antelope* (54), captured the French *Belliqueux* (60) which was then taken into the Navy with Thomas as her commander.

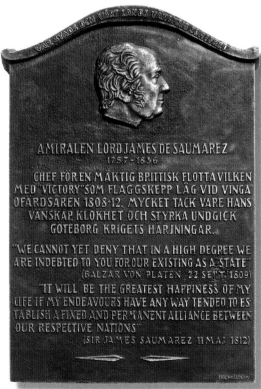

This plaque on the wall of the Town Hall in Gothenburg attests to the high esteem in which the Swedes held Saumarez: 'Our town and our country's friend in war and peace'.

Victory leaving the Swedish naval base of Karlskrona in 1809, escorted by the Swedish 64-gun *Dristigheten (Audacity)*.

received his first command, a galley called *Spitfire*. Nelson joined *Bristol* in Saumarez's wake.

Back in England Saumarez served in *Victory* (1778–81) and in the summer of 1781 he visited the Baltic for the first time in *Fortitude* (74), flagship of Vice-Admiral Hyde Parker.

At dawn on 5 August 1781 the British and Dutch fleets met over Dogger Bank and an intense fight at close quarters lasted three hours. Though there were many casualties, it was an indecisive battle, but the Dutch fleet took no real part in the rest of the war. Saumarez's reward was to be presented to the King and given command of the copper-bottomed, fast-sailing fireship *Tisiphone*, mounting eight 12-pounders with a crew of fifty-five. Saumarez was attached to Rear-Admiral Richard Kempenfelt's Channel Fleet when on 12 December 1781 he sighted an enemy convoy, with a strong escort downwind of the transports. Kempenfelt took fifteen sail, while the French ships of the line watched helplessly, and *Tisiphone* took a 36-gun frigate in an action lasting twenty minutes

– Saumarez's first victory as a commander.

Next, ordered to the Caribbean, Saumarez met two French 74s but by clever signalling he managed to deceive them and escape, sailing a narrow and uncharted channel between Nevis and St Kitts, a ploy he would use again off Guernsey later.

Saumarez was ordered to take urgent despatches home, which would probably have led to his promotion, but instead he reached captain's rank in February 1782 when he exchanged places with the sick captain of *Russell* (74) who was anxious to be in England. He found *Russell* a mutinous, shot-rolling ship, but soon formed the crew into a well-motivated, disciplined and effective fighting force.

A large French fleet had gathered in the West Indies where the British, now under George Rodney, caught up with them between Dominica and Guadeloupe. The fleets approached on opposite tacks and when the wind veered, Rodney luffed, as did others. After running up the French line,

Russell wore round before re-entering the battle and Saumarez found himself upwind of the French, to the pleasure and surprise of Rodney who thus broke the French line. *Russell* was one of the ships which fiercely engaged the *Ville de Paris*, Comte de Grasse's flagship, which struck and became the first first-rate flagship ever captured in battle. Rodney praised Saumarez for his efforts at the Battle of the Saintes.

Saumarez speedily repaired *Russell* and escorted a merchant convoy back to England. There he rewarded his crew for their loyalty: they had been drafted en bloc to sail to the East Indies, but Saumarez saw this as unfair, his protests were heard, and the crew were paid off.

The Treaty of Versailles of 1783 heralded a decade of peace during which Saumarez was presented to Louis XVI, who was in Cherbourg for the ceremonial opening of the new harbour. Saumarez also took the opportunity to marry his first cousin, Martha, to whom he was a devout, loyal and loving husband his whole life, corresponding nearly daily when apart.

On the renewal of war in 1793 Saumarez was given command of the frigate *Crescent* (36) in Rear-Admiral Hyde Parker's Channel Fleet, and there on 20 October *Crescent* fell in with the French frigate *Reunion* off Barfleur. *Crescent's* crew suffered one broken leg, while the French had over a third of their crew killed or wounded, and struck after just over two hours' fighting: Saumarez's victory earned him a knighthood.

On 8 June 1794, Saumarez sailed from Plymouth with a small squadron escorting merchant vessels to Guernsey when he was intercepted by a superior French squadron. He drew the French fire, allowing the merchantmen to return to England and the rest of his squadron to run for St Peter Port. Then, aided by a Guernsey pilot, he escaped through a narrow passage between reefs off the west coast. Saumarez persuaded the Admiralty to reward the pilot, Jean Breton, with £100.

In March 1795 Saumarez was given command of *Orion* (74) in the Channel Fleet now under Lord Bridport (Alexander Hood), and many of his

old crew from *Crescent* transferred with him. His first action was a chase of a French squadron off Île de Groix in June 1795, when the recently refitted and clean-bottomed *Orion* led and fired the first broadside, but the French were in no mood for an action and ran for Lorient leaving behind three ships. Later that year *Orion* was part of the landings in France at St-Nazaire, but the counter-revolution was unsuccessful and the remains of the invading army had to be evacuated.

At the Battle of Cape St Vincent on 14 February 1797, *Orion* engaged the *Salvador del Mundo* (112), which struck to Saumarez after an hour's fierce fighting, and then he engaged the *Santísima Trinidad* (130), which also struck. However, before Saumarez could take possession, Jervis recalled his fleet to defend Nelson's prizes (won by Nelson's patent bridge) and thus deprived Saumarez of the glory of taking two first-rates without a bridge.

When the Great Mutiny spread through the Navy, Jervis (now Earl St Vincent) dealt with mutineers severely. One mutineer was placed in chains in *Orion* prior to execution, but Saumarez persuaded St Vincent to commute the sentence. The saved man returned Saumarez's trust as the captain of a gun in *Orion* at the Nile and then by shoring up *Peuple Souverain* below the water line after she struck. Throughout his career Saumarez disliked severe punishment and never watched floggings. In another instance of his humanity, when Saumarez was ordered to cut out some gunships guarding the entrance to Cadiz but suspected a trap, he picked only unmarried men to follow him.

When the French massed troops and a large fleet at Toulon, Saumarez and Alexander Ball were dispatched under Nelson into the Mediterranean to gather intelligence. They discovered that the French had sailed from Toulon, and Nelson, reinforced with more ships of the line widened their search. Guessing that the French were headed for Egypt, the British overtook the French without seeing them, but eventually on the afternoon of 1 August they found the French in Aboukir Bay.

Technically, the fleets were fairly evenly matched but the ensuing battle showed how well-trained, skilled and highly motivated the original Band of Brothers were.

At 5pm Nelson signalled to attack the van and centre of the French line. *Goliath* saw a gap at the head of the French line and led five sail, including *Orion,* inshore to engage the French from the landward side, while the rest of the British engaged from the seaward side. The French had expected neither the action commencing so late in the afternoon nor being attacked from both sides. The French frigate *Sérieuse,* against the conventions of naval war, fired upon *Orion,* which returned fire and sank her with one broadside. Saumarez, together with *Defence,* engaged *Franklin* and *Peuple Souverain.* At 9pm fire was seen on the French flagship *Orient* and as it spread both French and British ceased firing and prepared for the inevitable detonation, which destroyed *Orient* and was heard in Alexandria. Meanwhile, *Peuple Souverain* cut her anchor and drifted out of the action, and *Franklin* struck after midnight. On hearing that Nelson was wounded, Saumarez, as second-in-command, signalled to those that could to slip anchor and lend assistance to those still fighting.

It was a great victory: some nine thousand Frenchmen were killed, wounded, or taken prisoner compared with the British butcher's bill of about nine hundred, and Bonaparte and his army were stranded in Egypt. Nelson's captains, the original Band of Brothers, formed the Egyptian Club and commissioned a gold crocodile-hilted sword to present to Nelson.

In 1799–1800 Saumarez commanded the blockade of Brest, and in 1801 he was sent to the Mediterranean to frustrate French plans for a renewed campaign in the east. There in one month he fought two battles. On 6 July 1801 at the Battle of Algeciras he attacked a French squadron at anchor under a line of forts; the fight ended indecisively but his ships were badly damaged. Just six days later his ships were refitted and in the Battle of the Gut Saumarez gave chase to the French ships and an escorting squadron of Spaniards. In light winds Saumarez ordered a general chase, and in the night the Spaniards mistook their own

ships for the enemy, two collided and both blew up. Nelson's maiden speech in the House of Lords started with his praise of Saumarez's victory.

After the breakdown of the Peace of Amiens, Saumarez once more commanded the Guernsey station, taking several French prizes and raiding Granville to destroy the invasion barges which were being gathered there. He was also in regular and friendly correspondence with Nelson, and received a letter from Nelson dated 18 October 1805 thanking him for wine, fruit and newspapers sent from Guernsey. This must have been in the final batch of letters ever sent by Nelson.

In 1807 Saumarez again blockaded Brest, but in March 1808 he was ordered to the Baltic. The political situation there was very complicated and the trade which Saumarez was sent to protect was vital to Britain and important economically to Sweden. He spent five years in the Baltic, returning to England in the winters escorting the merchant fleets which had assembled at Wingo (Vinga) off Gothenburg and at Hanö outside the Swedish naval base of Karlskrona.

Saumarez blockaded the Russian fleet in Rogervick, deciding not to attack as it might have alienated the Tsar who was becoming distrustful of Bonaparte, and when Russia forced a peace on Sweden in 1809, under which Sweden was to stop all trade with Britain and declare war, Saumarez played the skilful diplomat. When in 1810, one of Napoleon's marshals, Jean-Baptiste Bernadotte, was selected as heir apparent to the Swedish throne, Saumarez had built up a sound understanding of the complex politics of the region. Although Britain was technically at war with Sweden, he gave free passage to Swedish shipping and the new Swedish prince.

Saumarez's time in the Baltic is best summarised in a letter from the Swedish Baron Platen:

You have been the guardian angel of my country; by your wise, temperate and loyal conduct you have been the first cause of the plans which have been formed against the Demon of the Continent … You were the first cause that Russia dared make war against France;

had you fired one shot when we declared war against England all had been ended, and Europe would have been enslaved.

Saumarez, by his considered understanding of a volatile and complicated situation, on his own initiative, using restraint rather than ball and powder, and diplomacy rather than broadsides, had saved many lives, and shortened the length of the war. Sweden conferred on Saumarez the Grand Cross of the Order of the Sword, together with a beautiful and valuable diamond-encrusted sword, and in November 1812 he returned to England and struck his flag. This was his, and *Victory's*, last voyage in active service. Saumarez is still remembered with affection in Sweden, with a plaque to his memory on the wall of the town hall in Gothenburg.

In 1831, following the accession of William IV, Saumarez was ennobled.

Saumarez's charitable works after his retirement were aimed at causes dear to himself, giving considerable sums towards education in Guernsey (especially in helping to establish separate schools for girls), Sunday schools, the Bible Society and for the relief of the poor of Guernsey. He also gave time and money to building an Anglican Church for the English speakers of the island and was also instrumental in the formation of the Guernsey Savings Bank.

Admiral Baron de Saumarez, GCB, died at home on 9 October 1836. He was buried in the Castel churchyard, attended by an estimated 1,000 of his fellow islanders. A 99ft obelisk was erected to his honour in Guernsey – sadly pulled down by the Germans during their occupation in the Second World War. Saumarez was a loving, caring husband and father, a man who put loyalty and duty second only to devotion and trust in the Almighty. He was daring and courageous, but also fair-minded, and compassionate; he could show self-control and patience when the need arose. All these traits made his crews trust and want to follow him, and made him such a successful diplomat in the Baltic.

LORD DE SAUMAREZ

→ THOMPSON ←

Thomas Boulden Thompson (1766–1828) was almost certainly the love-child of Sarah Boulden of Barham, Kent (and thus a neighbour of Charles Middleton), and Edward 'Poet' Thompson (*c.* 1738–86), bon vivant, author, playwright and erstwhile naval officer.

Young Thomas went to sea in 1778 in his father's ship *Hyaena* (24), when he added Thompson to his name, and where his father ensured he had decent schooling and that his 'spirit, vigour and ability' were nurtured. In 1779 father and son returned with a convoy from the West Indies, and in 1780 they witnessed the Moonlight Battle and the relief of Gibraltar under Admiral Rodney. In 1781 Thompson was sent to take control of the Dutch colonies at Demerara and Essequibo, and in 1782 he promoted his son to lieutenant six weeks before his sixteenth birthday.

When *Hyaena* reached Barbados, Thompson found that Rodney was in England and his second-in-command, Samuel Hood, was in New York and he took it upon himself to escort a convoy home. In his absence the French captured Guiana and he was then tried by court-martial, for having

ABOVE: Sunset on 1 August 1798: the British fleet enters Aboukir Bay to attack the French fleet at anchor. Nelson's flagship, *Vanguard*, flies the signal for close action; the French flagship flies the signal to recall men from the shore, Robert Dodd (1748-1815).

LEFT: Thompson's monument in the Royal Navy Cemetery in the grounds of Devonport House, Greenwich.

INSET: The inscription records his naval, Admiralty and parliamentary career before becoming treasurer of Greenwich Hospital.

left his station without orders, but acquitted. Instead, in 1783 Edward Thompson was appointed to *Grampus* (50) as commodore of a squadron off West Africa, and there he died in 1786, having ensured that Thomas would be promoted to command *Nautilus* (16), which he brought home in 1787 and went on half pay.

Although advanced to post rank on 22 November 1790, Thompson was unemployed until late in 1796, when he was appointed to *Leander* (50) and joined Lord St Vincent off Cadiz in the spring of 1797. His friendship with Nelson started when he was detached in Nelson's flotilla for the attack on Tenerife. There he was in the boats which with Nelson attempted to land on the mole at Santa Cruz, and he too was wounded in the arm. Thompson left no reminiscence of the event, but the British had thought the attack would be a push-over, and one may suppose that he felt the defeat keenly. Nevertheless in the school of hard knocks, Tenerife, where Nelson, Fremantle, Hood, Miller, Troubridge, and Thompson first fought together, was an important step in establishing the Band of Brothers.

Thompson remained on station, while Nelson went home to recover from the loss of his arm. When in February 1798 Nelson, restored to health, led the British return to the Mediterranean after an absence of over a year, Thompson was sent to join him. In June 1798, east of Malta, Thompson reported four strange sail. These were the outriders of the French fleet, Nelson who was concerned not to scatter his own fleet, recalled Thompson and thus missed the opportunity to meet Bonaparte at sea and possibly to change the course of history.

In the opening phase of the Battle of the Nile *Leander* and *Mutine* (16) tried to assist Troubridge's *Culloden* but were ordered away to join Nelson in the battle. *Leander* was not a ship of the line but by squeezing between *Peuple Souverain* (74) and *Franklin* (84) she was able to rake these two French ships, and to get a few shots into *Orient* (118), without sustaining too much reciprocal damage. After the battle Nelson ordered Thompson to carry Berry home with his dispatches. The voyage ended badly when, on 18 August, *Leander* encountered the French ship *Généreux* (74), one of the two escapees from the Battle of the Nile, and, unable to out-sail her, resisted capture for six and a half hours. At the end *Leander* was a dismasted hulk and had been reduced to firing crowbars, nails and other langrage, and neither ship had a boat left. The Frenchmen had to swim to *Leander* in order to carry out their usual depredations against the British, even trying to take the surgeon's instruments while he was operating on Berry. The French captain told him (as reported in the *Naval Chronicle*), 'J'ensuis fâché, mais le fait est que les François sont bons au pillage.' Thompson and Berry were severely wounded and their captors

chivalrously allowed them to return overland to England.

At Thompson's court-martial for the loss of his ship he was acquitted and praised for his 'gallant and almost unprecedented' defence of *Leander* against such a superior force. Thompson was knighted in 1799 and awarded a pension of £200 per annum. In the same year he married Anne Raikes, daughter of Robert Raikes of Gloucester, the founder of the Sunday School movement.

Next Thompson was given command of *Bellona* (74), in which he joined the blockading fleet off Brest under Lord Bridport. After two years of this drudgery, *Bellona* joined Hyde Parker's expedition to the Baltic and was in Nelson's squadron for the attack on Copenhagen. *Bellona* did not make her designated station but stuck fast on the Middle Ground within range of the enemy, from where she was able to play long bowls against the distant Danes sufficiently well for Nelson to mention in his report Thompson's 'great service'. She suffered eleven dead and sixty-three wounded, including Thompson who lost a leg to a roundshot when he was standing on a quarterdeck gun to get a better view: later his only form of exercise was on horseback, which did nothing to forestall the onset of corpulence.

Upon his return to England Thompson's pension was raised to £500 (and to £700 in 1815) and his last command was the royal yacht *Mary* (6). In 1806–16 he was Comptroller of the Navy, and afterwards treasurer of Greenwich Hospital and director of the Chatham Chest.

He was elevated to the baronetcy in 1806, became rear-admiral in 1809, vice-admiral in 1814, KCB in 1815, and GCB in 1822. From May 1807 to June 1816 he was a Tory MP for Rochester, Kent; he voted against criminal law and parliamentary reform, and against Roman Catholic emancipation, but supported Christian missions to India.

Vice-Admiral Sir Thomas Boulden Thompson died at home at Hartsbourne Manor Place, Hertfordshire in 1828.

AGUSTÍN GUIMERÁ

✦ TROUBRIDGE ✦

Thomas Troubridge (c.1758–1807) was the first Troubridge to join the Royal Navy and achieve flag rank. I am the seventh baronet, also Sir Thomas Troubridge, and the first Troubridge for seven generations not to join the Royal Navy. However, I have taken a great interest in my illustrious ancestor's life and career and in particular his long friendship with Nelson, which began when they were both appointed midshipmen to *Seahorse* (24) at the tender age of fifteen and ended in early 1805 when Troubridge headed to the East Indies and Nelson started his pursuit of the French fleet finishing at Trafalgar.

His father was Richard Troubridge, a baker of Temple Bar and Cavendish Street, and his mother Elizabeth Squinch, of Marylebone. Somehow Richard Troubridge knew Sir Charles Saunders, who took an interest in the boy, but little else is known of Troubridge's early life or family background or how he came to be educated at St Paul's School, London.

Sadly, many of his possessions were with him in *Blenheim* (90) when she foundered in a typhoon off Madagascar and sank with all hands, although the family still retain some items. In 2005 I pur-chased two pewter plates at auction which came off *Culloden* (74), his command in 1794–9. I also have a scale model of *Culloden* built in 2005 in Mauritius from plans held at the National Maritime Museum and it was in *Culloden* that Troubridge came to the attention of Admiral Sir John Jervis, later Earl of St Vincent, at the Battle of Cape St Vincent.

Much of his early career was spent in the East Indies under Admiral Sir Edward Hughes, Troubridge advancing from midshipman in *Seahorse* in 1773 to post-captain in *Active* (32) in 1783 in the fiercely contested general actions between Hughes and the French Admiral Suffren. He came home in 1785 as Hughes's flag captain in *Sultan* (74).

During the Spanish Armament of 1790 Troubridge was appointed to *Thames* (32) and spent two more years in the East Indies. On his return to England he was appointed to *Castor* (32) where he had the misfortune to be captured by the French Brest fleet. Thus he had the unique and galling experience of being a prisoner in the French *Sans Pareil* at the Battle of the Glorious First of June. Imprisoned in the bosun's store, 'he amused himself in pouring forth every invective against the French and the man appointed to guard him,' and on hearing the *Sans Pareil*'s mainmast go overboard 'began to jump and caper with all the gestures of a maniac'. When *Sans Pareil* surrendered to *Majestic* (74, Captain Charles Cotton) Troubridge personally tore down her colours and had the satisfaction of taking her into port.

Shortly after this he was appointed to *Culloden*. One of my favourite stories of Troubridge was at the Battle of Cape St Vincent when *Culloden* led the British line and was the first to open fire on the Spanish ships. Troubridge anticipated a signal from Jervis and tacked his ship as Jervis hoisted his signal. Jervis was delighted: 'Look at Troubridge there! He tacks his ship in battle as if the eyes of England were upon him; and would to God they were, for they would see him to be, what I know him to be, and, by Heaven, sir, what the Dons will soon feel him to be!' This was one of Troubridge's finest hours and the name St Vincent lives on in our family with my youngest son, Nicholas Douglas St Vincent Troubridge, bearing the name for the eighth generation.

Troubridge was fortunate as a military man in that his career coincided with the American War of Independence, and the French Revolutionary and Napoleonic Wars. War tends to result in more opportunity to demonstrate courage and ability and achieve rapid promotion. Troubridge went from midshipman in 1773 at the age of fifteen to rear-admiral in 1804 at the age of forty-six, although not as fast as Nelson who was promoted to rear-admiral at the age of thirty-nine.

The Battle of the Nile was a turning point in Troubridge's life and career. *Culloden* ran aground on a shoal at the entrance to Aboukir Bay and he was forced to watch the battle without being able to take part. While en route to Naples with the French prizes, he received the sad news of the

The stained window at St Paul's School, London, commemorates one of its more famous pupils.

death of his wife, Frances, née Richardson, whom he had married in 1787. She died on 13 June 1798 and was buried at St Andrew's Church, Plymouth, leaving two children, Edward Thomas and Charlotte.

Unlike other captains he did not initially receive the traditional gold medal for the battle, although Nelson petitioned the Admiralty on his behalf and he was awarded the medal in 1799, the same year he became the first Baronet Troubridge of Plymouth. The family only have copies of Troubridge's gold medals from both Cape St Vincent and the Nile, so we assume that the originals went down on *Blenheim* in 1807. Much has been written of two relationships which marked the eight years from 1799 to Troubridge's death at sea in 1807. The first was his friendship with Nelson which had started in *Seahorse* in 1773 and endured through many of the great battles of the time as one of Nelson's Band of Brothers but which began to cool after Troubridge's appointment by St Vincent as one of the Admiralty commissioners in 1801; the second was his difficult relationship with Rear-Admiral Sir Edward Pellew, with whom Troubridge was supposed to share the East Indies station where he arrived in 1805.

Nelson and Troubridge had been friends since their formative years in the Navy and by 1796 both were captains under Jervis, though it was Troubridge whom Jervis said was capable of commanding the fleet, 'the best Bayard of the British Navy; the ablest adviser and best executive officer, with honour and courage bright as a sword'. The friendship started to cool after the Nile. When Troubridge joined the Admiralty under St Vincent, Nelson, sensing that Troubridge disapproved of his relationship with Lady Hamilton, began to interpret his orders as deliberate attempts to keep him at sea. Correspondence between the two men documents the deterioration in their thirty-year friendship which by 1803 was all but ended. Nelson did take Troubridge's son, Edward, into *Victory* in 1803 as a midshipman but otherwise contact between them was minimal thereafter. One of the items the family still possess is a silver inkstand presented by Troubridge while a captain to Nelson, probably after the Battle of the Nile. We do not know when or why the inkstand was returned to our family.

The second relationship was with Pellew, who was described as the best frigate commander the Navy had ever produced, and had been appointed to command the East Indies station in 1804, ironically with Troubridge's old ship, *Culloden*, as his flagship. The following year the Admiralty decided, without consulting Pellew, to divide the station in two and offered Troubridge one half and his choice of flagship, which was *Blenheim*. The family still have paintings by Thomas Buttersworth of Troubridge's squadron departing Spithead and anchored off Madeira en route to Penang in early 1805. This was a political decision and one can imagine the reaction of Pellew on Troubridge's arrival and his orders with which Pellew disagreed. There was a loophole in the orders which allowed Pellew to consolidate the command in the event of an emergency and such an emergency presented itself when Pellew received news of a French squadron on its way to India. In truth, both men were in an impossible situation, Pellew writing that 'even brothers' could not have agreed under the circumstances, and it was not resolved until early 1807 when Troubridge was ordered to the Cape of Good Hope. Modern communications would have dealt with the matter quickly, but in those days an exchange of letters with the Admiralty could take up to a year.

Troubridge must have taken some comfort from having his son and heir, Edward Thomas Troubridge, as a lieutenant in *Blenheim* and subsequently in command of *Harrier* (18). The young Troubridge, who was still only a teenager but already a veteran of Copenhagen, distinguished himself in July 1806 when he destroyed a Dutch brig and participated in the capture of a frigate and two Indiamen. His father pressed for his promotion to commander and would have been aware of the prize-money for the capture, some £26,000, and the award of a Lloyd's £100 patriotic sword. Pellew dispatched young Troubridge to look for his father's squadron in 1807 after *Blenheim* and

The inkstand which Troubridge presented to Nelson was somehow returned, and is one of the few artefacts not to have gone down with Troubridge, when his ship foundered.

Java disappeared in the Indian Ocean on the way to the Cape, but nothing was found.

Like many of his colleagues Troubridge spent most of his life at sea. He has been described as an exceptional naval officer and completely dedicated to the service and the framework of discipline that it provided. He had little sympathy for those who did not follow Navy rules and was known as a tough disciplinarian. The stress he was under in the last few years of his life appears to have made him less tolerant and may have contributed to the unfortunate decision to leave Penang in the unseaworthy *Blenheim*. The family motto is 'Ne cede arduis' or 'Do not yield to difficulties', and he had more than his fair share of difficulties in the years after the Battle of the Nile. One wonders if life would have been different if *Culloden* had not struck that shoal.

As he was lost at sea, I long assumed that there was no memorial to Troubridge. However, in 2007 by chance I discovered that St Paul's School, which he attended from about 1768 until he joined the *Seahorse*, has a stained glass window dedicated to Troubridge in the Montgomery room.

I am sure Troubridge would have been proud of the long line of Troubridge admirals who followed him and of the T-class destroyer, *Troubridge*, commissioned in 1942 and retired in 1970. I spent a weekend at sea on her out of Malta when I was a boy, and we have the ship's bell at home. As one of Nelson's Band of Brothers his place in history is assured.

TOM TROUBRIDGE

➤ WESTCOTT ➤

George Blagdon Westcott (c.1753–1798) was the son of Benjamin Westcott, believed to be a baker at Honiton, Devon, where he was baptised on 24 April 1753. Unusually, his mother, Susanna, had her obituary given in the *Naval Chronicle* after she died in 1813 at the age of eighty-two. According to family legend, young George often went to help at the local mill where he is said to have repaired a broken rope by splicing it, at which the miller recommended that he should become a sailor.

Starting as cabin boy in 1768, aged thirteen, he served five years in *Solebay* (28) under Captains Lucius O'Brien and George Vandeput, showed a quick grasp of his trade and was soon rated master's mate, able seaman and then midshipman. He served three more years as midshipman in *Albion* (74) under Captains Samuel Barrington and John Leveson-Gower before passing his lieutenant's examination on 10 January 1776. In 1777 he followed Leveson-Gower into *Valiant* (74) and was in her under Captain Samuel Granston Goodall at the first Battle of Ushant 1778 and was at the Relief of Gibraltar in April 1781.

It is not clear under whose patronage Westcott joined the Navy but he served under a succession of officers who all rose to flag rank in war (not by deadmen's shoes in peacetime) and in 1781, he joined *Victory*, wearing the flag of Rear-Admiral Richard Kempenfelt and took part in the second Battle of Ushant on 12 December 1781, Howe's Relief of Gibraltar and the Battle of Cape Spartel in October 1782.

Employment was scarce for naval officers during peacetime, but after a brief spell in *Medway* (60), Westcott's talent brought him an appointment in 1786 as first lieutenant of *Salisbury* (50), under Commodore John Elliot, commander-in-chief Newfoundland. In December 1787 he was promoted commander and 1789–90 commanded the brig-sloop *Fortune* (14). The Nootka crisis brought him the command of *London* (90) as flag captain to his former chief, now Rear-Admiral Goodall.

After a period on half pay, in late 1793 Westcott joined *Impregnable* (98) as flag captain to Rear-Admiral Benjamin Caldwell and they fought at the Battle of the Glorious First of June. Caldwell was a successful and battle-hardened officer who was overlooked in the plaudits after this battle and when he was relieved, in the West Indies, by the relatively junior Sir John Laforey he returned home in high dudgeon and refused to serve again. Westcott had followed Caldwell to *Majestic* (74), and seems to have been unaffected by his chief's disgruntlement, serving under Laforey until returning to Britain in June 1796.

Majestic then joined the Channel Fleet as a private ship (in other words, without the 'benefit' of bearing an admiral's flag), serving under Rear-Admiral John Colpoys off Brest in December, and then with Alexander Hood, Lord Bridport, at Spithead during the following mutinous spring. The crew of *Majestic* were enthusiastic mutineers, but they soon returned to duty, in common with most others, when their complaints were dealt with after Lord Howe's intervention.

Late in 1798, Westcott, still commanding *Majestic*, joined the fleet under the Earl of St

ERECTED AT THE PUBLIC EXPENSE.
TO THE MEMORY OF
GEORGE BLAGDON WESTCOTT,
CAPTAIN OF THE MAJESTIC;
WHO, AFTER THIRTY-THREE YEARS OF MERITORIOUS SERVICE,
FELL GLORIOUSLY
IN THE VICTORY OBTAINED OVER THE FRENCH FLEET OFF ABOUKIR
THE FIRST DAY OF AUGUST, IN THE YEAR MDCCXCVIII
IN THE FORTY-SIXTH YEAR OF HIS AGE.

Of his death, Collingwood remarked, 'A good officer and a worthy man; but, if it was a part of our condition to choose a day to die on, where could he have found one so memorable, so eminently distinguished among great days?' Westcott became one of only a handful of naval officers with a monument in St Paul's Cathedral, in which he is depicted expiring in the arms of Victory, who is holding a crown of laurels over his head, in a setting representing the connections with the Nile. Another monument to him was erected by subscription at Honiton.

Somehow, despite his near continuous thirty years at sea, Westcott found time to marry – apparently to a local Honiton girl. In January 1801, while passing through Honiton, Nelson invited Westcott's widow and her daughter to breakfast, and finding them in straitened circumstances presented them with his own Nile medal, saying, 'You will not value it less because Nelson has worn it.'

PETER TURNER

Memorial in St Paul's to 'George Blagdon Westcott, captain of the Majestic; who after thirty-three years of meritorious service, fell gloriously in the victory obtained over the French fleet off Aboukir'.

Detail from a large emblematic drawing presented to Nelson on his arrival at Naples on 22 September 1798.

Vincent, who detached her to join Nelson in the Mediterranean. At the Battle of Aboukir Bay *Majestic* was positioned towards the rear of the British line and she engaged the French *Tonnant* (80), but in the smoke and darkness she ran foul of the French *Heureux* (74), becoming trapped by her rigging, and for several minutes came under heavy fire from both ships. Westcott was shot in the throat by a musket ball, fired in the darkness from *Tonnant* and became the only British officer of his rank to fall in this battle. *Majestic*'s first lieutenant, Robert Cuthbert took command and was confirmed as acting captain by Nelson the day after the battle. Westcott was buried at sea in Aboukir Bay on 2 August 1798, with twenty minute guns fired in salute.

COPENHAGEN
AND THE
BALTIC

The Battle of Copenhagen by Nicholas Pocock (1740–1821), looking south along the King's Deep. Nelson's squadron is sailing up the Deep on the morning's light breeze, with the current helping too. In the foreground the bomb vessels are shown already anchored and turned to stem current, and have begun to fire over the British line-of-battle ships. In the distance to the left, some of the British ships have run aground. In the middle of the Deep the British ships are leapfrogging past each other as they take up their assigned stations, with the frigates moving into place last of all. In the third line are the Danish ships and floating batteries, and on the right is the city of Copenhagen itself.

✦ Introduction ✦

The Battle of Copenhagen in 1801 cannot be understood outside its context. On the one hand it was an unprecedented incident in the maritime history of the Baltic, whilst on the other it had its roots deep in history. How could this dualism be? The answer to that question is that London, together with the capitals around the Baltic, had several interests in the region, sometimes differing, sometimes coincidental.

Whenever the Royal Navy entered the Baltic it was, of course, primarily to protect British interests and if these coincided with the interests of one or several of the Nordic states, so much the better. However, even the interests of the government in London in general and of the Admiralty in particular were not always identical.

London's interests, as for Europe as a whole, were to see to that no regional power grew too powerful in the Baltic, a classic policy which maximised London's own influence. The Royal Navy's interests were to ensure the undisturbed delivery of naval stores: timber, hemp, tar and so on, all the goods needed to keep a wooden fleet sailing. During a large part of the eighteenth century these goods had been obtained from North America, but after the loss of these colonies in the American War of Independence, deliveries from the Baltic region increased in importance.

For Britain in the seventeenth century this had meant that the Royal Navy also had to keep other nations out of the Baltic, including Holland and France, resulting in shifting loyalties in London. A genuine balance of power policy in the region precluded a long-lasting alliance with any one country, though Sweden was, with some exceptions, London's usual ally in the Baltic from the mid-seventeenth century to the mid-nineteenth century, when Sweden–Finland and Denmark–Norway were two countries, not four. In the Swedish-Danish wars of 1643–5 and 1657–8 England supported Sweden, which resulted in the Danish loss of its eastern shore along the Sound, and in 1658 the provinces of eastern Denmark were incorporated into southern Sweden. However, when the Swedes tried to swallow the whole of Denmark in 1658–60, the English, as well as the Dutch, supported the Danes.

This story repeated itself in the Great Northern War (1700–21), when the Royal Navy sent several fleets into the Baltic to secure trade with Russian-controlled harbours against Swedish privateers. However, when Russian military power in the region threatened the balance of power, both in Scandinavia and in northern Germany where Russian troops had reached Mecklenburg, close to the homeland of the British Hanoverian royal family, British loyalty changed. In the last years of the war, 1720–1, British naval forces joined the Swedish Navy to prevent any further Russian attacks on Sweden.

In this way the British secured some kind of power balance in the Baltic Sea, where now three navies competed, the Danish, the Swedish and the new-born Russian Baltic Sea fleet. Russia soon objected to British insistence on the right of stop-and-search of neutral shipping, for what Britain regarded as contraband bound to her enemy France, and Catherine the Great brought into being the first League of Armed Neutrality (1780–3) which involved many other Baltic and, eventually, some Mediterranean states too. The Anglo-Dutch War of 1780–4 was fought to keep Holland out of the League.

The events of the Great War (1792–1815), and especially of 1801, cannot be understood without this historical knowledge. Around 1800 a new, powerful, actor entered into the region, Bonaparte's France. French troops by then controlled the northern coast of Germany, and France's lack of naval strength in the Baltic did not matter so much as long as it had allies with naval resources in the region, namely Russia and Denmark. Meanwhile, Swedish opinion was anti-Gallic. This might seem odd since France had been Sweden's ally during the Thirty Years War (1618–48), but the revolution of 1789 and the execution of the

French King and Queen had very much upset Swedish royalist, sentiments. (This anti-French policy of Stockholm did not change even in 1810, when the former French general Jean Baptiste Bernadotte was elected Crown Prince of Sweden and later became King Carl XIV Johan, and founder of the present Swedish royal dynasty.)

Meanwhile Britain continued to insist upon stop-and-search. Denmark was driven into the arms of Bonaparte, and Russia led in creating a second League of Armed Neutrality or League of the North. Then, after a reconnaissance in force in the autumn of 1800, the British prepared to send a fleet to the Baltic, and the Battle of Copenhagen or Slaget på Reden took place on 2 April 1801.

One of Britain's aims was to prevent Denmark from joining Bonaparte and giving him the navy he lacked in the Baltic, but the controversial attack and its aftermath only drove Denmark deeper into Bonaparte's arms. That the British were acting in their own interests can be seen from the orders given to Nelson in the early summer of 1801, namely not to commit any hostilities towards the Swedish Navy, but if it showed any intentions of joining force with the Danish or the Russian navies, then Nelson was to use 'every means in Your power to prevent' such a junction. Also later, when Nelson suspected that the Danes were rearming in contravention of the armistice which he had negotiated, he wrote to the Admiralty, from south of Copenhagen, threatening, 'I am here, will break the Armistice, and set Copenhagen ablaze.' Arguably, the collapse of the League of the North, following the assassination of Tsar Paul, saved the Baltic from further war that year.

So, 1801 was not the end but rather the beginning of the story. Hostilities between London and Copenhagen escalated, culminating with the British removing most of the Danish Navy in 1807, with the loss of the lives of 188 soldiers and some two thousand civilians; the Danes were forced to hand over seventeen ships of the line, seventeen frigates, and forty-three smaller vessels; an action considered locally as theft. Between 1807 and 1812 Russia was an ally of France and in 1808–9 conquered the eastern part of Sweden, modern Finland, so contributing further to anti-French feelings in Sweden. However, the British deployment to the Baltic did prevent the Russians invading parts of Sweden proper and any of the southern provinces being taken by Denmark; the British admiral, Sir James Saumarez, came to be regarded as a hero in Sweden.

In this part of Europe the Great War culminated in a British and Swedish naval blockade of Norway, which was then part of Denmark, and a Swedish invasion of Norway in August 1814. This resulted in a forced union between Sweden and Norway (a union which Norway broke free of in 1905, ironically with British support), leaving a mutilated Denmark, which in the war of 1863–4 against Prussia and Austria also lost Schleswig-Holstein, the Danish-speaking province of northern Germany.

This series of disasters for Denmark was brought about by British policy from James I through Oliver Cromwell to William Pitt, which was to some extent revived during the Crimean War and in the years 1919–20. Though exceptional in their brutality, the dramatic events at Copenhagen in 1801, exacerbated by the bombardment of Copenhagen in 1807, were entirely consistent with the policy of London towards the Baltic region.

LARS ERICSON WOLKE

The British fleet passed the strait into the Sound between Denmark and Sweden at the end of March 1801, giving as wide a berth as possible to the Danish guns at Elsinore, which opened fire, while the Swedish guns on the opposite shore at Helsingborg remained silent and maintained Sweden's neutrality.

→ BERTIE ←

Thomas Bertie (1758–1825) was born Thomas Hoar on 3 July 1758 in Middleton St George, Co Durham and was educated at Christ's Hospital, London. He joined the Navy aged fifteen in 1773 serving in the frigate *Seahorse* (24, Captain George Farmer), bound for the East Indies. In *Seahorse* he was a messmate of Horatio Nelson and Thomas Troubridge, with whom he maintained a close friendship until their deaths.

After *Seahorse* he served under Sir Edward Hughes in Salisbury (50) and with Captain Joshua Rowley in *Monarch.* Hoar followed Rowley into *Suffolk* and then to *Conqueror* (74), now as the first lieutenant. During the five years under Rowley he participated in the Battle of Ushant on 27 July 1778 and the action at Grenada on 6 July 1779, and in December 1779 Hoar distinguished himself in two boat actions off Martinique. Whilst serving in *Conqueror*, he also took part in Rodney's three actions with de Guichen in April and May 1782.

In 10 August 1782 Hoar, at the age of twenty-four, was made commander and received his first command, the sloop *Duc d'Estiac* (16) at Port Royal, Jamaica, retaining this post until she was paid off in England in August 1783.

He was unemployed and on half pay until,

in November 1790, he was made post-captain and given the frigate *Leda* (36) during the Spanish Armament or Nootka crisis, a spat between Britain and Spain over Vancouver Island. When the crisis was resolved, *Leda* was decommissioned and Bertie returned to half pay. During his long spell on the beach he had married Catherine Dorothy Bertie on 20 May 1788 whose surname he assumed under the terms of her inheritance from her father, Captain Hon Peregrine Bertie (1741–90). Bertie was the family name of the Earls of Abingdon.

Bertie got command of the former East Indiaman *Hindostan* (54) in 1795 and was deployed to the West Indies but a severe attack of yellow fever forced him to return to England in October 1796. A year later Bertie was appointed to *Ardent* (64): in a letter of congratulation Nelson called her 'the finest man-of-war upon her decks that I ever saw'. In August and September 1799 Bertie took part in the Anglo-Russian expedition to the Texel when some 250 craft of all sizes transported 17,000 troops from Margate Roads and the Downs across the Channel, and after landings at Den Helder, a Dutch fleet of twenty-seven ships, a dozen of them two-deckers, surrendered and many were purchased into the Royal Navy.

Then in August 1800 Bertie was part of a squadron which demonstrated against the Danes: they found three Danish 74s anchored between Kronborg Castle and the Swedish shore. The British and Danish squadrons manoeuvred indecisively off Copenhagen until matters were settled amicably.

The following year Bertie and *Ardent* joined Hyde Parker's expedition to the Baltic. There, on the morning of 2 April 1801, at anchor off Copenhagen, Bertie received the signal from *Elephant,* Lord Nelson's flagship, to weigh and proceed according to the battle plan which he had received orally from Nelson on board *Elephant* the evening before, and which was supplemented by written orders during the night. The Battle of Copenhagen had begun.

Not all the ships in the squadron could weigh at

the same time as there would be risk of collision. So the first division, *Edgar, Ardent, Glatton* and *Isis* were to weigh first and in that order sail around the Middle Ground and up the King's Deep and anchor by the stern opposite their assigned targets at the southern end of the Danish line. The rest of Nelson's squadron would follow and leapfrog along the unengaged side of the already anchored ships. At the end of this manoeuvre, the British line would be reversed so that the squadron's rear now was at the northern, head of the line and the van at the southern end of the line.

Nelson's carefully worked-out plan soon bordered on collapse. Some of his ships grounded at the southern tip of Middle Ground and several captains were very worried about passing on the unengaged side of the anchored ships: it seemed – and probably was – too close to the shallow waters of Middle Ground. The follow-on ships passed instead on the engaged side, Nelson's flagship among them, and other ships filled the planned positions of the grounded ships in order to concentrate the squadron's firepower on the southern part of the Danish line. Nelson personally hailed ships as they passed and gave them new orders and positions. But the leading ships did exactly what Nelson had ordered. *Edgar* anchored as planned at 10.45am, and Bertie passed *Edgar* on her engaged side and anchored by the stern ahead of her.

Bertie now faced the two primary targets that had been assigned to him in the battle plan, the blockship *Kronborg* and the floating battery *Svaerdfisken*. An artillery duel commenced at about 500–600 yards and continued for a little over three hours. *Ardent* did well and defeated her targets who ceased fire and hauled down their ensigns at 2.25. About an hour later, when a general flag of truce was flying, the crew of *Ardent* boarded their prizes, which also included the blockship *Jylland*, and began to evacuate prisoners. *Ardent* had received substantial damage. A Midshipman George Hoare was amongst the twenty-nine men killed and sixty-four wounded and *Ardent* was severely damaged in her hull, masts and sails.

Bertie had done everything right that day. He

Admiral Sir Thomas Hoar Bertie's gravestone lies by the porch of St Mary's, Twyford, Hampshire.

weighed successfully in the narrow waters, safely rounded Middle Ground, used his initiative to avoid grounding, anchored at the right spot and engaged the enemy at almost point-blank range, overcoming his designated targets and taking several prizes. It was a masterly example of good seamanship, good judgement and good fighting efficiency. Early next morning Nelson came on board *Ardent* to thank her captain and crew personally for their exertions, a compliment that was returned with six cheers on Nelson leaving the ship.

Bertie's immediate reward was command of a larger ship, *Bellona* (74), whose captain, Thomas Boulden Thompson, had lost a leg in the battle. *Bellona* stayed in the Baltic and cruised off Karlskrona, the Swedish naval base, and the Russian naval base at Kronstadt. Both Sweden and Russia were still formally members of the Armed Neutrality and therefore in opposition to British trade in the Baltic, until at the end of July the treaty was declared void. There was therefore no longer any immediate threat to British trade and the Baltic fleet returned to England.

As a result of the Baltic campaign of 1801 Bertie was now familiar with the political and nautical circumstances in the Sound and the Baltic, knowledge that would become very useful during his last command.

When war with France commenced again in May 1803 Bertie was appointed to *Courageous* (74) but had to give up his command after a few months due to family matters. In December 1805 he was given command of *St George* (98) and was deployed in the English Channel squadron until his promotion to rear-admiral on 28 April 1808. Vice-Admiral Sir James Saumarez, the British commander-in-chief in the Baltic, asked for Bertie and gave him the command of a squadron of small ships off Viken at the entrance to the Sound where he was active for two years, until illness forced him to strike his flag in February 1810. He saw no more active service.

Bertie was keen to improve his ship's efficiency and as a young lieutenant he experimented with a lifebuoy system, which later was introduced in all ships of the fleet. When commanding *Ardent* he modified the carriages of the 42-pound carronades which decreased the recoil and increased the power of their shot, as well enabling the piece to be worked with fewer men.

Bertie received the thanks of Parliament twice, first, after the evacuation of Texel in 1799 and, second, after the Battle of Copenhagen in 1801. He was knighted in 1813 and the same year also received a royal licence to wear the insignia of Commander of the Order of the Sword which was given to him by the Swedish King Carl XIII. So he joined the rare ranks of British officers who were awarded different grades of this order: among others were Captains Hope, Martin, Reynolds, Mansel and Lieutenant John Ross (later famous as a polar explorer). Three officers were awarded the highest grade: Vice-Admiral Sir James Saumarez, and Rear-Admiral Samuel Hood; the other was Sidney Smith, in 1790, during the Swedish–Russia War of 1788–90, which gave rise to one of the Duke of Bronte's less noble remarks in calling Smith 'the Swedish knight'.

Bertie never served at sea again but was promoted steadily until he reached admiral of the blue, only seventeen days before his death on 13 June 1825.

In Bertie's will his estate was carefully divided among family and friends. £100 was given to 'my dear friend Sir James Saumarez' and Bertie's brother got letters written to Bertie by Nelson and a ring containing 'the hair of my valued friend the said Lord Viscount Nelson'. Bertie specified that this was 'the forelock that Nelson used to wear and hang over his head to conceal the wound he received at the battle of the Nile'.

Admiral Sir Thomas Hoar Bertie's barely decipherable gravestone lies outside St Mary's Church at Twyford in Hampshire.

CHRISTER HÄGG

→ BIRCHALL ←

William Birchall (1769–1817) was the son of an upholsterer, cabinetmaker and auctioneer in Queen's Square, Bath, who may have been of Quaker stock and combined evangelical Protestantism with Freemasonry; his religious practice may only have been good business practice. Little is known of William's early life, even the spelling of his surname is not certain (Burchill and Burchell appear in contemporary newspapers), but from the few clues available, he was a capable officer, much-married and peripatetic.

He was examined for lieutenant in 1790 and promoted on 18 June 1793 when the *Bath Chronicle* proudly reported that he 'who has been a midshipman in His Majesty's navy near thirteen years' is promoted to lieutenant in *Montagu* (74) 'and will shortly sail for the West Indies with the gallant Captain Montagu who has not under his command a braver officer nor a better seaman'. It seems likely that Birchall was in *Montagu* at the Battle of the Glorious First of June in 1794.

By 1796 Captain Thomas Byam Martin had taken him as his first lieutenant into the Spanish-built *Santa Margarita* (36). On 23 October she was cruising in the chops of the Channel and captured the privateer *Buonaparte*, 16 guns and 137 men, but at nightfall two more ships were seen closing. They came nearly within hail before sheering away and standing off on different tacks. *Santa Margarita* fired a broadside at each ship and chased the larger, while Birchall got into a boat with five men armed with cutlasses to capture the smaller. Birchall urged his men on, telling them that they must fight for a bed or perish at night in the open sea, then 'with a high degree of zeal and intrepidity that does him the highest honour', Birchall boarded and retook the *Potomac*. She was a British merchantman, bound from Poole with provisions and merchandise for Newfoundland, in the possession of a French prize crew. Meanwhile, Byam Martin caught up with the privateer *Vengeur*, 16 guns and 120 men, which, after a few more shots from *Santa Margarita*, hauled down her colours. Having now nearly as many prisoners as crew, Byam Martin returned to Plymouth.

In 1797 Birchall was made commander and by 1798 he was commanding *Hebe* (14), formerly a 38-gun frigate which had been cut down *en flûte* and was being used as a fast troop carrier. In May *Hebe* formed part of a squadron of twenty-five small ships, the largest being Captain Home Popham's *Expedition* (26), which carried a major-general and some 1,140 troops to the continent. The British government had intelligence that a large number of barges were moving along the canals from Flushing to Dunkirk and was determined to stop this by destroying the lock gates and sluices at Ostend. The British squadron assembled at Margate, sailed on 14 May and, in the early hours of 19 May, landed the troops and their six field guns at Ostend under the cover of darkness and bad weather. Shore batteries badly damaged the smaller gun vessels, and *Hebe* kedged in as close as the low tide would permit to continue the bombardment. By mid-morning the troops reported that gates, sluices and several gunboats had been destroyed, but now the weather had deteriorated and, unable to re-embark, they were counter-attacked by a superior French force and capitulated next day. As Laird

Clowes said, it was 'doubtful whether the objects were attained and the troops ought never to have been landed when it would be difficult, if not impossible, to re-embark them until after a lapse of some days'.

In March 1800 Birchall was appointed to the sloop of war *Harpy* and in 1801 before the Battle of Copenhagen he helped to sound and mark the Hollander Deep, and then anchored to mark the Middle Ground shoal. Afterwards, Birchall towed the *Sjaelland* off as prize when it seemed that the Danes were going to warp her away, and then Nelson ordered him to remain in Copenhagen Roads to observe the Danes' compliance with the armistice, and to inform arriving British ships of the fleet's rendezvous off Bornholm. Birchall was made post-captain for his services.

The next news of Birchall is in 1803 when the *Bath Chronicle* reported that 'our gallant townsman' was appointed to command the Sea Fencibles in the Chester region. The newspaper later reported a riot on Boxing Day 1803 after Birchall had pressed a man who was a member of the local militia. After their Christmas parade, the militia attacked the prison and the rendezvous-house, tore down Birchall's colours, and the magistrates asked him to take his press-gang out of town until order had been restored by the Army.

Birchall married three times. He first married Esther Delany of Lyme Regis in 1786; one wonders about this marriage: she was older than him and he was a mere midshipman when they tied the knot. Esther died in 1806 at Bathampton and he almost immediately married, in Marylebone, Jane Cross, a Bath girl, but she died in June 1811 at Ilfracombe. Last, in 1815 he married Leonora Bingham, whose family had lived at Bingham's Melcombe in Dorset for six hundred years.

Captain William Birchall died at Exeter in 1817 and was buried at St Sidwell's, Exeter. He had no children (Lieutenant Thomas William Birchall (1779–1805) was his nephew) and any monument or memorial in Exeter was destroyed in the German Blitz of 1942.

PETER HORE

→ BLIGH ←

William Bligh (1754–1817) was born in St Tudy, Cornwall; among his ancestors and relatives were aristocrats, civil servants and naval officers. Bligh is recorded in *Monmouth*'s muster book as a captain's servant in 1762, in *Hunter* (10) in 1770 first as able seaman and then midshipman in 1771. The same year he transferred to *Crescent* (32), and in 1774 to the sloop *Ranger* (8). *Ranger* was employed in subduing smuggling in the Irish Sea, and when she visited the Isle of Man he met his future wife, Elizabeth Betham, the daughter of a customs officer.

Bligh did not take the lieutenant's examination at the minimum age of twenty. Nevertheless, his talents did not go unnoticed, since on 17 March 1776 he was appointed sailing master of *Resolution*, then fitting out for Captain James Cook's third and final voyage to the Pacific Ocean. Only now did he take and pass his lieutenant's examination.

A blue plaque marks the modest but elegant house in Lambeth Road where Bligh and his family lived from 1784 onwards.

Despite his youth, Bligh must have enjoyed an outstanding professional reputation, since James Cook, himself an excellent navigator, would not have accepted a less competent officer for the responsible position of sailing master. Like his patron, Bligh had wide scientific interests, and he and Cook had such a close relationship that the Tahitians thought they were father and son. But the voyage ended tragically: on 14 February 1779 Cook was killed by natives on the island of Hawaii.

After the return to Britain in October 1780, Bligh was omitted in the promotions that followed, not only due to the loss of his patron, but probably also because he had fallen out with Lieutenant John Gore, who had taken over command of the expedition after Cook's death, and Lieutenant James King, Gore's second-in-command. This is also one of the first hints regarding Bligh's troublesome character.

However, on 5 October 1781, Bligh finally received his commission, but was put on half pay after the end of the War of American Independence in 1783. He then accepted a position as master of a West Indiaman owned by the merchant Duncan Campbell, a relative of his wife Elizabeth, whom he had married in 1781. During his time in the merchant service Bligh met Fletcher Christian; they soon established a relationship almost as close as that between Bligh and Cook, and Bligh took Christian with him as a master's mate, when in 1787 he was offered command of a new expedition to the South Seas.

West Indian planters had approached the British Admiralty with the request to send a ship to Tahiti to collect breadfruit plants to be grown in the Caribbean as cheap food for their slaves. After Sir Joseph Banks, President of the Royal Society, had exerted his considerable political influence, King George III approved such an expedition. The merchantman *Bethia* was purchased by the Admiralty, renamed the *Bounty* and converted into a floating greenhouse. It was Banks who proposed Bligh for her command, not only as an experienced navigator but one who had been to Tahiti before. Bligh gladly accepted this chance to

William Bligh was buried beside his beloved Elizabeth at St Mary's, Lambeth, now the Garden Museum, where his tomb is adorned with a breadfruit.

Bligh's epitaph lists his merits as a scientist, navigator, and naval officer. In contrast to his popular image, he was not a brutal tyrant.

resume his naval career, and he and Banks established a lifelong friendship.

With a forty-six-man crew *Bounty* left Portsmouth in December 1787 and arrived at Tahiti in the following October, when the breadfruit trees were in their dormant period; *Bounty*'s crew therefore had to wait several months before they could pot the saplings. Little work, plenty of food and the generously granted sexual affections of the Tahitian women made the island a paradise for sailors accustomed to the hardships of life at sea. Inevitably, tight naval discipline eased during this period of idleness, and when, after the departure from Tahiti on 4 April 1789, Bligh tried to restore discipline on board, his men wished themselves back in Tahiti.

Bligh is often depicted as a despotic tyrant whose brutality drove his sailors into mutiny. Doubtless he was a difficult character, irascible, short-tempered and abusive, but he was genuinely concerned about the welfare of his men and only rarely resolving to the cat-o'-nine-tails as a means of maintaining discipline. Bligh was under tremendous pressure. For him, the expedition was a unique opportunity for professional advancement, since after a successful voyage he could expect certain promotion to captain. Another problem was that his officers obviously did not meet his high professional standards. Ever unwilling to tolerate incompetence, this brought out the worst side of his personality, ranting and raving at his officers at their slightest error. Bligh had promoted Fletcher Christian to acting lieutenant, but his young protégé failed his high expectations and he especially suffered from Bligh's tirades.

Finally, Christian broke under the pressure; in his desperation he saw no other way out but to take over the ship. The mutineers' core consisted of only nine men, led by Christian. In the early hours of 28 April 1789, Bligh was torn from sleep, when a group of them broke into his cabin, tied him up and brought him on deck, where he was told that Christian had seized command of the *Bounty*. The majority of the now forty-four-strong crew had no part in the mutiny.

Together with eighteen followers and provisions for five days, Bligh was set adrift in a 24ft open boat in the middle of the Pacific. The subsequent voyage of the *Bounty*'s launch was a nautical feat unparalleled in the annals of seafaring: in a direful seven weeks' journey, navigating from his memory, Bligh sailed the launch, overcrowded with starving men, over a distance of 4,000 nautical miles to Timor, while he surveyed and charted this virtually unknown region of the Pacific.

Upon his return to Britain in March 1790, Bligh was celebrated as a hero and honourably acquitted for the loss of the *Bounty*. He felt it a justification of his conduct that the Admiralty promoted him to captain and entrusted him with the command of a new expedition to Tahiti. But on Bligh's return in 1793, the situation had changed. Ten of the *Bounty*'s mutineers had been captured and brought to England to stand trial, among them Midshipman Peter Heywood, whose influential family tried to save his life by portraying Bligh as a despot, whose tyrannical behaviour had driven his crew into mutiny. Heywood, together with two other men who were sentenced to death, were pardoned by King George III and Heywood resumed his naval career. Fletcher's brother Edward Christian, a prominent lawyer, and James Morrison, one of the pardoned mutineers, later joined this campaign to undermine Bligh's reputation.

Ill and out of favour with the Admiralty, Bligh was put on half pay. Not until 1797 was he recalled to active duty and appointed captain of *Director* (64), in which he suffered his second mutiny. In April 1797, the seamen's discontent with the living conditions aboard British warships resulted in the Spithead mutiny. Although the Admiralty finally accepted the seamen's demands, on 12 May another mutiny broke out among the warships lying off the Nore, including the *Director*. This time, however, Bligh was in good company, since he was not the only captain sent ashore by a rebellious crew. The government, refusing to negotiate, cut off the mutineers from all supplies. This hard-line policy finally succeeded and on 13 June the Nore mutiny was ended. Bligh's *Director* now joined Vice-Admiral Adam Duncan's fleet on blockade duty off the Dutch coast, and on 11 October 1797, he and his ship distinguished themselves in battle, when Duncan engaged a Dutch squadron commanded by Admiral Jan Willem de Winter south of the Dutch island of Texel. The Battle of Camperdown was a massacre: Bligh forced the Dutch flagship *Vrijheid* (74) to surrender, suffering only seven men wounded. In total, their victory cost the British some 200 dead and 620 wounded, while the defeated Dutch counted about 950 dead and 520 wounded.

At the Battle of Copenhagen on 2 April 1801 Bligh again proved his bravery as captain of the *Glatton*, a converted East Indiaman, armed with fifty-four heavy carronades. Anchoring directly behind Nelson's flagship, *Elephant* (74), his guns hammered the Danish flagship *Dannebrog* (62) into pieces and set her alight. Despite fighting in the thick of the action, the *Glatton* suffered only seventeen dead and thirty-four wounded. Bligh once more showed his excellent seamanship, when after the battle he sailed his battered ship out of the narrow channel of the King's Deep. Bligh asked Admiral Nelson for a certificate of his good conduct, the reason for this rather unusual request being probably the smear campaign set up against him by the relatives of the *Bounty*'s mutineers, and in a letter to the Admiralty Nelson confirmed Bligh's character: 'His behaviour on this occasion can reap no additional credit from my testimony.'

In May 1801, Bligh was elected a Fellow of the Royal Society.

In 1805 Bligh was appointed governor of New South Wales, Australia, then a penal colony. Corruption was rife and most of the officers of the New South Wales Corps, which had been raised to guard the convicts, were involved in illegal transactions. Thus the British government had chosen the dutiful Bligh to restore order and to establish good government. But again, his efforts were thwarted by his difficult character. On the voyage to Australia he clashed with Captain Joseph Short of the armed transport *Porpoise*, and once in Sydney, Bligh relieved Short of his command and sent him back to Britain, where he was court-martialled, but to Bligh's embarrassment acquitted of all charges.

As governor, Bligh also quickly made enemies. The officers of the New South Wales Corps mutinied on 26 January 1809 in the so called 'Rum Rebellion', deposed Bligh and forced him into exile aboard the *Porpoise*. Instead of sailing back to England as expected by the mutineers, Bligh surveyed the coast of Tasmania, while the mutineers used their political contacts in London to end the rebellion with a rotten compromise. Thus Bligh was restored to office, only to be replaced one day later by a new governor. After his return to Britain, Bligh was promoted to admiral, but never called to active duty.

Although Bligh had distinguished himself in the wars against France, the *Bounty* mutiny haunted him all life. His only haven was the love of his wife and his four daughters. To this day, the dramatic events in *Bounty* are part of mass culture. But in contrast to popular image, Bligh was not a brutal tyrant. George Tobin, who served as lieutenant during Bligh's second Pacific voyage, remembered: 'It was in those violent Tornadoes of temper when he lost himself, yet, when all, in his opinion, went right, when could a man be more placid and interesting … Once or twice indeed I felt the Unbridled licence of his power of speech, yet never without soon receiving something like an emollient plaister to heal the wound.' This is an apt obituary for a man, who has been wrongly slandered as a despotic brute for more than two centuries.

Elizabeth died in 1812 and Vice-Admiral William Bligh died from cancer in 1817.

JANN DE WITT

➤ BRISBANE ⬅

James Brisbane (1774–1826) was a Scot, born in 1774 at Bishopton in Renfrewshire into a naval family, younger brother to Rear-Admiral Sir Charles Brisbane. He first went to sea as a midshipman in 1787 in *Culloden* (74): by 1794 he was signal midshipman in Lord Howe's flagship *Queen Charlotte* (100). She was heavily engaged at the Battle of the Glorious First of June, when Howe attempted to break the enemy's line, but was thwarted by the inadequacies of the signal book and his inability to communicate his intentions to his captains. Although Howe captured seven French ships, the convoy escaped and discharged its cargo of American wheat in France.

Brisbane was promoted to lieutenant, and sent to the Cape station in George Elphinstone's flagship *Monarch* and was present at the surrender of a Dutch squadron in Saldanha Bay in 1796. Aged twenty-two, Brisbane was given command of one of the captured Dutch ships and later of *Daphne* (20) as a commander, but on his return to Britain

in 1797 she paid off and he remained on half pay until 1800. On 17 June 1800 at St Peter-the-Less, Chichester, Sussex, Brisbane married Jemima Ann Ventham, shortly before he was given command of the new brig *Cruizer* (or *Cruiser*) (18).

In 1801 Nelson used *Cruizer* to take soundings and make charts of the approaches to Copenhagen prior to the British attack on the Danish fleet in its anchorage, and on the night of 1 April Brisbane anchored *Cruizer* as a marker at the entrance to the channel between Saltholm and the Middle Ground shoal, and so guided Nelson's squadron into battle.

Nelson was impressed by Brisbane and, following a private letter from Nelson to Earl St Vincent, Brisbane was given command of *Saturn* (74) and his promotion to post-captain was backdated to the day of the Battle of Copenhagen. She became flagship of Rear-Admiral Thomas Totty, who had been junior flag officer at Copenhagen, as commander-in-chief of the Leeward Islands, and Brisbane sailed from Portsmouth for Martinique on 13 December. When Totty died of yellow fever on 2 June 1802, the 27-year-old Brisbane assumed command of the station.

Between 1803 and 1805 Brisbane commanded the Kent Sea Fencibles, but in the autumn of 1805 he was given command of *Alcmene* (32) on the Irish station. There, on 4 January 1807, about 120 miles south-west of Cape Clear, Brisbane captured the French privateer cutter *Courier* (formerly HM Armed Cutter *Alert*), which mounted seven guns of various calibres including a 24-pounder and a 42-pounder carronade.

Brisbane had established his reputation as a frigate commander and in 1808 was given the newly captured, crack French frigate *Belle Poule*, and sent to the Adriatic, where he would become an expert in inshore and amphibious operations. He blockaded Corfu, cutting off supplies to the French garrison there, and when, on the night of 13 February 1809, the French attempted to run a supply of corn to the island from Brindisi, he chased the frigate *Var* for a day and night in stormy weather into the Gulf of Valona, where she sought the protection of two Turkish forts. On the afternoon of the 15th Brisbane anchored close in and opened fire, forcing the Frenchman to surrender.

At some time in 1809 the first game of cricket was played on the island of Vis.

In September 1809 Brisbane helped to free Cephalonia from French occupation, and on 21 March 1810 Brisbane was part of a squadron which took from the French the strongly-fortified island of Santa Maura (now Lefkada) in the Ionian Islands after a month's siege. In August 1810 he captured the Italian vessel *Saint Nicholo* and in December captured the Italian brig *Carlotta*.

On 4 May 1811 Brisbane was cruising in company off the coast of Istria when he chased a French 18-gun-brig into the small harbour of Parenzo (now Poreč in Croatia). Two ships of Brisbane's squadron stood in within a cable's length of the rocks at the entrance and opened fire on the brig and a shore battery, forcing her to haul out of range. That night 200 seamen and marines quietly landed on an island in the harbour, set up a battery of four guns, and at dawn commenced a five-hour bombardment in which the brig was sunk.

Brisbane left his mark in the Ionian Sea, being instrumental in re-establishing the Septinsular Republic, an island republic where for the first time since the fifteenth century Greeks enjoyed even limited self-government. Under the 1815 Treaty of Paris the islands became the United States of the Ionian Islands, held under British protection until they were gifted to independent Greece in 1864.

As the focus of the war shifted from the Mediterranean to the 'stab in the back' which became the War of 1812, *Belle Poule* on her way home in August 1812 captured an American privateer and several American trading vessels in the Channel. In September 1812 Brisbane moved to the new Blackwall-built *Pembroke* (74). He clearly had some problem handling his new ship as that autumn he had to accept the help of fellow Scot, Captain Donald Campbell in the frigate *Rosamund*, after he put *Pembroke* aground off the Dunnose, Isle of Wight.

'James Brisbane … conducted in person the naval force employed in the difficult and harassing war which ended in the submission of the Burmese empire … And landed at Sydney … Died on 10 December 1826'.

In 1813 the French fleet, blockaded by the British at Toulon, consisted of twenty-one sail of the line and ten large frigates ready for sea, but was badly manned owing to drafts of men being sent off to the Army. When the French did try to exercise at sea on 5 November they were met by the British under Admiral Pellew. The main body of Pellew's fleet had been blown from its station, but an inshore squadron, consisting of four 74s, one of them Brisbane's *Pembroke*, stood in to attack the superior French fleet which included the 130-gun *Wagram*. A running battle ensued during which Pellew's fleet clawed up to windward but the French escaped into Toulouse.

In 1816 Brisbane was flag captain to Lord Exmouth in *Queen Charlotte* at the successful bombardment of Algiers; afterwards Exmouth sent Brisbane home with dispatches and on 2 October he was knighted. He had already been made CB in June 1815.

In 1824 Brisbane was given command of *Boadicea* (42) and as a commodore sailed for the East Indies station, where the First Anglo-Burmese war in 1825 was fought in the Irrawaddy River. Leaving *Boadicea* at Rangoon, Brisbane continued upriver in his ship's boats to join the British army at its headquarters, making his mark by employing the Honourable East India Company's novel paddle steamer *Diana*, armed with Congreve rockets, both to tow his boats and to scare the Burmese.

In the words of the Governor-General of India, 'The important and essential aid afforded by his excellency Commodore Sir James Brisbane … rendered the most essential service in the various decisive and memorable actions which, in the month of December last, compelled the Burmese to sue for peace.'

However, Brisbane had contracted dysentery. On his way home he visited Port Jackson (as Sydney was then known) in *Warspite* (76), the first ship of the line to visit Australia, where a cousin, General Sir Thomas Brisbane, was governor of New South Wales. There he died on 19 December 1826 and was buried, far from the family mausoleum at Largs Old Kirk, Ayrshire.

PETER HORE

→ BRODIE ←

Thomas Charles Brodie (1779–1811) commanded the 28-gun sloop *Arrow* at the Battle of Copenhagen in April 1801. This statement corrects more than two centuries of mistakes: every historian from William James onwards has given another name, because Steel's 'original and correct' *Navy List* for 1801 was out of date. That the error should have been repeated so consistently since, argues strongly in favour of researching original papers in archives, for documents held at Kew allow no doubt that Brodie was in command. Brodie signed the ship's log and countersigned the ship's muster book from 25 February 1801 onwards.

The name erroneously given for the commander of *Arrow* in 1801 is William Bolton (1777–1830), a Norfolk man, related by marriage to Nelson, and with other strong connections to the great admiral, who later became a captain and was knighted. Quite why Bolton, an experienced officer with some practice in fighting the Danes, should be superseded on the eve of a major campaign in the Baltic is unknown, but the record allows no doubt that in April 1801 he was on half pay in England.

The mistake probably accounts for why Brodie is lost in the fine grain of history. He was the second son of William Brodie, of Scots descent and a magistrate at Great Marlborough Street, London, and a grandson of Captain David Brodie (*c.*1710–87). David Brodie had fought under Vernon at Porto Bello in 1739 and Cartagena in 1741, lost an arm, and when he died was, according to his monument in Bath Abbey, 'one of the oldest captains in the Navy' – and had plagued the Admiralty for years about his promotion and his pension.

Nevertheless the Brodies had enough interest to get young Thomas into the Royal Naval Academy, Portsmouth, in 1791, considered by some to be a 'back door' method of becoming an officer in the Navy. He was a midshipman in 1794 and passed for lieutenant on 17 February 1798, and later that year he was a lieutenant in Ralph Miller's *Theseus* at the Battle of the Nile. At the Siege of Acre in 1799 he commanded one of the small boats which enfiladed the French trenches and repulsed Bonaparte's army.

Brodie was made commander on 14 February 1801 and given *Arrow* (30). His station at Copenhagen was at the most northerly end of the British line, with the frigates and sloops under the command of Edward Riou. *Arrow* was the last ship to enter the King's Deep, about two hours after the first, and had to run the full length of Nelson's line, firing in gaps between the larger ships, and she was the last of all to arrive in position. Brodie had hardly dropped anchor and fired a first salvo at the Danes when Riou in *Amazon* reluctantly cut his cable in response to Parker's signal to break off action and ordered Brodie to follow. Consequently although the other frigates received a high proportion of casualties, *Arrow* received none. Brodie obviously did well in the subsequent campaign and he was made captain in 1802. This rapid promotion indicates a talented officer who had earned himself his own measure of interest.

He briefly commanded the Sea Fencibles between Dorsey Island and Sheep's Head in southwest Ireland, and in 1808 he was given command of the newly built 38-gun *Hyperion* and saw service in the Mediterranean and in the West Indies.

In early 1811 *Hyperion* touched at Gonaïves in San Domingo for wood and water, when Brodie was contacted by a Mr Simpson, an English merchant, who claimed the protection of the British flag. Suddenly and without warning the shore batteries opened up on *Hyperion*'s boats. Three men were killed and Brodie and two of his officers were captured. Next day at dawn his first lieutenant, James Morgan, beat up through an intricate channel and anchored the frigate in four fathoms, not more than a musket shot from the shore. Then, with one broadside presented to the batteries and the other to a Haitian frigate, he demanded that if his captain was not set free in fifteen minutes, the town would be destroyed and the man-of-war taken to Jamaica. The three officers were promptly released.

However, Captain Thomas Brodie died a few weeks later, at Jamaica on 14 March 1811, presumably of an illness he had caught while briefly held prisoner.

BOB O'HARA

→ CLAY ←

Edward Sneyd Clay (1768–1846) was a good seaman and a brave officer whose sea career came to an end on the shores of the Isle of May.

Clay entered the Navy as a midshipman in 1783 at the end of the American War of Independence, saw continuous service during the years of peace, was examined for lieutenant in 1792, and promoted in 1794 after the start of the French Revolutionary War.

Clay served under many famous names, including James Gambier, George Young, Robert Linzee and Joseph Bullen, without attracting any great patronage until he met Adam Duncan. He was at the Siege of Toulon, the capture of Corsica, and, in *Venerable* (74), the Battle of Camperdown. *Venerable* was the flagship of Admiral Duncan, was heavily engaged, and Clay was wounded, giving rise to his single mention in James's and in Laird Clowes's naval histories.

Once recovered he rejoined Duncan in his new flagship *Kent* (74) for the Anglo-Russian invasion of Holland, and was chosen by Duncan to deliver his dispatches concerning the surrender of the Dutch fleet. Duncan described Clay as 'an intelligent and

deserving officer' who could supply further details of this success. Clay was promoted to master and commander of the bomb vessel *Zebra* which had recently been converted from a 16-gun sloop.

At Copenhagen Nelson stationed the seven bomb vessels under his command on the unengaged side of *Elephant* close to the Middle Ground from where he intended them to bombard Nyholm. Starting from east of the shoal and working against the current the bomb vessels did not arrive until the end of the fight, *Zebra* not until gone 2pm. Consequently she suffered no casualties, though her company became entitled to the Naval General Service clasp 'Copenhagen', and Clay to an entry in this book.

Clay was promoted post-captain in 1802 but not until 1808 did he get command of *St George* (98), flagship of Rear-Admiral Sir Eliab Harvey, and the next year of *Temeraire* (98) flagship of Rear-Admiral Sir Manley Dixon. Clay served in the Baltic for two seasons under Saumarez, blockaded the Swedish fleet in Karlskroma in 1809, fought Danish gunboats, observed the Russian fleet at Revel, surveyed part of the coast, conducted convoys through the Baltic, and was back in Plymouth in November 1809.

He was apparently a competent and experienced officer and his next command *Nymphe* (36) was given to him presumably so he could earn a little prize-money. It all came to an end on the night of 18 December 1810 when, entering the Firth of Forth, the fires of a limekiln at Broxmouth were confused with the light on the Isle of May and *Nymphe* (and *Pallas*) ran aground and both were lost. A court-martial blamed the master and the pilot, but Clay never saw active service again. He commanded the receiving ship *Raisonnable* at Sheerness 1812–14, was placed on half pay and was eventually promoted to rear-admiral in 1837.

He married Elizabeth Knight in 1797: she died in 1837. Clay was given a grant of land in New South Wales but does not appear to have taken it up.

Rear-Admiral Edward Clay died at Southwell in Nottinghamshire, aged seventy-eight.

PETER HORE

→ CUMING ←

William Cuming (1760–1824) was Devon born and bred. The son of John and Elizabeth Cuming of Totnes, he died moderately wealthy and possessed of lands in the South Hams. His naval career was equally moderate.

Cuming entered the Navy in 1773, was examined for lieutenant in 1779, and was made commander in 1795; little else is known of his early career. However, in 1796 he commanded the storeship *Alliance* and in 1797 St Vincent made him post and appointed him to *Victory* 'as reward for his good services in the Mediterranean'.

On 2 April 1801 he commanded *Russell* (74) at the Battle of Copenhagen, when she ran aground close astern of *Bellona* on the southern tip of the Middle Ground and never reached her assigned station. Though aground, *Russell* fired at the Danish defences as opportunity offered, and Cuming sent his boats, despite heavy cross-fire from both sides, to take possession of one of Danish ships, *Prøvestenen*. By 1pm, few of the Danish guns had been silenced, and both *Bellona* and *Russell* were being fired upon and flying flags of distress, when Parker hoisted his signal to break off the action, to which Nelson turned his blind eye.

Cuming owed his reputation in the contemporary Navy to an entirely different cause. One of his lieutenants was the brave but unruly Nesbit Josiah Willoughby. When Willoughby returned with prisoners from *Prøvestenen*, after quelling a mutiny by the drunken crew, Cuming ordered him to be cheered. However, later in the 1801 Baltic campaign, when *Russell* was one of the ships which blockaded Karlskrona, Willoughby incurred Cuming's displeasure. Forbidden ever to leave the poop without permission, Willoughby brought charges against his captain of behaving towards his officers in a 'unofficerlike and oppressive manner, in having struck them or forcibly shoved them while in the execution of their duty … and made use of infamous and ungentlemanlike language, damning, blasting and threatening to cut them down'.

Cuming, the court understood, was particularly fond of a beverage called Ashburton pop, some type of fizzy beer which when uncorked 'gave a report louder than a pop-gun … and its contents would fly up to the ceiling if you did not mind to keep the mouth of the stone bottle into the white quart cup'. Unfortunately – or not – its recipe was lost when its brewer died. The court certainly heard enough evidence of Cuming's rages, his blasphemy and his use of his speaking trumpet to hit people, to justify the charges – to later, more sensitive ears – but he was acquitted. Willoughby had been heard to say, when he was given permission to go below for dinner, that he hoped that there would be plenty of Ashburton pop, and Cuming took this as an affront, and on counter-charges of insolence and contempt Willoughby was dismissed the service. (He was restored and became a knight and an admiral.)

Cuming might have been more famous but in June 1803 he took command of *Prince of Wales* (98) and became flag captain to Admiral Robert Calder. By March 1805 Calder was commanding a fleet on blockade off Ferrol and on 22 July fought the Battle of Finisterre, often denigrated as Calder's Action. The twenty-strong Franco-Spanish fleet, returning from the West Indies and making for Brest, were intercepted in fog by Calder's fifteen ships. As darkness fell after a four-hour battle, British losses were 39 officers and men killed and 159 wounded, while the enemy had suffered 158 dead and 320 wounded and lost two ships. Over the next two days the fleets manoeuvred indecisively until Villeneuve gave up his objective. It was undoubtedly a tactical and strategic victory, but when Calder learned that he was being criticised for not having achieved more, he demanded a court-martial, and Nelson allowed him to return home in *Prince of Wales*. There is no record of what Cuming felt about missing the imminent battle.

Subsequently he commanded *Isis* (50), flagship of Vice-Admiral Sir Erasmus Gower at Newfoundland, *Sampson* (64), *Bombay* (74) which was part of Vice-Admiral Sir Edward Pellew's

THY WILL BE DONE

SACRED TO THE MEMORY OF
ADMIRAL WILLIAM CUMING
WHO DEPARTED THIS LIFE...

AND OF
CATHERINE GRACE, HIS WIFE,
WHO DIED XXXth MARCH MDCCCXXVIII,
AGED LXXI

Admiral John Cuming's memorial in St Petroc's, South Brent, Devon.

fleet which blockaded Toulon, and *Royal George* (100). Postwar he was promoted rear-admiral: he had married a Devon lady, Catherine Lyde, but they were childless and he left his estate to his sister's son.

PETER HORE

→ DEVONSHIRE ←

John Ferris Devonshire (1774–1839), despite his name, was a Cornishman, born at Tregolls near Truro. Two of his brothers were also naval officers, Lieutenant Henry Devonshire (1775–?) who does not appear in the Navy List after 1804, and Richard Devonshire (1784–1860) who was a master's mate in *Prince* at the Battle of Trafalgar and who like John became a yellow admiral.

John went to sea as a volunteer in *Cumberland* (74, Captain John MacBride) in 1788. He served in a number of ships on the North American

station and in the West Indies between 1789 and 1795, until in *Boyne* (70), flagship of Admiral John Jervis, he was made acting lieutenant. Jervis liked what he saw in Devonshire and promoted him to lieutenant in *Terpsichore* (32, Captain Richard Bowen).

Bowen's *Terpsichore* saw service in the West Indies, the Channel and the North Sea before joining Jervis in 1796 in the Mediterranean where 'Old Grog' was now commander-in-chief. Bowen's crew had been reduced by sickness, but when he saw a strange frigate under full sail off Cartagena on 13 October, he gave chase. When he had closed his quarry sufficiently he fired a gun to test the frigate's intent, she replied with a full broadside and ran up Spanish colours. After an hour and forty minutes the enemy frigate surrendered, and was discovered to be the Spanish *Mahonesa* (36) one of the finest frigates in the Spanish Navy. Bowen reported to Jervis: 'The talents displayed by the first lieutenant, Devonshire, who was just out of the sick list, during the action, added to his uncommon fatigue in taking care of the prize, and the very able manner in which he conducted and prepared to defend her, entitle him to the distinction, and prove him highly deserving of the recommendation you gave him with his appointment in the West Indies.'

Devonshire enjoyed a satisfactory four months in command of *Mahonesa*, the Admiralty confirmed his promotion, and then put him on the beach for three years. However, in July 1800 he was given *Dart* to command, attached to Nelson's division at the Battle of Copenhagen, passing all the way along the King's Deep and anchoring with Riou's frigates opposite the Trekroner fort where she suffered three killed and one wounded.

He was rewarded on 8 April by promotion to post-captain and commanded *Alcmene* for a few days and *Glatton* until April 1802. No further command came his way until the War of 1812 when he commanded *Albion* (74) and *Sceptre* (74) on the North American station. Marshall's *Royal Naval Biography* says that he had no further opportunity of distiguishing himself, but he might have. On 5 December 1813 he was blockading Provi-

Admiral John Devonshire's over-large house in Stonehouse, Plymouth.

under Robert Man in *Prince Frederick*, *Cornwall* and *Lancaster*, in America and the West Indies. It is likely that he met Nelson's patron, Maurice Suckling, in *Lancaster* in early 1762 and moved with him to *Dreadnought*. He was examined for lieutenant at the relatively late age of twenty-three, but not promoted for a further twelve years, in 1777.

In his twenties he may have run into debt as a courtier to King Christian VII of Denmark, while the latter was in London.

However, in 1782 he was first lieutenant of *Gibraltar* (80, Captain Thomas Hicks), flagship of Commodore Sir Richard Bickerton sent to reinforce Sir Edward Hughes in the East Indies. When Bickerton reached Rio de Janeiro in 1782 he purchased a cutter, *Substitute* (14), and made Fancourt, aged forty, her commander. Hardly had *Substitute* reached India than she was sent home with seemingly unimportant dispatches and so missed the brilliant actions and the prize-money in the campaign against the French in the Indian Ocean. It is hard to avoid the suspicion that Fancourt was being removed from blocking the promotion of other, younger lieutenants.

dence, Rhode Island, when the American frigate *President* slipped out; a frigate saw *President*'s sail but Devonshire in *Albion* was too far off to prevent the American setting out on her third cruise.

Devonshire was not employed after June 1814. He married Harriet Kempe and built himself a house at the end of the then fashionable Durnford Street, East Stonehouse (now part of Plymouth) to accommodate his large family. The house was so large that in later years it became the hospital to the nearby marine barracks. Brother Richard's house in nearby St Andrew's Terrace was more elegant. Rear-Admiral Sir John Ferris Devonshire died on 19 February 1839.

PETER HORE

→ FANCOURT ←

Robert Devereux Fancourt (1742–1826) is at once one of the oldest, the most unusual and the blandest of the Band of Brothers. He was baptised on 29 August 1742, at St Clement Danes in London, the son of a London oilman who supplied the finest whale oil to light the King's palaces and the fine houses along the Strand.

Starting in about 1759, in Fancourt's early naval career he served as AB and midshipman

However, during the peace between the American and French wars Fancourt found some employment. In 1787–9 he commanded *Bulldog* (16); he was made post-captain in December 1789 and during the Spanish Armament was given command of *Ambuscade* which he took to the Mediterranean. His next command was *Chichester* (44) and in 1794 he helped capture the French corvette *Sirène*.

He commanded *Agamemnon* (64) in 1796–1802, a memorable command because she was one of the ships which in the Great Mutiny deserted from Admiral Duncan's rendezvous in the North

Sea. Fancourt was dining with his officers while the mutineers stole his ship. In 1800 she took part in Admiral Dickson's reconnaissance of the Sound and in 1801 she was in Nelson's squadron during the Battle of Copenhagen.

Marshall is firmly of the opinion that Fancourt 'from the unfortunate circumstance of the *Agamemnon* striking upon a shoal when approaching the Danish line of defence ... was prevented from participating in the glorious victory achieved by Lord Nelson'. Nelson himself was more charitable, writing in his dispatch: 'The *Agamemnon* could not weather the shoal of the middle [ground], and was obliged to anchor, but not the smallest blame can be attached to Captain Fancourt.' However, the absence of *Agamemnon*, and *Bellona* and *Russell,* which had also run aground, from Nelson's plan of attack did prevent the extension of his line by three ships which would, 'I am confident,' he wrote, 'have silenced the Crown Islands [Trekroner], the outer Ships in the harbour's mouth, and prevented heavy loss ... and which unhappily threw the gallant and good Captain Riou ... under a very heavy fire ... the consequence has been the death of Captain Riou, and many brave Officers and men in the Frigates and Sloops.' All reports agree that despite the contrary wind and current, Fancourt made strenuous efforts to warp his ship into the King's Deep.

After Copenhagen, *Agamemnon* served as guardship in Hollesely Bay (on the Suffolk coast, north of Felixstowe) and in 1805–7 Fancourt commanded *Zealand* (64), flagship at the Nore, without apparent incident. In 1808 he was promoted to rear-admiral and, though promoted again in peacetime, was never employed at sea again.

Vice-Admiral Sir Robert Fancourt married first, Margaret or Martha Clements in 1771, and in 1778 Margaret Brown, who was the daughter or sister or widow or aunt of naval officers. Robert died on 7 June 1826 in Ripley, Surrey.

PETER HORE

→ FREMANTLE ←

Thomas Francis Fremantle (1765–1819) was born in 1765 in Hampstead. His grandfather, John, came from a family of Lisbon merchants and had been a diplomat at Madrid, then Secretary to the Customs Board, and had married into the Spanish aristocracy. His father, also John, a colonel in the Coldstream Guards and a merchant, died in debt in 1784. His mother Frances (née Edwards) came from a wealthy Bristol family. His family patron was Lord Buckingham of Stowe, one of the Grenvilles. His elder brothers were colonels in the Army, and they and his aunts had all married into minor aristocracy while a younger brother was a prominent Whig MP. His sisters married men of influence. His nephew, John, was ADC to Wellington, and his second son, Charles, fought in the War of 1812. Fremantle spoke French, Italian and some Spanish.

Fremantle's first ships were *Tartar* (28) and *Hussar* (28), under Captain Elliot Salter on the Lisbon station. *Hussar* was impounded in the Tagus after colliding with the Portuguese ship *Sao Bonaventure* which she was trying to search, and she was only released after the personal intervention of the Portuguese Queen. He served in *Victor* (14) in the West Indies with Captain Sylverius Moriarty, and in *Jupiter* (50) with Lord Ducie. He was a midshipman in *Phoenix* (44) in 1780 with Captain Sir Hyde Parker, when she was wrecked in a hurricane on the coast of hostile Cuba but the crew entrenched themselves until rescued. Fremantle became one of Hyde Parker's 'boys', and was promoted lieutenant at the age of sixteen by Sir Peter Parker (commander-in-chief in Jamaica), no relation to Sir Hyde. It was Lady Parker who 'had been a mother to Fremantle', and had nursed Nelson after his ill-fated Nicaragua expedition. He served in *Ramillies* (74) for a year as midshipman and master's mate, the sloop *Vaughan* (14) and, when captured by the French *Triton* (64) in *Tickler* (14), was taken to Havana, where he was exchanged before returning to England from Jamaica in *Childers* (14).

From 1784 to December 1787 Fremantle served in *Camilla* (20) as first lieutenant under Captain John Hutt, on the Jamaica station. Hutt later achieved glory, a fatal wound, and a place in the nave of Westminster Abbey on the Glorious First of June. Fremantle also served in the sloop *Port Antonio* (12). A period ashore in London followed, when he met royalty through his elder brother, John, who was equerry to the Duke of York, and he confided in a letter to his brother William on 4 July 1788 from 31 Titchfield Street, London, that he had 'lived with the handsomest woman in England for five months', but doesn't name her.

During the Nootka Crisis of 1790 he joined Sir Hyde Parker in *Brunswick* (74) as third lieutenant. At the end of the year he was promoted commander but early 1791 found him living hectically in Bath until he was given command of the fireship *Spitfire* with James Brisbane, the third son of Admiral Brisbane, as one of his lieutenants and there followed an enjoyable, and amorous, spell based at Yarmouth, Isle of Wight, in command of a small squadron of guard boats. On half pay from September 1791 until early 1793, he visited France ('in a mess, best families fleeing') in August 1792, getting the clap that winter, and curing it with mercury. He had a brief command of the fireship *Conflagration* before being made post-captain in May 1793 when he was given command of his old ship, *Tartar*: his first prize-money in command was shared with John Trigge of *Mermaid* (32) when they took the French privateer *General Washington* (22).

Fremantle and Nelson both knew the Parkers in the West Indies and may have met there, but their first recorded encounter came after the capture of Toulon. *Tartar*, with Lord Hugh Seymour embarked, met *Agamemnon* on 31 August 1793 when Fremantle told Nelson of the burning of the French fleet. Nelson was on the way to obtain Neapolitan reinforcements for Hood.

The conversation in *Tartar* might have been interesting. In 1783 Seymour and 'Jacko' Willett Payne, both bachelor naval officers, had shared a house in Conduit Street, Mayfair, where the Prince of Wales was a visitor, and the friends led 'an irregular and convivial life'. There Payne seduced a penniless teenager called Amy Lyon. When in June 1794 Fremantle reached Naples he was entertained by Amy Lyon, now Lady Emma Hamilton, whom he found 'large and masculine'.

Meanwhile, *Tartar* joined Nelson on the blockade of Bastia, and his first known letter from Nelson is dated 25 January 1794: 'Sir You will proceed in His Majesty's Ship under your Command off Bastia in the Isle of Corsica, and in every means in your power prevent the Enemy's Privateers from leaving or getting into the Port … ' By the time Bastia surrendered on 21 May 1794 Fremantle had earned the respect of Nelson by his fearless use of *Tartar's* guns, though a walk ashore in April to inspect a new battery almost ended the lives of both as a shot from the defenders missed by inches: Nelson was bowled over.

Fremantle was making his name as a successful frigate captain, and in January 1795 was given *Inconstant* (36). His command started awkwardly when his commander-in-chief received a letter of complaint from his crew alleging cruelty.

Betsey Fremantle, who nursed her husband and Nelson after they had been wounded at Tenerife: a portrait made on the continent when she was a teenager.

Fremantle, who had experience of mutiny in *Camilla*, faced his men down, saying any punishment he gave would be less than a court-martial would have ordered and arrested the five ringleaders. Before the matter came to trial, Fremantle took part in one of the more famous frigate actions of the war. On 14 March the French battleship *Ça Ira* (80) had fallen behind a fleeing French fleet and Fremantle ranged up astern of the larger ship and repeatedly raked her, leading to her capture, and the capture of *Censeur* (80) when the British fleet caught up. Fremantle did not forget to obtain a pardon for the mutineers in view of their shipmates' 'sober, quiet and proper' action.

When the French armies entered Tuscany in June 1796, Fremantle persuaded local traders and the consul that British goods and people should be evacuated: among the naval stores, provisions, British subjects, and émigrés were the Wynne family, who embarked with their daughters in *Inconstant*. Soon Fremantle was seeking William's advice as to whether to marry eighteen-year-old Betsey Wynne whom he described as 'short, speaks German, Ital-

ian, French and English, plays incomparably well on the harpsichord, draws well, sings a little, and is otherwise a very good humoured, sensible dolly'. She in turn described him in her diary as 'not handsome but with fiery black eyes that are quite captivating, he is also good natured, kind, amiable, and lively, qualities that win everybody's heart'.

Betsey's diary describes the progress of their love affair while 'Old Jarvie', the unlikeliest of admirals to list matchmaking as one of his interests, kept the Wynnes in the fleet and entertained them on board his flagship. They married in Naples in the Hamiltons' house in January 1797, where Prince Augustus, George III's youngest son, gave away the bride. Betsey considered Emma to be 'beautiful and amiable'.

Tom and Betsey embarked in his new command, *Seahorse* (38), to join the close blockade of Cadiz. In a boat action Nelson was almost killed, writing afterwards: 'I feel particularly indebted to the successful conclusion of this contest to the gallantry of Captain Fremantle who accompanied me in my barge, and to my coxswain John Sykes who in defending my person is most severely wounded, as was Capt. Fremantle.'

Their next adventure was the disastrous attack on Santa Cruz in July 1797. Betsey dined with Nelson before the landing in which he and her husband were both shot through the right arm. Nelson's was amputated; Fremantle's remained painful to the end of his life and put him on shore for the next three years. Nelson's first note with his left hand was to Betsey, and she, though suffering from morning sickness herself, nursed them both on the passage back to Spithead, noting that Nelson was a 'very bad patient'.

They settled in Swanbourne in Buckinghamshire, in a house still occupied by their descendant, Betsy Duncan Smith.

In 1801, now in command of *Ganges* (74), Fremantle joined Hyde Parker and Nelson for their mission to the Baltic. There on 1 April Fremantle anchored *Ganges* ahead of Nelson's *Elephant* where, despite the fury of the battle *Ganges* suffered just seven dead and one wounded.

Hyde Parker was recalled. Nelson replaced him in command, and after a dinner to celebrate Emma's birthday on 24 April, he sent Fremantle to St Petersburg to negotiate the release of over a hundred interned British merchant ships, a measure backed by moving the fleet up the Baltic.

With peace in prospect Tom and Betsey went to Bath for further convalescence of his Tenerife wound. However, there was a problem with Henry Rice, his former first lieutenant, who accused him of bullying conduct, and challenged him to a duel. The Admiralty ruled that Rice had been disrespectful and Fremantle accepted an apology.

Fremantle resumed his command of *Ganges* in July 1803 when war broke out again. In October he was being battered by gales in Bantry Bay, before he joined Pellew on the blockade of Ferrol and Corunna, on the look-out for the frigate *La Poursuivante* carrying Bonaparte's brother Jerome from Baltimore to France. He dined ashore with the captains of the enemy ships being blockaded. They were personal friends, but professional enemies! In May 1805 he was given the new *Neptune* (98), joining the fleet off Cadiz in August. He told his brother that he was going to be second to Nelson in any battle, and had secret directions for the battle, which included instructions on how to attack in a letter of 9 October 1805.

At the Battle of Trafalgar *Neptune* was third in the weather column, having been ordered by Nelson to drop back so that *Victory* should be first to pierce the enemy line, but it was *Neptune* which did the real damage to the French centre. Midshipman William Badcock wrote that Fremantle was 'as cool in action as if nothing was doing' and 'we kept up such a brisk fire that the Spaniards could not keep at their guns'. The largest ship in the world, the *Santísima Trinidad* mounting 130 guns on four decks, surrendered to Fremantle, and she was in his hands long enough for him to remove part of her chapel contents, before she had to be scuttled. *Neptune* suffered just ten killed and thirty-four wounded. Fremantle even changed her tattered topsails for new ones when the enemy van threatened to join the battle. Later he interviewed

Fremantle died and was buried at Naples where now there is nothing to be seen, but successive generations of his family have maintained this monument on Malta.

the French Admiral Pierre-Charles Villeneuve and his flag captain Jean-Jacques Magendie to obtain a definitive list of the Franco-Spanish fleet. *Neptune*'s deeds in the battle are recorded in a poem by Lawrence Smith, Royal Marines.

Fremantle was recalled from Collingwood's blockade in October 1806 to become a Lord of the Admiralty and MP for Sandwich, and was in charge of erecting the seamark monument to Nelson on Portsdown Hill, modelled on the Axum pillar in Ethiopia.

Promoted to rear-admiral in 1810, Fremantle returned to the Mediterranean, seeing action off Catalonia, Minorca, Toulon, Sicily and in the Adriatic. Based at Palermo, he avoided the tangled politics of the exiled Neapolitan court, where the Queen was the aunt of Bonaparte's second wife.

His ships were in action along both coasts of Italy, and gave him a constant supply of naval intelligence. The command included eighty armed vessels manned by British and Sicilian troops under General Lord Bentinck. They instituted a joint plan in April 1812 to release the Sicilian slaves held by the Tunisians. He took Lady Bentinck, dressed as an officer of marines, with him in his flagship *Milford* (74) and by 3 May they had succeeded in liberating 380 captives, to the delight of the Sicilians.

After eighteen months spent driving the French out of the Adriatic, Fremantle was planning to take Venice when he was called home in March 1814. He was rewarded with a knighthood received from the Prince Regent and a barony from the Austrian Emperor. In May 1815, when Bonaparte briefly threatened Europe again, Fremantle had the Channel Islands command and launched his own invasion at Arromanches a week before Napoleon surrendered.

When the Great War 1792–1815 was over, Fremantle took his family to the Mediterranean, where in March 1818 he was appointed commander-in-chief with his flag in *Rochfort* (74), under the command of Captain Andrew Green who had served with him at Copenhagen and Trafalgar. Among his midshipmen were Augustus and Adolphus Fitzclarence, the Duke of Clarence's illegitimate sons.

Vice-Admiral Sir Thomas Fremantle died suddenly in December 1819 in Naples aged fifty-four. The King of Naples ensured that he was buried with full military honours. Betsey bore him nine children, including five sons, of whom three joined the Navy, and four daughters. His eldest son, Thomas, was made a baronet and entered politics to become Lord Cottesloe. Charles, his second son, founded Western Australia, and became an admiral, as did his grandson Edmund, and great-grandson Sydney, a family tradition of naval service which continued until the retirement of the present Lord Cottesloe and this author.

Charles Fremantle

↦ GRAVES ↤

Thomas Graves (1747–1814) was the third of four sons of the Reverend John Graves of Castle-dawson, Londonderry. It is easy to be confused by the numerous members of the extended Graves family, and some writers have conflated cousin Thomas Graves (1st Baron Graves, 1725–1802), who assisted the United States of America to its independence by failing to intercept the French fleet off Chesapeake Bay in 1781, with uncle Samuel Graves (1717–87), who fought at the Battle of Quiberon Bay in 1759, or even brothers Samuel, John and Richard, all of whom became admirals in the Royal Navy.

Thomas served in the Seven Years War (1756–63) and was made lieutenant in *Shannon* (28) in 1765 whilst serving off the coast of Africa under his cousin Thomas in *Edgar* (60).

In 1773 he was appointed to *Racehorse* (18) under Captain Constantine Phipps, who commanded a voyage of exploration that year which attempted to find the North-West Passage from the Atlantic to the Pacific, and which reached 10° degrees North. A young Horatio Nelson served as a midshipman in the second ship of the squadron, the bomb vessel *Carcass* under Captain Skeffington Lutwidge. Graves was prevented from duelling with another young officer over the carcass of a polar bear claimed by both, and Nelson is alleged to have shot a bear.

During the American War of Independence Graves was appointed lieutenant in *Lively* (20) in January 1774 and then, under his uncle Samuel, he was given independent command of various ships, including the schooner *Diana* (6). While aground at low water on the night of 27–28 May 1775 at Winnisimet Ferry, *Diana* was attacked by a large force of rebels and set alight; Graves, who was the last to leave her, carried the facial scars of his burns for the rest of his life. The next month at the Battle of Bunker Hill Graves commanded an armed sloop, *Spitfire* (6), and landed at Noddle's Island, opposite Boston; he fought a large group of rebels. One of them, more zealous than his comrades, advanced nearer to Graves's sailors, who were attempting to bring off some naval stores, and Graves, still suffering from his burns, was sufficiently incensed to offer single combat, but the rebel ran off and was missed when Graves slipped into a bog as he fired at him. This was reckoned by all who witnessed it as a fine instance of Graves's bravery.

Next Graves served under Commodore William Hotham in *Preston*, and in 1779 he commanded the brig-sloop *Savage* (14). In 1781 he achieved post rank. In the temporary absence of Commodore Edmund Affleck he commanded *Bedford* (74) at the Battle of the Chesapeake, and was Affleck's flag captain at the Battles of St Kitts and Dominica in 1782.

At the end of 1782 Graves was given *Magicienne* (32) and on 2 January 1783 he met the French *Sybille* (32). Both ships were reduced to wrecks and parted, *Magicienne* not reaching Jamaica until a fortnight later, but *Sybille* was later taken by *Hussar* (34).

During the peace Graves spent some time in France and during the first years of the French Revolutionary War he was unemployed, until in October 1800 he was appointed to *Cumberland*

(74) in the Channel Fleet under Lord St Vincent.

On 1 January 1801, as part of the general promotion to celebrate the union of Britain and Ireland, Graves was raised to rear-admiral and in March he hoisted his flag in *Defiance* (74) as third-in-command of the Baltic Fleet under Sir Hyde Parker and Nelson. At a council of war before the Battle of Copenhagen, Nelson conferred with Graves, who was against an attack: nevertheless Nelson took Graves as his second-in-command. *Defiance* was the last ship to enter the fray, running the gauntlet of the Danish line, to anchor as the northernmost ship of the line, opposite the Danish Trekroner battery, with only Edward Rioux's detachment of small ships to the north. *Defiance* suffered more casualties than most of the other British ships; she was also the nearest ship to Hyde Parker's reserve squadron and therefore best placed to read and repeat flag signals from the commander-in-chief. When the signal to discontinue the action was made, Graves repeated it by using the lee main topsail yardarm halyard whilst keeping Nelson's signal for close action on the main topgallant masthead, which meant Nelson and his ships would readily see the latter signal, but not the former. Graves claimed later that all other halyards were broken.

At a celebration meal given by Nelson on 26 April to celebrate the birthday of 'Santa Emma', as Nelson called her this time, he presented Graves with one of Davison's Nile medals, thus formally inducting him into the Band of Brothers.

After the excitement of the battle, Graves was unwell. Nelson's hypochondria may not have stretched to his people, however. In a letter to Emma dated 23 May, Nelson complained, 'I am coming home immediately or I shall be dead of consumption, the keen air of the North has cut me to the heart. Graves has kept his bed for a month.' However, Graves was well enough to attend a ceremony when Nelson informed him that Parliament had voted their thanks, and, on behalf of the King, conferred on him the Order of the Bath, with the words,

> In investing you with the ensigns of the most honourable and Military Order of

UNDERNEATH ARE INTERRED ALL THAT WAS MORTAL OF
SIR THOMAS GRAVES,
KNIGHT OF THE MOST HONOURABLE ORDER OF THE BATH.
AND ADMIRAL OF THE BLUE.
WHO DEPARTED THIS LIFE MARCH 28ᵀᴴ 1814.
ALSO OF HIS FIRST WIFE,
BRIDGET, DAUGHTER OF PHILIP BACON ESQᴿᴱ
OF BISHOP'S HALL, IN THE COUNTY OF SUFFOLK,
WHO DEPARTED THIS LIFE DECEMBER 25ᵀᴴ 1795.

'But I would not have you to be ignorant, brethren, concerning them which
are asleep, that ye sorrow not, even as others which have no hope.'
'For GOD hath not appointed us to wrath, but to obtain salvation by our
Lord Jesus Christ, who died for us, that, whether we wake or sleep, we
should live together with him.'
I Thes. IV. 9. 10.

ALSO OF
MARY GRAVES,
THEIR ONLY CHILD, WHO DEPARTED THIS LIFE
4ᵀᴴ MARCH 1860. AGED 87 YEARS.

Admiral Sir Thomas Graves' monument at St Nicholas Church, Combe Raleigh, Devon.

the Bath, I cannot but express how much I feel gratified that it should have fallen to my lot to be directed to confer this justly merited honour, and special mark of royal favour upon you; for I cannot but reflect, that I was an eye-witness of your high merit and distinguished gallantry on the memorable second of April, and for which you are so honourably rewarded. I hope that these honours conferred upon you will prove to the officers in the service, that a strict perseverance in the pursuit of glorious actions, and the imitation of your brave and laudable conduct, will ever insure them the favours and rewards of our most gracious Sovereign, and the thanks and gratitude of our country.

Graves's poor health continued, but when Nelson returned to England he stayed in the Baltic, as second-in-command to Admiral Pope, Nelson's successor, shifting his flag to *Polyphemus* (64) and subsequently to *Monarch* (74), in which he remained until January 1802.

From January 1804 to November 1805 he served on the Brest blockade as third-in-command, usually flying his flag in *Foudroyant* (80) and commanding the inshore squadron. He was criticised for taking his fleet to Quiberon Bay to collect water in January 1805, thereby allowing Missiessy's Rochefort squadron to slip out and begin the chain of events that led to the Battle of Trafalgar.

He was promoted to vice-admiral in November 1805 and removed from his command, causing

him to write to Cornwallis, explaining that 'a severe cold and inflammation in my eyes' prevented him expressing in person his 'surprise … disappointment, and mortification of being removed in so extraordinary a manner.' Nevertheless there were now too many vice-admirals chasing too few appointments and he was never employed again.

Admiral Sir Thomas Graves retired to Woodbine Hill, Honiton, Devon, and died there on 29 March 1814. He left a wife, Susanna (apparently his second wife), and a daughter, Mary.

PETER TURNER

⇢ HAMOND ⇠

Graham Eden Hamond (1779–1862) was born in London on 30 December 1779, the only son of Sir Andrew Snape Hamond. In his career he enjoyed considerable 'interest': his father becoming Comptroller of the Navy 1794–1806, and his sister marrying into one of the naval dynasties of the age, the Hoods.

Young Graham was borne on the books of his father's ship, *Irresistible* (74), when six years old but is unlikely to have left his mother's apron strings so early; however, by 1793 Hamond really was a midshipman in *Phaeton* (38), commanded by his cousin, Sir Andrew Snape Douglas, when she helped capture a valuable squadron of French ships, including the privateer *Général Dumourier* (22). The precise share-out of prize-money is unknown, but over the next few years Hamond enjoyed a steady income from prizes.

The next year in *Queen Charlotte* (100), the flagship of Earl Howe, Hamond took part in the Battle of the Glorious First of June. Hamond was made lieutenant in 1796, and served on several ships in the Mediterranean and on the home station, including the blockade of Le Havre in 1798, when he commanded *Echo* (18).

Just two years later Hamond was made post-captain, a promotion due undoubtedly to his father's influence, and the next year was given command of *Champion* (24) at the blockade of Malta, where he also served ashore in the Siege of Valletta until ill-health forced a return home.

Hamond was given command of *Blanche* (36) and in her he took part in the Battle of Copenhagen in 1801. Before the battle the British commander-in-chief, Sir Hyde Parker, sent Hamond to negotiate with the Danes, so he landed at Elsinore and took coach to Copenhagen; he returned with Nicholas Vansittart MP, the British government's special envoy, Mr Drummond, the British Minister to Copenhagen, various fleeing British subjects, and with the refusal of the Danes to accept terms. His part in the battle was at anchor between *Amazon* (38) and *Alcmene* (32) opposite the Trekroner battery. All the small ships under Captain Edward Riou took a hammering and *Blanche* suffered seven dead and nine badly injured. At church service the following Sunday, Hamond held Nelson's prayer book for him to read. Soon after, Hamond brought Hyde Parker back to England, and then *Blanche* did duty in the Channel, including attendance on George III at Weymouth.

Hamond commanded *Plantagenet* (74) throughout the season of 1803, when she captured the French *Courier de Terre Neuve* and the *Atalante*.

In 1804 Hamond was given command of the new frigate *Lively* (38), the prototype of one of the most successful British designs of the war: fifteen such ships were ordered over the next ten years. In *Lively* he took part in the notorious action on 5 October 1804 when, before a declaration of war, a squadron under Commodore Graham Moore waylaid four Spanish frigates laden with treasure intended to pay Spanish reparations to France. *Nuestra Señora de las Mercedes*, carrying many of the Spanish officers' wives and families, blew up early in the battle scattering her treasure on the seabed, which demoralised the other Spanish ships into surrendering with the vast fortune which they were carrying. The treasure was deemed droits of the Admiralty, so the captors only received a fourth of the usual prize-money. Two months later, in two separate incidents on the same day, Hamond helped capture two other treasure-laden ships, and all the bullion, worth approximately 5 million dollars, was entrusted to Hamond to bring home to England; this was probably the largest sum carried on board a ship up to that time, but the usual payment of freight-money was suspended for this trip, so that on this occasion also Hamond's reward was a share of a special bounty.

On 30 December 1806 Hamond married Elizabeth Kimber of Fowey, Cornwall. Hamond was well-connected and now wealthy and might have been expected to 'marry well', so this marriage may have been a love-match; they had five children.

Hamond commanded *Victorious* (74) at the unhappy taking of Flushing in 1809, but was invalided until 1824 when he was chosen to convey the British minister to Brazil in *Wellesley* (74).

As rear-admiral, flying his flag in *Spartiate* (74), he delivered the treaty of separation between Brazil and Portugal to the King of Portugal, but he was not allowed to wear the Portuguese Order of the Tower and Sword, as it had not been awarded on active service.

Hamond succeeded as the second baronet in September 1828. From 1834 to 1838 he was commander-in-chief on the South America station, and his steady rise through the flag list culminated in him becoming Vice-Admiral of

the United Kingdom in 1862 (an appointment in the monarch's gift). Admiral of the Fleet Sir Graham Eden Hamond died the same year at Norton Lodge, Freshwater on the Isle of Wight. Two of his sons served in the Navy, but he failed to found a dynasty and the baronetcy became extinct in 1969.
PETER TURNER

❧ HATHERILL ❧

Richard Hatherill (1769–1804) was born at Queenborough in north Kent on 20 September 1769 to Joseph and Elizabeth Hatherill. His father was ordained in 1775 and was appointed perpetual curate to the town in the same year. Joseph also served as a naval chaplain between 1779 and 1802, which may have proved useful in his son's future career.

Queenborough, placed near the confluence of the Medway and Thames, was a flourishing maritime and fishing centre. Nelson passed for lieutenant at nearby Sheerness in 1777 and is said later to have rented accommodation in Queenborough for himself and Lady Hamilton. The creeks and shallow waters of the river would have provided the young Hatherill with the ideal environment to learn how to sail. Richard attended Merchant Taylors' School, a charitable institution, in London between 1780 and 1784, but was absent because of illness for over a year during 1780–1. He seems also to have been apprenticed for seven years to a local oyster dredger, James Hall, in October 1785 at a cost of £15, perhaps as a back-up plan to a career in the Navy, since he is also recorded on the new, Thames-built *Dictator* (64, Captain William Parker) as the 'chaplain's servant' between 24 September 1783 and 11 March 1786. Then between October 1786 and June 1790, Hatherill was aboard *Maidstone* (28, Captain Henry Newcome), at first rated 'able' and then as a midshipman from 1788. This ship was in English Harbour, Antigua, in 1787, where her master was one of a number ordered to inspect supplies recently arrived from England, part of a small group of frigates under the command of Nelson in the *Boreas*. Hatherill

subsequently served briefly in *London* (90) and *Royal Sovereign* (100) and passed for lieutenant on 3 November 1790.

Research has failed to reveal where he served after this until he was appointed to *Repulse* (64, Captain James Alms) on 18 October 1794. He does not appear in the Biennial List of commissioned officers entitled to half pay for the years 1790–4. *Repulse* was caught up in the Nore mutiny of 1797 when her first lieutenant, Francis Douglas, was awarded a commemorative sword for bringing the ship to shore in spite of being fired on by other ships. Admiralty correspondence concerning pay shows that the ship was held by the mutineers, six of whom were court-martialled and four pardoned. During this period Hatherill also appears in the books of *Blenheim* (90, Captain John Bazely), in 1794–5, and in 1796 in *Director* (64, Captain William Bligh).

In March 1800 *Repulse* was on blockade duty off the coast of France when Captain Alms was injured in a fall. Under the command of her first lieutenant the ship struck rocks, and in spite of the best efforts of the crew over the next few hours, water rose rapidly to two feet above the orlop deck. Fortunately, they were near enough to shore to beach the ship and almost all the crew were saved and taken prisoner. The officers were soon exchanged, and the inevitable court-martial took place in Portsmouth on 26 and 27 June the same year. As fourth lieutenant, Hatherill had been on watch during the afternoon of the day before the wreck and was closely questioned by the court. The captain was exonerated, but the first lieutenant and the master were dismissed the service.

On 16 July 1800 Hatherill married Mary Pennall at Queenborough. She seems to have come from a seafaring family since several people of the same name are listed as mariners in the Queenborough directory of 1792 and another was Clerk of the Survey of the Ordnance at Sheerness.

In a great advance in his career, Richard Hatherill joined the *Hecla* bomb vessel as commander on 16 January 1801. In his log he records the ship's bombardment of the castle at Kronborg on 30

March and the various manoeuvres of the fleet. On 2 April he had orders 'to get to the northward, to throw shells at Crown Islands [Trekroner] and vessels within them', and grounding of other ships prompted him to sound carefully around the *Hecla* when forced to anchor because of the strength of the current. Having returned briefly from Copenhagen to Lowestoft in July, on 4 and 5 August *Hecla* took part in a bombardment of Boulogne in which five of the enemy's vessels were sunk in spite of 'heavy fire from the shore'. Later the same year the ship was paid off at the Nore, having been sent in by Nelson 'to make good her defects'.

On 29 April 1802 Hatherill was posted captain as part of a very large group (about seventy) promoted on that day, as a celebration of the Peace of Amiens.

Research has not found any further ships commanded by Hatherill. However, two letters have survived, one from 16 March 1803 and the other from 11 July 1804, in which he asks to be employed as 'whatever their Lordships in their Wisdom may Judge most proper'. Sadly, it was only three months later on 29 October 1804 when he made his will 'being at this time in an ill state of Body'. He died soon after at the age of thirty-five and was buried on 15 November 1804, leaving all his estate to his wife Mary, who went on to remarry in 1810 and made her will in 1855.

Richard Hatherill lived a short life, but an eventful one, travelling the world, seeing action, a serious mutiny and being shipwrecked. He is an interesting example of a man who made his way from the chaplain's servant to the quarterdeck. It may be that his father's connections in the Navy helped him on his way, since Evan Nepean, Secretary to the Board of Admiralty 1795–1804, was MP for Queenborough 1796–1802, and the two may have met during Joseph's time at sea, when Nepean was a purser. They would certainly have moved in the same circles in Kent. It may not be stretching imagination too far to think that Nelson came across the young Hatherill in Queenborough and perhaps they met again in the West Indies.

GILLIAN KNIGHT

◈ INMAN ◈

Henry Inman (1762–1809) was born in Burrington, Somerset, and educated at home by his father, the vicar, until in 1776, presumably under the influence of his father's Somerset friends the Hoods, he first went to sea in Samuel Hood's *Barfleur* (90).

The American War found Inman in *Lark* (32) which on 5 August 1778 at Rhode Island was beached and burnt with several other ships, to avoid capture by a French fleet under Vice-Admiral Comte d'Estaing, who had been sent to co-operate with the American rebels. Nevertheless, Inman manned a battery which deterred the French, whose storm-damaged fleet retired for repairs to Boston.

Inman was examined for lieutenant in 1780 and served in *Pearl* (32), *Camel* (26) and *Santa Monica* (36) in the West Indies. *Santa Monica* grounded off Tortola on 1 April 1782 and rapidly broke up, though the crew were saved.

When the French *Hector* (74) was taken at the Battle of the Saintes later that month, she was repaired and recommissioned as HMS *Hector*, even though there was already a ship of that name in Portsmouth. The French *Hector*, built in 1756, was in a poor state, old and badly battered at the Saintes, and twenty-two of her guns were taken out, her rigging and masts reduced, and she was manned by some two hundred invalids for the voyage to England. When on 5 September 1782 she fell in with two French frigates, *Gloire* (32) and *Aigle* (28), they realised her weakened state and were determined to recapture her. *Hector*'s newly promoted captain, John Bourchier, was wounded early in the action, and all the other officers were incapacitated except Inman, her first lieutenant. Unable to manoeuvre and repeatedly raked, Inman took command and resisted a boarding, and when the sails of a British fleet were seen, the Frenchmen made off. *Hector* had suffered forty-six casualties, and her 'previously crazy hull was almost torn to pieces, whilst her mast, sails and rigging were rendered useless by shot'.

With *Hector* in this condition 'a tremendous storm arose'; the 1780s saw a number of severe hurricanes which, in the days when they were not well understood and the art of forecasting not developed, were a particular danger to sailing ships. *Hector* lost her rudder and all her masts, the hold filled with salt water and spoiled the provisions and fresh water. To keep the pumps going, with a reduced, sickly crew, Inman enforced his commands with a pair of pistols and for a fortnight used 'entreaties, threats and commands' and 'never enjoyed one hour's repose'. Fortunately, with his ship slowly foundering, the Dartmouth snow *Hawke*, appeared and her master, John Hill, took *Hector*'s people on board and carried them to St John's, Newfoundland. There they arrived on short rations and almost out of fresh water, and for the third time Inman lost all his possessions, but the seamen whose lives he had threatened in order to force them to work the pumps now chaired him through the streets of St John's.

From 1783 to 1790 Inman was on half pay but during the Spanish Armament he was appointed to *Latona* (38, Captain Thomas Bertie) and remained in employment for the next twenty years. His first command was the cutter *Pigmy* (14), 'not a prime sailer', based on the Isle of Man. Around this time he also married Catherine Dalby, sister of Captain Thomas Dalby.

He was a lieutenant in *Victory* at the Siege of Toulon when Lord Hood gave him command of the captured French *Aurore* (32), in which Inman again endured an epic of survival and seamanship. *Aurore* was weakly manned and had on board more prisoners than crew; a mutiny, led by French officers who messed with their British captors, had to be put down. Next *Aurore* was dismasted in a storm off Corsica and Inman's turbulent prisoners again attempted to take her. When one of them bored a hole in her bottom, Inman ran before the wind until he made Gibraltar where he anchored her in shallow water and obliged the prisoners themselves to take to the pumps. This at first they refused, but when the water was up to their waists, Inman's fractious prisoners at last submitted to his will.

Inman's luck did not change. In 1797 while in the Channel in command of the captured French *Espion* (38), with his wife and children on board, she ran into heavy weather and only made Sheerness with great difficulty, where she was declared unfit to proceed to sea. Then in the winter of 1797/8 he commanded *Ramillies* on the blockade of Brest, 'struggling with continued gales, which for their violence, the oldest seaman had never seen exceeded'.

At last, at the beginning of 1799 Inman obtained command of *Andromeda* (32), 'one of the most beautiful models in the service', employed in the North Sea and on an attack on Dunkirk in July 1800. When the French *Desirée* (36) was cut out, Inman was given command and so proceeded to the Baltic under Parker and Nelson. At the Battle of Copenhagen Inman was in the King's Deep with Nelson, where in Nelson's words he 'performed the greatest service', and the men of *Monarch*, herself one of the more busily engaged ships, repeatedly exclaimed, 'Look at that frigate!' Though *Desirée* engaged one of the shore batteries, the Danish aim was too high, and she suffered just four men injured.

However, when after Copenhagen *Desirée* was ordered to the West Indies, Inman opted for family life and remained ashore.

In May 1805 Inman was given command of *Triumph* (74) and was in the thick of the fighting at Calder's action, the Battle of Finisterre in July, afterwards requiring a period of repairs. At Calder's court-martial – when in the words of the *Naval Chronicle* the admiral was tried and censured 'for an error of judgement after obtaining a victory' – Inman was asked, 'Why did he not inform the admiral of his crippled state?' to which Inman's immortal answer was, 'I did not think that a proper time to trouble the admiral with my complaints.'

Inman's health had suffered during his long career at sea, and although he was at sea again in 1806 in a squadron under Rear-Admiral Sir Richard Strachan, his ill-health forced him ashore in May. Initially, he was given command of the Sea Fencibles at King's Lynn, but then was reluctant to accept when offered the appointment of Naval Commissioner at Madras. The Indian climate ashore was not kind to Nelsonic heroes and he died there 'on 15 July 1809, just twelve days after arriving in the *Clorinde* frigate'.

PETER HORE

↣ **LAWFORD** ↢

John Lawford (1756–1842), the first son of John Lawford of Gosport and Sarah Gover of Portsea, was baptised at St Mary's Church, Portsea, on 3 July 1757.

He did not, it seems, join the Royal Navy until he was twenty-one years old, but the first record found of his service in the Navy is during the war with America. He was first lieutenant of *Namur* (90) at the Battle of the Saintes; this implies that he was already an experienced sailor when he joined. In October 1788 he took command of the new brig-sloop *Wasp* (16), and in 1790, he commanded the sloop *Hound* (16), and subsequently spent two years stationed at Jamaica.

At the outbreak of war with revolutionary France, in 1793, Lawford was promoted post-captain, and was given command of the recently captured *Convert* (36). In an incident known as the Wreck of the Ten Sail, he struck the shore off Grand Cayman three days into a voyage home. Acquitted at court-martial in Port Royal, Jamaica, his career seems to have continued smoothly thereafter. He commanded *Agincourt* (64) in 1798, but in March 1798 he swapped ships with Captain John Bligh (a cousin of William Bligh), taking over *Romney* (50).

In June 1798, Commodore Lawford, as he was then, instigated a short action against a Swedish frigate escorting a convoy of Swedish ships in the Channel, suspecting them of supplying cargoes of war materiel to France. This was a delicate situation, so Lawford sent an express to the Admiralty, from whom he received instructions to detain the convoy. Without being too heavy-handed, Lawford explained his requirements to the Swedish commodore, who, in turn, showed Lawford his orders to resist such action by the British. After a stand-off overnight, the Swedish were aware of their impossible position and so permitted the convoy to be brought into Margate Roads. This was one of the incidents that pushed Sweden, Denmark and Russia into the formation of the League of Armed Neutrality two years later. After a lengthy consideration the High Court of the Admiralty condemned the merchantmen and their cargoes as lawful prizes, worth £600,000, whilst the private adventures of the masters were released.

Romney joined Vice-Admiral Andrew Mitchell's squadron of Den Helder in August 1799, and was present at the Vlieter Incident, when a Dutch fleet mutinied and surrendered to the British. Later in that same August, Lawford took command of *Polyphemus* (64) – known to her sailors as the 'Polly Infamous' – and in her he joined the fleet under Sir Hyde Parker, sent out to force the Danes out of the League of Armed Neutrality that he had inadvertently helped to create. *Polyphemus* was detached into Nelson's squadron, sent to attack Copenhagen, and the Danish fleet at anchor before it, on 2 April 1801. As a result of the improvised changes that battle brings, *Polyphemus* anchored to the south of the line, from where she engaged the blockship, or floating battery, *Provesteen*, sustaining thirty-one casualties, including six dead.

Polyphemus returned to England after the battle and was paid off, after which, in April 1803, Lawford married Anna Maria Holden (1758–1853), of Great Yarmouth, Norfolk.

There followed a lucrative five months when Lawford's fortunes drastically improved as *Polyphemus*, sometimes in company with others, took several prizes, including in December 1804, the Spanish *Santa Gertrudis* which was found to be shipping specie from South America to the value of 1,125,000 dollars.

In June 1805 Lawford shifted into *Audacious* (74), thereby missing the Battle of Trafalgar in which his successor, Robert Redmill, fought *Polyphemus* with distinction. In October 1806 Lawford moved to the command of *Impétueux* (74). He served for a time in the Channel and the North Sea, where, on 25 July 1809, Lieutenant John Ball was tried for contempt of Lieutenant Jones, first of *Impétueux*, disobeying orders and disrespect of his captain, and was admonished by the court-martial. The following month *Impétueux* was engaged deploying gunboats in the attack on a fort at Flushing, sustaining two killed and three wounded.

After returning home *Impétueux* was sent straight off to Lisbon in March 1810. When the British troops retreated from Spain to the lines at Torres Vedras, her boats were engaged annoying the French troops camped on the banks of the River Tagus. The French amused themselves with artillery and rifle fire while *Impétueux*'s boats employed their carronades and small arms. On 1 August 1811, Lawford was promoted rear-admiral but not employed.

Lawford was promoted vice-admiral in 1829 and admiral in 1832. He was made a Knight Commander of the Order of the Bath in August 1838 for his role at the Battle of Copenhagen in 1801; he was the only veteran to have lived long enough for the decision to be made to award this honour.

In August 1837 Lawford wrote his own will, presumably without professional help; all twenty pages of it are closely written without punctuation, thus making it obscure and turgid and giving employment to lawyers for a long time.

Lawford died at his home in St John's Wood on 22 December 1842. Anna Maria survived him, but they had no children.

PETER TURNER

→ M'KINLEY ←

George M'Kinley (1766–1852) was born in Devonport; his father, a naval lieutenant, died when he was eleven, but he was allowed no time for grieving and was sent to sea, where he was fortunate to attract the patronage of Samuel Barrington, John Leveson Gower and later Lord Hood.

His first ship was *Albion* (74) in 1774 and he had only just been rated 'able' in the sloop *Ceres* (18, Captain James Dacres) in the West Indies when in 1777 he became briefly a prisoner of war. Dacres had decoyed the French *Iphigénie* (36) away from a troop convoy which *Ceres* was escorting, and after a chase of two days was captured, but with the gratification that her convoy escaped.

M'Kinley was evidently a bright young man. He served in *Alcmene* (32), *Belliqueux* (64) and *Barfleur* (98, Captain Alexander Hood, and flagship of Samuel Hood). He was at the Battles of Martinique and of the Saintes in the American War. Unlike many he found employment through the peace of 1783–93, and when the French War broke out he was first lieutenant of the frigate *Alcide* (74, Captain Robert Linzee).

By April 1795 he was commander of *Liberty* (14) in the Channel Isles where, 'in a dashing operation' under the command of Sir Sidney Smith, a small squadron took and burned a French corvette, four brigs, two sloops and a lugger. In May 1798 he became master and commander of the fireship *Otter* (14) and, unlike many another who held honorary rank in the marines, M'Kinley actually commanded a detachment of marines ashore during the British landings in Holland in 1798.

In April 1801 *Otter* sailed up the King's Deep and anchored near Riou's *Amazon* but did not take much part in the Battle of Copenhagen. However, M'Kinley was an officer of seventeen years' unbroken experience and was promoted post-captain and refitted *Bellona* (74) in succession to Sir T Boulden Thompson, and then was ordered to bring *Ardent* (64) home.

In October 1801 he carried the news of the Peace of Amiens to the West Indies in the sloop *Pel-*

ican (18). Accidents are seldom written about, but in 1803 M'Kinley certainly suffered a serious accident when, in *Roebuck* (44) and exercising his newly raised men, a full powder horn exploded close to his face and he was blinded for several weeks.

In 1806, when the French threatened Lisbon, he brought off the British factory and merchants, and in 1809 he commanded a squadron on the Galician coast which cooperated with local troops who, in a rare victory for the guerrillas, recaptured the pilgrim city of Santiago de Compostela from the marauding French army.

In 1810 M'Kinley's *Lively* (38) was wrecked off Malta; he was acquitted of blame and commended for his eight weeks' effort to get *Lively* afloat. In 1812 M'Kinley was once more in command of *Bellona*, and he saw out the war in the Channel. When he came ashore in 1817 he had been thirty-three years at sea with hardly a break, of which twenty-two years were in command, and in his record of captain's services he listed thirty-two ships.

Of M'Kinley's brothers, Samuel died in 1780 in the American War, and John died in 1782 in the West Indies. Admiral George M'Kinley died in Alverstoke in 1852.

PETER HORE

→ MARTIN ←

John Henry Martin (c.1753–1823), who sailed on Cook's third voyage, was most probably born in Pembrokeshire in west Wales and possibly in Manorbier. He had had nearly five and a half years at sea in Navy vessels before joining Cook, beginning as a midshipman in the 8-gun sloop *Peggy*. This was probably from 1765 under Commander James O'Hara, and followed by three months in *Yarmouth* (60, Captain James Gambier), which at the beginning of 1767 was guard ship at Sheerness.

When *Romney* (50) was recommissioned in March 1767 by Captain John Corner, Martin served for two and a half years, still a midshipman, in American waters, followed by a year and a half in the sloop *Bonetta* (10, Commander James Wallace). He rejoined James O'Hara (now a captain)

in *Alderney* (12) for three months, rated 'able,' in about 1772.

Martin appears to then have had a break of several years from active service before he joined Cook's third voyage in March 1776 as an AB in *Discovery*. Shortly after the ship sailed, her captain, Charles Clerke, had him rated midshipman.

On 30 October 1777, at Huahine in the Society Islands, a local, who had been in custody, escaped and William Harvey who had been on watch was disrated to midshipman. As a result, Martin was promoted to lieutenant in his place and transferred to Cook's *Resolution*. Martin was involved in an incident on 1 March 1779 at Kauai, one of the Hawaiian islands, when James King and two other men were chased down to the shore and Martin, who was in charge of the pinnace, fired muskets, killing one native.

During the voyage, Martin kept a journal on which an historian commented: 'Martin's entries are not long, even at their longest; but he seems to have looked at life for himself.'

After the voyage, Martin sat his lieutenant's examination on 19 October 1780 and received his commission in December that year. He was immediately posted to *Union* (90, Captain John Dalrymple) on the western station. Other details of his naval career are sketchy. He probably served in 1795 in *Syren* (32) and in 1797 in *Melampus* (36) both times under Captain Graham Moore.

In any event, Martin was made a commander on 17 February 1800 and given command of *Xenophon* (22, later renamed *Investigator*) for operations in the North Sea in 1800, but was relieved of this ship when she was selected for Matthew Flinders' expedition to Australia. Instead, Martin was given the bomb-ship *Explosion* and so took part in the Battle of Copenhagen in April 1801, and also in the unsuccessful attack on Boulogne in August 1801.

Martin married and he and his wife had a son, Henry Owen Martin, born about 1806. However, this first wife must have died, as Martin was married to a much younger woman called Margaret when he died in 1823.

John Henry Martin died on 10 May 1823 and was buried at St Elidyr's Church, Ludchurch, Pembrokeshire. A memorial in the churchyard reads: 'At the time of his death he was supposed to be the last surviving officer who accompanied Captain Cook on his third voyage round the world.'
JOHN ROBSON

∻ MOSSE ∻

James Robert Mosse (1745–1801) was born into a family that has for centuries produced naval officers, clergymen and doctors for Britain. His father was John Mosse, rector of Great Hamden and vicar of Great Kimble in Bucks. James entered the Royal Navy as a captain's servant in *Burford* (70) on 6 August 1757, when he was eleven years eight months old, and he took part in Hawke's raid on Rochefort that year and in November 1758 he joined *Lizard* (28) as ordinary seaman and master's mate, where he remained until May 1763.

He described these years in a memorandum of 1790: 'He served in the Fleet at the reduction of every place in North America and the West Indies during the former War, the Island of Guadaloupe excepted, and towards the end was made a prisoner, in which fate he continued till the Peace.' This would have been the Seven Years War, the first global war, which terminated with the Treaty of Paris in 1763, so his captors were presumably French. Between 1763 and 1771 he served in the Channel in *Hussar* (28), *Tweed* (32), *Yarmouth* (64) and *Bellona* (74). From March 1771 to May 1775 he served in the East Indies under Sir Robert Harland, initially as a midshipman in *Northumberland* (70), but on 4 October 1771 he was promoted to lieutenant and joined *Swallow* (14). Mosse saw little active service while in *Swallow* or subsequently in *Orford* (70) and *Buckingham* (70), writing in the same memorandum: 'Returned to England in the year 1775 in the Squadron, but with the loss of health occasioned by a blow from a piece of wood falling on his head when executing his duty and which rendered him incapable full 15 months or indeed till he returned to his native climate.'

During the American War Mosse served, from March 1776 until February 1778 in *Juno* (32), in which he recaptured the brigantine *Dinah* from the rebels, and then until January 1779 as second lieutenant aboard *Eagle* (64) with Lord Howe. During a brief interval ashore, on 16 March 1780 Mosse married Ann Grace, daughter of Rev Stephen Kinchin of Stoke Charity, Hampshire, and they set up home at Wickham.

From October 1780 until August 1781 he served on the West Indies station in *Alfred* (72) and later *Vengeance* (74), and in April 1782 he became first lieutenant in *Victory* at the relief of the Great Siege of Gibraltar, after which Lord Howe made him master and commander of the fireship *Pluto*. The National Maritime Museum still holds a Spanish flag which Mosse took as a trophy of war at Gibraltar. Afterwards he wrote:

Our loss is but a few killed and wounded – not a Captain hurt … The *Victory* did not fire a Broadside as did some of the other ships in the Centre – the Admiral did not think them near enough. Admiral Barrington … commanded the Van, and Vice Admiral Milbank with the Rear-Admirals Hood and Hughes in the Rear. We have only to regret it was not day instead of night; for I believe we should have made it as glorious and complete a victory as the annals has ever produced, notwithstanding their great superiority.

In April 1783 his rank was confirmed but he was placed on half pay before being sent on impressment duty to Bristol. Like many officers his career was advanced by the Nootka Crisis when he was made post-captain and appointed to *Wasp* (16). Then, between 1793 and 1797, Mosse commanded the depot ship *Sandwich* (98) at the Nore, and was there on 12 May 1797 when mutineers seized his ship. Mosse put down this mutiny with considerable humanity and a number of prisoners from *Sandwich* wrote to him pleading for him to intercede on their behalf. His conduct of the prosecution of the ringleaders was reported in *The Times* in June 1797, when Richard Parker was hanged onboard *Sandwich*: two months later the death sentences on other mutineers were commuted to imprisonment.

From September 1797 until April 1799 Mosse commanded the former Dutch *Braakel* (54) and then *Veteran* (64) on the North Sea station. He was in the North Sea at the time of the Battle of Camperdown, though not present during the action.

On 1 May 1799 Mosse took command of *Monarch* (74). In spring 1801 the British fleet sailed to the Baltic to break up the Northern Alliance of Denmark, Russia and Sweden which had placed an embargo on British trade. Admiral Sir Hyde Parker was commander-in-chief in *London* (98) and Nelson his second-in-command in *St George* (98*)*, when the fleet anchored north of Helsingør (Elsinore in Shakespeare's *Hamlet*) at the entrance to the Sound. Impatient for action Nelson wrote on 16 March 1801:

> Reports say we are to anchor before we get to Kronborg castle that our minister in Copenhagen may negotiate. What nonsense. How much better could we negotiate was our fleet off Copenhagen and the Danish Minister would seriously reflect how he brought the fire of England on his Master's fleet and capital. To keep us out of sight is to seduce Denmark into a war which I as an Englishman wish to prevent. I hate your pen and ink men, a fleet of British ships of war are the best negotiators in Europe, they always speak to be understood and generally gain their point, their

Detail of the monument in St Paul's cathedral to Captain James Robert Mosse who fell at the Battle of Copenhagen in 1801.

> arguments carry conviction to the breasts of our enemies.

Hyde Parker's negotiations were indeed unsuccessful and as the British prepared to sail south on the evening of 25 March, Mosse wrote to his wife:

> Lord Nelson has done the *Monarch* the honour of choosing her for his <u>Van Ship</u> and she is to lead on, as soon as the winds will permit. This my dear love is the <u>Post of Honour</u>, & I make no doubt we shall acquit ourselves with fresh laurels. Whatever may be the good fortune of the Day, you cannot avoid being a sharer in the Glory which I entrust & hope will follow.

On 30 March 1801 Mosse's *Monarch* led the fleet into the two-and-half mile wide Sound between Sweden and Denmark. When she came abreast Kronborg castle and hoisted her colours, she was fired on. Nelson's squadron sailed south and on the night of 1 April anchored just two miles from the city. There on the eve of battle Mosse wrote to his wife:

> Tomorrow it is likely, we shall approach nearer, in readiness for the most serious battle; – which induces me to write while I can write – Confirming all my affections on you and the dear children, hoping they will resolutely fix to live after God's Commandments, which will ensure them His Grace at the last. So God bless you, should it be my lot to fall – "God's will must be done"!!

After taking soundings overnight, Nelson's ships headed north on the morning breeze, up the King's Deep with the forts, the Danish hulks and then the Trekroner battery to port. The plan was that *Edgar* would lead and take up station alongside the Danish *Jylland*, then *Ardent* would pass *Edgar* and anchor next to the second Danish ship and so on up the line, but three ships went aground including *Russell*, dramatically changing the odds and warranting a change of plan.

Midshipman William Millard in *Monarch*, wrote: Observing [*Russell's*] awkward predicament, we reserved our fire until we came abreast of her opponents and honoured them with our first broadside. The crew of *Russell* gave us three cheers, to thank us for our assistance. We continued firing all the way down [the line] between our own ships; and when abreast of the Vice Admiral [Nelson], gave three hearty cheers, which compliment was returned by his men at their guns.

Monarch then continued north but much closer to the Trekroner battery than planned because of the missing ships, mooring ship abreast the two-decker *Sjaelland*. Millard saw, 'Captain Mosse on the poop; his card of instructions [Nelson's orders] in his left hand, and his right hand was raised to his mouth with a speaking trumpet through which he gave the word, "Cut away the anchor" … and in a few minutes the Captain was brought aft perfectly dead.'

Lieutenant Colonel William Hutchinson, whose soldiers of the 49th Regiment were serving as marines, suggested that the captain's body if taken below would dampen the men's spirits, and so Mosse was placed in the sternwalk covered by a flag. After the battle, Mosse's body was consigned to the deep.

Nelson wrote later, 'Amongst many other brave Officers and men who were killed, I have, with sorrow, to place the name of Captain Mosse, of the *Monarch*, who has left a wife and six children to lament his loss.' Hyde Parker wrote similarly.

His death, together with that of Captain Edward Riou, was the occasion of much public mourning. The playwright Sheridan proposed in Parliament that their respective families be made the subject of a royal bounty, and, on the motion of Prime Minister Henry Addington, a monument was placed in the crypt of St Paul's Cathedral.

Mosse's will is in The National Archives, Kew. Ann died on 21 January 1843 and was buried in Wickham churchyard and commemorated there with her husband; so also in due course were their children. A memo he wrote about his family history survives in an unpublished paper *The Mosse Family* by J R Mosse dated 7 July 1898.

Captain James Robert Mosse's great-great-grandson, Harry Tylden Mosse, commanded the converted Isle of Man passenger ferry *King Orry* at the end of the First World War. His great-great-great-grandson Commander John Pemberton commanded the sloop *Mermaid* in the Second World War and was awarded the DSC, and his great-great-great-great-grandson Peter John Mosse commanded the frigate *Ambuscade* during the 1982 Falklands War.

ANDREW MOSSE

→ MURRAY ←

George Murray (1759–1819): on Wednesday 10 November 1802, Nelson wrote from Merton to the then Captain George Murray, 'We shall be very happy to see you on Friday … I can assure you that at all times I am ever glad to see you, for I never shall forget your gallant support of me at the Battle of Copenhagen.'

Nelson and Murray were near contemporaries; Murray, six months younger than Nelson, was born in Chichester and baptised in the cathedral in April 1759. His father was a magistrate and alderman of the city and as an eleven-year-old, George Murray was enlisted as a midshipman on the *Niger* (32). His early career took him to the Mediterranean, the West Indies and Newfoundland, a rich experience that prompted the judgement, 'Like the departed Nelson, he knew not fear.'

He passed for lieutenant in 1778 and was appointed to *Arethusa* (32) but she was wrecked in March 1779, whilst chasing the French frigate *L'Aigrette* off the Île de Molène, and *Arethusa's* captain, Charles Everitt, his officers and crew were made prisoners of war. The officers were given parole and Murray took the opportunity to study the French language when a 'singular circumstance occurred'. The British officers observed the actions of an officer of an American privateer, 'paying his court to a young lady, the daughter, or relation of the mayor of the place'. The officer was wearing what seemed to be British naval uniform, including a cockade in which was set a British badge. Lieutenant Murray, drawn by lot from amongst the officers of *Arethusa*, remonstrated with the American; a scuffle ensued in which Murray was able to remove the badge, 'Coolly putting it into his pocket – though not without giving the pirate some sound reasons for remembering their encounter.' Though the American lodged a complaint to French officials, Murray's action was deemed to have been honourable and he was allowed to return to England.

In 1781 he was appointed to *Monmouth* (64), under Captain James Alms, another Chichester man. Monmouth was dispatched to the Indian Ocean to join Sir Edward Hughes's fleet where French warships under the command of the Bailli de Suffren were intent on driving the British, or more particularly, the East India Company, out of the subcontinent. In 1782 there were five engagements between Hughes and Suffren before the

Peace of Paris was declared in 1783, bringing an end to hostilities. The result was a 'no-score draw', though with sufficient damage inflicted on each side for the battles to rank amongst the most costly ever fought by the Navy.

Consequent on his conduct and bravery in the Indian Ocean, Murray was made captain of the frigate *Seahorse* (24) in October 1782, a ship in which both Horatio Nelson and Thomas Troubridge had served. The hostilities ended and Murray, along with many other naval officers, was reduced to half pay. He spent time in France, developing his language skills and appreciation of French culture, until in June 1790 he commissioned the frigate *Triton* and in the following April was sent to survey the Great Belt and the approaches to Copenhagen, an experience which proved invaluable ten years later.

When the French Revolutionary wars broke out in 1793, Murray was in the West Indies. He had many responsibilities, essentially ensuring the islands remained within the British sphere of influence, and on 15 December 1796 he was appointed to command *Colossus* (74) built ten years earlier in Gravesend. Murray was sent to join Admiral Jervis's squadron off the coast of Spain and in the blockade of the port of Cadiz. This was the first time that Murray was part of a squadron that included amongst its other commanders Horatio Nelson. At the Battle of Cape St Vincent on 14 February 1797 *Colossus* became an early casualty, having her bowsprit and foretopmast shot away. Following repairs in Lagos Bay in Portugal *Colossus* was sent to blockade Malta in 1798 and in November ordered to return to England carrying many of the possessions and treasures of the British Ambassador to Naples, Sir William Hamilton. Nearing the Scilly Isles on 7 December, *Colossus* was hit by a ferocious gale; she sought shelter off the island of Samson but her anchor cables broke and the ship was wrecked on the Southward Well reef. In the subsequent enquiry Murray was exonerated and over the following months many of Sir William Hamilton's treasures were recovered and are now in the British Museum.

At the turn of the century the war with France was not going well. Britain was isolated and even Denmark, a longstanding ally, had been induced by Russia to close its waters to Britain. The importance of this hostile act is that it affected significantly the supplies of timber and hemp that Britain needed to replenish, repair and rebuild its naval fleet: the wooden wall of England.

In February 1801 it was decided that Denmark must be persuaded to see the error of its ways and if it would not agree to reopen its waters to Britain then Britain would destroy Copenhagen. Murray was appointed to the *Edgar* (74) and joined Sir Hyde Parker's fleet. Parker's second-in-command was Admiral Lord Nelson. The expedition was characterised by indecision, lack of urgency and inadequate planning, much to the frustration of Nelson. However, he found in Murray an able captain who was knowledgeable about the seas round Denmark.

At the beginning of April Parker sent Nelson with a squadron of ships to press the attack on Copenhagen. Eighteen ships sailed out of range of the Danish batteries to anchor south of the city, and on the morning of 2 April 1801, with the wind and current with them, they weighed anchor and began to move north. Murray had been appointed to lead the attack and there survives an eyewitness account of *Edgar*'s passage:

A man-of-war under sail is at all times a beautiful object, but at such a time the scene is heightened beyond the powers of description. We saw her pressing on through the enemy's fire, and manoeuvring in the midst of it to gain her station; our minds were deeply impressed with awe, and not a word was spoken throughout the ship but by the

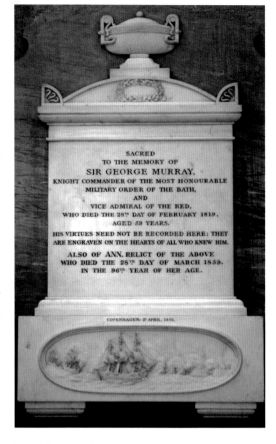

Memorial to George Murray in the Sailors' Chapel, Chichester Cathedral, also known as the Chapel of St Michael.

pilot and helmsmen; and their communications being chanted very much in the same manner as the responses in our cathedral service, and repeated at intervals, added very much to the solemnity.

Edgar took the full force of the defending fire from the Danes and lost 31 of her crew with 111 wounded.

On the second anniversary of the battle, Murray's wife Ann (they had married in Westminster on 15 September 1795) gave birth to a son and Nelson penned his congratulations, 'If one of his names is not Baltic, I shall be very angry with you indeed.' Ann used her judgement and Murray's son, and only child, was baptised George St Vincent Thomas Nelson Murray.

Nelson had been so impressed by the integrity, reliability and courage of Murray that when hos-

Home of
Admiral Sir George Murray
1759 – 1819
Nelson's Captain of the Fleet
'It must be Murray'
Nelson said,
'no other will do'.

Plaque on the Ship Hotel, North Street, Chichester, once the home of George Murray.

tilities against France broke out in 1803 he invited him to be his Fleet Captain, effectively his chief of staff. This was no easy task, as from May 1803 until August 1805 Nelson's squadron tracked the French and Spanish fleets across the Mediterranean and to the West Indies and back. Murray's responsibility was to ensure that the ships of the squadron kept their discipline and had adequate food, water and ammunition so that they were ready at any time to engage the enemy. In recognition of his competence Murray was promoted to the rank of Rear-Admiral of the Blue on St George's Day 1804.

On 20 August 1805, Admirals Nelson and Murray arrived back in Portsmouth in *Victory* for a period of leave and for Murray to discover that his father-in-law, Colonel Christopher Teesdale, had recently died. Leave was possible as the French and Spanish fleets were safely back in port, but by the beginning of September intelligence reports suggested that both fleets were about to put to sea. Nelson returned to *Victory* but Admiral Murray was excused in order to attend to the affairs of his late father-in-law. Nelson would not appoint anyone else as Captain of the Fleet, commenting, 'If ever I have another Captain of the Fleet, it must be Murray.'

In 1806 Murray was appointed in command of an expedition to South America and returned home in January 1808, his last period of service at sea. He spent the rest of his life supporting the civic development of Chichester; like his father he became an alderman and in 1815 was knighted and in the same year became Mayor of Chichester. He died suddenly in 1819. His obituary in *The Gentleman's Magazine* for March that year reads:

Feb 28 At Chichester, in his 59th year, Sir George Murray, KCB, Vice Admiral of the Red. Sir George went to bed in good health, and was seized with a spasmodic affection in his chest, which terminated his existence at eight o'clock. He had command of his Majesty's ship *Edgar*, of 74 guns, on the 2nd of April, 1801, and had the high honour to be appointed by Lord Nelson, to lead into action

before Copenhagen, on that memorable day.

Admiral Sir George Murray was buried in the precincts of Chichester Cathedral where there is a plaque to his memory; there is also one on the Ship Hotel in Chichester, his former home.

PHILIP E D ROBINSON

→ QUILLIAM ←

John Quilliam (1771–1829) was a Manxman, from an island whose population of less than thirty thousand provided some three thousand seamen to Nelson's navy.

The age of sail is well-represented in philately, but Quilliam is the only officer to share his portrait on a stamp with Nelson.

Some references state that Quilliam was press-ganged in Castletown harbour in 1794, but this cannot be true for, two years before, Quilliam was rated 'able' in *Lion* (64), under the Welshman Captain Sir Erasmus Gower who commanded the ships of Lord Macartney's embassy to the Imperial Chinese court. The rate of AB clearly indicates he was already an experienced seaman and it is likely that in Quilliam's case he messed with the midshipmen. Quilliam enjoyed Gower's patronage for several years, serving with him as quartermaster's mate in *Prince George*, and as master's mate in *Triumph*. He was not one of the officers turned out of *Triumph* by mutineers at Spithead in 1797 and after she was restored to discipline, under William Essington, Quilliam fought at the Battle of Camperdown following which he was made acting lieutenant. In September 1798 he rejoined Gower who now commanded *Neptune*.

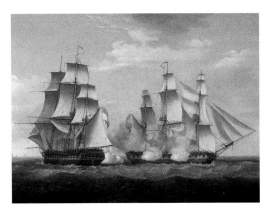

The capture in 1799 of the Spanish *Thetis* or *Tetis* by the British 38-gun *Ethalion* made Quilliam a very rich man.

In December 1798 Quilliam was commissioned and appointed third lieutenant of the new frigate *Ethalion* (38, Captain James Young) and took part in October 1799 in the capture of Spanish treasure ship *Thetis* (36), carrying freight and specie worth 1,385,292 Spanish dollars (£312,000), for which his share of the prize-money was more than £5,000. Just two months later *Ethalion* was wrecked on a reef off the Penmarks.

Then, at the Battle of Copenhagen, Quilliam was second lieutenant of *Amazon* (36, Captain Edward Riou), and when Riou was killed, he helped the first lieutenant, Joseph Masefield, to extricate *Amazon* from the battle, where she had been under fire from the Trekroner battery. Allegedly Nelson visited *Amazon* and enquired how Quilliam was getting on, receiving, in true Manx style, the single word reply, 'Middlin',' which apparently amused Nelson and earned his admiration.

When after Copenhagen Samuel Sutton was given command of *Amazon,* Quilliam became her first lieutenant: it was obviously a partnership which worked and when Sutton was fitting out *Victory* in 1803, he sent for Quilliam who would become first lieutenant. Evidently he was to be relied upon and at Trafalgar, while Nelson and Hardy, the flag captain, paced the quarterdeck during the battle Quilliam had charge of the ship, and after *Victory*'s wheel had been shot away, he and the master, Thomas Atkinson, spelled each other at steering her from the gunroom flat. It was appro-

priate that afterwards Quilliam should be promoted to post-captain, even if it was to the chagrin of *Victory*'s other senior lieutenants, like John Pasco, that they were only promoted to commander.

Quilliam was appointment captain of the Spanish prize *San Ildefonso* (74), captured by *Defence* and, once refitted at Gibraltar, he sailed her to England in May 1806. Apart from a few months when in 1807 he was elected to the House of Keys, Quilliam served at sea for the rest of the war: in 1808 he commanded *Spencer* (74), the flagship of Admiral Stopford; in 1809–10 the frigate *Alexandria* (32); and in 1811–15 *Crescent* (38) during the new American War, capturing the American privateer *Elbridge* (14) in September 1813.

In 1815 Quilliam retired to the Isle of Man. He took up residence at the White House in Kirk Michael, and was re-elected to the House of Keys in 1817. In his retirement he is credited with helping to improve the boat design for the Peel herring fleet. On 21 December 1817 he married Margaret Christian Stevenson of the Balladoole family at Arbory and they resided at Ballakeighen; there were no children.

Captain John Quilliam died at the White House in 1829 and was buried in the Stevenson family vault at Kirk Arbory.

PETER HORE

→ RETALICK ←

Richard Retalick (c.1759–1813) has left little mark on the pages of history, but was probably born in St Wenn, Cornwall.

He was examined for lieutenant in 1779 and promoted on 6 September. Presumably he was unemployed during the peace between the American and French wars. He may have been briefly recalled as a lieutenant in *Bedford* (74) during the Nootka Crisis, and in June 1790 he married Phoebe Downall or Downwell of Portsea. From January 1794 to March 1797 he commanded *Dolphin*, formerly a 44-gun frigate but re-rated as a hospital ship, on the Mediterranean station. On 12 August 1794 he was promoted commander.

A niece or possibly a natural daughter, Elizabeth Dolphina, was born in 1796 in Portsea and probably her mother was Betty Fuller, but Retalick acknowledged her to the extent of naming her after his first command and leaving her an annuity in his will.

In 1798 he was made post-captain and commanded the ship-sloop *Bonne Citoyenne* (22). When Nelson promoted Josiah Nisbet into *Bonne Citoyenne,* he gave the armed vessel *Earl St Vincent* to Retalick and employed him as liaison with the Portuguese squadron under Almirante Marques de Niza and on 3 August Retalick returned from the Mediterranean as a passenger in *Loire* (40).

He briefly commanded *Isis* (50) before taking charge on 24 December 1800 of *Defiance* (74). At the Battle of Copenhagen she was flagship of Nelson's second-in-command, Rear-Admiral Thomas Graves. *Defiance* anchored opposite the Crown Battery and in the absence of three other ships which had run aground on the Middle Ground, *Defiance* took much of the weight of battle. Several fires were started by hot 42-pounder shot fired from the battery, which caused severe damage, and she suffered twenty-four killed and fifty-one wounded. When Hyde Parker made the signal to discontinue the action, it was repeated in *Defiance* from the lee main topsail yardarm, from where it could not easily be seen in Nelson's *Elephant*, while Nelson's signal for close action was kept at the main topgallant mast. *Defiance* continued firing until 3.15pm when the cable on her spring was cut and she drifted aground. Retalick lightened ship by dumping thirty butts of water and quickly got her afloat. What Retalick did next has not yet been discovered, but his former ship *Defiance* was repaired and took part in Calder's action off Cape Finisterre and in the Battle of Trafalgar.

Captain Richard Retalick died at Padstow on 28 August 1813. He does not seem to have done well out of prize-money and his widow applied for help from the Charity for the Relief of Officers' Widows.

Peter Hore

✦ RIOU ✦

Edward Riou (1762–1801), 'the gallant and good', was born on 20 November at Mount Ephraim, near Faversham, Kent, the second son of Captain Stephen Riou of the Grenadier Guards.

In 1773 he started his naval career in *Barfleur* (90), flagship of Rear-Admiral Sir Thomas Pye, later transferring to *Romney* (50) on the Newfoundland station under Rear-Admiral John Montagu.

Back in Britain, Riou joined *Discovery* on 22 February 1776 as a midshipman under Captain Charles Clerke on Cook's third voyage. Riou remained in *Discovery* until 6 September 1779 when he was transferred to be a midshipman in *Resolution*. He kept a log and also made surveys and drew charts, including one of Avacha Bay in Kamchatka. During the voyage Riou, or 'Young Neddy' as he was known, acquired a native dog at Queen Charlotte Sound, New Zealand. The dog apparently bit several of Riou's colleagues so while he was ashore one day the dog was given a mock trial, found guilty, killed and cooked. This event came to be known as the 'Trial of the Cannibal Dog'.

After his return to Britain he passed his lieutenant's examination in 1780 and was appointed to the brig-sloop *Scourge* (14). Serving in the West Indies, he fell ill and in February 1782 was admitted to Haslar Hospital, Gosport. After his recovery he served from April 1783 to June 1784 in *Ganges* (74), the guardship at Portsmouth. After two years on half

Riou sprang to fame and popularity when, by a brilliant feat of leadership and seamanship, he saved the transport *Guardian* after she collided with an iceberg while en route to Australia.

pay, he was appointed in March 1786 to *Salisbury* (50), flagship of Rear-Admiral John Elliot, who as commodore-governor of the Newfoundland station was in command of the annual fishing convoy.

After six more months on half pay, in April 1789 Riou was appointed to commander of *Guardian*, a 44-gun fifth rate armed *en flûte* to serve as a transport bound for New South Wales. She sailed in August with a number of convicts and a cargo of plants, livestock and other stores for the new penal colony at Botany Bay. On Christmas Eve 1789, about half way between Africa and Australia, in dense fog, *Guardian* collided with an iceberg. Her rudder was smashed and her hull damaged, she began to leak and some of the crew and passengers panicked. With Riou's consent, 259 persons left the ship in four boats, but only 15 survivors in a single boat were later rescued by a French merchant vessel, and landed at the Cape of Good Hope on 18 January 1790.

By almost incredible effort and brilliant seamanship, Riou with his remaining crew of only

sixty-two kept the *Guardian* afloat. He divided his men into two watches for working the pumps. Stores, guns and livestock were jettisoned to lighten the ship. After two weeks, first symptoms of scurvy worsened the situation. After breaking his arm when subduing some rebellious sailors, Riou could take the necessary sights for his navigation only with great pain. On 21 February 1790, after an eight-week journey full of deprivations, the Cape of Good Hope was sighted: 'The ship had been running right for it,' Riou wrote. At his request, the surviving convicts who had helped to save the *Guardian* were pardoned.

In acknowledgement of his brilliant leadership, Riou was promoted to commander after his return to Britain and, on 4 June 1791, to captain. He was appointed to *Rose* (28), serving in the West Indies under Vice-Admiral Sir John Jervis. In November 1794, he was transferred to the frigate *Beaulieu* (40). Ill-health again forced his temporary retirement from active service in 1795. During this time he was appointed commander of the royal yacht *Princess Augusta*. In May 1796 he was elected a Fellow of the Royal Society. He also served on the courts-martial following the mutinies of 1797.

After his recovery, Riou in July 1799 was given command of the newly built frigate *Amazon* (38). On 14 February 1800 he captured the French privateer *Bougainville*. In April 1800 *Amazon* escorted the outward bound West Indies convoy. On 16 June she captured the French privateer *Julie* off Madeira and on 28 June recaptured the British merchantman *Amelia*, which had been taken by a French privateer.

In February 1801, *Amazon* joined Sir Hyde Parker's Baltic squadron where, on 1 April 1801, with Riou's assistance Nelson formed his plan of attack. Nelson gave one of the most dangerous tasks to Riou, who with his *Amazon*, two other frigates, some sloops and fireships was to attack the northern end of the Danish line.

When Admiral Parker gave his retreat signal, Riou, whose frigates were fighting the formidable Trekroner battery, reluctantly obeyed this order, remarking: 'What will Nelson think of us?'

When the Danes noticed the British retreat, they intensified their fire. With several men killed by the hail of Danish gunfire, Riou, himself wounded in the head and sitting on a gun-carriage, shouted: 'Come on, then, my boys, let us die all together!' Seconds later a Danish cannonball cut him in two. His first lieutenant, John Quilliam, who later served as *Victory*'s first lieutenant in the Battle of Trafalgar, led the *Amazon* safely out of the range of the Danish guns. Nelson, who was immensely impressed by Riou's abilities and the discipline on board the *Amazon*, lamented after the battle, 'In poor dear Riou the country has sustained an irreparable loss.' Parliament approved a monument to his memory and to Richard Mosse's in St Paul's Cathedral. Riou was not married and left no children.

Despite Nelson's praise, the accounts of Riou and his character are somewhat contradictory. Thomas Byam Martin, a contemporary naval officer, who knew him well, remembered: 'His eye was peculiarly striking, beaming with intelligence … There was a pensiveness of look and reserve in his manner which sometimes made strangers regard him as cold and repulsive, but this first impression was soon removed and all who knew him loved him.'

Riou's own writings indicate a man of high intelligence, but also a parochial pedant in all matters of discipline, for instance remarking on 'ships whose crews are neglected by their officers, to be constantly washing and scraping from no other cause than whilst one half of the ship's company are washing and scraping in one place the other half are making dirt in another place … Therefore it is repeated AVOID MAKING DIRT.' The American sailor Jacob Nagle, who had known Riou in *Ganges* and who as a pressed American seaman may not have been generalising, described him as 'a rail tarter [real tartar] to a seaman', a stern disciplinarian, despised by the sailors, 'he made it his study to punish every man he could get holt of, and gloried in having the name of a villen [villain] and a terror to seamen … He would tie them up in the rigging and gag them with a pump bolt till it frose in their mouth.'

JANN DE WITT

❖ ROSE ❖

Jonas Rose (1759–1820) was a born to a large family in Limerick.

Rose was a captain's servant in *Arethusa*, Captain Sir Andrew Snape Hamond, Bt, in 1771 on the American station. Between 1775 and 1795, from captain's servant to lieutenant, he served under George Murray (1741–97). Murray was the son of the Jacobite general Lord George Murray, and it may be assumed that religion was one of the causes which bound Rose to his patron. When Murray became commander-in-chief on the North American station in 1794 he cleared those waters of French men-of-war and French privateers, and Rose's reward for his twenty years' loyalty to Murray was command of *Esperance* (16); she had started life as a British privateer and changed hands several times before being captured off Chesapeake Bay in 1795. Rose brought her home, where she was sold off.

Two years later he was given the troopship *Espion*, previously the French *Atalante*, but after only a few months in command he had the misfortune to wreck her on the Goodwin Sands on 17 November 1799. This does not seem to have impeded his slow but steady progress, and on 1 January 1801 he was made post-captain and was given *Shannon* (32). In March that year he moved to *Jamaica* (22), the former French *Perçante*.

At Copenhagen in 1801, Rose was chosen to command the gun brigs which were intended to anchor at the southern end of the King's Deep and to rake the Danish line. However, Rose found himself in a south bound eddy which prevented him from taking his station. Nelson was appreciative of his efforts even if they were largely ineffective, writing in his dispatch to Parker: 'Captain Rose who volunteered his Services to direct the Gun Brigs, did everything that was possible to get them forward, but the current was too strong for them to be of Service during the Action, but not the less merit is due to Capt[ain] Rose, and I believe all the Officers and Crews of the Gun Brigs for their exertions.'

Now, having spent so long in the shadow of his patron, Rose showed himself a successful fighting captain at Boulogne later in 1801 and, when the war was resumed in 1803, in the chops of the Channel. Twice his dispatches appeared in the newspapers, once after Nelson's own and once, on another occasion, before James Saumarez's. Rose's

capture of a French flotilla off St Valéry on 21 August 1801 was ranked as one of the 'most remarkable events of the year'.

In 1804–6 Rose commanded the new-built *Circe* (32) in which he made some captures in the Atlantic, including a privateer which had sailed from France only twelve hours before. In June 1806 he took command of Nelson's old ship, *Agamemnon* (64), and was at the Second Battle of Copenhagen in 1807 and subsequent operations in the Baltic. In 1809 he sailed for the Tagus and then to South America, where on 16 June he ran *Agamemnon* aground off Maldonado on the Uruguayan coast and she was wrecked. He was never employed again.

Captain Jonas Rose died in Portsmouth on 20 July 1820.

PETER HORE

→ ROWLEY ←

Samuel Campbell Rowley (1774–1846) was born at Mount Campbell, Drumsna, County Leitrim, Ireland; his father, Clotworthy Rowley, was a lawyer and politician, but many others of his family for several generations were honest men, admirals and captains in the Navy. He was distantly related to another of the Band of Brothers, Clotworthy Upton.

Rowley entered the Navy though the Royal Naval Academy, Portsmouth, in 1785, and went to sea as a volunteer in 1789 in *Blonde* on the West Indies station. It may be assumed that it was his family's political interest which found him employment at sea during the years of relative peace between the American and French wars when many naval officers were on the beach. He passed for lieutenant in 1792 and he was promoted two years later into *Vengeance* (74).

On the night of 10 April 1795, while a lieutenant in *Astraea* (32, Captain Lord Henry Paulet), he assisted in the capture of the French *Gloire* (40) – William Pryce Cumby was Paulet's first lieutenant – and Rowley continued in *Astraea* in the Channel, the West Indies and the North Sea until promoted to commander on 30 January 1799.

Meanwhile, Rowley was also a member of the last Irish Parliament 1797–1800, when on one of his rare appearances he voted against the Union. Later he was persuaded to change his mind and between 1801 and 1806 was a member of the Westminster Parliament.

On 6 April 1799 he was made master and commander of the bomb vessel *Terror* and was on the expedition to Copenhagen in 1801. In June his brother, another politician, applied for him to be promoted, which he duly was on 29 April 1802. After this even John Marshall, who in his *Royal Naval Biography* was always keen to find the good so oft interred with men's bones, could find no mention of Rowley until his appointment to the frigate *Laurel* (36) in February 1811.

At first light on 12 January 1812, in heavy weather and low visibility and running at 8 knots under close-reefed topsails, Rowley hit a rock in Quiberon Bay. *Laurel* slid off into deeper water, one anchor cable broke and the other only brought her up when it had run out to the clench. Rowley had the unpleasant surprise of seeing *Laurel*'s false keel and part of her main keel bob to the surface and float away. He had no choice but to run for the shore. The guns were thrown overboard and all the boats, and the masts fell as she struck with great force and settled with the water already up to her quarterdeck. Rowley struggled through the day to save his people and some two hundred were rescued by other British warships, but ninety-six officers and men were taken prisoner, including two officers who had gone ashore to seek help and to ask the French commandant of a nearby fort to cease firing, 'but which he inhumanely refused notwithstanding a flag of truce and the signal of distress'. Rowley was acquitted at court-martial of all blame.

In 1815–21 he commanded *Impregnable* (104) then *Spencer* (76), flagship of his older brother, Rear-Admiral Sir Josias Rowley, in the Mediterranean and on the Irish station. In 1830–2 his last command was *Wellesley* (74).

He married, first in 1805, Mary Thompson of White Park, County Fermanagh, and when she died in 1821, he married Mary Frances Cronyn of Newtown, County Kilkenny. There were no children and Rear-Admiral Samuel Rowley died on 28 January 1846 at Mount Campbell.

PETER HORE

→ SUTTON ←

Samuel Sutton (1760–1832) was born in Scarborough. His siblings never left Yorkshire, but young Samuel's wanderlust saw him join *Monarch* (74) as a midshipman in March 1777; somehow he had fallen under the patronage of the Irish-born Captain Joshua Rowley, one of Britain's lesser-known hearts-of-oak.

Monarch led the van of the British attack on the French fleet at the Battle of Ushant on 27 July 1778. The battle is better known in naval history for the politically inspired controversy which followed between Whig Admiral Augustus Keppel and Tory Hugh Palliser. Keppel blamed the inconclusive nature of the battle on Palliser for not bringing his squadron into action: Palliser, though a member of the Board of Admiralty was junior to Keppel, and blamed him for general mismanagement. What began as a private squabble resulted in Keppel resigning his command after a court-martial acquitted him of blame and Palliser also being court-martialled and resigning his seat in Parliament.

Newly promoted, Rowley hoisted his flag in *Suffolk* (74, Captain Cloberry Christian), taking Sutton with him to the West Indies, where 19 March 1779 he again led the van division, this time in the fleet of Admiral Byron at the Battle of Grenada, when the French, though superior in force, failed to press home their advantage. Subsequently, Rowley's squadron made a number of captures including the large French frigate *Fortunée* (42), two other frigates, and a French convoy from Marseilles.

When Admiral Rodney arrived from England to command the station, Rowley shifted his flag to *Conqueror* (74) and fought at the Battle

The *Nuestra Señora de las Mercedes*, sunk by the British on 5 October 1804 when the two countries were still at peace with each other. *Mercedes* was carrying silver, gold, vicuna, cinnamon and quinoa, and many civilians home from Montevideo.

of Martinique on 17 April 1780, another indecisive battle because Rodney's captains failed to understand his orders to concentrate their ships against the retreating French rear. The fleets met again in May: the French were skilfully handled and Rodney was unable to communicate with his captains. *Conqueror*, however, was always in the thick of the fighting and suffered eighty-seven killed and wounded.

Sutton was made lieutenant in 1783 and when Rowley hoisted his flag as commander-in-chief at Jamaica in *Preston* (50), Sutton became first lieutenant in that ship. However, ill-health and the end of the American War brought a period of unemployment for him. He used the peace to marry a Norfolk lass, Mary Ann Gardner of Ditchingham.

The Spanish Armament in 1790 brought a short appointment to the frigate *Iphigenia*, but

Sutton had to wait until the outbreak of war with France in 1793 for full employment when he briefly joined *Culloden* (74, Captain Sir Thomas Rich). By November 1794 he was first lieutenant in *Mars* (74, Captain Sir Charles Cotton); this was a continuation of the Rowley patronage as Cotton was married to Rowley's eldest daughter. *Mars* was at the First Battle of Groix on 16 June 1795 when Cornwallis 'effected the most masterly retreat from an immensely superior French fleet'; *Mars* 'being the sternmost ship sustained the brunt of the enemy's attack, but fortunately not a man was killed and only 12 wounded'.

On 1 September 1795 Sutton gained his first command, the sloop *Martin* (16), and a rapid improvement in his luck. After a cruise to West Africa and to Jamaica, Sutton moved to the North Sea where he helped capture a privateer and her prize, and was at Leith when the future Charles X of France needed transport to Cuxhaven. For this service Sutton was made post-captain in June 1796.

Sutton briefly commanded *Monarch*, the

ship in which he had begun his naval career twenty-one years before, bearing the flag of Sir Richard Onslow in the North Sea, and then in *Prince* (98) he became flag captain 1799–1801 to Admiral Cotton.

In January 1801 Sutton took command of *Alcmene* (32) from Henry Digby: he owed this appointment to St Vincent at the Admiralty who wrote that he had chosen him 'for the express purpose of accompanying Sir Hyde Parker on the Baltic Expedition, where he has much local knowledge', presumably knowledge he had gained while in command of *Martin*.

Alcmene sailed from Portsmouth to Copenhagen in early March and on 2 April was part of the frigate squadron under Edward Riou which anchored, about 1pm at the northern end of the King's Deep. There she was one of the first ships to repeat and obey the signal made by Hyde Parker, number 39 'Discontinue the action'. While Nelson's number 16 'Engage the enemy more closely' was still flying, and others wondered which order to obey, Sutton, whose *Alcmene* had suffered five killed and fourteen wounded, did not hesitate and withdrew. John Quilliam in *Amazon* noted 'we continued our fire', as *Alcmene* 'cut her cable and stood off'. *Blanche*, the last of the frigates to anchor at the northern end of the British line followed suit, leaving Riou to the undivided attention of the guns of the Trekroner fort. No contemporary record attaches any blame to Sutton, nor did Nelson blame him. Rather, he was rewarded with the command of *Amazon* and orders to move deeper into the Baltic and to send a boat under a flag of truce into Karlskrona to acquaint the governor of the armistice with the Danes and to enquire how the Swedes would react.

Nelson and Sutton formed a close professional relationship during 1801 and 1802, when Nelson flew his flag in *Amazon* during his attacks on the French invasion fleet. The friendship included invitations to visit Nelson and Emma at Merton, and Nelson was pleased too to get Sutton to fit out *Victory* in 1803 in readiness for his new command in the Mediterranean. In July 1803,

according to James's *Naval History*, Nelson took 'Captain George Murray as his first captain, and Captain Thomas Hardy, as his second, the latter being succeeded in the command of the *Amphion* by Captain Sutton, late of the *Victory*.'

Sutton proved a successful frigate captain, and brought in plenty of prize-money for himself and for Nelson, but Nelson was surprised when Sutton turned down his offer of command of a ship of the line and the friendship began to cool. Nelson's holier-than-thou attitude, that he was not a 'money man' and would rather have Sutton take privateers than prize-money, was not convincing.

Then, in October 1804, Sutton took part in one of the less worthy actions of the Royal Navy. A British squadron, which included *Amphion*, was sent to intercept a Spanish squadron returning from America laden with treasure. At dawn on 5 October, four British frigates confronted four Spanish frigates. Neither country was at war with the other, and the Spaniards refused a request to stop and be searched. Firing broke out and after a very few minutes *Nuestra Señora de Mercedes* blew up, killing several hundred people, including a number of women and children who were passengers, and scattering the seabed with treasure (whose recovery by an American company in the twenty-first century would be disputed by Spain).

By early afternoon the other three Spanish frigates and their cargos of immense value had been captured. Nelson took secret delight that as war had not been declared, the prizes were declared droits of the Admiralty, so reducing Sutton's share of prize-money. Nevertheless Sutton was now a rich man, but he fell ill, and in mid-October 1805 Nelson had no compunction in replacing him with one of his favourites, William Hoste, and Sutton thus missed the Battle of Trafalgar. He was not employed again.

Sutton married Charlotte Ives and their sons bought commissions in the Army: Rear-Admiral Samuel Sutton died in 1832 and is buried at St Mary's Church, Woolbridge, Suffolk.

Peter Hore

→ UPTON ←

Clotworthy Upton (1768–1822) enjoyed only small fame in his lifetime but is unique among the Band of Brothers in that he was a legal bastard. He was the first-born of a union between well-connected parents; however, they did not marry until a year after his birth and the law then stated that 'a bastard was unable to be an heir to real property, and could not be legitimised by the subsequent marriage of his father to his mother'. The parents had their first son baptised at St Marylebone on 19 April 1768 and went on to have three legitimate children, the surviving boy of these, John Upton, inheriting the family baronetcy rather than Clotworthy.

Clotworthy Upton went to sea at age eleven, as captain's servant in the new *Alexander* (74, Captain Richard Kempenfelt) in June 1779, serving in six ships before passing for lieutenant in 1790. He had served with Captains Farnham, Duncan, Pellew and Milson, so there was no want of 'interest' in his career.

In 1791–2 and 1793–4 Upton, like some other unemployed officers, undertook voyages to the East, Upton going as a lieutenant in the East Indiaman *King George*, Captain Richard Colnett. His first command was the 10-gun *Zephyr* which was fitted out as a fireship at Woolwich in the winter of 1800–1 and commissioned by the new-made master and commander Upton in January ready for the Baltic campaign; she was in Nelson's division at Copenhagen in 1801.

Upton was made post-captain in April 1802 when about seventy officers were promoted in celebration of the Treaty of Amiens being signed. When the peace broke down he commanded a succession of ships, the frigates *Lapwing* (28), *Aimable* (32), *Camilla* (20), *Sybille* (44), *Junon* (38), and a ship of the line *Royal Oak* (74).

His father, who had died in 1785, set up a trust for all his children and, despite his legal status, Upton kept a place in good society. He married Eliza Walton, daughter of a New York merchant, at St Pancras Old Church in 1805, and their daughter,

Eliza Mary, married a Scottish lord.

The longest command which Upton held was *Sybille* between 1807 and 1813. He joined her in time to be present at the Second Battle of Copenhagen, and among the enemy ships taken by the *Sybille* in those six years were, in 1808, a French privateer *Grand Argus* (4), the brig-corvette *Espiègle* (16), renamed *Electra*, and in 1810 the French brig *Edouard* (14).

In the War of 1812, on the morning of 3 April 1814 in *Junon* (38), Upton and *Tenedos* (38, Captain Hyde Parker), chased the USS *Constitution* (44) into Marblehead, Massachusetts. Parker was determined to follow her into the port, which had no defences; but Upton was senior officer and for whatever reason gave the signal for recall.

Captain Clotworthy Upton's final appointment was as commissioner of the dockyard at Trincomalee in 1818, where he was sent to build six small frigates for the Navy. Upton 'did nothing but croak, growl and take physic; he was discontented, unhappy and quarrelling with everybody about him', while cholera ravaged the European officers. Upton survived four years, but died on his way home on board the Cochin-built *Samarang* (28) in 1822 and was buried at sea.

STEPHEN TREGIDGO

→ WALKER ←

James Walker (1764–1831) was a well-born Scot. His father was James Walker of Innerdovat, Fife, and his mother, Lady Mary Leslie, daughter of Alexander, Earl of Leven. Walker was maternally related to the Scottish clique which ruled the Royal Navy, Scotland and the British Empire: the Elphinstones, Dundases, Melvilles, even the Nisbets, and who were Whig, Protestant, Unionist, and Masonic. Little however is known of his father beyond an unsubstantiated claim that he was friendly with Admiral George Rodney.

Starting at age twelve, Walker served five years in *Southampton* (32) in the West Indies and in the Channel. In August 1780 off Portland *Southampton* captured an 18-gun French privateer, and Walker took off the prisoners and stayed on board to bale and pump, but she suddenly sank and he was nearly lost. Walker was appointed to *Princess Royal* (90), the flagship of Sir Peter Parker, who promoted him lieutenant in June 1781 and transferred him to *Torbay* (90) in which he took part in the Battles of Chesapeake, St Kitts and the Saintes, and was hoping for promotion when Rodney was superseded.

In the peace, Walker spent five years on the Continent, visiting France, Germany, Italy and Austria. In 1787, while in Vienna, he heard rumours of war and attempted to return home in hope of an appointment, but was robbed and left for dead by highwaymen. In 1788 at the outbreak of the Russo-Turkish War he was offered a command in the Russian Navy but the Admiralty vetoed this and, helped by local freemasons, Walker reached England in 1789 after an absence of five years.

He was appointed to the Leith-based *Champion* (24), followed by appointments to *Winchelsea* (32), *Boyne* (98) and *Niger* (32). *Niger* was one of the repeating ships at the Glorious First of June, and Walker the signal lieutenant, for which service he was promoted to commander.

In 1795 Walker was in command of *Trusty* (50) in which he escorted five East Indiamen past Spain to safety. Learning that there some three dozen merchantmen with valuable cargo waiting in Cadiz for convoy, Walker used his initiative to collect these and escort them home. The Spanish were irked, arrested some of his officers on the accusation of smuggling money out of the port, and demanded that Walker be court-martialled. Curiously, he was found guilty of disobeying orders and dismissed from the Navy. Walker sailed for the West Indies in a merchant ship, but his ship was driven back by bad weather and when Spain joined France against Britain he was promptly restored.

Monmouth (64) had been badly handled by Captain Lord Northesk and Bullen, her first lieutenant, during the Nore mutiny and Walker, as an acting captain, was tasked to restore morale. A

few weeks earlier he had been planning to attack the mutineers with a squadron of gunboats; now at the Battle of Camperdown he told his ship's company, 'My lads, you see your enemy before you. I shall lay you close on board, and thus give you an opportunity of washing the stain off your characters with the blood of your foes. Go to your quarters, and do your duty.' *Monmouth* engaged in heavy combat with the Dutch ships *Delft* and *Alkmaar*, capturing both.

Walker continued in a series of temporary commands until he was appointed to *Isis* (50) in 1801, in the Baltic fleet, and was part of Nelson's squadron that attacked Copenhagen. In the battle he engaged three targets: a fourteen-gun battery, his own allotted blockship target and that of *Elephant* (74), Nelson's flagship, which had temporarily run aground. When *Elephant* got free and moved up the line to find a new opponent, Nelson took off his hat, waved it and cried, 'Well done, brave Walker! Go on as you have begun; nothing can be better.' After four-and-a-half hours *Isis* silenced her three targets, but suffered 121 casualties (including 33 killed) out of a complement of 350.

Back in the West Indies, Walker, now in *Vanguard* (74), took part in the blockade of Haiti, the capture of the French *Duquesne* (74) on 25 July 1803, and the capture of St Marc, taking off its garrison of 1,100 men and saving them from the vengeance of the freed slaves. Walker took *Duquesne* home, was appointed to the frigate *Thalia* (36) and employed on convoy duties. In 1805 he made a passage to the East and back in only ten months and on another occasion in 1806 he was caught in gale on the Newfoundland Banks and ran 1,250 miles in five days under bare poles.

Walker was given command of *Bedford* (74) in October 1807 and, under Sir Sydney Smith, escorted the Portuguese royal family into exile. Walker stayed for two years in Brazil, during which he was awarded the Portuguese Order of the Tower and the Sword, then returned in *Bedford* to serve in the North Sea and in the

Rear-Admiral James Walker: 'a most brave and distinguished officer who served, fought and conquered with Rodney, Howe, Duncan, St Vincent and the immortal Nelson'.

SACRED TO THE MEMORY OF
JAMES WALKER, ESQUIRE,
REAR ADMIRAL OF THE RED,
A MOST BRAVE AND DISTINGUISHED OFFICER,
WHO SERVED, FOUGHT, AND CONQUERED WITH
RODNEY, HOWE, DUNCAN, S.ᵗ VINCENT,
AND THE IMMORTAL NELSON!
IN THE GLORIOUS VICTORY OF CAMPERDOWN, HE COMMANDED
THE MONMOUTH, IN THAT OF COPENHAGEN THE ISIS;
AND AFTER SERVING HIS KING AND COUNTRY
FOR FIFTY FIVE YEARS
WITH CONSPICUOUS VALOUR, ZEAL SKILL AND FIDELITY,
HE DEPARTED THIS LIFE AT BLATCHINGTON, JULY 13ᵀᴴ 1831
IN THE 67ᵀᴴ YEAR OF HIS AGE.

IN AFFECTIONATE REMEMBRANCE OF HIS MANY VIRTUES
THIS TABLET IS ERECTED BY HIS WIDOW.

Walker's tombstone in the graveyard of Seaford parish church, Sussex.

Channel, until sent to the Gulf of Mexico, where he was senior officer.

After the peace in 1815 Walker had command of *Albion* (74), *Queen* (74) and *Northumberland* (74). His sea career ended on 10 September 1818 when *Northumberland* was paid off, after the crew had been praised for having fought a dangerous fire in Sheerness Dockyard that was threatening to destroy the entire yard. He was promoted rear-admiral in 1821.

Walker's first wife was a daughter of General Sir John Irvine; as a widower he then married Priscilla Sarah, a daughter of Arnoldus Jones Skelton MP, with whom he had three sons, two of whom followed him into the Navy.

Rear-Admiral James Walker died on 13 July 1831, taken ill while visiting one of his sons at Blatchington, near Seaford, Dorset.

PETER TURNER

↠ WATSON ↞

James Watson (c.1762–1833) was undoubtedly a Scot and born about 1762.

His first ship in 1776 was the armed tender *Africa* in which he served as able seaman and as midshipman. However, in the American war he quickly found the patronage of Robert Digby, whom he followed from *Ramillies* to *Prince George* and *Lion*, and on 29 May 1782 he was made lieutenant in *Charlestown* (28), the former USS *Boston* which had been captured at Charleston, South Carolina, two years before. In the ten years' peace which ensued he was unemployed.

For six years Watson commanded two small Leith-based ships, but on 5 January 1800 his gun-brig *Mastiff* was wrecked near the Cockle Sands, when the fishermen of Winterton-on-Sea were awarded 150 guineas for saving more than thirty of her crew at great risk to themselves. Watson was acquitted of all blame at the subsequent court-martial.

Watson was next appointed as a lieutenant in *Kent* (74, Captain William Johnstone Hope), flagship of Admiral Duncan. This Scots faction soon saw him promoted to command the cutter *Saxe Cobourg* on the North Sea station and, when promoted commander in January 1801, to the bomb ship *Volcano*.

On 25 July 1801 there was an incident in the Channel between British warships and the Danish *Freya* (40) and her convoy. The British wished to search the convoy for supplies intended for France and *Freya*'s Captain Krabbe refused until there had been a token exchange of fire. *Freya* kept her ensign flying, but the convoy was detained.

The British government lost no time and on 8 August sent Lord Whitworth to the Baltic to settle the matter amicably. To give additional weight to his diplomacy, he was accompanied by a squadron of ten sail of the line, three 50-gun ships, and several frigates and smaller vessels, including *Volcano*, all under the command of Vice-Admiral Archibald Dickson. By 29 August the matter had been settled between the British and the Danes, and by 14 September Dickson's squadron was back in Yar-

Watson's memorial is cared for by the Friends of the Canongate Kirkyard, Edinburgh.

mouth. However, the Russians had taken offence and embargoed British shipping in Russian ports; by December Russia and Sweden had reimposed the League of Armed Neutrality, and over the winter Denmark and Prussia were induced to join.

The consequence was that in March 1801 a powerful fleet under Admiral Sir Hyde Parker sailed from Yarmouth for the Baltic. There on 2 April Nelson's plan was that *Volcano* and six other bomb vessels would anchor close to the Middle Ground and fire over the British line anchored in the King's Deep. In the event the bomb vessels were so late coming into action that they only played a limited part in the fighting. Nelson, however, was satisfied that they had tried against the eddying stream.

Next Watson commanded the sloop *Hermes* (18) until April 1802. When the war was renewed he commanded the Sea Fencibles at Hartlepool until May 1804, and subsequently *Epervier* (18) and *Alonso* (16) in the Channel and the North Sea, until on 22 January 1806 he was made post-captain. From 1807 until the end of 1810 Watson commanded the impress service at Dundee.

Captain James Watson, who married Elizabeth Clark, died in Edinburgh on 19 May 1833.

JOSEPH STONE

→ WHITTER ←

Hender Whitter (1770–1809) was a Cornishman born in East Looe: little is known of his parents John and Rebecca, except that John came from a long line of John Whitters of Looe. Several versions of Hender occur as a surname in Devon and in Cornwall, so presumably he was a second son, named after some local patron. Hender was examined for lieutenant in 1793, promoted in 1794, paid land taxes in East Looe in 1798, promoted to commander on 1 January 1801 and commanded the bomb vessel *Sulphur* at the Battle of Copenhagen later that year.

Sulphur was originally a merchant ship called *Severn*: fitted as a bomb vessel her principal armament was two 10in mortars, four 68-pounder carronades and six 18-pounder carronades, and at the battle she moored on the Middle Ground from where she fired her mortars into the Danish lines, but, as Nelson's dispatch implies, the bomb vessels had much difficulty in getting into a position and played little part in the fiercest hours of the exchange of shot between the British and the Danes.

The Peace of Amiens was long enough for Whitter to be elected into office as Mayor of Looe.

Whitter was promoted to post-captain on 22 January 1806, and in March 1807 he commissioned the Bideford-built *Garland* (22). After supervising her fitting out at Plymouth, he sailed for the West Indies in November 1807; yellow fever was raging in Jamaica and on 17 April 1808 in Port Royal Whitter, presumably also a victim of the 'black vomit' was superseded by Captain Rowland Bevan, and sent home to die, sailing from Jamaica as a passenger in the Falmouth packet *Prince Ernest* on 6 June.

On 31 January 1809 'Hender Whitter esq late a post-captain in the Royal Navy who departed this life January 20 1809, aged 38 years' was buried at St Martin by Looe.

PETER HORE

→ YELLAND ←

John Yelland (1755?–1827) hailed from the West Country. In 1776–1778 he was a volunteer and then midshipman in *Torbay* (74) when she hardly seems to have left Plymouth, and in May 1778 he joined *Duke* (90). He was a midshipman in *Duke* at the Battle of Ushant in 1778; served 1778–81 in *London* (90), flagship of Rear-Admiral Thomas Graves; and was an acting lieutenant in *Royal Oak* (74) at the Battles of Chesapeake in September 1781 and the Saintes in 1782. Mostly on half pay during the years of peace between the American and the French wars, Yelland spent a few months in 1790 as a lieutenant in the fireship *Tisiphone*.

When war broke out again he was appointed a lieutenant in *Egmont* (74) and then *Britannia* (100), flagship of Admiral William Hotham, and was at the action off Genoa – when he would have witnessed Nelson and *Agamemnon* in action – and the Battle of Hyères in 1795. Yelland now served in *St George* (100) and *Chichester* (44): bloody war and sickly season ought by now to have given promotion to a battle-hardened officer who had served under some of the more prominent naval officers of the age, but luck failed him.

Throughout 1797 Yelland was unemployed, until in January 1798 he became first lieutenant of *Veteran* (64). Captain James Mosse assumed command of *Veteran* in June, and Mosse took Yelland with him when he removed into *Monarch* (74) in the summer of 1799.

They sailed for the Baltic in early spring 1801,

where a sharp light is thrown on Yelland in a unique pen-picture of him at the Battle of Copenhagen, by a then eighteen-year-old midshipman, William Millard:

This brave veteran had taken care to have the decks swept, and everything was clean and nice before we went into action. He had dressed himself in full uniform with his cocked hat set on square, his shirt-frill stiff starched, and his cravat tied tight under his chin as usual. After the fall of our captain he sent down to desire the lieutenants from the different quarters to come on deck, when he informed them of the captain's death and appointed himself, of course, commanding officer; the remaining officers having as it were sworn fealty to him, returned to their different stations. How he escaped unhurt seems wonderful; several times I lost sight of him in a cloud of splinters: as they subsided I saw first his cocked hat emerging, then by degrees the rest of his person, his face smiling, so that altogether one might imagine him dressed for his wedding-day.

In the sanguinary battle *Monarch* suffered 56 killed and 164 seriously wounded and many more with minor wounds. Mosse had fallen early in the battle, and Yelland was the only junior officer mentioned in either Nelson's report to his commander-in-chief, Parker, or in Parker's dispatch to the Admiralty, Parker adding a postscript: 'I cannot close this without acquainting their Lordships, that Captain Mosse being killed very early in the Action, Lieutenant John Yelland continued it with the greatest Spirit and good Conduct; I must therefore, in Justice to his Merit, beg Leave to recommend him to their Lordships' Favour.'

Under the circumstances it seems a little unjust that Yelland was not immediately promoted, causing Millard to complain that 'a stranger was sent on board of us, who had 'borne none of the burthen and heat of the day'. Parker used his patronage to promote his own favourites: he did offer to make Yelland first lieutenant of his flagship, *London*, but the latter 'very properly considered

this an insult, and preferred being first lieutenant of the ship in which he had fought, and trusting to his country for reward, rather than to receive it from Sir Hyde Parker when he might grant it as a favour'. In fact the stranger who was given command of *Monarch* was William Bligh, who had fought *Glatton* in the battle. The damaged *Monarch* sailed from the Sound on 15 April and on the day she reached the Nore, 27 April, Yelland was made commander 'for rank only', but not given a command.

So for the second time in the war Yelland was without a ship until, in March 1805, he was given the fireship *Fury* (16) though she was his for just nine months. Time enough, however, for William James, in his *Naval History*, to hold up Yelland's service in *Fury* as an example to others of the different actions fought between British cruisers and the French invasion flotilla. Under cover of darkness on the evening of 23 April a fleet of thirty-three gun-vessels and nineteen transports laden with stores for Bonaparte's Grande Armée had attempted to pass down Channel, and in a running battle over the next two days, made chaotic by the wind and tide, and under fire from French shore batteries, British vessels including *Fury* had made short work of the French.

In a general round of promotion on 22 January 1806 Yelland was made post-captain, but he never went to sea again, and on 2 November 1809 be became an out-pensioner of Greenwich Hospital. John Yelland 'Captain in His Majesty's Royal Navy of Ranelagh Street Pimlico' died in December 1827, and was buried on New Year's Eve at St George's Field, Bayswater, survived by his wife, Sarah.

PETER HORE

THE
CAMPAIGN
OF
TRAFALGAR

The Battle of Trafalgar at the end of the day: the French ship *Achille* is on fire and will shortly blow up, while British boats rescue her people from the water, by Robert Dodd (1748–1815).

✦ Introduction ✦

The tactics of the Battle of Trafalgar are sufficiently written about. However, the tactical victory off Cape Trafalgar on the afternoon of 21 October 1805 was the culmination of several centuries of British effort at sea, of two years of strategic preparation and of several months of operational planning.

The strategic planning took place in London, largely around the Admiralty Board table where so much else had been, and continues to be, decided since the seventeenth century.

The Peace of Amiens was a brief respite in the Great War (1792–1815), a peace whose treaty terms neither the British nor the French wholly respected. Nevertheless, between late 1802 and 1803 crews were paid off and ships decommissioned, as though the peace would be long-lasting. Meanwhile, Bonaparte placed orders for over 2,000 invasion craft, began to mass troops on the Channel coast and paraded at his headquarters at Boulogne in preparation to invade Britain. In Britain after some initial fervour, enthusiasm for the treaty waned and in the early months of 1803 the demobilisation of the Navy was reversed: the battlefleet increased from 32 to 60 ships and by the end of the year there were 75 ships of the line in commission and 320 smaller warships. New ships were started on the stocks too, and in November 1804, as a demonstration of Britain's industrial and financial might, *Hibernia* (120), *Circe* (32) and *Pallas* (32), were launched and *St George* (98) undocked, all on the same tide at Plymouth.

Naval strategy was directed by the First Lords of the Admiralty, who were John Jervis, Earl of St Vincent (1801–4), Henry Dundas, Viscount Melville, and from May 1805 Charles Middleton. Eighty-year-old Middleton, who took the title of Lord Barham, was a veteran of the Seven Years War and the American War, and had first gone to sea in 1741. Barham was a Scot and an evangelical Christian, who lived with his wife, Margaret Gambier, at Barham Court, Teston, in Kent which was owned by her close friend, Elizabeth Bouverie.

When Barham was not in London, he was a model farmer at Teston which also, as a leading campaigner for the abolition of slavery, he turned into 'the Runnymede of the slaves'.

Barham was a brilliant administrator, whose reforms of the Navy included the sheathing of the ships of the fleet in copper. In the years from 1779 to 1782, over three hundred ships were fully coppered, effectively increasing the size of the fleet, since coppered ships sailed faster, required fewer dockings to clean their bottoms, and so freed docks for other repairs and more new construction. The effect of coppering was to make ships one to two knots faster: for example, in early 1805 *Royal Sovereign* was known as the 'The West Country Wagon' for her poor, lumbering speed, but when she had returned, newly coppered, to the fleet off Cadiz, she sailed better in light airs than most other ships and on the morning of the battle was the first to break the line of the Franco-Spanish fleet.

The Campaign of Trafalgar lasted two years, its aim to stop any French invasion of the British Isles. Bonaparte's strategy was for the French squadrons to sail independently from French ports to attack colonies overseas and to rendezvous in the West Indies. The British ships were supposed – by Bonaparte – to respond by lifting their blockade of France, when the French Navy would sail up Channel in overwhelming force to protect an invasion fleet: 'Let us be masters of the Channel for six hours and we are masters of the world.' Bonaparte's spies had not reported St Vincent's words: 'I do not say, my Lords, that the French will not come. I say only they will not come by water.'

And when his hour came Barham, the mastermind of the Campaign of Trafalgar, showed himself to be a naval strategist somewhat greater than Bonaparte, with a thorough command of detail. From his offices in the Admiralty, Barham deployed several hundred ships under a dozen commanders-in-chief in the North Sea, the Channel, off Ireland and the Americas, in the East Indies, and, of course, the Mediterranean. There, in a north-easterly gale on 30 March 1805, Villeneuve broke out of Toulon, leaving Nelson to search the Mediterranean until he learned that Villeneuve had united with a Spanish fleet and sailed for the West Indies. Nelson followed, nearly a month after Villeneuve, but by early June he was only a few days behind. The news that Nelson had arrived in the West Indies was sufficient to make Villeneuve start for Europe again. Fast-sailing frigates brought Barham fragmentary intelligence, which he correctly interpreted and sent orders for Vice-Admiral Sir Robert Calder to block Villeneuve's route to the west coast of France or into the Channel.

On 22 July 1805 Villeneuve's combined fleet emerged from the fog very much where Barham's orders had put Calder. The ensuing two-day Battle of Cape Finisterre, fought in poor visibility and baffling winds, was desultory but decisive. Calder attacked the larger fleet, captured two of the enemy, and prevented Villeneuve from entering any French port. Meanwhile, Nelson arrived off Gibraltar on 20 July; he was physically and mentally exhausted and soon took passage in his flagship, *Victory*, to Portsmouth. After, in Nelson's words, only 'twenty-five dinners', he sailed again on 14 September to take command of the fleet blockading Cadiz, where the Combined Fleet was awaiting further orders from Bonaparte.

Nelson's command covered the largest area that had ever been granted to a British commander-in-chief, and included the Mediterranean and much of the North Atlantic. The focus of his operations, however, was the Bay of Cadiz. With winter approaching, Nelson had to guard several valuable convoys to and from the Mediterranean, the West Indies and India and Australia, while maintaining the blockade. He did not know for how long this would be necessary and his nearest bases were Gibraltar and Lisbon and, for food and water, the ports of North Africa.

To the north he placed *Nautilus*, Commander John Sykes, to stay off Cape St Vincent to tell other ships where to find him and to warn if more French ships came south. To the south-east he kept *Juno*, Captain Henry Richardson, in the Gut, 'a fixture between Cape Spartel and Gibraltar'. Inshore, close off Cadiz, he placed his smallest ships to watch events there, an advanced squadron lay further out into the bay, and the main body of his fleet he kept over the horizon 'fifteen to eighteen leagues West of Cadiz'. Nelson told Alexander Ball in Malta: 'There will be moments when it might be wished that we were closer; but I have considered all possible circumstances, and believe that there will often be times, in strong gales of Westerly wind, when we may often wish ourselves farther off, as we shall be in danger of being driven into the Mediterranean.'

Nelson's ships were provisioned for a maximum of six months, and two of them were crank. So on 3 October *Victory*'s log recorded that *Zealous* and *Endymion*, whose mainmasts were sprung, and Rear-Admiral Thomas Louis's squadron, *Canopus*, *Spencer*, *Tigre* and *Queen*, had parted from the fleet: the first two for repairs and Louis's ships for water and victuals. Louis had protested: 'You are sending us away, my Lord, the enemy will come out, and we shall have no share in the battle.' Nelson replied, 'My dear Louis, I have no other means of keeping my fleet complete in provisions and water, but by sending them in detachments to Gibraltar. The enemy will come out, and we shall fight them, but there will be time for you to get back … I send you first to insure your being here to beat them.'

Nelson clearly did intend his ships to provision in rotation for on 5 October he informed Collingwood that '*Britannia*, *Temeraire*, *Achille*, *Bellerophon*, *Polyphemus*, and *Donegal* are the next ships for Gibraltar and Tetuan … but I must have an Admiral with the Squadron.'

Nelson's operations were compounded by another problem: Robert Calder's wish to leave the fleet off Cadiz where he might, in Collingwood's words, 'have settled his account with Villeneuve'. However, John Bull (as Nelson referred to the great British public and its newspapers) was not content with the scale of Calder's victory on 22 July. Calder insisted on a court-martial to vindi-

The First Kiss this Ten Years! – fighting faltered in 1801 and the Peace of Amiens was signed in March 1802. This James Gillray cartoon shows Bonaparte kissing King George III dressed as Britannia, who remarks, 'I am sure you would deceive me', and in May 1803 war was resumed.

cate his honour, upon going home with his flag captain, William Cuming, and his flagship, *Prince of Wales* (when Nelson wanted him to take *Dreadnought* which 'sail[ed] very ill'), and taking with him four captains as witnesses to the Battle of Finisterre. The captains were William Brown (*Ajax*), William Lechmere (*Thunderer*), Philip Durham (*Defiance*) and William Prowse (*Sirius*); the two first agreed, Durham refused and, it seems, the question was never put to Prowse. Nelson procrastinated for two weeks, but on 13 October he allowed Calder to leave. Afterwards Hardy told Durham, 'One of the last things Nelson said before the action began was "Hardy, tell your friend Durham he was the most sensible man of the party

to stick to his ship."' Such were the vagaries of the wind that Calder barely arrived home before the news of a crushing victory over the Franco-Spanish also arrived. Ironically, Calder's court-martial did not take place until the end of December when Durham, who had distinguished himself at Trafalgar, was also home.

Several other ships passed through Nelson's area of operations, including the frigates *Amphion* and *Eurydice*, and when Samuel Sutton fell ill, one of Nelson's favourites, William Hoste, was given *Amphion* on 10 October and sent to Algiers with letters and presents for the Dey. Nelson's brother-in-law, Sir William Bolton, who had missed being at Copenhagen, was appointed in Hoste's place. Nelson wrote, 'This is the last chance of Sir Billy's making a fortune,' but Bolton missed Trafalgar and he reflected: 'Billy, Billy, out of luck!'

In the event, *Donegal*, Captain Pulteney Malcolm, also missed the battle. She had been out of dockyard hands since the start of 1804, and with Nelson on his chase to the West Indies, she was in such a parlous state generally, and short of wood and water, so she too was sent to Gibraltar on 17 October.

One other ship took a significant part in operations off Cadiz and that is the little *Weazel* (or *Weazle*, Nelson used both spellings), Commander Peter Parker. At 6am on the morning of 20 October he saw the enemy's fleet getting under way, signalled to *Euryalus*, and was sent by Blackwood to carry the news to Gibraltar and to find Louis, which he did on 22 October. The fast-sailing *Weazel* had time to return to Trafalgar and back, reporting to Louis on the 26th, 'Enemy defeated but our fleet off Cadiz in want of assistance.'

The only other ship able to beat out of the Gut was *Donegal*, which rejoined Collingwood's fleet on the day after the battle. Against the prevailing wind, Louis's squadron, which Nelson had been expecting back since 18 October, was unable to rejoin Collingwood until 30 October.

When the news of victory reached London in the early hours of 6 November, the architect of success, the octogenarian Barham, was roused from his bed and spent the next several hours dispatching reinforcements and supplies to Collingwood from other fleets and from the home ports. Only at 9am did Barham write to the King, apologising because, he had been 'engaged in giving the requisite orders for dispatching reinforcements to Admiral Collingwood, which he trusts will enable him not only to renew the blockade of Cadiz, but to complete the measures which his truly great and much lamented predecessor had in contemplation'.

The Campaign of Trafalgar was not over immediately and there were other fleet and squadron actions in the wake of Trafalgar, perhaps the most significant being Strachan's Action, when four French stragglers from Trafalgar were snapped up, and the Battle of San Domingo in February 1806 when some of those who had been denied a role in the Battle of Trafalgar were able to take their revenge upon the enemy.

The war lasted a further ten years, and it fell to the American historian, Alfred T Mahan to make the judgment that 'Those far distant, storm-beaten ships upon which the Grand Army never looked, stood between it and the dominion of the world.'
PETER HORE

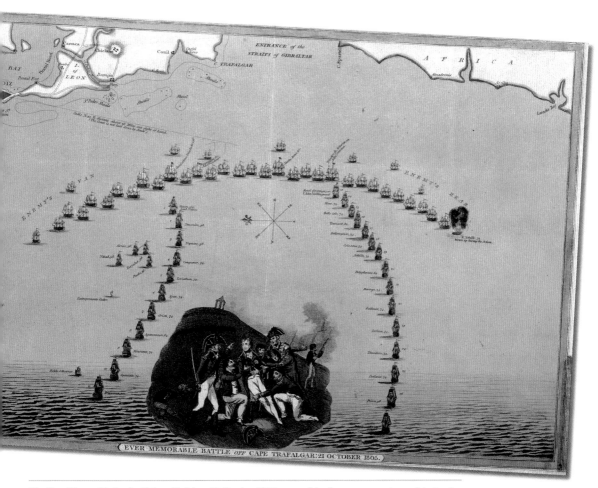

The Ever Memorable Battle off Cape Trafalgar 21 October 1805 – one of the first representations of the battle, drawn by Robert Dodd, who worked in Whitehall 'six doors from the Admiralty'. Presumably drawn in early November 1805 under the guidance of John Lapenotiere, who was then the only person in London who had been eyewitness to the battle. As other participants arrived, more accurate plans were published.

❖ BAYNTUN ❖

Henry William Bayntun (1766–1840) was one of Sir John Jervis's followers, whose connection with Nelson did not get under way until 1804 when Baytun's *Leviathan* joined Nelson on the blockade of Toulon.

Bayntun's father was a former soldier, wealthy and well-married, and British consul-general at Algiers where Henry was born in 1766. He was rated captain's servant in *Levant* (20, George Murray) in 1775 and enjoyed Murray's patronage for the next eighteen years. He was a midshipman 1775–83 and was made lieutenant on 16 April 1783. The pattern of his appointments suggest that he was not at sea for all of this time. Nevertheless, he was with Jervis in the West Indies at the

Silver Boulton Trafalgar restrike purchased by Captain Henry Bayntun in the 1840s.

capture of Martinique and was made commander of *Avenger* (16), following the death in action of her captain while on a cutting-out operation which captured the French frigate *Bienvenue* (32) at Fort Royal in March 1794. He then commanded *Nautilus*, *Veteran* (64) and *Solebay* until September 1795 when he took command of *Reunion* (36).

While commanding *Reunion,* he ran aground on Sunk Sand in the Thames in December 1796. Bayntun and his men survived and he was acquitted of blame at court-martial. There followed appointments to *Quebec* (32), *Nereide* (36), *Thunderer* (74) and in April 1801 to *Cumberland* (74), in which on 28 June 1803 he captured the French corvette *Mignonne* (16), and on 30 June the French frigate *Créole* (40), both returning to France with troops embarked.

Having gained command of *Leviathan* (74) in July 1803, he returned to England in 1804 with a convoy of over a hundred sail. Merchants from London, Bristol and Liverpool presented him with a sword. As soon as his ship was refitted, Bayntun joined Nelson in the Mediterranean, remained with Nelson for the chase to the West Indies and was at the Battle of Trafalgar.

At Trafalgar, *Leviathan* was the fourth ship in the larboard line in the wakes of *Victory, Temeraire* and *Neptune*. *Neptune* and *Leviathan* passed under the stern of the *Bucentaure*, raking her fully with broadsides. Then, as *Neptune* engaged *Santísima Trinidad* (the heaviest-armed ship in the world), Bayntun conned *Leviathan* towards the French *Neptune* (80), which had been giving Harvey's *Temeraire* trouble; Harvey in his turn was supporting *Victory* by engaging the *Redoutable*. The French *Neptune* fell off to leeward and so Bayntun turned his attentions toward *Santísima Trinidad*.

Bayntun now saw a large group of French ships, Dumanoir's squadron, change course and bear down on *Victory*, so he disengaged from *Santísima Trinidad* and in company with a number of late-arriving British ships set a course to intercept the French squadron. Hardy, from the deck of *Victory*, also saw Dumanoir's squadron turn towards him and signalled that the British ships should come to the wind on the larboard tack and block the enemy. *Leviathan* led this group and engaged the rearmost of Dumanoir's squadron, the Spanish *San Agustín* (74). Having exchanged broadsides at very close quarters, Bayntun grappled the Spanish ship, called for boarders and carried her without much resistance.

Following Trafalgar, Bayntun took part in Lord Nelson's funeral and carried the guidon during the water procession from Greenwich. In 1807 he took part in the failed expedition to Buenos Aires.

On 23 August 1809 he married Sophia Mayhew at Stoke Damerel (then a suburb of Plymouth). In the same year he commanded *Milford* (74), and in 1811 he was appointed to the command of the royal yacht *Royal Sovereign*, but he saw no further active service. He became a rear-admiral in 1812 and steadily advanced through the flag list until he became a full admiral in 1837. Admiral Sir Henry William Bayntun died at Bath in 1840.

SIM COMFORT

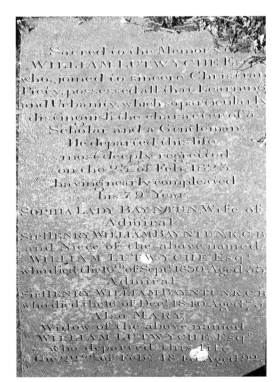

Bayntun's tomb at St Swithin's, Weston, Bath.

→ BERRY ←

Edward Berry (1768–1831) was one of Nelson's closest professional friends, and a key member of the original Band of Brothers at the Battle of the Nile. As well as serving with Nelson at the Battles of Cape St Vincent, the Nile and Trafalgar, he took part in six other fleet battles and a large number of smaller actions. A slight, rather delicate man with fair hair and piercing blue eyes, Berry was quick-witted, impulsive and aggressive to the point of recklessness. When he joined the fleet off Cadiz in *Agamemnon,* on 13 October 1805, just prior to Trafalgar, Nelson laughed, 'Here comes that damned fool, Berry. Now we shall have a fight!'

He was born in 1768 in Norwich, the son of a London merchant. His father died young, leaving a large family with little means of support, and so young Edward was sent to sea aged eleven as a midshipman in *Burford* (70).

Promoted lieutenant in the West Indies in 1794 for bravery in boarding a French man-of-war, his conduct came to the attention of the commander-in-chief, Admiral Sir John Jervis. So when later, in 1796, Commodore Horatio Nelson was looking for a new first lieutenant for his ship, *Agamemnon* (64), Jervis recommended Berry. The two took an instant liking to each other and formed a close

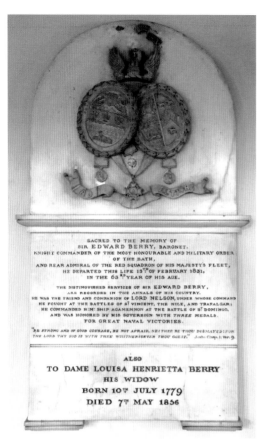

SACRED TO THE MEMORY OF
SIR EDWARD BERRY, BARONET.
KNIGHT COMMANDER OF THE MOST HONOURABLE AND MILITARY ORDER
OF THE BATH,
AND REAR ADMIRAL OF THE RED SQUADRON OF HIS MAJESTY'S FLEET,
HE DEPARTED THIS LIFE 13TH OF FEBRUARY 1831,
IN THE 63RD YEAR OF HIS AGE.

THE DISTINGUISHED SERVICES OF SIR EDWARD BERRY,
ARE RECORDED IN THE ANNALS OF HIS COUNTRY.
HE WAS THE FRIEND AND COMPANION OF LORD NELSON, UNDER WHOSE COMMAND
HE FOUGHT AT THE BATTLES OF ST VINCENT, THE NILE, AND TRAFALGAR;
HE COMMANDED HIS SHIP AGAMEMNON AT THE BATTLE OF ST DOMINGO,
AND WAS HONORED BY HIS SOVEREIGN WITH THREE MEDALS.
FOR GREAT NAVAL VICTORIES.

"BE STRONG AND OF GOOD COURAGE, BE NOT AFRAID, NEITHER BE THOU DISMAYED: FOR
THE LORD THY GOD IS WITH THEE WHITHERSOEVER THOU GOEST." Josh: Chap: I: Ver: 9.

ALSO
TO DAME LOUISA HENRIETTA BERRY
HIS WIDOW
BORN 10TH JULY 1779
DIED 7TH MAY 1856

Berry's monument in St Swithin's, Walcot, Bath.

partnership. When Nelson transferred to *Captain* (74) in 1796, Berry went with him.

Jervis continued to support Berry and obtained his promotion to commander in early 1797, but there was no ship ready for him and so he remained in *Captain* as a passenger. He was thus with Nelson at the Battle of Cape St Vincent on 14 February and was in the boarding party which captured two Spanish ships. Running out along *Captain's* bowsprit, he led one division onto the poop of the *San Nicolas* (80) while Nelson led another through her stern windows.

On 12 December that year he married his cousin Louisa, eldest daughter of Rev Dr Forster, headmaster of Norwich Grammar School, Norfolk, where he himself had been taught.

In March 1798, Berry was made a post-captain and Nelson, who was in England recovering from

the amputation of his arm, asked him to be his flag captain in *Vanguard* (74). He fought with distinction at the Battle of the Nile on 1 August 1798, and it was into his arms that Nelson reeled when he was hit on the forehead by a piece of flying shrapnel, with the words, 'I am killed. Remember me to my wife.'

Given the honour of carrying Nelson's dispatches home in *Leander* (50), *Berry* was captured by *Généreux,* one of the French battleships which had escaped from Aboukir Bay. Badly wounded in the arm, Berry was exchanged and finally reached England in December, where he was knighted and presented with the freedom of the City of London.

He was then given command of *Foudroyant* (80) and sent out in her to the Mediterranean in June 1799, to replace Nelson's battered flagship *Vanguard.* He commanded the *Foudroyant* during the capture of Malta from the French occupying force and also at the capture of his nemesis, *Généreux,* and her fellow-escapee from the Nile, *Guillaume Tell.*

Nelson left the Mediterranean overland in the summer of 1800 while Berry took the *Foudroyant* home to England. He remained there until the summer of 1805 when he was appointed to *Agamemnon* and joined Nelson in time for Trafalgar.

Agamemnon was towards the rear of Nelson's line and so did not get into action until nearly 2pm. She joined the *Neptune* and *Conqueror* in pounding the mighty four-decked Spanish battleship *Santísima Trinidad* until she was forced to surrender. In the closing stages, when the enemy van, under Dumanoir, threatened an attack on the badly damaged British ships, *Agamemnon* was part of the hastily formed line of battle that drove them off. As the smoke of battle began to clear away, Berry felt a premonition that something was wrong on board the *Victory* and had himself rowed across to the stricken flagship, but he arrived just too late to bid farewell to his friend Nelson.

The following year, Berry, still commanding the *Agamemnon,* took part in the Battle of San Domingo and was made a baronet. He remained in active service until 1813 when he was given command of one of the royal yachts, but his health was broken and although he became a rear-admiral in 1821 he never hoisted his flag.

Sir Edward Berry died in Bath in 1831 and was buried in the graveyard of St Swithin's, Walcot.

COLIN WHITE

❧ BLACKWOOD ❧

Detail from Blackwood's monument in Killyleagh Church, Co Down, Northern Ireland.

Henry Blackwood (1770–1832) was the eleventh child and seventh son of Sir John Blackwood, Bt, and Dorcas (later Baroness Dufferin), born in County Down, Ulster, on 17 December 1770, possibly at Ballyleidy (later renamed Clandeboye) or more probably at Killyleagh Castle, both of which were owned in part by his mother. His father's family was originally from Scotland, where one of his forebears, Adam Blackwood (or Blackwode), had been secretary to Mary, Queen of Scots.

Blackwood's chances of succeeding to the title were remote, and he entered as captain's servant at the age of eleven in *Artois* (40, Captain John MacBride). He saw action at the Dogger Bank in 1781 in the Fourth Anglo-Dutch War, and in a number of frigate actions before passing his examination for lieutenant. His next ships were *Proserpine* (28), *Active* (38), and, as first lieutenant, *Invincible* (74, Captain Thomas Pakenham). *Invincible* was fully engaged at the Battle of the Glorious First of June, and after Blackwood brought the French *Juste* (74) into Portsmouth, in the general promotion afterwards he became master and commander the fireship *Megaera* (14).

He was disappointed when his frigate *Brilliant* (28) joined the Nore Mutiny, but it was a mark of the man that Blackwood appeared at the court martial of one of the *Brilliant*'s crew to try and obtain a fair judgement for him.

In 1799 Blackwood moved to *Penelope* (36) and on 29 March 1800 was watching Malta, then in French hands, when *Guillaume Tell* tried to slip past the blockade. Though vastly out-gunned, Blackwood gave chase and by dint of fine seamanship, criss-crossed the stern of the *Guillaume Tell* to rake her and bring down her mizzen mast and render the Frenchman open for capture by *Foudroyant* and *Lion*. Nelson wrote to thank Blackwood: 'Your conduct and character, on the late glorious occasion stamps your fame beyond the reach of envy.'

In 1803 Blackwood was appointed to *Euryalus* (36), building at Buckler's Hard, Hampshire. In the summer of 1805 Blackwood carried the news from Collingwood that the French and Spanish fleets had ended up in Cadiz: in his impatience, Blackwood landed by boat at Lymington and took a post chaise to London, calling at Nelson's home at Merton en route. After Nelson had been appointed to command the fleet, Blackwood in *Euryalus* accompanied Nelson from Portsmouth to Spain, spending some time aboard the flagship playing dice with the admiral. (The actual dice are in the private Dufferin collection.) Nelson at one time offered Blackwood command of one of the ships of the line, but Blackwood preferred to serve as the senior captain of frigates. Later he and Hardy were signatories to the codicil to Nelson's will in which Nelson left Lady Hamilton and their daughter Horatia as a legacy to his King and country.

Off Cadiz Blackwood was given the command of the inshore squadron while Nelson waited over the horizon out of sight of the French and Spanish fleet. As Nelson formed his order of battle, *Euraylus* repeated his signals, and Blackwood was frequently on board *Victory*, including when Nelson made his famous signal. Later *Euryalus* took the damaged *Royal Sovereign* in tow, and when Collingwood shifted his flag to the frigate, Blackwood interpreted for Villeneuve. He also entered Cadiz and negotiated the exchange of prisoners.

At the end 1805, Blackwood was given command of *Ajax* (74), ironically one of the two ships offered him by Nelson before Trafalgar, and joined Admiral Collingwood's fleet cruising off the Spanish coast.

In January 1807 *Ajax* was ordered to the Dardanelles, where, on 15 February, she caught fire and was lost despite the exertions of Blackwood and his people. At the subsequent court-martial, Blackwood was absolved from blame for the loss, the fire probably being caused by two of the crew smoking in the bread room. Blackwood was transferred to *Royal George* (100) and took an active part in an action against the Turks on 21 February 1807.

Later in 1807 Blackwood was appointed to *Warspite* (76) building at Chatham. Her first deployment was to the North Sea, but she was mainly in the Mediterranean under Admiral Sir Charles Cotton. Blackwood watched the port of Toulon and the actions of the French fleet based there. In July 1810 a British squadron under Blackwood in *Warspite* with *Ajax* and *Conqueror* (74) were faced

with a French squadron of six ships of the line and four frigates, but Blackwood drove of them into port, and in 1813 in two weeks in the Channel he captured five American privateers.

When a naval review was planned for June 1814, the Duke of Clarence asked for Blackwood as his captain of the fleet in *Impregnable* (98). Blackwood met King Friedrich Wilhelm III of Prussia and Tsar Alexander I of Russia at Boulogne and escorted them to Spithead. Blackwood was promoted to rear-admiral of the blue and created a baronet.

In 1820 Blackwood was appointed commander-in-chief in the East Indies in succession to his friend Richard King, and sailed for the Indian Ocean in *Leander* (58). He occupied the long days at sea by writing to the Admiralty on a wide range of topics, including a proposition to substitute cocoa for rum, an idea which might have earned him a certain reputation on the lower deck.

His last appointment was as commander-in-chief at the Nore.

Blackwood was married three times: in 1795 to Jane Mary Crosbie; in 1799 to Elizabeth Waghorn; and in 1803 to Harriet Gore. In December 1832 Henry Martin Blackwood, his son by Elizabeth, caught typhoid fever, and was nursed by Blackwood at Ballyleidy, where there were no other children who might catch the disease, but he caught the contagion himself. Another son, Francis Price Blackwood, surveyed the Australian coast in *Fly* (24) and in 1848–50 commanded *Victory* in ordinary at Portsmouth.

It was said of Blackwood that 'He rejoiced to encourage merit in all, high and low; and few officers of his standing … were evermore instrumental in advancing the deserving as Sir Henry.' Typical of this was the case of a young black West Indian, Harry Piper, in whom Blackwood recognized potential talent and ability. Piper became gunner of a ship of the line, and when he was old Blackwood found him a home on the family estate at Ballyleidy where Piper is buried in the grounds.

Vice-Admiral Sir Henry Blackwood, 1st Baronet, died on 13 December 1832.

LESLIE H BENNETT

→ BULLEN ←

Charles Bullen (1769–1853) was an officer of great personal courage, who saw much service before and after Trafalgar. He was closely associated with Lord Northesk in the years before the great battle, but only then did his career intersect Nelson's.

Born in 1769 at Newcastle and entering the service in 1779, young Bullen gained his lieutenancy in 1791, and in the same year he married a distant relative, Miss Eleanor Wood. At Lord Howe's victory of the Glorious First of June he was in *Ramillies* (74), and afterwards joined *Monmouth* (64), whose captain was the Scottish Earl of Northesk. They were both swept into the maw of the Nore Mutiny of 1797. As John Marshall relates:

> on which occasion [Bullen] was brought to trial by the rebellious crew, one of whom a man who had received many favours from him went so far as actually to throw a noose over his head. He, however, had the good fortune not only to escape with his life, but also to see the deluded part of the ship's company return to obedience and redeem their character by conduct more natural to British seamen in the glorious battle off Camperdown, 11 October, 1797.

At Camperdown, Bullen was first lieutenant of *Monmouth* and Northesk his captain. They fought a brutal battle with *Alkmaar* (56) and *Delft* (56), both surrendering to their guns. Marshall recounts that *Delft*, 'was taken possession of by Lieutenant Bullen, who found her in very shoal water and so dreadfully cut up that it was with great difficulty he could get her clear of the shore'. Two days after the action while under tow she sank under him; many Dutch and British seamen were lost, but many more were saved under Bullen's direction as they were picked up by the boats. Bullen himself 'sprang into the sea … at the very moment of her going down'. Bullen was promoted to commander early in 1798. He took command of *Wasp* (16) in 1801 and served a very arduous time off Sierra Leone, then a struggling colony of resettled black loyalists from America who were at risk from local tribes and of being re-enslaved.

Bullen next commanded a district of Sea Fencibles and the flotilla equipped in the Thames and Medway, all in anticipation of imminent invasion in 1804. In August 1805, Northesk, whose flag was in *Britannia* (100), sent for Bullen to be his flag captain.

At Trafalgar, Nelson wanted to punch through the Franco-Spanish line with a battering ram of his heaviest ships and he placed *Britannia* high in the order of sailing close behind *Victory*, but *Britannia* was such a poor sailer that she hauled to windward of the line and was overtaken by *Leviathan* and *Conqueror*. According to family tradition, as *Britannia* struggled to get into battle, Bullen and Northesk quarrelled. Bullen refused to take in sail, but then *Britannia* ranged up the windward side of the enemy and though she opened fire early, she did not pass through the line until two hours and ten minutes later. When she did, Marine Lieutenant Lawrence Halloran described how she raked the 130-gun *Santísima Trinidad*: '[our guns] shattered the rich display of sculpture, figures, ornaments and inscriptions with which she was adorned. I never saw so beautiful a ship.'

Britannia had ten killed and forty-two wounded, Northesk resigned his command due to ill

A 100-guinea sword in its case, such as was presented to many of the victors of Trafalgar

Bullen's hatchment in St James, Shirley, Southampton, where his house, Trafalgar House, was demolished in the twenty-first century. He is buried at South Stoneham outside the city.

during the 1830s, and captain of the royal yacht *Royal Sovereign* during the same period. Bullen rose to the rank of admiral in 1852 and died at his home, which he named Trafalgar House, Shirley, then a village outside Southampton, aged eighty-six and the last surviving captain of Nelson's fleet at Trafalgar.

SIM COMFORT

→ CAPEL ←

health and Bullen refitted *Britannia* at Gibraltar before escorting three of the prizes to England.

Following Trafalgar, Bullen rose in rank and responsibility, ultimately commanding the frigates *Volontaire* (30) and *Cambrian* (40) during the Peninsular War. In spring 1811 he was senior officer off the coast of Catalonia when, whilst in a battery at Puerto de Selva near the French border, he was severely wounded. Recovered, he commanded *Akbar* (50) at Antwerp and on the North American station in 1814–17. In *Maidstone* (42) he commanded a squadron in the Gulf of Guinea engaged in the suppression of the slave trade; between April 1824 and June 1827 he freed more than 10,000 slaves.

He was commissioner of Chatham Dockyard and superintendent of Pembroke Dockyard

Thomas Bladen Capel (1776–1853) became one of Nelson's protégés in 1798 when, having just been confirmed as lieutenant, he was made flag lieutenant of *Vanguard* (74), Nelson's flagship at the Battle of the Nile (1798). His ability and, no doubt, his aristocratic pedigree caught Nelson's eye and, although junior to many of *Vanguard*'s other lieutenants, Capel was given the honour of taking a copy of the Nile dispatches to London, first as commander of the brig *Mutine* (16) and then overland across Europe.

The original dispatches were captured by the French and so it was Capel's copies that brought the news of the victory to London. This welcome news (First Lord of the Admiralty Earl Spencer passed out with relief when reading the victory dispatch) ensured that the Admiralty would approve Nelson's promotion of Capel to commander, Nelson calling him 'a most excellent officer'.

Capel was the youngest son of William, 4th Earl of Essex, born on 25 August 1776 in Hanover Square, London. In order to gain sea time, Capel was entered on the books of the frigate *Phaeton* (38) in 1782 although he actually joined the Royal Navy in 1792 on board *Assistance* (50) off Newfoundland as captain's servant. He was soon made midshipman in *Syren* (32) and Captain Graham Moore wrote that he was a 'remarkable fine young man and one whom I am convinced will turn out a meritorious officer' and later, when Capel was transferred to another ship, 'I shall regret Capel [leaving]'. After serving as a midshipman in a number of ships he saw his first major fleet action in *Sans Pareil* (80) when Lord Bridport's fleet took three French men-of-war off Lorient on 23 July 1795. On 16 May 1796 Capel was made acting lieutenant and this promotion was confirmed in April of the following year.

After delivering the Nile dispatches Capel was made commander and was shortly after given post rank as captain of *Alecto* (12). In the next eight and a half years Capel became one of the Navy's star frigate captains, particularly distinguishing himself in operations off the coast of Spain. However, in June 1800 he had the misfortune to run his ship, *Meleager* (32), onto rocks off the Gulf of Mexico where, after burning the ship to stop it falling into Spanish hands, he transferred the crew onto a nearby island from which they were subsequently rescued.

During the Trafalgar campaign Capel commanded *Phoebe* (36). While Nelson pursued Villeneuve to the West Indies and back Capel was put in command of a small squadron of five frigates and two bomb vessels and ordered to cover Sardinia, Sicily and the approaches to Egypt. At the Battle of Trafalgar, *Phoebe's* task was to repeat signals and to stand by to assist in any way she could, but she took no direct part in the fighting. During the gale that followed the battle *Phoebe* 'by extraordinary exertions' helped save the French prize, the *Swiftsure* (74), not to be confused with the British ship of the same name, from destruction.

Capel's grave in Kensal Green Cemetery, London, before and after conservation, illustrating the work of the 1805 Club to conserve the monuments to Britain's Georgian naval heroes.

Following the Trafalgar campaign Capel's *Endymion* (40) was part of Sir John Duckwood's fleet which forced the Dardanelles in February and March 1807. *Endymion* was struck by two gigantic Turkish marble shot from a giant siege cannon (which reputedly had last been used in the Siege of Vienna in 1683): the shot were 2ft in diameter and weighed over 800lb each, but *Endymion* survived the experience.

In 1811 Capel was made captain of the newly constructed *Hogue* (74) and commanded a small squadron of ships blockading US frigates off the coast of New London during the War of 1812. Following this, in 1814, he married Harriet Smyth. At the end of the war Capel commanded one of the royal yachts, became rear-admiral in 1825 and hoisted his flag as commander of the East India station from 1834 to 1837.

In 1847 Capel sat on the Board of Admiralty that decided to issue the Naval General Service Medal for service between 1793 and 1840.

Admiral Sir Thomas Bladen Capel died in London in 1853 and is buried in a family plot in Kensal Green cemetery.

NICK SLOPE

↦ CARNEGIE ↤

William Carnegie, Earl of Northesk (1756–1831) was born at Leven outside Edinburgh on 10 April 1756. His father, George, Earl of Northesk, had been born in Edinburgh Castle during the Jacobite Rising of 1715, and became an admiral; his mother was the eldest daughter of the Earl of Leven.

Young William went to sea in 1771, the same year as Nelson, in *Albion* (74, Captain Samuel Barrington), and afterwards served with Captains MacBride in *Southampton* and Stair Douglas in *Squirrel*.

In 1777 Carnegie was made lieutenant in *Nonsuch* (64) and confirmed by Lord Howe in *Apollo* (32, Captain Philemon Pownall). His next ship was *Royal George* (100), and then he went to the West Indies in *Sandwich* (98) with Sir George Rodney, serving under him at the Battle of Martinique in April 1780. Rodney thought well enough of Carnegie to promote him commander, though this was not confirmed until several months later, and gave him command of the fireship *Blast* and then of the ex-Dutch *St Eustatius* (also *Eustatia*) (20). Carnegie was present at the capture of the Dutch island of St Eustatius in February 1781, and in April 1782 he was made post-captain and given command

of the frigate *Enterprise* (28) which he brought to England and paid off at the peace in 1783.

In 1788 he married Mary Ricketts, niece to Sir John Jervis (her brother William Henry Ricketts would change his name and eventually inherit the St Vincent earldom). Unlike Nelson, who had married a few months previously, Carnegie found his marriage happy and fruitful, and again unlike Nelson, who was unemployed during the Spanish Armament of 1790, Carnegie was given command of *Heroine* (32).

His succession to the earldom of Northesk in 1792 scarcely interrupted his sea time and in 1793 he commanded the frigates *Beaulieu* and *Andromeda* in the West Indies.

In 1796 Northesk was elected one of the sixteen representatives of the peerage in Scotland in the parliament of Great Britain, a role which he fulfilled until 1830.

Northesk was captain of *Monmouth* (64), one of the ships in the North Sea squadron which mutinied at the Nore in May 1797. Northesk was held prisoner in his own cabin until the mutineers sent for him as 'one who was known to be the seaman's friend'. Richard Parker, the chairman of the delegates, presented him with the terms 'on which alone, without the smallest alteration, they would give up the ships' or they would immediately put the fleet to sea. They ordered Carnegie to wait upon the King, present the resolutions of their committee, and return with an answer within fifty-four hours. Northesk informed the delegates that 'he certainly would bear the letter as desired, but he could not, from the unreasonableness of the demands flatter them with any expectation of success'.

He did carry the mutineers' letter to the Admiralty where the First Lord, Lord Spencer, took him to the King. When the demands were rejected, the mutiny quelled, and the mutineers tried, Northesk resigned his command.

He was briefly unemployed by the Navy until in 1800 he was given command of *Prince* (98) until the Peace of Amiens, and when the peace broke down, his next ship was *Britannia* (100), employed first as a guard at St Helens and then on the blockade of Brest under William Cornwallis. When he was promoted rear-admiral in April 1804, he sent for Charles Bullen to be his flag captain and remained in *Britannia*, and in August 1805 joined a squadron under Admiral Calder which sailed to reinforce Admiral Collingwood on the blockade of Cadiz.

So far Northesk and Nelson had never served together, and when Nelson arrived to take command of the fleet off Cadiz, he invited Northesk to dine alone with him on at least two occasions, making, as was his custom, some attempt to get to know his new subordinate and win his confidence. However, though third in seniority on 21 October 1805, Northesk seems to have played very little part in planning the battle. It may be wondered what Nelson thought of Northesk, so different from him, descended on both side from earls, a sitting member of the House of Lords who had been favoured by Admirals Howe and Rodney, and was related by marriage to St Vincent.

However, all does not seem to have been well in *Britannia* on the day of battle: she sailed so badly that Nelson ordered her to haul out of the line; Northesk and his flag captain were heard to shout angrily at each other; she failed to break the line as Nelson wanted; and though she engaged the largest Spanish ship, *Santísima Trinidad*, her casualties were light, ten dead and forty-two wounded.

Northesk received the usual honours after the battle including a knighthood and a vase worth £300 from the Lloyd's Patriotic Fund, but he did not serve at sea again, though he received the royal honour of being made Rear-Admiral of the United Kingdom in 1821 and was commander-in-chief at Plymouth 1827–30.

However, he suffered the devastating loss of his eldest son who was drowned when a midshipman in *Blenheim* (90, Captain Thomas Troubridge) when she foundered in a storm off Madagascar with the loss of all hands.

Admiral William Carnegie, 7th Earl of Northesk, died in Albemarle Street, London, on 28 May 1831 and he was buried in St Paul's Cathedral near Nelson and Collingwood.

PETER HORE

❖ CODRINGTON ❖

Edward Codrington (1770–1851) had never served with Nelson before September 1805 and yet he quickly became an admirer. Moreover, he showed by his actions at Trafalgar that he both understood, and fully supported, Nelson's battle plan and style of fighting. Alone of the Trafalgar captains, he later commanded a British fleet in battle, at Navarino in 1827.

The third son of a Gloucestershire landowner and baronet, Codrington was born on 27 April 1770 and educated at Harrow before joining the Royal Navy in 1783. He became a lieutenant in 1793 and was signal officer of Admiral Lord Howe's flagship, *Queen Charlotte* (100), at the Glorious First of June in 1794. A personal protégé of Howe, he was given the honour of taking home the admiral's duplicate dispatches and, as was customary, was rewarded with promotion to commander. The following year he was made a captain and was present, in command of the frigate *La Babet*, at Bridport's action off Groix on 23 June.

On 27 December 1802 at Old Windsor Church, Berkshire, he married Jane Hall, daughter of a Jamaican planter.

He remained in frigates until May 1805, when he was appointed to command *Orion* (74) and, after a short spell with the Channel Fleet, was detached to reinforce Collingwood off Cadiz. He

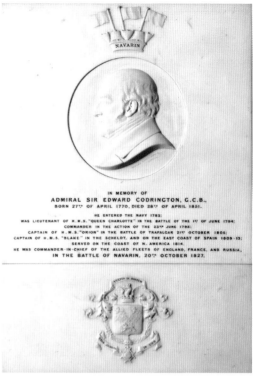

IN MEMORY OF
ADMIRAL SIR EDWARD CODRINGTON, G.C.B.
BORN 27ᵀᴴ OF APRIL 1770, DIED 28ᵀᴴ OF APRIL 1851.

HE ENTERED THE NAVY 1783;
WAS LIEUTENANT OF H.M.S. "QUEEN CHARLOTTE" IN THE BATTLE OF THE 1ˢᵀ OF JUNE 1794;
COMMANDER IN THE ACTION OF THE 23ᴿᴰ JUNE 1795;
CAPTAIN OF H.M.S. "ORION" IN THE BATTLE OF TRAFALGAR 21ˢᵀ OCTOBER 1805;
CAPTAIN OF H.M.S. "BLAKE" IN THE SCHELDT, AND ON THE EAST COAST OF SPAIN 1809-13;
SERVED ON THE COAST OF N. AMERICA 1814.
HE WAS COMMANDER-IN-CHIEF OF THE ALLIED FLEETS OF ENGLAND, FRANCE, AND RUSSIA,
IN THE BATTLE OF NAVARIN, 20ᵀᴴ OCTOBER 1827.

Codrington has a monument (*above*) in St Peter's, Eaton Square (though the crypt has been cleared), and two fine monuments (*left*) overlooking the Bay of Navarino, modern-day Pylos, where he fought his last battle.

found Collingwood's regime uncongenial and was delighted when Nelson was appointed to command the fleet. At their first meeting, Nelson bound the young captain to him with one of his characteristic gestures: he handed Codrington a letter from his wife saying that 'being entrusted with it by a lady, he made a point of delivering it himself'.

At Trafalgar *Orion* was towards the rear of Nelson's line and so did not arrive in the thick of the fighting until about two hours after the first shot was fired. Codrington planned his approach carefully, holding his fire so as not to obscure his view with smoke, and even when he reached the action, he passed through the clusters of ships until he came across a suitable victim. She was the French *Swiftsure* (74) into whose stern *Orion*'s gunners poured a series of murderous broadsides, forcing her to surrender. Codrington

then attempted to take on *Principe de Asturias* (112), flagship of the Spanish commander-in-chief, but she pulled away, so he moved on northwards to assist the British ships there in repelling the attack by Dumanoir and the French van. *Orion* then played a key role in the capture of the gallantly defended *Intrépide* (74), sailing right round the stricken ship pouring in a deadly, accurate fire from close quarters. It was a classic demonstration of the sort of mobile, intelligent fighting that Nelson wanted. Like the other captains, Codrington was rewarded with the naval gold medal and a sword from Lloyd's Patriotic Fund.

Codrington remained with Collingwood in the Mediterranean until December 1806, and continued in active service throughout the rest of the war, serving in the disastrous amphibious attack on the Dutch island of Walcheren in 1809 and off the coast of Spain, commanding a squadron support-ing Wellington's land campaign, during 1811–13.

Promoted rear-admiral in 1814, he was cap-tain of the fleet to the commander-in-chief of the North American station, Sir Alexander Cochrane, during the closing stages of the War of 1812, and took part in operations in the Chesapeake River and in the attack on New Orleans.

In 1826, by then a vice-admiral, he became commander-in-chief in the Mediterranean, with his flag in *Asia* (84). The Greeks were in open revolt against their Turkish overlords, and Britain, though not formally at war with Turkey, was generally sympathetic to the Greek cause, placing Codring-ton in a difficult position politically. The growing tension eventually led to a full-scale battle in the Bay of Navarino in southern Greece, on 20 Octo-ber 1827, where the Turkish fleet was annihilated by a combined British, French and Russian fleet under Codrington's overall command, thus pav-ing the way for Greek independence, which came two years later. It was the last major naval battle fought wholly under sail. Although the victory was popular, the government was embarrassed by such overt intervention and recalled Codrington for an explanation. However, he was cleared of blame and received the Grand Cross of the Bath. He contin-ued to serve, commanding the Channel squadron in 1831–2, and ending a long and distinguished ca-reer as commander-in-chief at Plymouth 1839–42.

Codrington had the inconsolable grief of losing his eldest son, Edward, drowned when a midship-man in the frigate *Cambrian* in 1819 by the up-setting of a boat; Jane died in 1837; his other sons and daughters served in or married into the Navy and Army.

Admiral Sir Edward Codrington lived long enough to claim his Naval General Service Medal with four clasps in 1848, and died at his home in Eaton Square in 1851. He was buried at St Peter's but when the crypt was cleared in 1953 the body was moved to Brookwood cemetery and its where-abouts is now unknown. He is, however, memori-alised in St Paul's Cathedral and at Pylos in Greece.
COLIN WHITE

↣ COLLINGWOOD ↢

Cuthbert Collingwood (1748–1810) was born in Newcastle on 26 September, the eighth child and eldest of three sons of Cuthbert Collingwood, a less than successful merchant, and his wife Milcah Dobson. Educated at the Royal Grammar School under the Rev Hugh Moises, he was rated 'able' in *Shannon* (28) on 28 August 1761, under the aegis of his cousin, Captain (later Admiral) Rich-ard Brathwaite. His brother Wilfred, younger by a year, joined a week later as captain's servant and the two served together in *Shannon*, *Gibraltar* (20) and *Liverpool* (28); the brothers both passed for lieutenant on 7 April 1772. Cuthbert felt greatly indebted to Brathwaite, 'to whose regard for me and the interest he took in whatever related to my improvement in nautical knowledge, I owe great obligation'. In his turn he took an interest in the education of the youngsters serving under him.

Collingwood next served in *Lennox* (74) under another relation, Captain Robert Roddam. So far he had only seen the Baltic and the Mediterranean but in February 1774 *Preston* (50) took him, un-der the command of Vice-Admiral Samuel Graves, to America and the American Revolutionary War. At Boston he was part of the naval brigade which fought at the Battle of Bunker Hill on 17 June

1775, when Graves made him a lieutenant.

His promotion was confirmed in 1776 when he sailed for Jamaica in the *Hornet* sloop. It was an unhappy year: his commanding officer, Robert Haswell, had been on the lieutenants' list for eighteen years, the Hornets were mocked for their inability to take prizes, Haswell flogged a large number of his crew, and Collingwood, feeling the strain of this and taking control of most of the day-to-day working of the ship, was eventually court-martialled in September 1777 but acquitted with no more than an admonition for a 'want of cheerfulness' and urged to conduct himself in future with 'more alacrity'. This experience gave him a distaste for flogging.

However, whilst in the West Indies, Collingwood and Nelson, who had met some years before, became firm friends, though, given their opposite personalities, they were the unlikeliest to do so. Every time Nelson got a step up, Collingwood succeeded him, first in *Lowestoffe* (32), then *Badger* brig, *Hinchinbroke* (28) and *Janus*. *Hinchinbroke* was engaged in operations against the Spanish Central American colonies after Spain had allied with France in aid of the American colonists, but an expedition against San Juan was a disaster, with British forces decimated by fever. Collingwood wrote. 'I survived most of my ship's company, having buried in four months 180 of the 200 which composed it.' Nelson was himself sent back to England suffering from fever.

Collingwood was then given command of the *Pelican* (24), but in August 1781, after a successful cruise in which a French frigate and five privateers were taken, she was wrecked on the Morant Keys near Jamaica. In the *Naval Chronicle* he explained: 'the next day with great difficulty the ship's company got on shore on rafts, made of the small and broken yards, and on those small sandy hills, with little food and water, we remained ten days, until a boat went to Jamaica, and the *Diamond* frigate came and took us off.'

His next ships were *Sampson* (64), *Mediator* (44) and *Boreas* (28) in the West Indies where he and Nelson made themselves unpopular in upholding the Navigation Acts, even against the wishes of their commander-in-chief. He and Nelson also developed their lasting attachment to Mary Moutray, the wife of the Commissioner for the Navy Board in Antigua. They drew portraits of each other which have survived, Nelson's by Collingwood showing him wearing a wig after his fever. This, and a self-portrait, are workmanlike, but not particularly accomplished in comparison with Nelson's effort. Of the station, Nelson wrote to Captain Locker: 'Had it not been for Collingwood, it would have been the most disagreeable I ever saw.'

Cuthbert's brother Wilfred was also in the West Indies at this period, commanding the *Rattler*, engaged in the same protection duties, with Nelson and, later, with Prince William Henry, third son of George III, in the *Pegasus*. Cuthbert returned home in the late summer of 1786, only to receive a long letter from Nelson telling him that Wilfred had died (he was thirty-eight). The Prince had also extended his sincere condolences which Nelson forwarded to Cuthbert. Meantime, Collingwood took the opportunity of four years in Northumberland 'making my acquaintance with my own family, to whom I had hitherto been as it were a stranger'. His youngest brother, John, had joined the Customs service and there were surviving sisters.

The Nootka Sound incident, or Spanish Armament, reignited Collingwood's career. He took himself to the Admiralty, like many another naval officer hoping for a command. A letter to his sister Mary reveals what a sea captain thought necessary for a cruise:

Here we are in the most delightful confusion. War is inevitable and every preparation making ... Every body pushing their interest for ships. We who have none must be content to wait until those who have are out of our way, but I think I can hardly miss being employed very soon, therefore have enclosed to you the key of my bureau. The keys of my trunks are in it. Every thing that is in my bureau except the ragged shirts leave in it, fill it with linen from the trunk, so as to prevent its shaking, but with such things as are least heavy. All the papers that are in it leave just in the state they are, all the plans and draft books put into the larger chest, with such books of navigation and signals as are on the book shelves and, in the drawers under them, three spy glasses. The shortest night glass not to be packed, it may stay; in a right hand drawer in the top of the bureau is the great object glass of the largest telescope, it must be screwed in its place. My quadrant with the brass at the key hole must be put into the chest, the glasses might be rolled in the cloaks to preserve them from injury, a few books might be put in where there is room, the Spectator and Shakespear. Of plate my plain spoons, fish things and teaspoons, those I bought last, no salts, cups nor castors: of linen, 4 prs sheets, and my sea table cloths and breakfast cloths, towels etc. In short, where I say that my very best things, I wou'd not have come. My new shoes are in a box – I do not know where. May I beg of my brother John to get those things in readiness for me, that if I am appointed to a ship they may be sent to the port where she is, by the earliest opportunity that offers.

Collingwood was given *Mermaid* (32) in which he made an uneventful cruise to the West Indies.

Afterwards, on 18 June 1791, he married Sarah, daughter of John Erasmus Blackett, Mayor of Newcastle. They were to have two daughters, Sarah and Mary Patience. Though an absentee father Cuthbert took a great interest in their education, urging the teaching of maths, Spanish ('the most elegant language of Europe and very easy') and swimming: having seen 'women and children running from death and when they come to the Po or the Pavia find the bridges broken down, it was scenes like these, to which human creatures are now daily exposed, that made me so desirous my girls should learn to swim, then they might set such chance and circumstance at defiance, and a river or two would have been no bar to their safety.' In addition, he felt they should avoid reading novels.

In 1793, when war broke out with France, Collingwood was appointed flag captain to Admiral Bowyer in *Prince* (98), 'the most miserable sailer in the fleet'. They transferred to *Barfleur* (90) and fought at the Glorious First of June, where Bowyer was wounded early in the action and it was left to Collingwood to fight the ship and command Bowyer's subdivision. Bowyer was created a baronet but Collingwood was not mentioned in Lord Howe's report, did not receive the gold medal and was understandably aggrieved.

In July 1794 he moved to *Hector* (74) and then to *Excellent* (74), which became renowned for the rapidity of her gunnery. After a few months off Ushant he was directed to the Mediterranean to blockade Toulon and guard Corsica. When the Spanish fleet was brought to battle off Cape St Vincent on 14 February 1797, *Excellent* fought first with the *Salvador del Mundo* (112), and, believing that she had surrendered, proceeded under the lee of the next ship, *San Ysidro* (74), which also struck to him. Collingwood then went to the assistance of Nelson in *Captain*, firing on the *San Nicolas* (80) and causing her to run on board the *San Josef* (112) and allowed Nelson to take both ships.

Following the engagement, Nelson wrote to Cuthbert: 'My Dearest friend. "A friend in need is a friend indeed" was never more truly verified than by your most noble and gallant conduct yesterday in sparing the *Captain* from further loss.' Vice-Admiral William Waldegrave wrote: 'Nothing could exceed the spirit and true officership which you so happily displayed yesterday … May England long possess such men as yourself – 'tis saying everything for her glory.' Gold medals were again to be awarded, but Collingwood refused to accept his unless the injustice of the previous oversight was reversed, which it was.

The next two years were spent blockading the Spanish fleet in Cadiz. He was briefly made commodore by St Vincent but returned home in November 1798 and in January 1799, when *Excellent* was paid off, returning to Morpeth, Northumberland, where his family was established. He was promoted rear-admiral in May and hoisted his flag in *Triumph* (74). The next few years were spent searching for the French fleet and blockading the French

ports. In January 1801, when he had transferred to *Barfleur*, his wife and elder daughter and the dog Bounce travelled from Morpeth to Plymouth to see him, but on the evening of their arrival he was obliged to sail for Brest. They waited six weeks for him, but it was another year before he was able to return to the north. Writing in January 1802 he reported that he had already sent off his heavy baggage in a collier to Newcastle 'and Bounce amongst the valuables'.

By May 1803 Collingwood and Bounce were at sea in *Diamond* (38), in which he hoisted his flag, war having been resumed. For the next seven years he was constantly at sea and never saw his family again. He was appointed to command a squadron blockading the enemy fleets on the Atlantic coast, and moved from one ship to another to stay on station.

On 21 May 1805 he sailed for Cadiz with eleven ships of the line, though by 20 August he was reduced to only three ships and a frigate. As Villeneuve's fleet approached, Collingwood deceived his enemy as to the size of his force by standing towards him and Villeneuve took refuge in Cadiz.

Collingwood has perhaps the grandest monument of all the Band of Brothers, on a headland looking out to sea at Tynemouth, and a fine monument in Newcastle Cathedral, as well as a tomb in St Paul's.

For this, Nelson told him, 'Everybody in England admired your adroitness.' Now Collingwood transferred his flag into the *Royal Sovereign* (100).

At Trafalgar, in the hours before the battle, Collingwood visited the decks to encourage the men and said to his officers: 'Now, gentlemen, let us do something today which the world may talk of hereafter.' Collingwood's *Royal Sovereign* was the first to break the enemy line, prompting Nelson to say to Blackwood, 'See how that noble fellow Collingwood carries his ship into action.' The battle is described elsewhere. Following Nelson's death, Collingwood succeeded to the command. There remains some controversy as to whether he should have ordered the fleet to anchor and the destruction of some of the prizes, but he is remembered by the Spanish for his humanity in the treatment of the enemy prisoners and wounded.

His famous dispatch prompted a personal letter from George III, and he was appointed commander-in-chief in the Mediterranean, with the same authority Nelson had held. He was created Baron Collingwood of Caldburne and Hethpool. He wrote home of Bounce's reaction to this elevation: 'The consequential airs he gives himself since he became a Right Honourable dog are insufferable. He considers it beneath his dignity to play with commoners' dogs, and truly thinks that he does them grace when he condescends to lift up his leg against them. This, I think, is carrying the insolence of rank to the extreme.'

Now he had to contain the French in their Mediterranean ports, although he would dearly have loved to engage them in one further decisive battle. At the same time he demonstrated a rare talent to understand the shifting alliances of the European powers, dealing with the difficult Queen of Sicily (he got on well with the King, talking companionably about gardening), and dispatching ships to obtain intelligence around the Mediterranean. As Piers Mackesy put it, 'The splendour of the navy's work in the theatre after Trafalgar has been obscured by the absence of fleet actions; and the name of Lord Collingwood has equally been dimmed by his inability to bring an enemy fleet to battle.' Mackesy also writes of his skill as a diplomatist and his 'real stature'.

The strain of this tedious work continued while his health deteriorated. His inability to delegate did not help. At the same time, matters at home were distracting. His wife, now 'the extravagant party', and his father-in-law had invested in shares in fire insurance and he became convinced that the reason that his request to return home had been rejected was that the King would not admit an insurance merchant into the house of peers. Added to these burdens, Bounce had fallen overboard and drowned. 'I have few comforts, but he was one, for he loved me. Everybody sorrows for him. He was wiser than [a good many] who hold their heads higher and was grateful [to those] who were kind to him.'

Vice-Admiral Cuthbert Collingwood, 1st Baron Collingwood, finally relinquished his command early in 1810, and he died on 7 March, shortly after he had sailed from Menorca. He lay in state at Greenwich before an impressive cortège took him to St Paul's and he was laid in a tomb alongside his friend Nelson, the contrast between the two memorials reflecting their different personalities, the flamboyance of Nelson, and the austerity of Collingwood.

JUDY COLLINGWOOD

❧ CONN ❧

John Conn (1764–1810) was baptised on 5 August 1764 in Stoke Damerel, Plymouth; his father was a commissioned gunner in the Navy.

He first went to sea in 1778 at the age of thirteen and served in his father's brig-sloop *Weazle* (18). He then went on to *Arrogant* (74) as a midshipman and master's mate and saw action at the Battle of Saintes in April 1782. In June 1788 he was made an acting lieutenant but had to wait for five years before being given his first commission in 1793. During that period he married a cousin of Nelson, Margaret, the daughter of Rev Isaac Nelson.

Conn was appointed to *Royal Sovereign* (100) and present at Admiral Lord Howe's victory at the Glorious First of June in 1794. His first command, *Staunch* (12), followed in June 1797, but he left her a year later to join *Foudroyant* (80) and was under Commodore Sir John Borlase Warren at the defeat of a French squadron off Donegal during an attempted landing in Ireland on 2 October 1798.

Next came promotion to master and commander of the bomb vessel *Discovery* (10) in August 1800. At the Battle of Copenhagen, Conn anchored his ship off the Middle Ground. There were no casualties in *Discovery*.

In mid-August 1801, he commanded a division of eight howitzer flatboats during Nelson's disastrous attack on the French invasion flotilla in Boulogne harbour. It failed because the intention to capture French ships was thwarted as they were secured by chains and anti-boarding rigging. Although the British were repulsed, Conn continued firing at French camps and batteries 'until the enemies fire totally slackened'. Three days later Nelson sent in Conn again with his howitzers to try and set fire to the French brig *Etna*. Nelson told Earl St Vincent that 'a more zealous and deserving officer than Conn, never was brought forward'.

Conn was promoted to post-captain on 29 August 1802 and was given *Culloden* (74), in which he was joined by his nine-year-old son Henry, as first-class volunteer, and who followed him into several other ships including *Dreadnought* at Trafalgar.

In April 1803 he transferred to the large and powerful French-built *Canopus* (80), which as *Franklin* had been taken at the Battle of Aboukir Bay, and he joined the blockade off Toulon. In January and February 1805 he joined the pursuit of the French to the West Indies, but in March he was superseded by Francis Austen, the brother of Jane. Back in England he became acting captain of *Victory* while Nelson and Hardy were on leave. He was ordered to take her to join Admiral Cornwallis's Channel Fleet, an order which was cancelled when the news came that the Combined Fleet was in Cadiz. As reinforcements prepared to sail from Portsmouth, Nelson, fresh from his home in Merton, briefly met Conn at the George Inn.

Subsequently, Conn transferred to the newly refitted *Royal Sovereign* (100) and took her to join Collingwood. When Nelson joined the fleet Conn changed ships again, this time swapping with Collingwood and his flag captain, for the new *Dreadnought* (98), her highly drilled crew trained to produce rapid firepower, but a slow sailer; Conn missed the dinners when Nelson explained his plans for battle.

As the British fleet squared up to the enemy on 21 October 1805, *Dreadnought* was some way down the line of Collingwood's division, and by the time she had entered the fray, Nelson in the weather line had already been shot. *Dreadnought* engaged the *San Juan Nepomuceno*, which was bearing down on the crippled *Bellerophon* (74), forcing her to surrender in fifteen minutes. Next, Conn went after the Spanish flagship *Principe de Asturias* (112) in which Admiral Gravina was mortally wounded, though his ship escaped to Cadiz. After the storm which followed the next day, Conn was able to reclaim his prize and *San Juan Nepomuceno* was one of the four enemy ships to survive.

Conn was awarded a gold medal and a sword of honour from the Lloyd's Patriotic Fund, and he remained in *Dreadnought* until 1806 when he commanded in succession, *San Josef* (112) and *Hibernia* (110).

In 1810 he took up his final command, *Swiftsure* (74), in the West Indies. There on 4 May, while giving chase to a small French ship off Bermuda, tragedy struck. Henry, Conn's son, had been captured in December 1809, while third lieutenant of the frigate *Junon*, off Guadeloupe, in a fight against four French frigates. (*Junon* suffered heavy causalities and was so badly damaged that she was burned by her captors; the British got their revenge by later taking all four of the French, and young Henry escaped from captivity in 1812.) John Conn was so deeply affected by the news of his son's capture that he became delirious and, though he was apparently recovered, when left alone for a few minutes in his cabin, he fell overboard from the windows of the quarter gallery. The alarm was raised by a boy who saw him from the gunroom port, but *Swiftsure* was under all sail in a strong breeze and heavy swell. His body was not found.

Admiral's rank and the nation's honours would no doubt have come his way and his passing was mourned in Britain, especially in the Navy in which he was a popular and respected figure. Admiral Sir John Borlase Warren wrote of how much he regretted the loss of 'so deserving an officer as Captain Conn'.

JOHN R GWYTHER

→ COOKE ←

John Cooke (1763–1805) joined Collingwood on the blockade off Cadiz on 10 June 1805 in *Bellerophon* (74), built in 1786 and affectionately known to her crew as the *Billy Ruffian*. Four months later, on the evening of 19 October, he was looking forward to dining with Nelson in *Victory* when the signal that the enemy were coming out of port changed everything.

The order of sailing placed Cooke's ship fifth in line of Collingwood's division. Foreseeing the bloodiness of the ensuing battle, he felt that he could be 'bowl'd out' at any time, and in an act of leadership worthy of Nelson took his first lieutenant, William Pryce Cumby, and the master, Edward Overton, into his confidence. He showed them Nelson's memorandum so they knew clearly what they were expected to do. When he made out the admiral's signal, 'England expects that every man will do his duty', Cooke went below to pass it on to the gun crews.

After *Bellerophon* had broken through the enemy line, the fighting became furious and men were falling all around Cooke as he stood with Cumby and Overton on the quarterdeck. He was locked in combat with the French ship *Aigle*, whose captain had filled her fighting tops and rigging with sharpshooters. Cumby pointed out to his senior

that he was wearing his epaulettes, which marked him out to the enemy sharpshooters in the tops and rigging. Unperturbed, Cooke exclaimed, 'It is too late to take them off. I see my situation, but I will die like a man.'

He continued discharging his pistols at the enemy, even killing a French officer on his own quarterdeck. After a short time, he directed Cumby to go down to the gun decks to ensure that the starboard guns kept firing at all costs. Even before Cumby got back to the quarterdeck, he was met by the quartermaster, who had come to inform him that Cooke was mortally wounded while reloading his pistols. When Cumby reached the quarterdeck, Cooke was dead. His last words were, 'Let me lie quietly one minute. Tell Lieutenant Cumby never to strike!'

John Cooke was born in 1763. His father, Francis Cooke, was an Admiralty cashier. His name was put on the ship's books of *Greyhound* in 1774 but for the next two years he attended 'Mr Braken's celebrated naval academy at Greenwich', thus, in the words of the *Naval Chronicle* 'no time might be lost for acquiring thoroughly the first elements of nautical science and military tactics … and thus obtained the double advantage of prosecuting his naval studies, and reckoning his time as though in actual service'.

Somewhere he acquired the patronage of Samuel Hood (later Lord Bridport) which served him well throughout his career.

His first ship, at age thirteen, was Hood's flagship *Eagle* (64, Captain Henry Duncan), Lord Howe's flagship at the beginning of the American War, and at the Battle of Rhode Island he was 'one of the first who entered the fort'.

He passed for lieutenant in 1779 and sailed for the East Indies in *Worcester* (64) but bad health soon brought him home. While convalescing he spent a year in France, before joining *Duke* (98, Captain Alan Gardner) and was a senior lieutenant in her at the Battle of the Saintes in April 1782. A fall again invalided him and Cooke spent more years on half pay, being briefly recalled during the Spanish Armament by Bridport to be third lieutenant of *London* (90).

Cooke 'having evinced the most consumate skill and bravery … fell in a moment glorious indeed to his country' has a monument at Donhead St Andrew in Wiltshire and this monument in St Paul's.

When the French war broke out Bridport again summoned him, this time as first lieutenant of his flagship, *Royal George* (100, Captain William Dommett). At the first opportunity Bridport gave Cooke the fireship *Incendiary* which he commanded as a lieutenant at the Glorious First of June. Before he could be confirmed as a commander, Bridport seized the opportunity, when her captain fell ill, of giving *Monarch* (74) to Cooke. There ensued an argument between Bridport and Lord Spencer at the Admiralty that Cooke 'was too young to keep a 74 at home', out of which he emerged as post-captain of *Nymphe* (36), never having been to sea as a commander.

Cooke justified the confidence in him by taking, with another frigate, two French frigates almost at the mouth of Brest Roads, *Resistance* (48) and *Constance* (24) (which had landed an invasion force in Fishguard Bay) on 9 August 1797. Nemesis quickly followed when *Nymphe* joined the fleet mutiny at the Nore and his crew put him ashore; when they relented he declined to go back. Cooke had a reputation as an excellent officer but a strict disciplinarian.

Two years later, now in command of *Amethyst* (38), he took the Duke of York to Holland on his ill-fated expedition, immortalised by the famous nursery rhyme. He was still in *Amethyst* when he joined the operations under Lord Bridport, off Quiberon Bay, and in 1800 the expedition to Ferrol under Rear-Admiral Warren. In 1801, Cooke was in the Channel where he met and captured the French frigate *Dédaigneuse*, sank the Spanish privateer *Nuestra Señora del Carmen* and took the French privateer *Général Brune*.

At the Peace of Amiens he could look back with satisfaction: he had enjoyed the patronage of Lord Bridport and other great men, he had married well and inherited wealth, and done well through prize-money, and was laying out a park around his house at Donhead, Wiltshire. Cooke had been at every major engagement of the fleet except the Nile and Copenhagen, and his one unfulfilled ambition was to fight a battle under the command of Nelson. Little could he know that they were both doomed to fall in the same manner and almost at the same moment, but he could not resist when invited to take command of *Bellerophon*.

Cooke left behind a wife, Louisa Hardy, daughter of the quondam Governor of New Jersey, whom he had married in 1790, and an eight-year-old daughter. His widow received the naval gold medal for the battle, and a silver vase from the Lloyd's Patriotic Fund. One of his pistols can be seen at the National Maritime Museum at Greenwich.

PETER WARWICK

❖ CUMBY ❖

William Pryce Cumby (1771–1837) was born on 20 March 1771 at Dover where presumably his father was temporarily stationed. He came from generations of worthy naval officers, the Cumbys and also the Jepsons, whose family home was Heighington, County Durham; none of them made more than master and commander until Cumby was thrust into the captaincy of *Billy Ruffian* at Trafalgar.

Young Cumby entered the Navy aged thirteen in the cutter *Kite* (12), which cruised against smugglers on the north-east coast of England for two years. Cumby then undertook several voyages in merchant ships trading between Holland, the Baltic and Canada, before he found a berth in 1789 in *Brazen* (12). As the Navy rapidly expanded during the Spanish Armament, he moved successfully into *Alfred* (74), *Meleager* (32) and *Leviathan* (74), where he won the patronage of his fellow north-countryman Captain Constantine Phipps (late Lord Mulgrave), who got him an appointment under Captain Henry Savage (later admiral of the white) in *Pomona* (28).

He passed for lieutenant in 1792, and became third lieutenant of *Hebe* (38) under Captain Alexander Hood who had sailed with Cook, and then in *Assistance* (50), flagship of Richard King (later admiral of the red) under another north-countryman and former shipmate, Captain Nathan Brunton. Next another former shipmate, Lord Henry Paulet, asked for Cumby as first lieutenant of *Astraea* (32); on 10 April 1795 *Astraea* ran down three French frigates in thick fog in the Channel, and despite the odds exchanged broadsides with the *Gloire* (42) for an hour until the Frenchman surrendered. Cumby shifted into *Thalia* (36) with Paulet, who had all the makings of a successful frigate captain and made several captures, but he was court-martialled in June 1798 for striking one of his other lieutenants. The court found him guilty and he was dismissed his ship. The partnership had been broken up, and though Paulet was reinstated, Cumby had moved on to *Excellent* (74, Captain Cuthbert Collingwood) as third lieutenant.

There followed three years on half pay until Orkneyman Admiral Alexander Graeme, Laird of Graemeshall, and friend of Nelson (and who like Nelson had lost an arm in battle) took Cumby as his flag lieutenant in his flagship *Zealand* when commander-in-chief at the Nore. On the renewal of the war Cumby saw a return to a familiar duty: command of the cutter *Swift* in the North Sea, and then a brief period in command of the Sea Fencibles in Norfolk, from which he was recalled in 1804 when the Massachusetts-born Captain John Loring asked for him as first lieutenant of *Bellero-*

Cumby has a memorial in his local church St Michael's, Heighington, Co Durham (upper), but the graveyard where he was buried at Park Street, Pembroke Dock, has been cleared and little is left of his tomb (lower).

phon (74) – the *Billy Ruffian* to her. When Loring was superseded in April 1805, Cumby stayed as first lieutenant to Captain John Cooke.

Cumby wrote an account of the Battle of Trafalgar for his son. He claimed to have been the first man in the main body of the fleet to have seen the distant signal from the frigate on the horizon that the enemy had put to sea. 'Our joy', he wrote, 'at the prospect this afforded of an opportunity of bringing the enemy's fleet to action, and consequently terminating the blockade which we had been so long and so disagreeably employ'd was considerably checked by the apprehension that it was merely a feint on their part and having no intention of giving us battle that they would re-enter the harbour of Cadiz so soon as they discovered us in pursuit.'

Overnight Cumby kept watch-and-watch with his captain and had retired to his cabin when he was rudely awakened by his friend Edward Overton, the ship's master: 'Cumby my boy, turn out,' he shouted, 'Here they are all ready for you; three and thirty sail of the line close under our lee.' Before going on deck he knelt down and prayed to the great God of battles for a glorious victory and 'committed myself individually to his all wise disposal and begging his gracious protection and favour for my dear wife and children, whatever his unerring wisdom might see fit to order for myself'. Afterwards he reflected with pride that his sentiments were so similar to Nelson's prayer before the battle. On deck he found everyone staring at the eastern horizon and the enemy ships silhouetted against the dawn light.

Cooke and Cumby breakfasted together, as they usually did at 8am, when Cooke allowed Cumby to read Nelson's memorandum, setting out how he intended to break the enemy line. When Cumby had finished, Cooke asked if he understood the admiral's instructions, and Cumby told him that they were so distinct and explicit that it was quite impossible that they could be misunderstood. Cooke wanted Cumby to know what his orders were should he be 'bowl'd out', when Cumby replied, 'On this I observed that it was very possible that the same shot which disposed of him might have an equally tranquilizing effect on me and under that idea I submitted to him the expediency of the Master (as being the only other officer who in such case would remain on the Quarterdeck) being also apprised of the Admiral's instructions.' Cooke agreed and Overton was summoned so that he also could read Nelson's memorandum.

Bellerophon was fifth into battle in Collingwood's lee division. Cooke wanted to hold his fire until she was passing through the line, but relented when she came under sustained, accurate fire. At 12.30 she passed close under the Spanish *Monarca* (74) raking her with a murderous broadside which temporarily silenced the Spaniard and then she crashed into the French *Aigle* (74). On board were 150 soldiers who from her bulwarks and tops sniped at *Bellerophon's* officers. In an episode similar to that in *Victory*, Cumby advised Cooke to remove his distinctive epaulettes, to which Cooke replied, 'It is now too late to take them off. I see my situation, but I will die like a man,' and he sent Cumby below to give directions to the gun crews.

Between decks Cumby heard the sound of fighting above him and rushed on deck to find the mortally wounded Overton, who told him of Cooke's death in hand-to-hand combat with a French boarding party and of his last words, 'Tell Lieutenant Cumby never to strike!' Cumby's presence changed the tide of battle; taking command, he withdrew his men from the poop deck and into the waist of the ship, where they were less exposed, and ordered the guns trained onto the French boarding parties. When a grenade landed at his feet he calmly extinguished it, and then he rushed *Aigle*, capturing her.

He was promoted to captain in 1806 and in the following year was appointed to *Dryad* (36) on the Irish station. From 1808 to 1811 he commanded *Polyphemus*, another Trafalgar veteran. He served in the squadron which blockaded and took San Domingo in 1809, when he was praised by the inhabitants for his courteous conduct towards them. From 1811 to 1815 he commanded *Hyperion* (32), in the Davis Strait protecting the whale fishery, on convoy duty in the Atlantic, and in the Channel.

Cumby later held a sinecure, command of the royal yacht *Royal Sovereign,* and was made a Companion of the Order of the Bath in 1831, but saw no other sea service. In 1837 he was appointed superintendent of Pembroke Dockyard but died in the same year.

PETER HORE

✧ DIGBY ✧

Henry Digby (1770–1842) was my great-great-great-grandfather, born into a family which produced naval officers and Protestant prelates for the church in Ireland and England over several centuries. Henry Digby is famous for three things: his success in winning prize-money, his role at the Battle of Trafalgar, and as the father of Jane Digby.

Henry went to sea in 1782 in *Vestal* (28) at the end of the American War, and he remained at sea through the peace which followed. The names of his captains are a roll call of the best and most blue-blooded officers in the Navy. At the start of the French wars he was a lieutenant in *Eurydice* (24), but it was his appointment as commander to the sloop *Incendiary* (16) on 10 August 1795 and subsequently to the *Aurora* (28) which made his fortune. In three years on the coasts of Holland, France, Spain, Portugal and the Azores, Henry captured forty-eight merchant ships and ten enemy frigates, corvettes and privateers. Henry paid his crew's prize-money in advance out of his own pocket, enabling him to recruit only the best men.

In 1798 he commanded *Levathian* (74), flagship of Commodore John Duckworth, at the recapture of Menorca, but in early 1799 he returned to the business he knew best in command of *Alcmene* (32). According to family legend, on

16 October 1799 Henry had a recurring dream in which he was urged to steer north; he acted on his dream and next morning found the British *Naiad* and *Ethalion* in pursuit of two Spanish frigates. Digby joined the chase and on the 18th they took *Thetis* (36) and *Santa Brígida* (36) both carrying fabulously rich cargoes – in *Santa Brígida* alone there was over one and half million dollars. It took sixty-three wagons to carry the riches from Plymouth to London.

An ordinary seaman's prize-money for this capture came to £182 or about ten years' pay. Digby's share was £40,731, but it was not won without a further fight, this time in court, and by proxy through their agents, between St Vincent and Nelson, who wanted his portion of the flag officer's share. Nelson won, but he was not grateful to Digby and was spiteful. However, in January 1801, Henry was sent to America in command of *Resistance* (36), thus missing the Battle of Copenhagen, but prize-taking had become a habit and he took several more prizes. On 30 November the French letter-of-marque *Elizabeth* was the last capture of the war before the Peace of Amiens.

Despite his success at sea, Henry had no experience of fleet action and little of fleet work, and in, June 1805 he had been ashore for three years and was not expecting another command. He was on horseback on his way to Bath when he saw he was being followed by another rider, and he reined in expecting to deal with a highwayman, but his pursuer was an Admiralty messenger with an order to commission *Africa* (64), which was then fitting out at Northfleet on the Thames.

Digby and *Africa* joined Nelson off Cadiz on 14 October, one of the last ships to do so. During the night before the battle, *Africa* lost touch with Nelson's fleet. Family history does not record the conversation on the quarterdeck of *Africa* when at first light on 21 October *Africa* was alone, almost becalmed, 8 or 9 leagues from Cape Trafalgar. At 6am (*Africa*'s ship's time seemed to have been set about half an hour ahead) Digby wore ship. At 8am he made out the Combined Fleet to the south and the British away to the southwest. At

Africa at Sea off the Streights Nov.r 1.st 1805

My Dear Uncle

I write merely to say I am well after having been closely engaged for six hours on the 21.st of October, I have not time to detail, being busy to the greatest degree. I have lost all my Masts in consequence of the Action, & my Ship is otherwise cut to pieces but sound in bottom, my killed & wounded 63 – & many of the latter I shall lose if I dont get into Port. Out of so many great Prizes, it has pleased God that the Elements should destroy most perhaps to lessen the Vanity of Man after so great a Victory, I will just give you a rough sketch of the lines going into action more minute it I shall

10am the Combined Fleet was 6 or 7 miles away, and at 10.53am *Africa* received her first rebuke from Nelson: signal number 307 'Make all sail with safety to the masts'. At 11.40am by *Africa*'s time, she opened fire on the Spanish ship *Neptuno*, at the head of the enemy line. At 12.00 Nelson made signal number 16 'Engage the enemy more closely' to *Africa* and at 12.15pm he made number 16 general to the fleet. For the next two hours, *Africa* ran down the enemy line, on the opposite tack, firing broadsides until at 1.30am she engaged *Santísima Trinidad*.

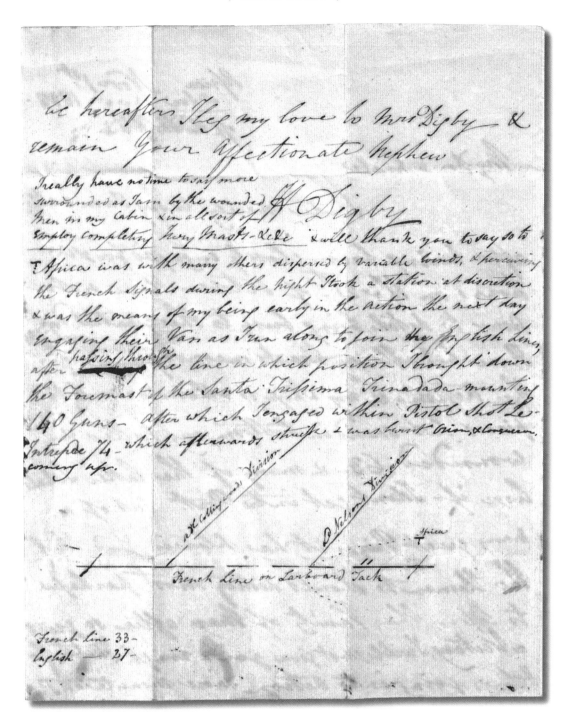

be hereafter I beg my love to Mrs Digby — &
remain Your Affectionate Nephew

I really have no time to say more
surrounded as I am by the wounded,
Men in my cabin & in all sort of
employ completing her Masts-&c &c

H. Digby

& will thank you to say so to

T. Africa was with many others dispersed by variable winds, & perceiving
the French Signals during the night I took a station at discretion
& was the means of my being early in the action the next day
engaging their Van as I run along to join the English Line,
after passing through the line in which position I brought down
the Foremast of the Santa Trissima Trinadada — mounting
140 Guns — after which I engaged within Pistol Shot Le
Intrepde 74 — which afterwards struck & was burnt Orion, & Conqueror,
coming up.

A. Collingwoods Division

D Nelsons Division

Africa

French Line on Larboard Tack

French line 33 —
English — 27 —

When *Santísima Trinidad's* masts went by the board and her guns fell silent at 1.50 Henry concluded that the four-decker had surrendered, and sent across his first lieutenant, John Smith. However, when Smith reached the quarterdeck and asked whether she had surrendered, in reply a Spanish

Digby's *Africa* lost touch with Nelson's fleet on the night before battle and he hurried to join the battle: his letter to his uncle written in his cabin, when surrounded by the wounded, is a poignant reminder of the battle, and contains a sense of urgency and of the desperation to control his damaged ship in the storm afterwards.

officer gestured to Dumanoir's squadron which had also worn and seemingly had pursued *Africa*. Smith as 'he had only a boat's crew with him quitted the Spanish ship (the crew of which, singularly enough, permitted him to do so), and returned on board the *Africa*'.

Despite *Africa* being one of the smallest ships in the British fleet she had acquitted herself well. Her bowsprit and lower masts would not stand, her yards, rigging and sails were cut to pieces, and she had several shot between wind and water; her casualties were high, eighteen killed, and thirty-seven wounded, but *Africa* had performed as gallant a part as any ship in the British line.

Henry's letter to his uncle is a poignant reminder of the battle:

I write merely to say that I am well after having been closely engaged for six hours … I have lost all my masts in consequence of the Action, & my ship is otherwise cut to pieces but sound in bottom, my killed and wounded 63 & many of the latter I shall loose if I don't get into Port but of so many great Prizes, it has pleased God that the Elements should destroy most perhaps to lessen the Vanity of Man after so great a Victory … I really have no time to say more surrounded as I am by the wounded men in my cabin and in all sort of employ completing jury masts etc … *Africa* was with many others dispersed by variable winds and

A book from Digby's library onboard, shivered by a shot knocking his bookcase to pieces.

perceiving the French signals during the night I took station at discretion and was the means of my being early in the action the next day engaging their van as I ran along to join the English Lines.

Henry was superseded in command in early 1806. He received the usual rewards for Trafalgar, but did not serve at sea again, though he lived long enough to be promoted admiral of the blue in 1842.

In 1806 he married the beautiful Lady Jane Elizabeth Coke, daughter of Thomas Coke, 1st Earl of Leicester, and in 1815 he inherited the family estate at Minterne Magna from his uncle, Admiral Robert Digby (1732–1815). Their daughter Jane Digby (1807–81) was also beautiful; she had everything: beauty, aristocratic connections, money, and, as revealed in her letters, poetry and intimate diaries, a highly original mind. Jane was an intrepid traveller, but her marriages and affairs scandalised Victorian society.

A twentieth-century scion of the Digby family was Pamela Harriman, who through marriage became an American citizen and was President Clinton's ambassador to Paris. When the New Trafalgar Dispatch stopped in Dorset in 2005, my father, the Lord Lieutenant of Dorset and 12th Baron Digby, wore the hundred-guinea sword presented by Lloyd's to Henry after the Battle of Trafalgar.

HENRY DIGBY

Digby's grave at St Andrew's, Minterne Magna, Dorset.

✦ DUFF ✦

George Duff (1764–1805) was my great-great-great-grandfather. I am called James Norwich Arbuthnot, the Norwich after his son who was also at Trafalgar; as a midshipman Norwich served in *Mars* (74), which was captained by his father, George Duff, who was known in the Navy as 'Worthy Duff'.

George Duff was born at Banff, a kinsman to the Earls of Fife and great-nephew of Admiral Robert Duff. When not yet a teenager he ran away to sea in a merchant ship, and at thirteen he joined Robert Duff who was commander-in-chief in the Mediterranean. Robert Duff assisted in the early stages of the Great Siege of Gibraltar, but when the government could not reinforce him he was recalled in 1780, though not before he had promoted sixteen-year-old George to lieutenant.

As a lieutenant in the newly built *Montagu* (74), Duff was present at most of the significant naval engagements of the next few years, including the Battle of Chesapeake in 1781 and the Battle of the Saintes in 1782. Notwithstanding that precocious start to his naval career, Duff justified the strong family 'interest' in him. By 1790 he was a commander and in 1793 a captain; his commands included *Martin* (16), *Duke* (90), *Resource* (28), *Glory* (98), *Ambuscade* (32), *Glenmore* (36),

Courageux (74) and *Vengeance* (74). It was sign of Duff's leadership that when there was an outbreak of ill-discipline in a squadron at Bantry Bay, which instead of being sent home at the beginning of the Peace of Amiens in 1801 was ordered to the West Indies, the good and fair discipline maintained by Duff ensured that no one from *Vengeance* joined the mutiny.

When the peace ended, Duff was given *Mars* (74), and thus in August 1805 she was one of just five ships, under Collingwood, watching more than five times that number of French and Spanish ships in Cadiz. When Nelson arrived in September 1805 to assume overall command, Duff was given command of the inshore squadron of four sail of the line, stationed midway between the frigates which cruised close to the harbour of Cadiz and the main fleet which kept out of sight.

So on 19 and 20 October, the *Mars* was busy transmitting signals from the frigates to the fleet about the movements of the French. On the morning of the 21st it became clear that the enemy fleet could not escape, and Captain Duff's ships were told to return and take their places in order of battle, *Mars*'s place being to lead the lee division of the fleet and to break the enemy's line.

Unfortunately the *Mars* was rather less worthy than her captain. She was exceedingly slow, and not very seaworthy. Duff ordered every stitch of canvas to be set, and told his gunners not to waste their fire as he would 'take care to lay them close enough to the enemy'.

Duff's monument in St Paul's, on the wall by the tomb of his chief, Nelson.

And indeed he did. They charged at the French fleet, but immediately after the first three British ships broke the enemy line, the wind dropped, so that they were isolated from the British fleet and surrounded by the French. Another Scot, Midshipman James Robinson, wrote:

It unfortunately became calm and left us three ships in the centre of the fleet. Judge of our situation, we engaged five ships at one time. Captain Duff walked about with steady fortitude and said, 'My God, what shall we do, here is a Spanish three-decker raking us ahead, a French one under the stern.' In a few minutes our poop was totally cleared, the quarterdeck and forecastle nearly the same, only the Boatswain and myself and three men left alive. It was then the gallant Captain fell. I saw him fall. His head and neck were taken entirely off his body, when the men heard it, they held his body up and gave three cheers to show they were not discouraged by it, and then returned to their guns. We fought two and a half hours without intermission, and when the smoke cleared away we found five ships had struck.

Duff had married his childhood sweetheart, Sophia Dirom, to whom he wrote every day while at sea. The approach to battle had been at walking pace and so there had been time for one last letter:

Dearest Sophia, I have just time to tell you we are going into Action with the Combined Fleet. I hope and trust in God that we shall all behave as becomes us, and that I may yet have the happiness of taking my beloved wife and children in my arms. Norwich is quite well and happy. I have, however, ordered him off the quarterdeck. Yours ever, and most truly, George

Norwich had indeed been sent off the quarterdeck. He was, after all, thirteen years and two and a half months old, one of the youngest officers at the battle. Afterwards he wrote his mother a famous letter, starting as follows:

My Dear Mama, – You cannot possibly imagine how unwilling I am to begin this melancholy letter. However as you must unavoidably hear of the fate of dear Papa, I write you these few

lines to request you to bear it as patiently as you can. He died like a hero, having gallantly led his ship into action, and his memory will ever be dear to his king and his country and his friends. It was about 15 minutes past 12 in the afternoon of 21st Oct: when the engagement began; it was not finished till five. Many a brave hero sacrificed his life upon that occasion to his king and his country. You will hear that Lord Viscount Nelson was wounded in the commencement of the engagement and only survived long enough to learn that the victory was ours, 'then,' said that brave hero, 'I die happy since I die victorious,' and in a few minutes expired.

What a remarkable letter. And for him to have written it at the age of thirteen, when his father had just been killed, must make one wonder whether our education system has improved since then. At least he too, like Nelson, ended up a Vice-Admiral. You will understand why I am proud to be called Norwich and to be descended from a naval family.

Captain Duff's memorial is next to Nelson's in St Paul's.

JAMES ARBUTHNOT

→ DUNDAS ←

Thomas Dundas (1765–1841) entered the Navy on 23 May 1778 as a captain's servant in *Suffolk* (74) and was quickly made midshipman. In 1778 he met Nelson, who reported that 'he keep the fourth watch' and 'he agrees tolerably well', and in 1779 Nelson clearly admired Dundas for leading a storming party of seamen and marines from *Lowestoffe* at the taking of the fortress of Saint Fernando de Omoa in Honduras.

Dundas was not, however, examined for lieutenant until 1788 and not commissioned until 1793; however, just two years later he was a commander. His commands, 1795–98, of *Weazle* and the sloop *Merlin* in the North Sea and Bristol Channel were apparently uneventful. Promoted to post-captain in 1798 he was given the captured French *Prompte* (20), and in the West Indies in 1799 he captured and burnt a Spanish frigate. His next command was *Solebay* (32) but he hardly had time to make his mark when the Peace of Amiens was declared.

Nevertheless, in 1804, propelled by little more than his name and his relationship to the Dundas dynasty, he was given command of *Naiad* (38). He made a number of captures, including a Spanish ship carrying some 200,000 dollars and the French privateers *Fanny* (16) and *Superbe*. In 1805 *Naiad* patrolled the Portuguese and Spanish coast and reported the flight southward of the Combined Fleet, and she was one of the repeating frigates at the Battle of Trafalgar. Afterwards Dundas towed the battered *Belleisle* to Gibraltar; there is a dramatic description of this, and the highly skilled seamanship which Dundas displayed, in Tim Clayton and Phil Craig's *Trafalgar: The Men, the Battle, the Storm* (2004).

After Trafalgar Dundas commanded *Africa* (64), *Vengeur* (74) and, postwar, *Bulwark* (76), and in 1825 he was promoted rear-admiral, but never flew his flag at sea. He is credited with inventing an incendiary shell for bombarding towns.

Vice-Admiral Sir Thomas Dundas died on 29 March 1841 in Reading, Berkshire.

NICK SLOPE

Dundas's tomb at St Nicholas Church, Hurst, near Reading, Berkshire.

➢ DURHAM ➣

Philip Charles Durham (1763–1845) was one of the last survivors of the *Royal George* disaster of 1782, and the first and the final captured tricolour flags of the Great War 1792–1815 were surrendered to his guns.

Descended on both sides from renowned Scottish historical figures, he was born at Largo, in Fife, in 1763, and was distantly related to Charles Middleton, later Lord Barham. In 1777 Durham joined his first ship *Trident* (64), commanded by fellow Scot John Elliot, bound for North America, but when the martinet Anthony Molloy assumed command and the ship's company grew restive, Durham returned to England in 1779, in order to rejoin Elliot in *Edgar* (74), and took part in the Moonlight Battle of Cape St Vincent.

In 1781, having been trained by Richard Kempenfelt in his innovative numeral signal code, Durham became acting lieutenant and signal officer in *Victory* (100). He was present at the rout off Ushant of the Comte de Guichen's Caribbean-bound squadron, and he followed Kempenfelt to *Royal George* (100). When, in August 1782, she

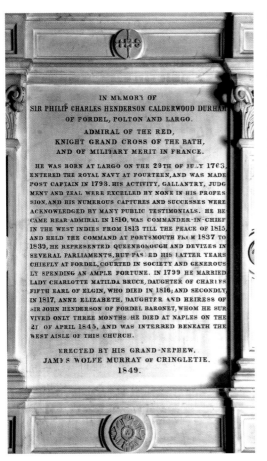

IN MEMORY OF
SIR PHILIP CHARLES HENDERSON CALDERWOOD DURHAM
OF FORDEL, POLTON AND LARGO.

ADMIRAL OF THE RED,
KNIGHT GRAND CROSS OF THE BATH,
AND OF MILITARY MERIT IN FRANCE.

HE WAS BORN AT LARGO ON THE 29TH OF JULY 1763,
ENTERED THE ROYAL NAVY AT FOURTEEN, AND WAS MADE
POST CAPTAIN IN 1793. HIS ACTIVITY, GALLANTRY, JUDG
MENT AND ZEAL WERE EXCELLED BY NONE IN HIS PROFES
SION, AND HIS NUMEROUS CAPTURES AND SUCCESSES WERE
ACKNOWLEDGED BY MANY PUBLIC TESTIMONIALS. HE BE
CAME REAR-ADMIRAL IN 1810, WAS COMMANDER-IN-CHIEF
IN THE WEST INDIES FROM 1813 TILL THE PEACE OF 1815,
AND HELD THE COMMAND AT PORTSMOUTH FROM 1837 TO
1839, HE REPRESENTED QUEENBOROUGH AND DEVIZES IN
SEVERAL PARLIAMENTS, BUT PASSED HIS LATTER YEARS
CHIEFLY AT FORDEL, COURTED IN SOCIETY AND GENEROUS
LY SPENDING AN AMPLE FORTUNE. IN 1799 HE MARRIED
LADY CHARLOTTE MATILDA BRUCE, DAUGHTER OF CHARLES
FIFTH EARL OF ELGIN, WHO DIED IN 1816; AND SECONDLY,
IN 1817, ANNE ELIZABETH, DAUGHTER AND HEIRESS OF
SIR JOHN HENDERSON OF FORDEL BARONET, WHOM HE SUR
VIVED ONLY THREE MONTHS. HE DIED AT NAPLES ON THE
21 OF APRIL 1845, AND WAS INTERRED BENEATH THE
WEST AISLE OF THIS CHURCH.

ERECTED BY HIS GRAND-NEPHEW,
JAMES WOLFE MURRAY OF CRINGLETIE.
1849.

Durham's fine monument records his many appointments and that he died at Naples but was buried at Largo, but omits to mention that he fought at Trafalgar.

capsized at Spithead with the loss of Kempenfelt and most of her company, Durham leapt overboard and was saved. Several historians, mindful that Acting Lieutenant Durham was officer of the watch at the time and mistaking him for the lieutenant who, according to survivor James Ingram's account, had brusquely ignored the carpenter's warnings of impending disaster, have unjustifiably blamed him for the tragedy.

The court-martial found none of the survivors culpable, and Durham joined *Union* (90), which sailed with Howe to the relief of Gibraltar and took part in the indecisive action off Cape Spartel on 20 October. In December she joined Admiral Hugh Pigot's West Indies squadron and Durham was commissioned lieutenant; in 1783

he became fourth lieutenant in *Raisonnable* (64). On the advent of peace he lived for some time in France, where he had expatriate Jacobite relatives, acquiring fluency in French. In 1786–9 he was third lieutenant in Commodore Elliot's *Salisbury* (50) on the Newfoundland station, where he became the boon companion of the future William IV, commanding *Pegasus* (28), and in 1790 during the Spanish Armament, second lieutenant in *Barfleur* (98), wearing the flag of his first patron, Elliot. In November 1790 he was made master and commander, taking *Daphne* (20) to the West Indies and returning in command of *Cygnet* (18), which upon arriving home with dispatches was paid off.

On the outbreak of war with France in 1793 Durham took command of the swift-sailing but under-armed, under-manned *Spitfire* (pierced for 20 guns) at Spithead, and on 14 February, the very day she weighed, made the first capture of the war, the French privateer *Afrique*. Several captures quickly followed. In March he received the first piece of plate awarded by the newly formed Committee for Encouraging the Capture of French Privateers, in June the Admiralty appointed him to *Narcissus* (20), and in October to *Hind* (28). In June 1794 he escorted 157 British merchantmen from the Gulf of Cadiz safely into the Downs, two other escorts, commanded by more experienced captains (one was Richard Grindall, who would command *Prince* at Trafalgar), having become separated off the Lizard.

That October, over the heads of sixteen hopefuls senior to him, an appreciative Admiralty gave him command of the new *rasée* frigate *Anson* (44), and in the six years in which he commanded her, he sealed his reputation as one of the Navy's ablest captains, as when, at the Battle of Tory Island on 12 October 1798, with his ship disabled and dismasted, he withstood the fire of five French frigates, one of which he captured six days later. Among those he impressed was Lady Charlotte Matilda Bruce, sister of the Earl of Elgin. A marriage notice in the *Edinburgh Magazine* stated: 'Captain Durham has realized about 50,000

l. by prize-money this war; a sum not greater than his courage and skill deserve.' This is about £5,000,000 in today's money. (Several thousand that he accrued when commanding *Spitfire* had been lent to his eldest brother, and lost when the bank into which the loan was repaid collapsed.)

Until the Peace of Amiens he commanded *Endymion* (44), receiving 400 guineas (about £45,000 in today's money) from the East India Company for safely escorting its fleet home from St Helena. In March 1803 he was appointed to *Windsor Castle* (98), but that June, shortly after the renewal of war, was transferred to *Defiance* (74). He fought under Sir Robert Calder at the Battle of Cape Finisterre on 22 July 1805, and was furious with Calder both for neglecting to give him the credit for having first sighted the enemy and for failing to re-engage on the day after the battle. Returning to Spithead with his damaged ship, Durham helped to stoke prejudice against Calder.

At a chance meeting in the Admiralty waiting room on 9 September, Nelson told him that he would like to have had him in his fleet had not the *Defiance* been under repair, at which Durham urged Nelson: 'Ask Lord Barham to place me under Your Lordship's orders and I will soon be ready.' When he did join Nelson off Cadiz on 7 October he refused a request from Calder, conveyed by Nelson, to return home with Calder to give evidence on the latter's behalf at the court-martial which Calder had felt compelled to request. Durham reminisced:

> I went on board Sir Robert Calder's flag-ship, and found there the Captains who were going home [William Brown of *Ajax* and William Lechmere of *Thunderer*]. Sir Robert presented me with a public letter, addressed to Lord Nelson, signed by the Captains, requesting permission to go home. I said, 'Sir Robert, I will neither sign the letter nor go home.' I then *ran* out of the cabin, got into my boat, and returned to my ship.

He endeared himself to Nelson by writing: 'I cannot volunteer quitting the Command of a Line of Battle Ship entrusted to me at so critical and momentous a period.' The next day Durham, Fremantle, Harvey and Durham's friend Pulteney Malcolm (who as part of Louis's squadron would miss the coming battle) dined together, when Fremantle considered Durham's refusal 'justified … under the present circumstances'. Codrington of *Orion*, however, noted acerbically that of all the captains at Calder's action only Durham was 'under obligations to Sir Robert' yet 'begged to decline leaving his ship *at so important* [Codrington's emphasis] a moment!' What those obligations were is unknown.

Although she was the fastest sailing ship of her class in the Navy, *Defiance*, hampered by lack of wind and her place towards the rear of Collingwood's lee column, did not get into action until 3pm, but still caused two of the enemy to strike, her struggle with *Aigle* being one of the most stirring episodes of the engagement. Her casualties were seventeen killed and fifty-three wounded. Durham was injured in the leg and side by a splinter: 'slightly' according to diagnosis and Collingwood's dispatch, yet nearly losing his leg and being troubled by the wound for years afterwards, according to the account in his own memoir.

At Portsmouth in late December, while *Defiance* was undergoing repairs, Durham testified at Calder's delayed court-martial, where the two men's contempt for each other was palpable.

As captain of *Renown* (74) from 1806 until July 1810, when he achieved flag-rank, he served under St Vincent in the Channel Fleet (1806–7) and Collingwood in the Mediterranean (1807–10). As a rear-admiral he commanded squadrons off Sweden in 1811, later that year off the Texel, and in 1812–13, off the Basque Roads. Durham's mercenary instincts led him during this last command to shift his flagship's position northwards, the better to pick off the enemy's coastal trade, until the Admiralty sharply ordered him back to his proper station. One of the ships captured was carrying the American consul to Tunis, Mordecai Noah, who dined with Durham and his officers and attended a play put on by the sailors, when he was startled to find a female part played by 'a real woman', an amused Durham explaining: 'We are compelled in a fleet to have a few women, to wash and mend, &c.' Durham also showed Noah 'a list of American vessels captured … the value of which … exceeded £800,000 sterling … he assured us … that his share of the prizes would not fall far short of £10,000 … and under such circumstances, I have no objection to the continuance of the war'.

As commander-in-chief in the Leeward Islands (1813–16), Durham collaborated with the Army in proceeding against Martinique and Guadeloupe, when they declared for Bonaparte following his escape from Elba. The fall of the fort near Basse Terre on 10 August 1815 under bombardment from Durham's flagship achieved the final surrender of the tricolour flag in the wars that had begun twenty-two years before.

His wife died in 1816, and when in 1817 he married the heiress Anne Isabella Henderson of Fordel, a cousin of 'sea wolf' Lord Cochrane, and 'the most valuable prize the gallant Admiral has yet obtained', he added Henderson to his names.

In 1817 Durham listed his total financial assets, including his 'Guadeloupe Prize-money' of an anticipated £5,000 and the estimated worth of his London house, but excluding income from annuities and half pay, as £53,359. Most of this sum (equivalent to £5,500,000 today) presumably derived from prize-money, quite an achievement for a younger son who as an unemployed lieutenant in 1790 had 'just money enough to get my dinner, and at this moment not even that'.

A gala function which he gave when commander-in-chief at Porstmouth on 21 October 1836 for every officer in the Portsmouth area who had served at Trafalgar brought so many together that a club was immediately formed, with him presiding at its inaugural dinner. In 1838 he chaired the banquet at the Royal Naval Club in New Bond Street in honour of Commodore Sir Charles Napier, the hero of Acre. He was instru-mental in founding in 1837 the Army and Navy Club and was its first naval president, and in 1844, to mark its move into new premises in St James's Square, he presented it with a full-length portrait of himself. He was on the committee which was responsible for the erection of Nelson's Column, and he assisted Sir Harris Nicolas in compiling his multi-volume *The Dispatches and Letters of Lord Nelson*.

Durham was an entertaining raconteur with a fund of tall tales (George III dubbed any improbable anecdote he heard 'a Durham'), and he shone in company, but he was avaricious, impatient, and prone to what one who knew him well described as 'caustic sarcasm'. Nevertheless, he was widely considered good-natured and pleasant, an admirer, Edinburgh publisher James Hogg, observing not long after Durham's death: 'All the qualities necessary for success in the profession he had adopted seem to have met in his person. Kind, generous, and open-hearted, he was the very *beau ideal* of the British sailor'.

In 1841 he might, but for rheumatism, have assumed the Mediterranean command. In 1843 he added Calderwood to his forenames on inheriting his maternal family estate from his brother.

Both Durham's marriages were childless. However, in 1790, Durham did father a girl, Ann, with Christian [*sic*] Dick of Largo, who was summoned before the kirk elders to be 'properly admonished', but Durham escaped such humiliation. Durham acknowledged his responsibility as far as educating and providing for Ann, but she was never welcomed into his social circle.

Admiral Sir Philip Charles Henderson Calderwood Durham died of bronchitis on 2 April 1845 in Naples, personal business having taken him to Italy after the death three months earlier of his second wife. The monument to his memory in Largo church mentions his naval career in glowing terms, but ironically forgets its proudest episode, Trafalgar.

HILARY L RUBINSTEIN

❧ GRINDALL ❧

Richard Grindall (1751–1820), who sailed on Cook's second voyage, was born on 19 April 1751 and baptised at St Sepulchre, London, the second of six sons of Rivers and Martha Grindall.

Grindall joined the Royal Navy as captain's servant to Henry St John in *Tartar* (28) in early 1763, following St John into *Garland* (20), based at Halifax, Nova Scotia; he spent nearly five years in her, firstly as an able seaman and then as a midshipman, before joining *Pearl* (32) for six months as an able seaman. Then, in November 1770, Grindall passed for lieutenant, though he would have to wait seven years before being promoted.

Meanwhile, he joined Cook's *Resolution* on 7 January 1772, still as an able seaman, though he messed with the midshipmen during the voyage. A fellow midshipman, John Elliott, described him as 'a Steady Clever young man'. At the end of the voyage in 1775 and to the great surprise of his messmates, Grindall climbed up outside Cook's coach taking him from Portsmouth to London. According to Elliott, 'The same day Captn Cook

ABOVE: Grindall's grave at St Nicholas, Wickham, Hants, before and after conservation.
BELOW: A rare family portrait of one of the Band of Brothers.

with Messrs Forster, Wales, Hodges, and my Mess-mate Grindal set out for London. The latter we now found (and not till now) had Married a very handsome young Lady, and left her, within an hour after, on our leaving England.'

Grindall had indeed married eighteen-year-old Latitia London on 27 March 1772, though what romance lies behind this story is not known. There seems to have been nothing disgraceful in it, be-cause when he was married again in 1779 to Kath-arine Festing, a Dorset vicar's daughter (and sister to another naval officer, Henry Festing), he was described as a widower, and one of their daughters was christened Catherine Latitia(h). Katharine, his second wife, came from a musical background, her grandfathers being Michael Christian Festing, a violinist virtuoso and composer; and Maurice Greene, a composer and organist.

In 1777 Grindall was appointed a lieutenant in *Egmont* (74, Captain John Elphinstone) and then moved to *Princess Royal* (98, Captain Wil-liam Blair) in 1778, the flagship of Vice-Admiral John Byron – another Pacific explorer and grand-father of the poet, but best known as 'Foul Weath-er Jack'. Grindall took part in the Battle of Gre-nada in 1779 when Commodore Samuel Hood made him commander and gave him the captured Spanish *St Vincent* (14) and in early 1783 he was made post-captain. Grindall commanded *Thalia* (36) from 1793, and on 20 February 1795 he cap-tured the French brig *Requin* off Dunkirk. He was wounded while in command of *Irresistible* (74) at the Battle of Groix in 1795, but recovered to take command the next year of *Carnatic* (74).

In quick succession, Grindall then commanded *Colossus, Russell* and *Ramillies* (74): there was trou-ble in *Ramillies* and in 1799 two of her seamen were tried for mutiny and one of them, George Gear, was hanged.

In 1801 Grindall took command of *Formida-ble* (90); she was part of a squadron at anchor in Bantry Bay in December that year when there was as serious and mutiny on board *Temeraire*. The sail-ors had heard the (accurate) rumour that though hostilities with France had been suspended, they

were about to be sent to the West Indies. Though *Temeraire* was in a state of mutiny for some ten days, the men of *Formidable* showed their loyalty to Grindall by writing to him, distancing themselves totally from the mutiny and any crimes committed.

Grindall's next ship was *Prince* (98), which he commanded at the Battle of Trafalgar in 1805. Though Nelson's order of sailing and of battle placed *Prince*, as one of the heavier ships, at the head of Collingwood's division, intended to punch through the enemy line, her bottom was so foul and she such a poor sailer that, unfortunately for Grindall's hopes of action, she did not open fire until two hours and fifty minutes after *Royal Sovereign*. By then the bat-tle was almost over. She did fire her massive broad-sides on the Spanish flagship *Principe de Asturias* and the already blazing French ship *Achille,* but was not attacked and suffered no damage or casualties. Grindall launched boats from his undamaged ship and rescued many struggling survivors from the wa-ter, including a number from *Achille*.

In the week of ferocious storms which followed the battle the sturdy *Prince* was invaluable, provid-ing replacement stores to more battered ships and towing others, saving some 350 men from the sink-ing *Santísima Trinidad* who would otherwise have drowned. After his laden ship arrived at Gibraltar, she was ready to sail again in a matter of hours.

Nevertheless, Lloyd's of London presented him with a sword and scabbard inscribed 'from the Patriotic Fund at Lloyd's to Rich.d Grindall Esq.r Cap.tn of HMS *Prince*, for his meritorious services in contributing to the signal victory obtained over the combined fleets of France and Spain off Cape Trafalgar on 21st October 1805'. He was promoted to rear-admiral on 9 November 1805, vice-admiral in 1810, and appointed Knight Commander of the Order of the Bath on 2 January 1815, but his active career was over.

His retirement was unhappy: two of his sons who had joined the Navy in their father's foot-steps, Edmund and Festing Horatio, died in 1811 and 1812 from unconnected illnesses. The latter had also been present at Trafalgar, as a midshipman in *Victory*. Grindall himself died at

Wickham in Hampshire on 23 May 1820, Katherine died in 1831, and the family are interred at St Nicholas Church, Wickham, Hampshire.

Matthew Flinders named features in Northern Territory, Australia, after Grindall, and George Vancouver named Grindall Point in Clarence Strait, Alaska, after Grindall. Grindall is also one of the real-life characters whom C S Forester used to authenticate his book *Hornblower and the Hotspur.*
JON ROBSON

→ **HARGOOD** ←

William Hargood (1762–1839) was born in Chatham on 6 May 1762, the son of Hezekiah Hargood, a naval purser.

His early patrons included Maurice Suckling and George Keith Elphinstone, but it seems that he did not serve at sea until 1775, when he joined *Romney* (50), flagship of Rear-Admiral Robert Duff off Newfoundland. Next he moved to *Bristol* (50), carrying the broad pennant of Sir Peter Parker and was present at the Battle of Sullivan's Island on 28 June 1776. He followed Parker to *Chatham* (50) and then back to *Bristol*, where he met Lieutenants Horatio Nelson and Cuthbert Collingwood in 1778. While Nelson left *Bristol* on promotion to master and commander of the sloop *Badger*, Hargood stayed with Parker until January 1780, when he was made lieutenant and given

Hargood, 'who served his sovereign and his country with zeal and fidelity for seventy years', has his monument in Bath Abbey.

command of the sloop *Port Royal* (18), which was involved in the unsuccessful defence of Pensacola. Under the terms of the British surrender to the Spanish in May 1781, Hargood was obliged to return home, via New York, and then was appointed to *Magnificent* (74) to join Rodney in the West Indies and at the Battle of the Saintes.

At the end of the American War, *Magnificent* returned home, whereupon Hargood was appointed to *Hebe* (38, Captain Edward Thornbrough), in which Prince William Henry (later King William IV) was a junior lieutenant. After Hargood had insisted that the Prince obey him when Hargood was in command of a ship's boat, the two young men formed a lifelong friendship. When in 1786 the Prince was given command of *Pegasus* (28), he asked for Hargood. The prince took him as his first lieutenant in *Andromeda* (32) in 1788, and when she was paid off in April 1789, Hargood became commander of the sloop *Swallow* (18). After a year on the coast of Ireland, he reached post rank on 22 November 1790.

During a period ashore, Hargood probably saved Prince William's life and his own, when they were aboard a wherry on the Thames and the Prince's high jinks were only got under control by Hargood's admonitions – an act for which the Prince, when sober, was grateful.

In April 1792 he took *Hyaena* (24) to the West Indies; Hargood became ill, probably from yellow fever, and was about to be sewn up for burial when signs of life were spotted. Off Cape Tiberon on 27

May 1793 he met the powerful French frigate *Concorde* (44), the advance ship of a French squadron consisting of two 74s and three or four frigates. Hargood put *Hyaena* before the wind in light airs but against a heavy head sea and was soon overhauled. As *Concorde* approached her on the quarter, *Hyaena* fired a few of her main deck guns, and then, without waiting to receive any fire in return, hauled down her colours. For a second time Hargood became a prisoner of war. He and his officers were landed on their parole at Cape François, Haiti, but when a rebellion broke out they fled for their lives by swimming to the *Concorde*, whose captain generously gave them passage to Jamaica. Hargood was honourably acquitted for the loss of *Hyaena* by the court-martial held at Plymouth in October 1793.

Hargood was given *Iris* (32) in April 1794, and then, in August 1796, *Leopard* (50). On 31 May 1797 when ships at Yarmouth joined the Mutiny at the Nore, Hargood went forward to speak to his men in the crowded peak, but when they cried 'No!' he ran aft to his cabin where he fainted. Hargood was forcibly landed at Yarmouth; subsequently his officers repossessed *Leopard* and sailed her into the Thames, despite fire from those ships still in mutiny. Hargood never resumed command, but was both prosecutor and a witness at the subsequent courts-martial.

Instead, on 12 July he was appointed to *Nassau* (64), which formed part of the North Sea Fleet under Duncan, but missed the Battle of Camperdown because *Nassau*, damaged in a storm, was in refit at Sheerness.

In February 1798 Hargood was appointed to *Intrepid* (64), and in April he sailed for China in charge of a convoy, afterwards joining Admiral Peter Rainier, commander-in-chief in the East Indies. There, while assembling a homeward-bound convoy, he found himself confronted by a squadron of four Spanish and two French ships; in boisterous weather Hargood trailed his wing, his enemies gave chase and when Hargood determined that they could not catch him, he turned back to rescue his convoy. Rainier was happy with Hargood and frequently hoisted his flag in *Intrepid* during her service in India and China un-

til, in urgent need of dockyard attention, she was sent home and paid off at Chatham in April 1803.

Hargood came under the command of Nelson on the blockade of Toulon, when in March 1804 he was given *Belleisle* (80), and, over a period of twenty-one months, *Belleisle* was only in harbour on one occasion, for three days collecting bullocks, fruit and onions from Naples. Hargood stayed under Nelson during that year and the next, taking part in the watch off Toulon throughout 1804, and in July and August, while Nelson watered his ships, he was trusted with the close blockade. In February 1805 he accompanied Nelson on his false cast to the east, and he was with Nelson on the chase to the West Indies and back between April and August 1805.

After a brief stay in Plymouth to refit, *Belleisle* joined the fleet off Cadiz on 10 October, in time for the Battle of Trafalgar. He was the next to enter the fight about fifteen minutes after Collingwood's *Royal Sovereign* (100). His orders were brief: 'Gentlemen, I have only to say that I shall pass under the stern of that ship [*Santa Ana*], put in two round shot and a grape, and mind not to fire until your gun[s] will bear with effect.' He had made the approach with his crew lying between the guns while he climbed onto a carronade to see better and to con his ship, 'Steady! Starboard a little, steady so!' He dismissed his first lieutenant's suggestion of a protective smoke-screen as a waste of powder, and even after he was knocked from his perch by a large splinter of wood, he continued to munch on grapes picked from the potted vines growing in his cabin.

Belleisle was one of the hardest-fought ships in the battle, becoming totally dismasted and suffering ninety-three wounded and thirty-three killed, but even when she lay like a log she continued to spit fire at any enemy within range.

It says much for his seamanship that a few months later, in February 1806, Hargood sailed for the West Indies in Sir Richard Strachan's squadron. When in August they were scattered by a hurricane south of Bermuda, Hargood sailed northward and, joined by *Bellona* (74) and *Melampus* (36), cruised off the mouth of the Chesapeake. There on 14 September he fell in with the French *Impétueux* (74) which was jury-rigged, having been dismasted in the same storm which had dispersed the French as well as the British. *Impétueux* ran herself ashore and Hargood took off her crew and burned her.

In 1808, in his next ship, *Northumberland* (74), Hargood joined the fleet at Lisbon whence Collingwood sent her into the Adriatic to co-operate with the Austrians.

Hargood was promoted rear-admiral in 1810 and hoisted his flag at Portsmouth as second-in-command. Shortly afterwards, in 1811, he married Maria Cocks, a banker's daughter, but they had no children; Admiral William Hargood (1801–88) was his nephew.

Admiral Sir William Hargood received the usual peacetime promotions and decorations. In addition, in 1831 his friend, now King William IV, with whom he had kept up a personal correspondence, made him a Knight Grand Cross of the Hanoverian Guelphic Order. He died at Bath on 11 September 1839.

PETER TURNER

→ HARVEY ←

Eliab Harvey's coffin lies in the crypt of St Andrew's, Hempstead, Essex, with many members of his family.

Eliab Harvey (1758–1830) was one of the more colourful of the Band of Brothers who, fortuitously for him, did not test Nelson's patience unduly, unlike others who crossed the admiral's path. However, the memory of the maverick Harvey is with the passage of time upstaged by his command of *Temeraire* (98), as recorded on canvas by J M W Turner. He combined success as a naval officer with a career in Parliament. Privately, his reckless gambling, extravagance and fiery temper were nearly his downfall.

Harvey was born on 5 December 1758 at Rolls Park, Chigwell, in Essex into what Marshall called 'an opulent family', the fourth, and only the second surviving, son of William Harvey and Emma Skynner. An earlier William Harvey, Eliab's great-great-uncle, was the discoverer of the circulation of the blood. Eliab's father died when the boy was five years old and he grew up on the family estate under the guardianship of his uncle, General Edward Harvey. He attended Westminster School for two years and then went on to Harrow School in 1770.

Whereas the names of many boys were placed on fighting ships' books, young Harvey's was first

Temeraire ended her days at the breaker's yard at Rotherhithe, where some of her timbers were used to make furniture for St Mary's Church.

entered on the books of the royal yacht *William and Mary*, but then on the books of *Orpheus* (32), as a protégé of Captain John MacBride (1735–1800). However, Harvey's first sea-going appointment was to *Lynx* (16) in the Leeward Islands. In 1775, at the outbreak of the American rebellion, Harvey transferred to *Eagle* (64), Lord Howe's flagship, and after a short spell in England, he returned to the North American station in 1776–8, and served in several ships, *Mermaid* (28), *Eagle*, *Liverpool* (28) and again *Mermaid*, until the last was wrecked in Jamaica Bay on the southern side of Long Island on 11 February 1778.

He was promoted to lieutenant on 25 February 1779 and appointed to *Resolution* (74) but did not join her. Maldon in Essex had been represented in Parliament by the Harveys since the Civil War, and on the death of his elder brother, Eliab Harvey took possession of a sizeable fortune and was elected to the House of Commons, a confirmed royalist and an old Tory.

With his new-found wealth he took to the flesh-pots of London and gambled with wild abandon. In a much told, and no doubt embellished, tale, in a high stakes game of hazard on his twenty-first birthday in 1779 he lost £100,000 in a single session to a Mr O'Byrne. The latter, realising the consequences for his opponent, refused to accept more than £10,000, with the request to roll the dice once more to decide who kept the remaining £90,000. Harvey won that bet, but seemingly failed to pay the £10,000 still due to O'Byrne.

Harvey was probably done a favour when the Admiralty appointed him in August 1781 to *Dolphin* (44), serving in the Downs station, albeit for only four months. He then transferred to the sloop *Fury* (16) at Spithead. Just as peace with France was agreed, he was promoted to commander on 24 March 1782 and entrusted with the newly built sloop *Otter* (14). In her he was employed in the North Sea until, at the behest of George III, he was promoted to captain a few months later on 20 January 1783. (Robert Nugent had lent the King's father large sums of money which were never returned; Nugent was ennobled and, it is alleged, his future son-in-law, Harvey, promoted as compensation.) Harvey completed his parliamentary term in 1784, the same year that he married Louisa Nugent; however, he was not employed on active service for another seven years.

In 1790 Harvey's career was resurrected by the Nootka Crisis and he commanded *Hussar* (28) for six months until tension subsided in October that year.

In 1793, at the outbreak of the French Revolutionary War, Harvey was recalled again and was made captain of the captured Spanish-built *Santa Margarita* (36) and sailed with her to the Leeward Islands. One of his master's mates was John Lapenotiere who would later distinguish himself by carrying the news of Trafalgar and of Nelson's death to London. Harvey served under Vice-Admiral Sir John Jervis at the capture of the French colonies of Martinique and Guadaloupe in the spring of 1794, and he later saw action in the squadron of Sir John Borlase Warren, which drove the French frigate *Félicité* and two corvettes ashore near the Penmarks off Brittany.

Early in 1796, Harvey left the Channel Fleet for the West Indies but, his health broken, he returned to England and was given command of the Sea Fencibles, the naval militia newly established as a defence against invasion, in his native Essex. However, in 1799, he was well enough to command *Triumph* (74) until the Peace of Amiens, when he returned to politics. Harvey represented Essex from 1802 to 1812, even while he was in command at sea.

He was appointed captain to his most famous command, *Temeraire*, after the breakdown of the Peace of Amiens. Before him there had been a mutiny by sea-worn men of whom four of the twelve found guilty were hanged in 1802, and Harvey commissioned her with a new crew. She is known now after Turner's 1838 painting as the *Fighting Temeraire* but her seamen called her the *Saucy Temeraire*.

Temeraire was stationed with the Channel Fleet on the blockade of French ports until the autumn of 1805, and Harvey had been her captain for fifteen months when he took his ship to join Vice-Admiral Nelson off Cadiz.

This was the overture of the Battle of Trafalgar in which Harvey greatly distinguished himself. At that time he had been a captain for twenty-two years, and in spite of being the most senior present, had seen little action. And so, the most documented of sea battles took place on 21 October 1805. The British fleet of twenty-seven ships bore down in two columns against the combined French and Spanish fleet of thirty-three, with Nelson leading one column and Vice-Admiral Collingwood leading the other. Nelson had been persuaded to let *Temeraire* go ahead of him, but it was a half-hearted decision, *Victory* did not give way and when *Temeraire* was close to her quarter, Nelson called across, 'I'll thank you Captain Harvey to keep your proper station which is astern of the *Victory*.' Harvey wrote that he had almost touched his admiral's ship.

Harvey noted that the Spanish four-decker *Santísima Trinidad* was the first to fire on *Victory*, but as the melee intensified, he wrote afterwards that locked in death-grips with his opponents, muzzles touching, and wreathed in gunsmoke, he was, 'So nearly engaged, that I can give you no other account of this part of the most glorious day's work.'

Victory and the French *Redoutable* became locked together, and it was possibly Harvey's arrival on the Frenchman's unengaged side which prevented *Redoutable* from boarding the British flagship. Nelson was killed by small-arms fire from *Redoutable*'s crosstrees, before her mizzen mast fell across *Temeraire* and Harvey's boarding party was able to take possession of her. However, *Redoutable* was so battered that she sank in the ensuing storm with the loss of thirty lives from Harvey's prize crew. The three ships drifted into the French *Fougueux* and she also struck to *Temeraire*. Again, Harvey had to forfeit his prize as the *Fougueux* was wrecked two days later.

Collingwood was later to single out Harvey's *Temeraire*: 'Nothing could be finer. I have not words in which I can sufficiently express my admiration of it.' The conclusion of the battle brought personal thanks from the British Parliament, promotion, a gold medal and a sword of honour which he declined for some unspecified reason. He was also honoured by being one of the four pall-bearers at Nelson's funeral.

Promotion to rear-admiral came on 9 November 1805, but Harvey's opinion of himself did not sit well with others. 'His head is turned,' wrote Captain Thomas Fremantle. 'Never having been in action before, he thinks every ship was subdued by him, and he wears us all to death with his incessant jargon.' Undeterred, Harvey took *Redoutable et Fougueux* as his personal motto, underscoring his boastfulness and further alienating him from the Band of Brothers.

In the following spring he hoisted his flag in *Tonnant* (80) in the Channel Fleet under Earl St Vincent, and later joined Lord Gambier for blockade duties off the Basque Roads, where a French fleet had been thwarted in its attempt to get to the West Indies. Harvey took leave for two months in April 1809, and on his return he found that preparations were under way to attack the French fleet with fireships and he had been passed over to lead the assault in favour of Captain Lord Cochrane. Harvey was so aggrieved that he went to the flagship, marched into Gambier's cabin and 'used vehement and insulting language to Gambier … shewn great disrespect to him … as commander-in-chief and treated him in a contemptuous manner', and he was then rude about Gambier on the flagship's quarterdeck. For this he was court-martialled and sentenced to be dismissed the service, but he had already resigned his commission. His behaviour was evidently in line with his reputation. 'His intemperate manner is such,' wrote Gambier, 'that, had I been told

Harvey's grand monument in the church, claiming that his *Temeraire* was selected by Lord Nelson to be his supporting ship, is accompanied by his hatchment showing his motto 'Redoutable et Fougueux', and has survived the collapse of the steeple, roof and chancel of St Andrew's.

the circumstances without a name being given, I should have supposed it to be Admiral Harvey.'

Harvey was, however, reinstated in the Navy with rank and seniority secured on 21 March 1810 'in consideration of his long and meritorious service', but never again hoisted his flag in command. He achieved further promotions and honours in peacetime, and served a third term in Parliament.

Admiral Sir Eliab Harvey died at his estate of Rolls Park and is buried in the family crypt at St Andrew's church at Hempstead in Essex which contains over fifty of his kin. His coffin is still in the crypt and can be viewed on request. On the church wall is a hatchment in his honour, originally placed shortly after his death and restored in 1958 after it was destroyed in the partial collapse of the church in 1884. His eldest soldier son was killed in action at the Siege of Burgos in 1812.

The crest of the Harvey Grammar School, Folkestone, was designed by Harvey himself and bears his motto as well as his ship's name *Temeraire*.

JOHN GWYTHER

⋋ HENNAH ⋌

William Hennah (1768–1832) is one of those who had greatness thrust upon him. At approximately the same moment that Lord Nelson received his fatal wound, Captain George Duff of *Mars* (74) was decapitated by a cannon ball fired from the French ship *Fougueux* and Hennah, as first lieutenant, assumed command.

He was the son of Rev. Richard Hennah, vicar of St Austell, Cornwall, and domestic chaplain to Viscount Falmouth. He was baptised on 7 January 1768, and the *Gentleman's Magazine* states briefly that he entered the Navy under Samuel Wallis who had circumnavigated the world in 1766–8. Closer research shows that he was entered in *Alderney* (10, Commander Philip Walsh) as a captain's servant on 1 November 1778, was rated midshipman on 27 December 1779, and passed for lieutenant on 3 January 1788. He was made lieutenant in 1793.

Many churchyards have been cleared and here at St Cuby's, Tregoney, Cornwall, Hennah's tombstone is propped up with others and its identity lost.

Little or nothing appears to be reported of his early career until 7 November 1800, when he first made a name for himself in command of a gallant boat action at Morbihan, in which the French corvette *Réloaise* was boarded and destroyed. The historian William James remarked, 'The enterprise thus entrusted to Lieutenant Hennah was conducted with great judgement and gallantry.'

On 19 October 1805 *Mars* was the first ship to hoist the signal '370' meaning 'the enemy's ships are coming out of port, or are getting under sail'. On the 21st, she sailed third in Collingwood's column between the *Belleisle* and *Tonnant*. Trying to find an opening in the enemy's line, she was fired upon by the French *Pluton*. To avoid a collision with the Spanish *Santa Ana*, *Mars* was obliged to turn her head to the wind, thus exposing her stern to the guns of another Spaniard, *Monarca*, and the French *Algésiras*, which punished her severely until *Tonnant* was able to come to her aid. *Mars* with difficulty paid off, only to be further punished by the broadsides of *Fougueux*, one of whose shots took off Duff's head.

Hennah fought *Mars* as well as he was able, given her damaged condition. Including her captain, a total of ninety-eight officers and men were killed or wounded in her and for his role Hennah received a lieutenant's share of the prize-money, a vase worth 100 guineas from Lloyd's Patriotic Fund (the naval gold medal was presented to Duff's widow), and on 1 January 1806 he was promoted captain but not employed again. He also received the unusual honour of a letter of commendation from the ship's company. In 1815 he was made a Companion of the Order of the Bath.

He married, but Marshall merely records that he had 'a large family' and at least three of his children were born in Tregony on the Roseland peninsula, Cornwall.

Captain William Hennah died at Tregony on 23 December 1832, when *The Times* in a short obituary, described him as 'one of the old school of British sailors, having entered the Navy under Wallis, the circumnavigator, and finished his active career in the wake of Collingwood at Trafalgar'.
ANTHONY CROSS

❖ HOPE ❖

George Hope (1767–1818) was not one of the inner circle of the Band of Brothers, but nevertheless enjoyed Lord Nelson's confidence and sincere friendship. A portrait of him by Charles Turner, now in the National Portrait Gallery, shows an earnest expression, and, in the way he clutches his telescope, a man devoted to duty.

Born in Edinburgh on 6 July 1767, he was the son of the Honourable Charles Hope-Vere,

by his third wife, Helen, the daughter of George Dunbar. His grandfather was Charles, 1st Earl of Hopetoun. He was related also to the Dundas family, a connection that would prove beneficial to his later career.

Young Hope entered the Navy at the age of thirteen on 8 March 1781 when he was rated captain's servant in *Iphigenia*. On 27 September 1782, he was promoted midshipman, gained his lieutenancy on 29 February 1788, and two years later, on 22 November, was made master and commander of the sloop *Racehorse*. He had done well to proceed so far so soon in peacetime.

At the outbreak of war with France in 1793, he was in command of *Bulldog* (16) in the Mediterranean, employed on convoy duty under the command of Vice-Admiral Lord Hood. On 13 September the same year, he was promoted captain and given the *Romulus* (36), serving under Vice-Sir William Hotham; he saw action against the French off Genoa in 1795.

In May 1798, Hope, in the frigate *Alcmene*, was sent by Lord St Vincent to join Nelson in the Mediterranean on his search for a French expeditionary force. Hearing that Nelson's flagship, *Vanguard*, had been badly damaged in a storm, Hope erroneously supposed that Nelson would make for Gibraltar for repairs and took his ship and the rest of Nelson's frigates there, thus depriving the admiral of his scouts at a critical point in the campaign. 'I thought he would have known me better,' Nelson said in frustration.

Hope continued to serve in the Mediterranean, firstly off Alexandria, where he chased and captured the French gunboat *Légère* and seized dispatches intended for Bonaparte, despite a French officer attempting to jettison them. Then he served with Nelson again during the civil war in Naples in 1798–9 when he helped to evacuate the King and Queen of Naples and their entourage from Naples to Palermo. Later, in August 1799, he received a letter from Nelson:

I have his Sicilian Majesty's orders to present you in his name a Diamond Ring, as the dispatch states it, 'To Captain Hope, who embarked his Majesty and the Prince Royal in his barge, on the night of December 21st 1798,' and which his Majesty desires may be accepted by Captain Hope, as a mark of his Royal gratitude. Ever yours, my dear Hope, faithfully and affectionately, Nelson.

In 1801, he commanded *Leda* (38) in the Egyptian campaign and continued in active service – so much so that shortly before Trafalgar, it was reported that he had been at home only fourteen months in the previous eight years.

However, in 1803 he married his cousin, Jemina Johnstone, a daughter of the 3rd Earl of Hopetoun, when he added Johnstone to his name: their son was Admiral of the Fleet Sir James Hope (1808–81).

At Trafalgar, *Defence* sailed at the rear of Collingwood's column, and thus was unable to engage the enemy closely until nearly two and a half hours after firing had commenced. Then, for nearly half an hour, she engaged the French *Berwick*. As that ship pulled away from the *Defence*, only to be attacked by the British *Achilles*, Hope turned his attention to joining the *Revenge* in pounding the Spanish *San Ildefonso* into submission. The *Defence* had thirty-six killed and wounded, and, by comparison with other British ships, suffered relatively minor damage. Hope managed to anchor with his prize and weathered the gale that ensued; as a result, *San Ildefonso* was one of the few trophies to survive both battle and storm. For the part he played, Hope received the naval gold medal, the thanks of Parliament, and a sword of honour from the Lloyd's Patriotic Fund.

After Trafalgar, he served in the fleet in the Baltic under Sir James Saumarez. He was made rear-admiral in 1811, and in 1812–13 he was sent to bring the Russian fleet to England during the French invasion of that country. He was a member of the Board of Admiralty 1813–18 and was knighted in 1815.

He was married a second time in 1814, to Georgiana Kinnaird, daughter of a Scottish baron.

Rear-Admiral Sir George Johnstone Hope died in the Admiralty on 2 May 1818 and was buried at Westminster.

ANTHONY CROSS

→ KING ←

Richard King (1774–1834) was the only son of Admiral Sir Richard King, an exceptionally active and lucky officer who had founded his family's wealth by capturing a richly laden Spanish galleon in 1762, and was created a baronet in 1784 for his success as second-in-command to Admiral Sir Edward Hughes in the campaign to end French influence in India. The older King married Susannah Margaretta, daughter of William Coker, a landowner at Mappowder, Dorset, and young Richard was born on 28 November 1774.

Aged six, young King was entered on the ship's books of *Exeter*; more than likely he did not go to sea until 1788 when *Crown* (64) sailed for the East Indies, under Commodore (afterwards Sir William) Cornwallis, making King the third generation of his family whose fortunes were linked to the success of the British in India. Cornwallis promoted King to lieutenant in 1791 and in just three years to post-captain aged twenty. These promotions were confirmed by the Admiralty and in November 1794 King was given command of *Aurora* (28) in the North Sea, and in the summer of 1795 of *Druid* (32), which was employed escorting trade to and from Portugal, and then *Sirius* (36). He carried out another duty in June 1797: he was one of thirteen officers of the court-martial convened off Greenhithe which tried Seaman

King died of cholera at Sheerness, but his second wife and all twelve of his children survived him.

Richard Parker and condemned him to be hanged for his part in the Nore Mutiny.

In October 1798 *Sirius* was off the Texel when she captured two Dutch ships, the corvette *Waakzamheid* (26) and the frigate *Furie* (36) with nearly 300 French troops on board. Success came again in July 1800 when he captured *La Favorie* of six guns off the coast of France followed by a Spanish brig; both were loaded with merchandise. Then, on 27 January 1801, after a two-day chase, *Sirius* and *Oiseau* (36) took *La Dédaigneuse* (36) which was carrying dispatches and 300 men from Cayenne to Rochefort. In his report Captain Samuel Hood Linzee of *Oiseau* expressed his gratitude for the firepower provided by King.

In November 1803 Richard King married Sarah Anne, the only daughter of Rear-Admiral Sir John Duckworth, and it was Duckworth who used his influence and his friendship with Nelson

to have King appointed to command *Achille* (74) and to join Nelson's fleet off Cadiz later that year.

So, on 21 October 1805, King and his ship were sixth in Collingwood's column. *Achille* first duelled with the Spanish *Montanes* (74), but then King sailed to the assistance of *Belleisle* (74), which was under fire from several enemy ships. Later, however, he was obliged to engage the Spanish *Argonauta* (80) and in a fierce encounter both ships were heavily damaged. After an hour, the Spanish ship broke off the fight and thwarted King's attempt to assemble a boarding party. As *Achille* tried to follow, she was prevented by two French ships, her namesake *Achille* (74) which passed on one side, and *Berwick* (74) on the other. King now engaged *Berwick* in a further hour of intense firing which ended with *Berwick* striking her colours after her captain had been killed. In spite of such murderous activity, King, whose ship had barely any superstructure remaining, reported only thirteen killed and fifty-nine wounded amongst his spent crew. King received the naval gold medal and a sword of honour from the Lloyd's Patriotic Fund.

King remained in command of *Achille* and in 1806 fought under Commodore Samuel Hood when he captured four French frigates off Rochefort.

In November 1806 King succeeded to the baronetcy but remained in *Achille*. He took part in the blockade of Ferrol in 1807, the attempt on Walcheren in 1809, and the defence of Cadiz in 1810–11, before being sent to the Mediterranean in February 1811 as captain of the fleet to Admiral Sir Charles Cotton.

King was promoted to rear-admiral on 12 August 1812. For the rest of the war he flew his flag in *San Josef* (112) and was off Toulon as second-in-command to Sir Edward Pellew.

Further honours and promotion accrued and he was commander-in-chief on the East India station, from 1816 to 1821, where in 1819 Sarah, his first wife, died onboard his flagship, *Minden* (74). His command stretched to the Red Sea and in 1820 he sent a small squadron to Mocha in south-west Yemen to seek redress for injuries in-flicted on British subjects by a local potentate, the Iman of Sanaa.

King's second marriage was to Maria Susanna on 14 May 1822, the daughter of his old friend Admiral Sir Charles Cotton. Most of his thirteen offspring married or became naval officers, includ-ing his second son, whom he burdened with the name George St Vincent Duckworth King, but who lived up to expectations by coming a full ad-miral in the Victorian Navy.

Vice-Admiral Sir Richard King, 2nd Baronet, was appointed commander-in-chief at the Nore in 1833, but died of cholera on 5 August 1834 at Admiralty House, Sheerness, and was buried nearby. The baronetcy became extinct in 1972.
JOHN GWYTHER

❖ LAFOREY ❖

Francis Laforey (1767–1835), my ancestor, was born into a family of Huguenot émigrés, aristo-crats, and military officers. It was a family of ac-complishment, courage and loyalty. Laforey's life was the epitome of these virtues.

Louis Laforey, formerly La Forêt, was Francis Laforey's great-grandfather, an ordained Hugue-not minister, originally from Poitou, who came to England with William III in the 1690s. Lafo-rey's grandfather was John Laforey, a governor of Pendennis Castle, protecting Carrick Roads and the Falmouth anchorage. Mary Clayton was his grandmother; her father was Lieutenant-General Sir Jasper Clayton of Clayton Hall, Yorkshire. One of Francis's uncles, a soldier also named Francis, died at the Siege of Pondicherry, in 1748, and an-other uncle, Loftus, was a lieutenant in the Navy.

Francis Laforey's father was Admiral Sir John Laforey (1729–96), who in 1758 led a division of boats and 300 men at Louisbourg, which succeed-ed in destroying the French *Prudent* (74) and help-ing to capture *Bienfaisant* (64), the only instance of a ship of the line being cut out of a harbour by boats, and in 1759 he was at the taking of Quebec. John Laforey was naval commissioner at Antigua

in 1779 and naval commissioner at Plymouth in 1783, when he was repeatedly passed over for promotion on the grounds that he had accepted a civil office; more probably his support of Ad-miral Augustus Keppel at his trial after the Battle of Ushant and his dealings with Admiral George Rodney over the purchase of naval stores during the American Revolutionary War had made him political enemies. John Laforey appealed and was eventually promoted rear-admiral in 1789, taking rank according to his seniority as post-captain. He was created a baronet in 1789 and returned to the West Indies as commander-in-chief on the Lee-ward Islands station until his death in 1796.

In 1763 John Laforey married Eleanor Farley, daughter of Lieutenant-Colonel Francis Farley of the Royal Artillery, who was a major landowner, a judge and a member of the Council of Antigua. Francis Laforey was born on the last day of 1767 in the colony of Virginia, while his father was there on personal business. At the age of eight and a half Francis was entered on the ship's books as a captain's servant in *Amazon* (32), and at nine and a half he was rated midshipman in his father's ship, *Ocean* (90). Whether he ever served at sea in these years is not known but unlikely. Certainly, in 1779 Francis went up to Trinity College, Cambridge, and graduated in 1784.

Next he was entered as a midshipman in *Car-natic* (74), where his father made him a lieutenant in 1789, and at age twenty-one gave him his first command, the sloop *Fairy* (16). When in 1793

St Nicholas church, Brighton, where Sir Francis Laforey, KCB, 2nd Baronet of Whitby, Devon is buried in the northern extension: his tombstone is laid flat.

news reached the Leeward Islands of war with France, Sir John Laforey immediately undertook an expedition with Francis and 500 British troops, to capture the sugar-rich island of Tobago. Young Laforey was sent to England with his father's dispatches and as a reward he was made captain.

In *Carysfort* (28) in 1794 he captured the frigate *Castor* (32), a British ship that had been taken three weeks previously by the French. When the Navy tried to establish the value of the prize as salvage, instead of as a warship, Laforey appealed and won his case, just as his father had won an appeal four years earlier. The *Castor* case established the important precedent that the prize-money for the recapture of a Royal Navy ship was 100 per cent of her value, not 12.5 per cent.

In 1795 Laforey was given command of *Aimable* (32) and took his father back to Antigua. Then sailing in *Scipio* (64), as second-in-command to his father, Laforey helped quell a slave rebellion in the Dutch Guiana Islands. In so doing, he captured three more islands for Britain: Demerara, Berbice and Essequibo. When Sir John succumbed to yellow fever on 14 June 1796, while returning to England on his son's ship *Majestic*, Francis Laforey became the 2nd Baronet of Whitby, Devon.

Laforey was subsequently appointed to *Hydra* (38) and when, on 31 May 1798 off Le Havre, he drove ashore *Confiante* (36) he became one of only three British frigate captains to be victorious twice in single-ship frigate versus frigate actions (the other two were Edward Pellew and Robert Barlow). *Hydra* then served in the West Indies 1798–1801. In 1801–2 Laforey commanded *Powerful* (74), which saw service in the Baltic, Mediterranean and the West Indies.

In March 1804 Laforey took command of *Spartiate* (74), a French ship taken at the Battle of the Nile, and set out for the West Indies. When Nelson himself arrived in the West Indies in June 1805 in search of the French fleet, *Spartiate* joined the pursuit. At Trafalgar, *Spartiate* was the last ship in Nelson's weather line; consequently, it was about 2.45pm before *Spartiate* and *Minotaur* came into action. The two ships bore down on the five ships of the van squadron of Admiral Dumanoir. Being aware these five ships could very effectively counter-attack the *Victory* and *Temeraire,* (both of which were heavily damaged and almost helpless), Laforey asked Captain Mansfield of *Minotaur* (who was his senior) for permission to pass because the *Spartiate* was the faster ship.

Laforey then led the *Spartiate* and *Minotaur* across Dumanoir's bow. Though significantly outnumbered and outgunned, neither of the two British ships flinched. They passed the French *Formidable* at pistol-shot range, firing broadsides into her bow, and then engaged all four of the other ships.

Such was the rate of fire from the two British ships that *Formidable* turned and fled, taking with her the three French ships and leaving the Spanish *Neptuno* (84), which fought valiantly but struck her colours after an hour, with thirty-eight killed and thirty-five wounded. *Spartiate*'s losses were three killed and twenty wounded. The two British captains, Laforey and Mansfield, had shown initiative, independent decision-making, courage, aggressiveness and an understanding of strategy: qualities that were the epitome of what Nelson expected and spoke of in his Battle Memorandum.

Following Trafalgar, Laforey returned to England for Nelson's funeral, where he was one of six Trafalgar captains present. Laforey was the bearer of the standard in the first funeral barge and walked behind the coffin with the standard.

Laforey retained command of *Spartiate* until 1810; most notably in 1809 he covered the landing of British troops who successfully returned the Neapolitan Islands to the Two Sicilies. In 1810–14 Laforey followed his father as commander-in-chief, Leeward Islands, and in March 1813 he was present for the commemoration ceremony of the statue of Lord Nelson in Trafalgar Square, Barbados.

Laforey retired from active service in 1814, and lived in Brighton until his death in 1835. In his will he left £2,000 to Statira Milton, neé Statira Laforey Beckles, my great-great-grandmother. She was born in Barbados on 19 August 1800. According to family history, she was Sir Francis's natural daughter, whom he brought to England with him when he left the island.

Admiral Sir Francis Laforey lived a life that honoured his ancestral heritage and was befitting of his profession. He demonstrated remarkable courage in the performance of his duties while remaining true to the family motto of 'Loyal until death'.

ROB COVERT

→ LAPENOTIERE ←

John Richards Lapenotiere (1770–1834) was born at Ilfracombe in Devon, the descendant of a family who had followed William of Orange to Britain.

Aged fifteen, he was one of 'several young gentlemen' from Christ's Hospital who, having 'evinced an inclination to engage in a seafaring life, were put under Mr Portlock's care, for the purpose of being initiated in the knowledge of a profession which requires length of experience, rather than supereminence of genius'. Nathaniel Portlock was about to set off in the merchant ship *King George* on a commercial expedition to the Pacific.

Between 1785 and 1788 Portlock visited the Sandwich Islands, the north-west coast of America, and China. Lapenotiere served 1788–91

in home waters in *Scout* (14, Captain Charles Cobb), and *Magnificent* (74, Captain Richard Onslow). Meanwhile, William Bligh was preparing his second breadfruit expedition and his ship, *Providence*, was to be accompanied by *Assistance* commanded by Nathaniel Portlock, who invited Lapenotiere to join him, first as AB and then as midshipman.

In 1793 as master's mate, Lapenotiere joined *Santa Margarita* (36, Captain Eliab Harvey) in Admiral Sir John Jervis's squadron in the West Indies. While others distinguished themselves, there is no mention of Lapenotiere. Nevertheless, in April 1794 he was given brief command of *Berbice* (8).

In 1800 Lapenotiere was given command of *Joseph* (8), and:

> was several times engaged with the enemy, near Brest, and then employed in affording protection to the Mediterranean trade. On each of these occasions, his gallant conduct obtained him the high approbation of his commander-in-chief, Earl St Vincent and Sir James Saumarez: that of the Admiralty was also conveyed to him, in a flattering letter from the former officer.

Joseph was paid off in early 1802 and Lapenotiere, aged thirty-two, took command on 24 May 1802 of the schooner *Pickle*.

Pickle's original name was *Sting*, 'a clever fast sailing schooner of about 125 tons, coppered and in every respect suited to the Service', almost certainly built at Bermuda in 1799 and purchased in the West Indies in December 1800 for £2,500.

Pickle's complement was a microcosm of the British fleet. The youngest boy in her was fourteen and the oldest man, an Irishman who deserted before Trafalgar, aged forty. Most men were in their early twenties. A quarter of her crew were from two counties, Devon and Cornwall, another quarter from the rest of England, and a third quarter were Irish, and the remainder came from Scotland and Wales, Norway and America. In 1803 and 1804 there were two courts-martial for mutiny, but when *Magnificent* (74) sank after striking on

the Pierres Noires on 25 March 1804, the Pickles acquitted themselves well in the rescue of *Magnificent*'s crew.

In early 1805 *Pickle* was back in the Caribbean, where an American, George Almy of Newport, became her acting second master and pilot. Then, in July 1805 on passage from Plymouth to Gibraltar, *Pickle* got into a scrap with some Spanish gunboats. Collingwood, reading Lapenotiere's dispatch, thought he had acted with 'great spirit and propriety', but the Admiralty confined themselves to an expression of approbation.

Pickle had a grandstand view of Trafalgar but played no great part in the fighting. Of Nelson's famous signal, Almy noted in the log 'at ten the commander in chief made signal to prepare for action with a number of other signals'. Some years later Lapenotiere reminisced that when the French *Achille* blew up, *Pickle* rescued from the water two women and a hundred men. According to him:

one of the Women thus saved was floating on an oar, and perfectly naked, a seaman immediately pulled off his trowsers and gave them

The boats from *Pickle* and other ships rescued men and one woman from the water, as the French ship *Achille* burned. Leslie Arthur Wilcox (1904–1982) painted this picture of Jeanette, naked but for her earrings, which now hangs in Fortnum and Mason, Piccadilly.

to her: when she got on board the schooner, she immediately began to relate with much seeming pleasure, the number of men she had sent to the bottom, for endeavouring to take the oar from her; and she appeared as happy and contented as if nothing had happened, although her husband had fallen in the battle.

Where the tiny *Pickle* would have put so many prisoners is source of puzzlement.

On the morning of 27 October Collingwood gave his famous dispatch to Lapenotiere with orders for home and Almy noted 'at 12 wore and made sail to the NW & parted company with the commander in chief up main topmast set the gaff top sail'. *Pickle* reached Falmouth on 5 November, where 'At 9.45 Shortened sail and hove to & out Boat our Commander landed at Falmouth with his Dispatches.' In the next thirty-seven hours he rode the 266 miles to London where he announced his arrival with the words: 'Sir, we have won a great victory, but we have lost Lord Nelson.'

At last Lapenotiere was promoted commander, and the Patriotic Fund gave him a sword worth 100 guineas. He received his share of the prize-money and, after a bureaucratic struggle, a £500 reward as 'the bearer of dispatches of importance'.

In 1806–11 Lapenotiere commanded *Orestes* (16) in home waters, where he made a number of captures and was praised by his commander-in-chief, Admiral Sir Robert Calder, who wrote of one incident: 'This capture does very great credit to the captain, officers, and men of the *Orestes*, from the prompt and neat manner in which it has been effected, without any loss to his Majesty's service; and confirms the good opinion I have long since entertained of Captain Lapenotiere as an officer, whilst serving under my command at different times.'

Lapenotiere obtained post rank in 1811, but did not serve again at sea. He retired to live quietly in Cornwall with his wife, Mary Ann, daughter of the late Lieutenant John Graves, whom he had married in 1805. He died in 1834 following a fall from his horse.

PETER HORE

Lapenotiere is unique among the Band of Brothers in having died after a fall from his horse; his box-tomb, before conservation, sits on a slight rise in the graveyard of St Lalluwy's, Menheniott, Cornwall.

⇝ MANSFIELD ⇜

Charles John Moore Mansfield (1760–1813) spent his early childhood in Plymouth dockyard where his father was Master Caulker and named his two youngest sons after heroes of the Seven Years War.

With two brothers working in the dockyard, and four others already in the Navy, Mansfield joined *Kent* (74, Captain Charles Feilding [*sic*]) in 1772, rated as captain's servant. For much of the next three years, *Kent* was moored in the Hamoaze below Mansfield's home in the officers' terrace above the dockyard, although how much time he spent on board and not ashore in school is not clear.

In 1775 Feilding was superseded by Captain John Jervis, whom Mansfield briefly followed into *Foudroyant* (80). Next year he rejoined Feilding in *Diamond* (32) and was soon in action against the American rebels; here Mansfield formed two lasting friendships with fellow midshipmen James Hawkins (later Admiral of the Fleet Sir James Hawkins Whitshed), and Seymour Finch, seventh son of the Earl of Aylesford, who would prove to be important in both Mansfield's private and professional lives.

Mansfield was promoted lieutenant just ten days after his eighteenth birthday, joining *Albion* (74, Captain George Bowyer) at Rhode Island as fifth lieutenant, and sailed for the West Indies. Next he transferred to *Sultan* (74, Captain Alan Gardner) and was at the Battle of Grenada in July 1779, when *Sultan* headed the first group of three British ships into action. Immediately astern was Admiral Samuel Barrington's flagship with Mansfield's younger brother Barrington on board. Unsupported for a considerable time, the leading British ships suffered heavy losses, *Sultan* also being fired on by her own side in the confusion. *Sultan* was again in action in Rear-Admiral Hyde Parker's action off Martinique in December.

In 1780 Mansfield became first lieutenant of the captured French frigate *Fortunée* (40, Captain Hugh Cloberry Christian) on the West Indies and North American station, but when he sailed for England in October 1780, after four years' absence, he was too late to see his father, who had just died.

Fortunée next joined Admiral Sir George Rodney in the West Indies, and then Admiral Samuel Hood's squadron at New York, and she was a repeating frigate at the Battle of the Chesapeake.

Mansfield saw action in Hood's skilful but unsuccessful attempt to relieve St Kitts. On 25 January 1782, Hood had occupied the anchorage at Basseterre Road in a brilliant manoeuvre, anchoring while engaged with the superior fleet of the French Admiral de Grasse. That night, Mansfield was sent on foot to gain communication with the garrison on Brimstone Hill, twelve miles up the coast, surrounded and under bombardment by French troops, and he returned with the garrison's assurance that they needed no help. Brimstone Hill eventually fell after holding out for a month, and Hood's fleet, unable to assist further, escaped during the night.

Mansfield served in *Fortunée* until September 1782, returning home as second lieutenant in the frigate *Southampton* (32), before being appointed first lieutenant in the former French privateer *Monsieur* (32), under Captain Seymour Finch, who had been his fellow midshipman in *Diamond*.

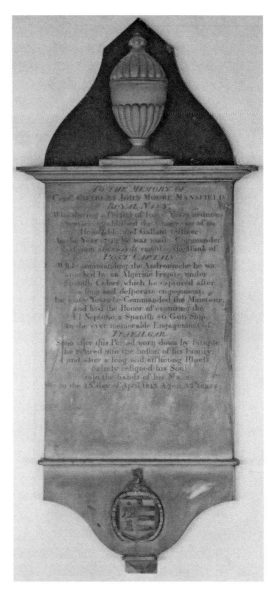

Mansfield's memorial at St Margaret's, Rochester, Kent, records his naval career in detail.

Unlike Nelson, Mansfield was employed throughout much of the peace following the end of the American War, but with little prospect of promotion. He joined *Irresistible* (74), a guard ship at Chatham, where, with little to keep men occupied, discipline was difficult to maintain, and Mansfield appears to have been harsh. Finding two men absent from duty, he ordered the boatswain's mates to start them with their canes, or according to an eyewitness, to 'give them a damned good hiding'. On their grumbling, he ordered it repeated and, after further complaint, had them put in irons, where they remained for three days. Despite this, they were soon given shore leave when they deserted, making a revenge attack on Mansfield during an evening ashore, beating him so severely that it was five weeks before he was back on his feet.

In March 1788, Mansfield was on half pay and very likely met his future wife, Anna Spong, on a visit to his friend Finch's family home at Aylesford, where Anna's brother lived on the opposite bank of the Medway. They set up home in Malling, Kent, but their idyll was broken by the Nootka Sound crisis, and Mansfield joined *Lion* (64) as first lieutenant, again under Finch, and sailed for the West Indies.

After serving briefly in *Assistance* (50), *Bonetta* (18), and *Stately* (64), and after nearly fifteen years as lieutenant, a new war finally brought Mansfield command of the fireship *Megaera* (14) in 1793. He was made post-captain on 4 October 1794, and was given first *Sphynx* (20), and then *Andromache* (32) in March 1795. When *Andromache* was caught by a hurricane en route to Newfoundland in July, and was dismasted and helplessly entangled in the wreckage, broadside-on to the mountainous seas, Mansfield and his people veered a cable to bring the ship head-to-sea and struggled through the night to cut clear the wreckage.

By the beginning of 1797, having joined John Jervis's Mediterranean fleet, Mansfield's *Andromache* consistently outsailed the other frigates of Lord Garlies's small squadron, and twice he took her into action unsupported. On 26 January he engaged a Spanish 74, suffering one man killed and four wounded before the squadron came up and Garlies ordered him to disengage. Five days later, *Andromache* again left the squadron far behind, chasing and engaging what Mansfield believed to be a Spanish frigate, but proved to be an Algerine corsair of twenty-four guns, which in turn took *Andromache* to be Portuguese. In the fierce forty-minute fight the Algerine made a desperate attempt to board, which was repelled in brutal hand-to-hand fighting. When Garlies came up,

the Algerine lay silently, having lost sixty-six men killed, and fifty wounded, while *Andromache*'s casualties were three killed and six wounded.

He was again in action on 5 November, driving off several gunboats while escorting a convoy into Gibraltar Bay, under fire from the forts and a Spanish frigate at Algeciras. On 1 May 1798, a gun burst, killing two men, including John Sykes, Nelson's former coxswain in *Theseus* who had saved the hero's life in the hand-to-hand fighting off Cadiz, and had been rewarded by being made *Andromache*'s gunner.

In February 1799, when Mansfield took command of *Dryad* (36), destined for the Irish station, one of his midshipmen described Mansfield's wife and two of their children living on board. Anna dressed eccentrically in trousers, epaulettes, a man's round hat and cockade, and had little authority over their unruly children, but was popular because, unlike other captain's wives, she did not interfere in the ship's business.

Mansfield was responsible in February 1801 for an incident which helped to push Sweden into the Armed Neutrality. Under orders to detain Swedish vessels, he met the warship *Ulla Fersen* (18) and her convoy. Despite being outgunned, the Swede refused to comply with Mansfield's orders, and only struck after a short but fierce engagement. She was released in Portsmouth following diplomatic negotiations.

In Cork, Mansfield had the rare opportunity of seeing his younger brother Barrington, now a lieutenant in command of a hospital ship, but Barrington died later that year. At the age of forty, Mansfield had now outlived all six of his brothers. A few months later he suffered still greater loss when his eldest son, Seymour, died aged twelve.

When the Peace of Amiens broke down, Mansfield was appointed to *Minotaur* (74), a veteran of Nelson's victory at the Nile. Having sailed to Plymouth with half her full complement, he sent a lieutenant to the receiving ship with orders to pick seamen by selecting those who were chewing tobacco, but on getting only pressed men cursed, 'Damn these fellows, they are all tailors, barbers, or grass-combers – I want seamen!' Nevertheless, by the end of May *Minotaur* was sufficiently well-manned and well-drilled to capture the French frigate *Franchise* and five merchant ships. The next two years saw arduous service on blockade duty as part of Cornwallis's Channel Fleet and then in March 1805, as part of Collingwood's blockade of Cadiz.

At the Battle of Trafalgar, *Minotaur* was tenth of the eleven ships in Nelson's weather column. Mansfield had pledged to his people to bring the ship into action as soon as possible and, 'Never to quit the ship I may get alongside of, till either she strikes, or sinks – or I sink,' but as the wind died, *Minotaur* with her fouled bottom logged only one knot and two hours after Nelson had broken the line, Mansfield was yet to engage. Then, recognising the threat from the enemy van led by Pierre Dumanoir, Mansfield changed course to head off these ships. While Nelson lay dying in *Victory*'s cockpit, *Minotaur* and *Spartiate* engaged the five fresh enemy ships within pistol shot, cutting off the Spanish *Neptuno* (80), which at 5pm, with the light fading and the wind increasing, struck to *Minotaur*.

After a month refitting at Gibraltar, *Minotaur* resumed her blockade duties. However, a third winter in the Atlantic took its toll on Mansfield's health. Home briefly a year later, he took the waters at Bath, while twice Collingwood wrote hoping that Mansfield would rejoin him in the Mediterranean. Instead, *Minotaur* and Mansfield were sent to the Baltic and took part in the Second Battle of Copenhagen.

Mansfield's health did not hold out, and in November 1807 he asked to be relieved. Briefly he served as a commissioner responsible for seamen's wages, but in January 1809 his failing health forced him to resign. Collingwood commiserated, writing shortly before his own death: 'I do not believe there is a man in the service, who has served in it more zealously, or more laboriously than you have done.'

Mansfield died aged fifty-two on 23 April 1813 and was buried at St Margaret's, Rochester, where his memorial can be found. He was then second on the captain's list, and would have been made

rear-admiral at the December round of promotions, but after thirty-five years of active service, interrupted by less than three years ashore, his death went almost unnoticed, recorded in *The Monthly Magazine* in no more than a dozen words: 'Died … at St. Margaret's Bank, Rochester, Captain Mansfield, of the Royal Navy.'

TONY BEALES

→ MOORSOM ←

Robert Moorsom (1760–1835) was my mother's great-great-grandfather. He was born in the busy seaport of Whitby, Yorkshire and his career was closely linked to another North Country family, the Phipps.

His father was a Whitby ship-owner and family lore says that Robert was apprenticed in one of his father's ships until, at the relatively old age of seventeen, he joined the expedition of a neighbour, Captain Constantine John Phipps (1744–92), to explore the North-East Passage, when he was rated AB in *Ardent* (64). He followed Phipps into *Courageux* (74) and served for five years as a midshipman and acting lieutenant, 1777–83.

Constantine Phipps combined his naval career with politics and was also a member of the Board of

This simple tablet in St Peter's, Cosgrave, Northants, commemorates Robert Moorsom.

TO THE MEMORY OF
SIR ROBERT MOORSOM, K.C.B.
ADMIRAL OF THE BLUE SQUADRON
OF THE FLEET;
WHO DIED 11ᵗʰ APRIL 1835,
IN HIS 75ᵗʰ YEAR.

Admiralty 1777–82, and it appears that his younger brother, Charles Phipps (1753–86), actually commanded *Courageux* for some months. However, Moorsom saw plenty of action. He took part in the First Battle of Ushant, 1778, when Constantine Phipps led the attack on the French *Ville de Paris* (90) – in the politically driven courts-martial which followed, Phipps, a Tory, gave evidence for his fellow North Countryman, Hugh Palliser. He also took part in the Affair of Feilding [*sic*] and Bylandt on New Year's Day 1779 (a dispute between the British and Dutch about stop-and-search), the capture of the French *Minerve* (32) in 1781, the Second Battle of Ushant at the end of 1781, the relief of Gibraltar in 1782, and the Battle of Cape Spartel against a Franco-Spanish fleet.

So when Moorsom was examined for lieutenant in 1784 he was older than most candidates, but unusually experienced and battle-hardened.

In 1787 he was given command of *Ariel* (16) and two years later sailed in Commodore William Cornwallis's expedition to the East Indies. At Tenerife, Cornwallis promoted him to commander, and in 1789–90 he conducted a survey of East India Company ports. However, during the capture of the Andaman Islands he fell ill and was invalided home.

In November 1790 he was made post-captain but held no appointment. However, in his three years of unemployment Moorsom married a neighbour's daughter, Eleanor Scarth of Stakesby, Whitby. Two of their three sons would join the Navy.

His commands in the French war were *Niger* (32), *Astraea* (32), *Hindostan* (64) and *Majestic* (74), before in April 1805 he took command of *Revenge* (74).

At Trafalgar some ships sailed better than others and in Collingwood's lee column something of a race developed. Moorsom wrote: 'All our ships were carrying studding sails and many bad sailors a long way astern, but little or no stop was made for them. Admiral Collingwood dashed directly down supported by such ships as could get up and went directly through their line. Lord Nelson the same and the rest as fast as they could.'

Moorsom's *Revenge* was tenth in the order of sailing when line-astern, but Collingwood's signal, number 42, 'Form the larboard line of bearing', had the effect of throwing *Revenge* closer to the enemy line. When Moorsom saw the signals 'Make more sail' from Collingwood and 'Engage the enemy more closely' from *Victory* he needed no further encouragement to sweep down on the enemy line and become one of the first ships to open fire. Moorsom described it thus:

I have seen several plans of the action but none to answer my ideas of it – indeed scarce any plan can be given; it was irregular & the ships got down as fast as they could, & into any space where they found the Enemy without attending to their place in the Line – A regular plan was laid down by Lord Nelson some time before the Action, but not acted upon; his great anxiety seemed to be to get to leeward of them, lest they should make off for Cadiz before we could get near.

Moorsom added: 'I am not certain that our plan of attack was the best, however it succeeded.'

Revenge was severely damaged and suffered twenty-eight men killed and fifty-one wounded, among then Moorsom, but by his account of the battle 'in about three hours they gave way'. This would have been 4pm. Elsewhere, the battle still raged until about 5.45pm. It was punctuated by the explosion of the French *Achille* which blew up with great loss of life. One of the survivors was a woman called Jeanette and Moorsom gave the only contemporary account of her:

> I must tell you an anecdote of a French woman the *Pickle* Schooner sent to me about Fifty people saved from the *Achille* which was burned & blew up amongst them was a young French woman about five and twenty & the wife of one of the Main Topmen when the *Achille* was burning she got out of the gun room Port & sat on the Rudder chains, till some melted lead ran down upon her, and forced her to strip & leap off; she swam to a spar where several men were, but one of them bit & kicked her till she was obliged to quit & get to another, which supported her till she was taken up by the *Pickle* & sent on board the *Revenge* amongst the men she was lucky enough to find her Husband – We were not wanting in civility to the lady; I ordered her two Pussers shirts to make a Petticoat & most of the officers found something to clothe her; in a few hours Jeanette was perfectly happy & hard at work making her Petticoats.

Constantine John Phipps had been Lord Mulgrave (in the Irish peerage) since 1775 and when he died in 1792 he was succeeded by another brother Henry Phipps (1755–1831). Notwithstanding Henry's career as a soldier in the West Indies during the American War and at the Siege of Toulon in 1793, he became First Lord of the Admiralty in 1807–10 and made Moorsom his private secretary. Then, in 1809, Moorsom himself became a member of the Board of Admiralty. When Mulgrave became Master-General of the Ordnance in 1810, Moorsom became his Surveyor-General of the Ordnance: they were both superseded when Wellington became Master-General of the Ordnance in 1820.

Admiral Sir Robert Moorsom retired to Cosgrove Priory, Northampton, where he died in 1835. There is stained glass in the church windows to commemorate his sons, who continued

their father's exploring tradition and became pioneers of the railway. One of Robert's grandsons, also an engineer and explorer, was killed at the relief of Lucknow in 1858 and his memorial is in Westminster Abbey.

Toby Young

✦ MORRIS ✦

James Nicoll Morris (1763–1830) was a thirteen-year-old midshipman when he saw his father John Morris killed in command of *Bristol* (50) during the unsuccessful attack on Sullivan's Island, Charlestown, in June 1776 during the War of American Independence. The dying Morris left his family to the providence of God and the generosity of his country: this amounted to a pension of £100 a year to his widow.

In 1778–9 young Morris was in *Prince of Wales* (90, Captain Benjamin Hill), flagship of Samuel Barrington, at the Battle of St Lucia in December 1778, and flagship of John Byron at the Battle of Grenada in July 1779, and was promoted lieutenant a year later.

He was a lieutenant in *Namur* (90, Captain Robert Devereux Fanshaw) at the Battle of the Saintes on 12 April 1782, and by 1792 he was commander of *Flirt* (14) in the West Indies. In 1793 on the Newfoundland station, now commanding the fireship *Pluto*, he took part in the capture of the French *Lutine* and in the same year he was promoted captain and given *Boston* (32), in which in 1797 he enjoyed a successful cruise in the chops of the Channel against French privateers.

Five years later, his frigate *Lively* (32) was lost on Rota Point, near Cadiz. No blame attached to him at court-martial and in his next ship, *Phaeton* (38), he conducted Lord Elgin, 'his lady, and numerous suite' to Constantinople as ambassador, and then entered the Adriatic to co-operate with the Austrians. Briefly he commanded *Leopard* (50), before taking *Colossus* (74). She was 'an excellent sailer', according to Collingwood, on the blockade of Brest and the watch off Cadiz. When Morris first assumed command, she was a sickly ship with an unpromising

The words of Morris's monument in All Saints' Church, Marlow, Buckinghamshire, do not make him sound very lovable.

to rear-admiral and third-in-command in the Baltic.

Vice-Admiral Sir James Nicoll Morris accrued the usual honours and died at Marlow on 15 April 1830. He had married in 1802 Margareta Sarah Cocks, sister-in-law to another of the Band of Brothers, William Hargood, and niece of Lord Somers. She wrote of him that his 'strict sense of honour rendered him universally respected and esteemed', and that he was 'distinguished in simplicity and singleness of heart for which he was remarkable'.

PETER WARWICK

✈ PELLEW ✦

Israel Pellew (1758–1832) was born in Dover, but everything else about him was Cornish. His father, Samuel, commander of a Post Office packet, hailed from Flushing on the Fal, and his mother was Constantia Langford of Penzance. When Samuel died and their mother remarried, the six Pellew siblings were brought up by their grandmother at Madron, and the boys sent to Truro Grammar School. The eldest son, also Samuel, combined the

After *Conqueror* had lost her figurehead in the Battle of Trafalgar, her ship's company insisted that a new one should be made and that it should be of the conqueror Nelson. This is the design paid for by Pellew.

crew, but by October 1805 he had transformed her into a formidable fighting vessel. She gave a good account of herself at Trafalgar, where she was the sixth ship in Collingwood's division.

Once engaged, Morris's ship suffered heavy fire from the French *Swiftsure* and *Argonaute*. The latter collided with *Colossus*, sandwiching her between the two enemy ships so that she endured furious and heavy punishment from their great guns. Even though the *Colossus*'s carronades were able to clear the enemy upper decks of men, *Argonaute*'s crew prepared to board and were only prevented when the two ships were driven apart by the swell.

Morris next engaged the Spanish *Bahama* and was able to bring down her mizzen mast, before being supported by Codrington in *Orion*. Thus, at the end of the battle, Morris was able to claim a share in the defeat of three enemy ships. However, the *Colossus* had suffered the highest casualties of all of the British ships: 40 killed and 160 wounded. Morris was among the wounded, hit in the knee. The pain was great, but he applied his own tourniquet to stop the bleeding and refused to leave the quarterdeck. Only at the close of the action did he faint from loss of blood and was finally carried below. He recovered in Gibraltar and subsequently received the thanks of Parliament, the naval gold medal and a vase from the Lloyd's Patriotic Fund for his part in the battle.

In 1810–11 Morris commanded *Formidable* (90) under James Saumarez and in 1812 was promoted

Plymouth lost many memorials and monuments in the Blitz during the Second World War, both at Stonehouse and here in the still ruined Charles Church.

Israel Pellew was unlucky in his commands. On 22 September 1796 *Amphion* was in the Hamoaze and on the eve of sailing. He was dining in his cabin with his first lieutenant and another captain and there were a large number of people on board, at least three hundred of both sexes. It may be assumed that there was relaxed discipline and a certain amount of licentiousness between decks. Pellew heard 'a kind of rumbling noise', an observer saw *Amphion* lift out of the water 'almost to her keel', the bows shattered, the 'masts shivered almost to pieces', bodies and wreckage 'were thrown as high as her main-top-gallant masthead', and the stern sank. Pellew, thrown by the explosion onto the deck of a hulk, was one of only forty survivors of this accident.

On another occasion, in an otherwise successful command of *Cleopatra* (32), she was swamped in a hurricane at night; the ship sank in the trough between two peaks, and when Pellew struggled on deck the taffrail and quarterdeck were underwater, the jib and spanker booms and several yards lost or sprung, and several ropes broken. Later *Cleopatra* struck on one of the outlying islands of the Bahamas and Pellew had to throw her guns and part of the ballast overboard before he could get her afloat. Then, in a thwarted attack on shipping in Cuba, he lost his first lieutenant and several men.

Nevertheless, when the Peace of Amiens broke down, he was appointed to the new *Conqueror* (74) in April 1804, succeeding Thomas Louis as her captain. In her, he joined Nelson in the Mediterranean in September 1804 and took part in every stage of the Trafalgar campaign, including the chase to the West Indies and back in the summer of 1805.

At Trafalgar *Conqueror* was fifth in Nelson's line and Pellew first positioned her off the *Bucentaure*'s quarter, forcing the already badly damaged French flagship to surrender. Not wishing to waste time with the formal ceremony, Pellew sent his captain of marines, James Atcherley, to receive Villeneuve's sword.

When Villeneuve asked who it was to whom he surrendered, Atcherley answered that it was Captain Pellew. 'It is a satisfaction to me that it is to so

duties of doctor of medicine in Mylor and customs officer at Falmouth; the next brother, Edward, became Admiral Lord Exmouth; Edward's twin sister, Katherine, married a Swedish count and was great-great-grandmother to Carl Gustaf Mannerheim, the liberator of Finland; a younger brother, James, was killed at the Battle of Saratoga in 1777; and there was a younger sister, Jane.

Israel Pellew went to sea in 1771. He became a lieutenant in 1779, and while in command of the *Resolution* cutter of twelve guns and seventy-five men, fought and captured in January 1783 a Dutch privateer, and was promoted commander in 1790. There was no ship for Israel and so he was serving with brother Edward in *Nymphe* (36) when she captured the French *Cleopatre* (32) in June 1793. It was the first single-ship action of the new war and the brothers were summoned to Windsor where the King knighted Edward and Israel was made post-captain.

fortunate an officer as Sir Edward Pellew that I have surrendered,' remarked the courteous Villeneuve. 'It is his brother, sir,' blurted an embarrassed Atcherley. 'His brother! What, are there two of them? Helas!' Atcherley requested the admiral to accompany him on board *Conqueror*, so as to surrender his sword in person. *Conqueror*, however, had made sail, and was then in close action with the Spanish four-decker, *Santísima Trinidad*, so Atcherley took his prisoner to *Mars*, where he delivered his sword to William Hennah who had succeeded George Duff in command. The sword was afterwards given to Collingwood, who kept it, much to the chagrin of Pellew, who considered that by the custom of the service it belonged to him. Meanwhile Pellew had moved to attack the French ship *Intrépide*; few other British warships were quite so busy off Trafalgar.

After the battle Pellew attempted to take *Bucentaure* in tow, putting a party of sailors on board under the command of Lieutenant Richard Spear, who was captured when in the storm which followed the Frenchman went ashore off Cadiz.

Pellew received the usual rewards for Trafalgar, as did his ship's company, and *Conqueror* received a new figurehead. The head of her old one had been shot away and the crew petitioned that it should be replaced with a bust of Nelson, which was duly done at Plymouth, paid for by Pellew and his officers. He continued in command of *Conqueror* until 1808, stationed off Cadiz and Lisbon.

He was promoted rear-admiral in 1810, and served in the Mediterranean as captain of the fleet to his brother Edward when he was commander-in-chief, but he did not serve at sea after 1816. He was knighted in 1815 and eventually reached full admiral in 1830. He was buried at Charles Church, Plymouth, in 1832.

Pellew married Mary Gilmore in 1792; their only son, Edward, was killed in a duel with a fellow officer in Paris in 1819.

Some 150 years later the Pellew brothers had the distinction of having two ships of the same class named after them at the same time, *Pellew* and *Exmouth*.

COLIN WHITE

❧ PILFOLD ❧

John Pilfold (1769–1834): my ancestor came from an extended family of yeoman farmers who worked land near Horsham in Sussex, but also at Effingham in Surrey and Donhead in Wiltshire. There has been a John Pilfold in the family since at least the sixteenth century.

What 'interest' or patronage the Pilfolds enjoyed in Nelson's Navy is unknown, but John's older brother Charles joined the Navy in about 1776, served with Nelson as a junior officer, and met Nelson again in New York in 1782 when

Pilfold's coat of arms, which he acquired to mark his ascent from seafarer to gentleman, carries his Trafalgar medal in the dexter field.

Nelson (already a captain) tried to use his influence to advance Charles. However, during the lull in warfare 1783–92, between the American and the French Revolutionary Wars, Charles joined the East India Company in 1787 and sailed on three voyages to the East, the third in 1791 in the East Indiaman *Ocean*. He died on 28 August 1792 in China.

Meanwhile, John also entered the Navy in 1780 and learned his trade under William Cornwallis in *Crown* (64). In 1788 Pilfold was promoted midshipman and accompanied Cornwallis to the East Indies, when Cornwallis was appointed

This mosaic was laid down in 2005 to mark the bicentenary of Trafalgar and to commemorate Pilfold as 'Horsham's Hornblower'.

commander-in-chief. It is not known if the brothers met in the East, but John returned home in May 1792 to find that his father had died.

James, a younger brother, had taken charge of the Pilfold lands and John decided to remain in the Navy, was made lieutenant in *Brunswick* (74) and fought at the Battle of the Glorious First of June in 1794. There Howe ordered his captains to pass through the French line, raking the enemy ships to port and starboard as they did so, but few of Howe's captains understood the order. One of those who did was John Harvey in *Brunswick*, but as he burst through the French line his anchor fouled *Vengeur du Peuple* (74). When *Brunswick*'s master asked if he should cut the anchor cable, Harvey replied, 'No, as we've got her, we'll keep her,' and a vicious fight ensued in which both ships suffered terrible casualties. There were 44 dead in *Brunswick* and 114 wounded, including Harvey, who lingered for a month before dying on 30 June.

Harvey was a popular figure and the memorial to him, and to Captain John Hutt, in Westminster was one of the first of many in the Great War 1792–1815. Pilfold, however, must have learned some valuable lessons which he would demonstrate at Trafalgar eleven years later. The dying Harvey had recommended Pilfold for his bravery and competence to Howe, and Howe took him into his flagship as a lieutenant, aged twenty-five.

John Pilfold next removed into *Russell* (74), which was heavily engaged on 23 June 1795 at the Battle of Groix, and he removed again into *Kingfisher* (18) as first lieutenant, making some money from prizes captured during operations off the Spanish and Portuguese coasts. When the crew of *Kingfisher* mutinied on 1 July 1797, her captain drew his sword and assisted by Pilfold, and supported by the other officers and the ship's marines, put an end to disobedience by killing or wounding several men.

In 1798 Pilfold returned to service in large ships when he removed into *Impétueux* (74), one of the prizes at the Glorious First of June, and he

gained some fame in 1800 when he led a raiding party into the Morbihan river to destroy French shipping. By now John was in a position to exercise his own patronage, which he did by taking his nephew to sea with him in *Impétueux*: William Grove became a ten-year-old first-class volunteer.

When he took his nephew home to Donhead during the Peace of Amiens, Pilfold courted and married in 1803 Mary Anne Horner South: she was a descendant of Thomas Horner of Mells in Somerset, allegedly the source of the nursery rhyme about 'Little Jack Horner'.

On the renewal of the war Pilfold soon found himself in *Ajax* (74), commanded by Captain William Brown. *Ajax* was heavily engaged at the Battle of Cape Finisterre on 22 July 1805, the strategic success which prevented the combined Franco-Spanish fleet from joining French ships waiting in western France, and tactically was a victory, in that Robert Calder's inferior fleet captured two of the enemy, but England wanted and expected an annihilation to end the possibility of invasion and 'John Bull' criticised Calder in the press.

After the battle *Ajax* and *Thunderer* (74, Captain William Lechmere) were sent to Plymouth for repairs throughout August. Nelson sailed from Portsmouth on 14 September and four days later off Plymouth made the signal for *Ajax* and *Thunderer* to join him. Nelson brought with him to Cadiz the British newspapers, and when Calder read what was being said about him asked to go home to be court-martialled. He also asked for Captains Brown, Lechmere and Durham as witnesses to his conduct at Cape Finisterre.

It says much about the manners of the time that Nelson allowed Calder to return home in the 98-gun *Prince of Wales*, a heavy ship which Nelson would have wanted for his tactic of breaking the line at the coming epic battle. It says more about Nelson and his confidence in the officers under his command that he left John Pilfold in command of *Ajax*.

Whatever patronage Pilfold had enjoyed as a youth, it was not strong and aged thirty-six he was a very experienced officer, but still only a lieutenant, and he had never held a command. Nevertheless, Nelson trusted him sufficiently, a trust which must have drawn as much upon Nelson's memory of brother Charles as it did upon Nelson's knowledge of John.

Pilfold left no memoir of the Battle of Trafalgar, but the master's log shows that at 12.18pm and at 12.32pm *Ajax* repeated the general signal number 16 for closer action, and at 1.12pm *Ajax* engaged the enemy 'firing from both sides as we broke through the line', about fifty minutes after *Victory* had led the way. At 3.26pm *Ajax* 'bore away a little to engage part of the enemy's van which was attempting to escape to leeward' and at 4pm 'a Spanish ship bearing a rear-admiral's flag struck. Kept up a raking fire on the enemy's ships running to leeward.' At 10pm *Ajax* took in tow the French *Intrépide* (74), and in the storm after the battle Pilfold was ordered to scuttle the Spanish *Argonauta* (80).

Pilfold returned home to rapturous praise in December 1805, and was promoted post-captain, but he was now a married man with young children and he did not seek active employment at sea. Pilfold assumed his ancestral role of farming; in 1808 he became a gentleman when he was granted a coat of arms, and in 1815 he was made a Companion of the Order of the Bath.

He also supported his nephew, the poet Percy Bysshe Shelley, during Shelley's elopement and in his unconventional lifestyle. John's literary connections included another poet, his cousin Thomas Medwin, who was Shelley's biographer and author of a memoir about Lord Byron – who was, of course, the grandson of an admiral, 'Foul Weather Jack' Byron.

In later life John seems to have mismanaged his finances. It was charity when in 1828 after more than twenty years' absence from the Navy, he received an appointment as captain of the ordinary, the reserve ships at Plymouth, where he suffered a stroke which left him 'quite childish', and he died in 1834. He was buried at the church of St George of Lydda, East Stonehouse, at the head of the then fashionable Durnford

street. The church was bombed in 1941 and postwar the monuments were broken up and the graves removed to Efford public cemetery, where nothing remains of a man who found his 'fifteen minutes of fame' at Trafalgar.

JOHN PILFOLD

➤ PROWSE ✦

William Prowse (1752/3–1826) commanded *Sirius* (36) during the Trafalgar campaign. On 19 October *Sirius* was the closest inshore ship to Cadiz and Prowse had the honour to signal to Henry Blackwood, commander of the British frigate squadron, that the Combined Fleet had hoisted topsails and was coming out of port. In light airs it was not until the next day that the enemy fleet cleared Cadiz and *Sirius* had to sail smartly away to avoid being taken: her captain's log records that 'one of the enemy's squadron fired a broadside at us'.

There is some debate as to William Prowse's origins, but he was born in Stonehouse, Plymouth and his lieutenant's passing certificate shows that he joined *Dublin* (74) in November 1771. One source says that he was raised as a child on a trading vessel and it is implied that he was of humble birth.

In 1776 Prowse transferred to *Albion* (74, Captain George Bowyer), rated 'able', midshipman, and then master's mate. He fought at the Battles of Grenada, Martinique and the Saintes, where he was severely wounded in the head. After passing for lieutenant in 1782, he served on the North American station in the frigate *Cyclops* (38).

During the peace that followed Prowse served under Robert Calder in *Barfleur* (98) and *Stately* (64).

In July 1793 Prowse's first patron, now Rear-Admiral Bowyer, hoisted his flag in *Prince* (90, Captain Cuthbert Collingwood), and in January 1794 he and Collingwood transferred to *Barfleur* (98) in which they took part in Lord Howe's victory at the Battle of the Glorious First of June. Lieutenant Prowse had followed Bowyer and at the battle he was again severely wounded, this time by a large shot which tore the flesh from his thigh and disabled the gun which he was in the act of

Nothing remains of Prowse in St Pancras Church, London, only this nearby street name.

pointing, while Bowyer lost a leg and fell into the arms of Collingwood.

Prowse was made commander in 1796 and at the Battle of Cape St Vincent on 14 February 1797 his *Raven* (16) was one of the repeating ships. His commander-in-chief, possibly advised by his captain of the fleet, who was Robert Calder, thought well enough of Prowse to make him post-captain and to give him command of one of the Spanish prizes, the mighty *Salvador del Mundo* (112). When in July 1800 the newly promoted Calder hoisted his flag in *Prince*, he took Prowse as his flag captain. The partnership lasted two years until in August 1802 Prowse was given command of *Sirius* (36).

Prowse was not content with his role as mere repeating frigate at Calder's Battle of Cape Finisterre in July 1805 and daringly attempted to cut out a Spanish treasure galleon which was being towed by the Franco-Spanish fleet, but he was thwarted by the arrival through the mist of the enemy van.

As a frigate at the Battle of Trafalgar, *Sirius* was stationed on the windward side of the weather column where she was expected to repeat signals and to assist ships in distress. The frigate commanders waited on board *Victory* until shot began to pass over her, when Nelson sent them back to their ships. (However, one account states that Prowse was delayed on board the *Victory* and did not return to *Sirius* until the battle was over.) Following

the battle *Sirius* took the crippled *Temeraire* (98) in tow. As she did so there was still firing from the tops of the French *Redoutable*. In a letter written by *Sirius*'s master, William Wilkinson, to his uncle who lived in Dublin, Wilkinson claimed that the sharpshooter who mortally wounded Nelson was shot by the marines of *Temeraire*:

> We [*Sirius*] towed the *Temeraire* out from between two French line of battle ships that had struck to her. One of them, the *Redoutable*, was engaged some time by the *Victory*, and it was one of the villains on board her that shot Lord Nelson from out of her Top. And when alongside of the *Temeraire* they threw a stink pot on board her which was near blowing up the three ships. The [French] officers called out for Quarters and desired the men in the Top to cease firing, but they killed several of the *Temeraire*'s men notwithstanding but when they surrendered the Marines shot everyone as they came down from the Tops and among them the villain that shot Lord Nelson.

Research shows that William Prowse was uncle to Charles Adair, the captain of marines who had been shot in *Victory* a few minutes before Nelson, and that also serving in *Sirius* was Master's Mate William Adair, Charles's brother. So it seems likely that shooting the men from *Redoutable*'s tops was as much to revenge Charles's death as Nelson's.

Following Trafalgar, Prowse was in the Mediterranean under Collingwood, when in April 1806 he fought and won a bitter action 'within pistol-shot', against a superior force at the mouth of the Tiber, and after a two-hour action captured the French ship-corvette *Bergére* (18) along with three brigs and five gun vessels, but unfortunately his nephew William Adair was killed.

Between 1810 and 1813 he commanded *Theseus* (74), seemingly without further incident. Prowse died unmarried in 1826, when his estate was split between his five surviving sisters.

Rear-Admiral William Prowse was buried in St Pancras New Church.

NICK SLOPE

↣ REDMILL ↢

Robert Redmill (1758–1819) was the son of Lawrence and Mary Redmill of Stamford, Lincolnshire. From the terms of his will, the Stamford connection seems to have remained strong throughout his life. It is not known when he joined the Navy, but he was made acting lieutenant on 24 December 1783 and it is probable that he had fought in the American War of Independence.

In June 1786 he and a fellow naval officer and friend, George Blake, made one of the early balloon flights in England, remaining aloft for more than six hours. They thought they might reach France, but the wind changed direction and they landed near Yalding in Kent, where a crowd of 500 gathered to witness their descent to a field known for long afterwards as Air Balloon Field.

On 5 May 1791, at St Martin's in the Fields, Redmill married the well-connected Susannah Douglas. Redmill and his wife had one child who died in infancy; the marriage appears not to have been a happy one.

Redmill was appointed commander in 1795 and given the fireship *Comet* (14). He was present at Vice-Admiral Hotham's inconclusive encounter off the Hyères Islands on 13 July 1795 (in which Nelson commanded the *Agamemnon* (64), but was not mentioned in Hotham's dispatch. However, in October 1796 he was entrusted with Sir John Jervis's dispatches from the Mediterranean in the hired cutter *Fox* and was made captain on 16 December 1796.

In 1799 he was given his first command as captain, *Delft* (64), the former Dutch *Hercules*, in which he was to remain until 1802. *Delft* carried troops to Sir Ralph Abercromby's invasion of Egypt in 1801, when Redmill and Thomas Louis of *Minotaur* (74) gave covering fire from armed launches against the French who vigorously opposed the landings. Redmill remained off the coast of Egypt until September 1801 and was awarded Sultan Selim III's gold medal.

On 16 June 1805 Redmill was given *Polyphemus* (64) and on 21 October 1805 she stood eighth in Collingwood's lee division. Although recently recoppered and accounted a fast sailer, the *Polyphemus* did not engage until about 2.30 in the afternoon, but thereafter fought the French *Berwick* (74) and the Spanish *Argonauta* (80) and drew some of the fire from Hargood's dismasted *Belleisle* (74). Ordinary Seaman Henry Blackburn told his mother that *Polyphemus* 'lay alongside of the *Achille* until we dismasted her and set her on fire and about six she blew up'. The inventory taken by Master's Mate Samuel Wise reveals that she expended no less than 1,000 24-pounder shot and 900 18-pounder. *Polyphemus* was relatively little damaged, with nine men wounded and two killed. Redmill was temporarily struck down by a recurrence of an old illness (which seems to have recurred throughout his career) and his first lieutenant, George Moubray, took command while *Polyphemus* took *Argonauta* in tow, but on the 24th she was required to tow the badly damaged *Victory*. Gales on the evening of the 25th nearly caused the *Victory* to run into *Polyphemus* and at 6pm the hawser had to be severed. However, late in the afternoon of the 29th Redmill, now back in command, took the French *Swiftsure* in tow, one of only four prizes to survive the battle and the storm, and he finally reached Gibraltar.

Polyphemus reached Spithead on 22 December 1805 and was quickly refitted, being back on station in early March 1806 after which she captured two valuable Spanish ships, *Estrella* and *San Pablos*. Redmill was still in command when on 14 July 1806, under Commodore Sir Samuel Hood and cruising off Rochefort, *Polyphemus*'s boats under the command of Lieutenant Edward Reynolds Sibly cut out the brig-corvette *César*. Owing to the apparent recurrence of his old illness, Redmill was superseded in *Polyphemus* in September 1806.

He spent his last months with his illegitimate son, William Redmill Craddock (or Cradock), the landlord of the Swan Inn in London Colney in Hertfordshire, where he died on 19 February 1819 and was buried in the churchyard of St Nicholas's Church, Stevenage, although it appears that no monument or headstone has survived.

In his will he provided for his relations in Stamford, but excluded his estranged wife Susannah. She challenged the will unsuccessfully, and it was admitted to probate in 1821.

One of his executors, Thomas Renouard, had been a midshipman in *Pandora*, which had been sent to track down the *Bounty* mutineers. Renouard's own epic voyage in the *Matavy* tender, which was separated from the *Pandora* and had to make her own way from the mid-Pacific to Java, was on a par with William Bligh's famed open-boat voyage. It is ironic that Redmill's ultimate successor as captain of the *Polyphemus* was *Bounty* mutineer Peter Heywood, who had been captured by the *Pandora*, shipwrecked, brought home, tried, condemned to death and subsequently reprieved.

MARK WEST

Rotherham died frustrated and friendless, but 'a brother officer' erected this marble tomb and a memorial inside the church of St Mary Magdalene, Bildeston, Suffolk.

→ ROTHERAM ←

Edward Rotheram (1753–1830) sometime spelt Rotherham, was a doctor's son born in Hexham, Northumberland, and educated at Head School, Newcastle upon Tyne, before going to sea in a collier.

Rotheram entered the Royal Navy in April 1777 at the late age of twenty-four, joining *Centaur* (74), serving under four captains as able seaman, midshipman and master's mate, and was present at the First Battle of Ushant. In 1780 he moved to *Barfleur* (98, Captain Benjamin Hill), flagship

of Samuel Barrington, and later that year as acting lieutenant to *Monarch* (74, Captain Francis Reynolds). *Monarch* was in Sir Samuel Hood's squadron in the Battles of Martinique, off the Chesapeake in 1781, at St Kitts in January 1782, and in Rodney's victory at the Saintes in April 1782.

He was unemployed 1783–7, during which time he married Dorothy Harle of Newcastle, before finding a berth as a lieutenant in *Bombay Castle* (74, Captain Robert Fanshawe). He then struggled to find steady employment until he met Captain Thomas Rich and under him he served in *Culloden* (74), *Vengeance* (74) and, as first lieutenant, again in *Culloden*. At the Glorious First of June in 1794, Rotheram commanded one of the British boats which helped save many of the French from *Vengeur* before she sank.

Rotheram was promoted but it was some months until, in January 1795, he was given the storeship *Camel* to command in the Mediterranean, and in June 1800 the sloop *Hawke* in the West Indies. He returned home in *Lapwing* (28), which he commanded until she paid off in 1802.

So far Rotheram's career had been workmanlike, but without any of the star qualities of his contemporaries. He was also older than many of his equals in rank, and seems not to have attracted much patronage.

Now in December 1804, after two years ashore, Rotheram's career received sudden acceleration to

Collingwood Collecting his Fleet the Morning after the Battle by Wyllie, from a watercolour by Lieutenant Colonel James Fynmore RMLI, the last surviving officer of the Battle of Trafalgar. Sixteen-year-old Fynmore was a Volunteer 1st Class in HMS *Africa* (64) where his father, also called James, commanded the Royal Marines, of whom there were eighty-seven in Henry Digby's well-manned ship. Young James later also entered the Royal Marines and in 1816 was a second lieutenant in HMS *Hebrus* at the Bombardment of Algiers. The inset photograph is of James Fynmore aged ninety-two; he died in 1887.

command of *Dreadnought* (98), as flag captain to fellow North Countryman Vice-Admiral Cuthbert Collingwood. Sadly, after a few months he no longer impressed Collingwood who wrote, 'He is a man of no talent as a sea officer, and of little assistance to me.' Nevertheless, when on 10 October 1805 Collingwood shifted into *Royal Sovereign* (100) Rotheram went with him. Nelson detected the tension between Collingwood and Rotheram and when Collingwood came alone for dinner, Nelson sent the boat back for Rotheram, telling both men, 'In the presence of the enemy, all Englishmen should be as brothers.' Awkwardly, Collingwood preferred to leave the management of his flagship to Lieutenant John Clavell, who he called 'my right arm and the spirit which puts everything in motion', telling Nelson, 'Mr Clavell wants none [appointment] as his commission moves with me.'

Nevertheless, *Royal Sovereign* fought gallantly at Trafalgar where she led the lee division into action and was hotly engaged. Rotheram dressed for the occasion in an oversized cocked hat, which he claimed he always wore when fighting. The newly coppered *Royal Sovereign* was a fast sailer, broke the Franco-Spanish line astern of the towering *Santa*

Ana, and engaged her so fiercely that Collingwood called out, 'Rotheram, what would Nelson give to be here!' unaware that Nelson at about the same time was remarking, 'See how that noble fellow Collingwood carries his ship into action!'

After the battle, Collingwood appointed Rotheram to *Bellerophon* (74), whose captain had been killed, while Cumby remained her first lieutenant, and he stayed in command of *Bellerophon* until she paid off in 1808. Rotheram's older brother, John, had studied in Sweden under Carl von Linné, the founder of modern taxonomy, and was a distinguished professor of natural philosophy at St Andrews University. Perhaps this inspired Rotheram to make his own unique attempt to classify his ship's company. There are other, occasional analyses by captains who researched their people by nationality and former trade, but Rotheram went further and listed height, colour, shape of faces, dialect, tattoos, scars, injuries, family background and previous occupations ashore, which revealed men from every walk of life.

In April 1807 he was court-martialled for unacceptable conduct towards his lieutenants and the chaplain, and reprimanded. 'I was sorry to hear of poor Rotheram,' wrote Collingwood again,

'Though I think him a stupid man I was in hope he might have gone on in the ship I put him in.' After Rotheram left *Bellerophon* in June 1808, he was never employed at sea again.

His actions at Trafalgar were rewarded with the naval gold medal and a sword from the Lloyd's Patriotic Fund, but Rotheram was not content even when he was appointed CB in 1815, and he campaigned angrily but unsuccessfully for a knighthood. He died a widower in 1830 in Bildeston, Suffolk, where he was buried.

SIM COMFORT

⇸ RUTHERFURD ⇷

William Gordon Rutherfurd (or Rutherford) (1765–1818) was born in Wilmington, North Carolina, in 1765 and entered the Royal Navy in August 1778 on board *Suffolk* (74), following an education at Edinburgh and St Andrews Universities and spent thirteen years on different ships' books, but presumably not all of them at sea, before passing for lieutenant in September 1793. He received his lieutenant's commission in January 1794 and served in *Boyne* (98), the flagship of Vice-Admiral Sir John Jervis during the British invasion of Martinique in 1794. Rutherfurd commanded a detachment of sailors ashore and led a storming party which captured the important post of Monte Mathurine. Following this action Rutherfurd was made commander in July 1794, captain in November 1796 and it is around this time that he married. He took part in the capture of the Dutch island of Curaçao in 1800 and served for some time in the West Indies and assisted the British blockade of the French Atlantic ports. In 1805 he was appointed to command *Swiftsure* (74) in which capacity he served during the Trafalgar campaign and subsequent battle.

At the Battle of Trafalgar *Swiftsure* was the tenth ship in the British leeward column commanded by Collingwood. As she reached the enemy line, the dismasted British *Belleisle* (74) was being fired on by three enemies; *Swiftsure* gave her a rousing cheer and then poured a devastating broadside into the stern of one of the *Belleisle*'s tormentors, the French *Achille* (74). *Achille*'s mizzen mast quickly went by the board and fire broke out in her foretop. Soon she was ablaze and, despite the danger of explosion and the fire setting off the French guns, Rutherfurd sent the *Swiftsure*'s boats aided by those of the *Prince*, *Pickle* and *Entreprenante* to rescue as many men as they could. *Swiftsure* lost two men killed and several wounded during this mission, but succeeded in rescuing many of the *Achille*'s crew. Shortly afterwards, *Achille* exploded killing the remaining crew on board.

After the battle *Swiftsure* took the French prize *Redoutable* in tow. However, as the gale increased it became clear that the *Redoutable* was sinking and, after rescuing as many men as he could, Rutherfurd cut *Swiftsure* free. *Redoutable* then sank taking around three hundred of her French crew down and with them went five Swiftsures.

In 1814 Rutherfurd was appointed captain of Greenwich Hospital and made Companion of the Bath in 1815. Captain William Rutherfurd died at Greenwich on 14 January 1818 and was buried in St Margaret's, Westminster, where a tablet was erected to his memory and that of his wife Lilias, who died in 1831.

NICK SLOPE

STOCKHAM

John Stockham (1765–1814) is one of the more elusive of Nelson's Band of Brothers, who has been unfairly ignored by some historians. It is known that his family were from Exeter and that in two centuries they never moved more than a few miles from the city centre: presumably it was trade which kept them there. Stockham was baptised, married and buried at St Sidwell's, the shrine of a local saint.

How, when and where he joined the Royal Navy is not known, but he was promoted lieutenant on 29 April 1797, at thirty-two years old, when many newly made lieutenants were in their late teens or early twenties. So, either he was in the Navy before the end of the American War of Independence and lacked 'interest', or maybe he served in the merchant navy, possibly the East India Company. Whatever his background, his competence was recognised by Nelson in the early months of 1801 when he served briefly as a lieutenant in *San Josef* (74), a Spanish prize from the battle of Cape St Vincent. When Nelson shifted his flag to *Elephant* in March, he took Stockham with him and so Stockham became a veteran of the Battle of Copenhagen.

Stockham was married twice, first in 1795 to Betty Viney, and second in 1803 to Martha Collett, both local Exeter girls, of course.

Stockham does not reappear at sea until after the Peace of Amiens, by which time he was first lieutenant of *Thunderer* (74, Captain William Lechmere), at the Battle of Cape Finisterre in July 1805. The battle was a tactical and strategic success, which prevented the junction of the Franco-Spanish fleet with French ships at Brest, but the admiral, Robert Calder, was criticised in the press for not having won an even more decisive victory. Calder insisted upon returning to England to be court-martialled, and took Lechmere with him as a witness. *Ajax*'s Captain William Brown also opted to return to testify in *Calder's* defence, and this left their first lieutenants in command. Philip Durham, captain of *Defiance* (74), declined a similar request from Calder.

Not long before this, Stockham had written to Nelson, requesting a transfer to serve in *Victory* as a lieutenant; he now found himself commanding a 74. *Thunderer* was towards the rear of Collingwood's lee division and so was unable to join the action until late, but Stockham made up for lost time by engaging both the Spanish flagship *Principe de Asturias* (112) and the French *Neptune* (84). *Thunderer* suffered only sixteen casualties, and was relatively undamaged, and so in the storm after the battle Stockham was able to offer much-needed assistance to *Revenge* (74) and some other badly damaged ships. *Thunderer*, and others, tried unsuccessfully to make an offing, and seven days later she was the first British ship to make Gibraltar with a prize in tow, the Spanish *San Juan Nepomuceno* (74).

Some have argued that Stockham (and Pilfold in *Ajax*) did not fight their ships as effectively as some of the more experienced captains, but it is an indication of the standards expected – then and now – that to take on two superior enemy ships, to help save one British ship, and to ride out the storm whilst towing a prize, could be seen as under-achievement.

Stockham's promotion to post-captain was confirmed in December 1805: he was granted a gold medal, the thanks of Parliament, a sword of honour from Lloyd's Patriotic Fund, and the freedom of his native city for 'the many services he has rendered his country, particularly when commanding *Thunderer* during the glorious battle of Trafalgar', but after a few more months in command of *Thunderer*, there was no other ship for him.

He lived on half pay in Exeter until his death in 1814 and he was buried in the family plot, since destroyed by a German bomb during the Blitz.

Given his short naval career, Stockham had little opportunity to garner prize-money. He received only a lieutenant's share of the financial rewards for Trafalgar, and died impecunious. So Martha, with several small children, was obliged to ask for charity. When she had produced a marriage certificate and proved 'that she is not possessed of a clear annual income to double the amount of ninety pounds', she was granted a captain's widow's pension.

Like many naval officers Stockham was a Mason, though the evidence is seldom available, but in this case a rarely seen certificate issued by the Grand Elected Masonic Knights Templars to 'Sir [*sic*] John Stockham' has survived.

PETER HORE

→ TYLER ←

Charles Tyler (1760–1835) was born in 1760, the son of Peter Tyler, who was a captain in the Oxford Light Infantry, and Anne Roper, a daughter of Henry, 8th Lord Teynham.

In 1771 the boy was entered on the books of *Barfleur* (90, Captain Andrew Snape Hammond), guardship at Chatham, as captain's servant. When Hammond transferred to *Arethusa* (38), he took Tyler with him to the North American station, and there Tyler served in *Preston* (50) under Vice-Admiral Samuel Graves and later Commodore William Hotham. In 1777 Tyler was invalided for two years by an injury to his left leg which left him with a limp.

Nevertheless, Tyler was made a lieutenant on 5 April 1779 and for the next decade or so served at sea, even during the years of peace between the American War of Independence and the start of the French Revolutionary War, in *Culloden* (74), *Britannia* (100), and *Edgar* (74). He was promoted and in succession commanded *Chapman* (24), then *Trimmer* (14) and next *Tisiphone* (18) on revenue patrols in the Irish Sea and the Channel.

He was promoted in 1790 to post-captain. He was in command of *Meleager* (32) at the occupation of Toulon and the reduction of Calvi where Hood gave him command of *San Fiorenzo* (40). Formerly the French *Minerve*, she had been sunk at San Fiorenzo in Corsica by British batteries on 19 February 1794 but chiefly through Tyler's efforts she was raised and made serviceable. Over the next few years Tyler became close to Nelson.

His next command in February 1795 was *Diadem* (64) in which he was involved in the Battle of Genoa which led to the capture of the French *Ça Ira* and *Censeur*.

However, Tyler's time in *Diadem* was marked by another issue. His authority was challenged by a detachment of soldiers, in lieu of marines, under one Lieutenant Gerald Fitzgerald. Fitzgerald held that he and his men were outside naval control and he showed contempt to Tyler. Tyler complained and Fitzgerald was court-martialled by a board consisting of four admirals and nine post-captains, which Fitzgerald refused to recognise. He declined to defend himself and was cashiered. The Duke of York took the matter up and gave an order that soldiers serving in men-of-war should not be subject to naval discipline but should be sent ashore and tried by a military court. Admirals and captains met in Portsmouth to 'consider the situation', they argued that it was subversive of all discipline and contrary to an Act of Parliament, and the government 'very wisely decided that no alteration should be made to the naval Articles of War and that officers and privates of the army, serving in HM ships should be subject to the laws of naval discipline'.

In 1796 Tyler was joined by his son Charles when he removed into *Aigle* (38), and then took several enemy privateers and North African pirates. However, on 18 July 1798 off Tunisia, while carrying dispatches to Nelson, *Aigle* struck a rock off Île Plane, nearly 3 miles due east of Cape Farina, and was lost. Tyler saved his crew and though the loss was attributed to an error in navigation, he was acquitted at court-martial and given *Warrior* (74). At the Battle of Copenhagen on 2 April 1801 *Warrior* was a part of Hyde Parker's reserve squadron. Three weeks later, Tyler received an invitation with brother officers from Nelson to celebrate 'Santa Emma's birthday', though how comfortable he felt at celebrating an event in the life of his friend's absent lover can only be guessed at.

When the Peace of Amiens broke down, Tyler was appointed to the Sea Fencibles, but in February 1805 he commissioned *Tonnant* (80) and was asked for by Nelson for the Cadiz blockade, and so was sent there to join the British fleet.

However, Tyler had an awkward private matter: he asked Nelson to intervene in to extricate his son Charles from disaster. The boy had jumped ship in Malta and, burdened by debt and love for a ballerina, was incarcerated in a Naples jail. Nelson did intercede and unknown to the father, offered to pay for the son's release. Earlier that year, he had also saved the lad from being removed from the lieutenants' list: 'I still hope the young man, who does not want abilities, will recollect himself,' Nelson told Tyler, adding, 'I will not dwell longer upon this very unpleasant subject.' The exasperated father would not have needed being reminded that Nelson had assisted in getting his son on the list in the first place.

At Trafalgar Tyler's *Tonnant* was fourth in Collingwood's line and as *Belleisle* (74) crawled past *Tonnant* the captains exchanged greetings. Tyler exclaimed, 'A glorious day for old England! We shall have one a piece before tonight!' Eventually they were warmly engaged. His first action was to drive off two of the enemy's ships which had crippled *Mars* (74); *Monarca* (74) struck her colours but being unable to surrender to *Tonnant* or any other British vessel, briefly rehoisted her flag. In the meantime, *Tonnant*'s attention was turned to the second ship, the *Algésiras* (74). The two ships collided and the Spaniards made several attempts to board but were repelled, though Tyler was seriously wounded from a musket ball in the thigh. A lieutenant and sixty men took possession of her whilst *Tonnant* now confronted *San Juan Nepomuceno* (74), which also struck her colours but as a prize went to *Dreadnought*. In the storm after the battle, Tyler's prize crew in *Algésiras* were overpowered and the Spaniards made good their escape back to Cadiz with some of his crew as their prisoners.

The Tyler memorial in St Nicholas Church, Glamorgan, is one of the very few in Wales.

At the close of battle, *Tonnant* struggled back to Gibraltar with over seventy casualties on board, including Tyler. He briefly returned to London to recover and received the thanks of Parliament and numerous awards from the nation. He was awarded the naval gold medal and the Lloyd's sword of honour together with a disability pension of £250 before returning to his ship in the Mediterranean.

He was promoted rear-admiral in 28 April 1808 and in May hoisted his flag as second-in-command at Portsmouth before being sent to Lisbon, and was there with Sir Charles Cotton in September to receive the surrender of the Russian fleet as a consequence of the Anglo-Russian War (1807–12). In 1812–15 Tyler was commander-in-chief at the Cape of Good Hope. His active naval career ended in March 1816, though he continued to accrue honours and promotion.

Tyler was twice married, the first time to Anne Pike, daughter of a naval surgeon, Charles Rice, and said to be the widow of 'Captain Pike RN'. Anne died in 1784 and Tyler married his second wife, Margaret, in Pembrokeshire in 1788. Admiral Sir Charles Tyler died at the spa in Gloucester on 28 September 1835.

JOHN GWYTHER

→ YOUNG ←

Robert Benjamin Young (1773–1846) was born on 15 September 1773 in Douglas, Isle of Man, and came from a naval family. He was entered in the books of his father's ship in 1781, but probably did not go to sea until five years later. He passed for a lieutenant in May 1791 although he did not receive his commission until 1796. In May 1795 Young distinguished himself during the capture in a spirited night action by the British *Thorn* (16) of the French *Courier-National* (18). Young further marked himself out in 1795 when he landed 100 British soldiers on the island of St Vincent during the Carib war, in heavy surf and under enemy fire. At the end of the action he found his hat and clothes had been shot through, although he was unhurt.

All that remains of Young's grave at St James', Exeter, after German bombing and postwar redevelopment: the site is now home to the city's football ground.

He was appointed lieutenant in the sloop *Bonne Citoyenne* (20), a captured French vessel. Young served at the Battle of Cape St Vincent in 1797, but a few weeks after the battle he was injured during an action with a Spanish vessel when part of the *Bonne Citoyenne*'s foretopmast was shot away and fell on him. Young recovered to fight further actions against the Spanish in defending Gibraltar. *Bonne Citoyenne* then joined Nelson for the campaign against Napoleon in Egypt which culminated in the Battle of the Nile. Although not present at the battle, the *Bonne Citoyenne* joined the fleet shortly after and assisted with repairs. Young returned to Britain on *Colossus* (74) and survived that ship's wreck off the Isles of Scilly. Young was appointed first lieutenant of *Goliath* (74) and in 1801 during a hurricane in the West Indies the *Goliath* was laid on her beam-ends and lost her masts. Within twenty-four hours Young had her back in order and taking prizes, a remarkable testament to his sea-going skills.

Lieutenant Young was appointed to command the cutter *Entreprenante* (10) and assigned to Nelson's fleet before Trafalgar. Young always claimed that the day before Trafalgar Nelson instructed him to keep the *Entreprenante* close to the *Victory*, as he would be given the task of taking his dispatches. In the event, Vice-Admiral Collingwood sent the dispatches home in the schooner *Pickle* (10). Young was 'mortified' by this decision, as the bearer of such dispatches was guaranteed honours and promotion, and he was bitter about it until the end of his days.

Entreprenante was a small ship and took no direct part in the battle, though when Young saw the French ship *Achille* (74) on fire, he sent her boats to rescue as many of the crew as they could. A total of 161 Frenchmen were packed into the *Entreprenante,* a vessel that only had a crew of 40. *Achille* blew up before more men could be saved. During the great storm after the battle, the overcrowded *Entreprenante* was almost overwhelmed, Young recording in his log 'lost the jolly boat … split the after jack of the mainsail and carried away the topmast … made signal of distress'. Despite this battering, Young took the *Entreprenante* in search of the drifting prizes and alerted the fleet to the fact that the crew of the Spanish ship *Bahama* (74) had recaptured that vessel. This action allowed the *Bahama* to be taken again and a valuable prize kept in British hands. Young then took Collingwood's duplicate dispatches to Faro in Portugal, but had the misfortune to run aground in the river entrance.

Following the Trafalgar campaign, Young continued to serve in *Entreprenante*, assisting in the blockading of the enemy coastline, but due to ill-health left the ship in 1807. He subsequently served in a number of vessels and in 1810 was made commander but was then put on half pay. Young married in 1835 and four years later was given a Greenwich pension.

Commander Robert Young died of heart disease in 1846, leaving his wife Mary and five offspring, and he was buried in St James' Church, Exeter.
NICK SLOPE

Robert Dodd (1748–1815) had his studio six doors from the Admiralty and it is clear that officers returning from battles in distant waters would call at Dodd's, after they had delivered their despatches, to tell him how the battle had been fought and presumably were tipped by Dodd who then hurriedly painted the picture and sold engravings. Sometimes, as others arrived, the pictures were brought up to date.

✦ North Americans in Nelson's Navy ✦

The Royal Navy in Nelson's time was varied and international in composition. Analysis of the Ayshford Trafalgar Roll, a database of some 18,000 officers and men at the Battle of Trafalgar, reveals that:

Approximately 367 came from the USA.

Approximately 58 came from provinces that now form Canada.

Of these, 75 are simply listed as from 'North America' or 'America'.

Of the roughly 425 Americans and Canadians at Trafalgar, 55 per cent are identified as volunteers, 21 per cent as pressed men, and 24 per cent 'unknown'.

At the height of the wars with France, it appears that roughly 2 per cent of the British fleet's personnel consisted of North Americans, ranging from the less skilled men or 'landsmen' to admirals.

It is not surprising that Canadian sailors found their way into the Royal Navy's ranks. However, as a newly sovereign nation, the United States was a quite different matter. After winning their independence in 1783, the Americans were forced to walk a fine line diplomatically between the era's two global superpowers, Great Britain and France. The primary objective of the US government at that time was to stay out of European political and military affairs at all costs, particularly the conflict brewing between Great Britain and France.

However, when the US government attempted to prevent British seizure of American merchant vessels, resulting in the 1794 Jay Treaty, it led to precarious relations with France, which considered the treaty too pro-British in intention. This brought about an undeclared war between the United States and France – taking place primarily at sea – that raged through the late 1790s. Meanwhile, American relations with Great Britain also soured. Manning the ships of the Royal Navy (a three-decker needed some 850 officers and men) was always a challenge. This problem was particularly acute in wartime, when there were rival claims on manpower from the mercantile marine as well as the Army. Short of manpower, the Royal Navy turned to impressment to fill its ranks and routinely conscripted men against their will, including many Americans.

Legally, impressed recruits had to be British subjects, but throughout a global empire, there were multiple interpretations as to who actually qualified as a British national. For instance, it was debatable as to when a British immigrant to the United States stopped being a British subject. The Crown's criterion was 'Once an Englishman, always an Englishman.' Thus foreign sailors fell victim to press gangs on land and were even sometimes captured forcibly on the high seas. The Royal Navy sometimes released individuals who could prove foreign citizenship, but nevertheless thousands were forced to serve against their will. Overall, the issue though more complex than commonly believed, presented an affront to national sovereignty, particularly for the United States.

Estimates vary, but upwards of 2,400 Americans were pressed between 1792 and 1802; around another 7,200 Americans were forcibly seized over the next decade. To try to protect its citizens and also to preserve the pool of American seamen, the US Congress passed legislation, such as the 1796 Act for the Protection and Relief of American Seamen. However, impressment continued and led to several incidents between the British and American governments. This enraged American politicians and was a primary factor in causing the War of 1812. To a lesser extent Canadian sailors were also pressed. Understandably, many pressed American and Canadian sailors deserted at the first opportunity, often fleeing to foreign merchant ships for asylum as well as employment. However, others made a career of the Royal Navy, going on to enjoy distinguished service. For instance, James Sutter Britton, a pressed able-bodied seaman from Charleston, South Carolina, served in *Thunderer* (74) at the Battle of Trafalgar and went on to become a lieutenant, and lived to claim the Naval General Service Medal.

It is likely that a few thousand Americans also joined the Royal Navy voluntarily. For instance, of the 367 American-born sailors at Trafalgar only about 77 or 20 per cent had been pressed while at least 200 or 54 per cent were there voluntarily. Similar proportions of the 58 Canadians present: at least 20 per cent were pressed men while approximately 35 (or 60 per cent) were there as volunteers. Thus volunteering represented another primary path to service in the Royal Navy for Americans as well as Canadians. To be sure, there were many shades of grey within the realm of volunteering for service in the Royal Navy. Some truly volunteered of their own free will, being lured by the attraction of prize-money and adventure. Others volunteered reluctantly, likely seeing no other option if faced with the prospect of impressment. As with North Americans who had been pressed, some volunteers deserted at the first opportunity while others made a career for themselves in the Royal Navy. David Ferris of New York, an able-bodied seaman who served in *Britannia* (100) at Trafalgar, was not discharged until 1831, and James Nipper, an able-bodied seaman from Rhode Island, who served in *Victory* (104) at Trafalgar, continued in the Royal Navy until 1839.

A well-known Canadian volunteer was Richard Bulkeley (1784–1809) of Nova Scotia. His father was a British Army captain with New England roots who had served with Nelson at the 1780 San Juan expedition in Nicaragua, when Bulkeley's father and Nelson became lifelong friends. Bulkeley junior was a midshipman in *Victory* at Trafalgar, and Hardy's aide-de-camp during the battle. He was one of the last individuals to speak to Nelson, the dying admiral instructing Bulkeley: 'Remember me to your father.' Bulkeley went on to serve as a lieutenant in *Garland* (22), but died at Port Royal, Jamaica, on 29 December 1809.

Whether pressed or volunteers, it is difficult to ascertain the specific areas from which the North Americans came, and their recorded places of origin only partly reveal this. For the Canadians, the vast majority hailed from Newfoundland, Nova Scotia, and Quebec. For the Americans, the largest number hailed from the East Coast states of Pennsylvania, New York, Massachusetts, and Virginia, especially the seaport-cities of Philadelphia, Boston, New York, Norfolk, Charleston, and Baltimore.

An interesting question for future research concerns how many of these Americans and Canadians returned home at the end of the war in 1815. Some were likely rootless 'sons of the sea', but many others probably did return to those regions with fascinating wartime stories to tell. For example, Nova Scotia native Sir James Pearl (1790–1840) reached the rank of commander and retired to Newfoundland. A Trafalgar veteran, knighted by King William IV, Pearl became a local celebrity of sorts in his adopted community, which was later named 'Mount Pearl' in his honour. Conversely, some may have married British women and stayed on in Britain. Others may have opted to stay in Great Britain to take advantage of military benefits such as the Greenwich Hospital. Ultimately, more analysis is needed to help answer these intriguing questions.

Whether Americans or Canadians, the majority served on the lower deck. While a few of these sailors would go on to become junior officers, the higher-ranking Royal Navy officers from America and Canada were generally professionals. A few of these individuals came from established British families, and just happened to be born in North America. Usually, this occurred because their father had been stationed there as a British military or government official. More often than not, they quickly left North America at a young age; despite being American-born, they did not have any significant personal connection to that part of the world.

Sir Robert Barrie (1774–1841) and Sir Francis Laforey (1767–1835) were examples of career officers who were North American by accident of birth. Born in St Augustine, Florida, Barrie was the son of a Scottish surgeon who was stationed there in the British Army. Following his father's death in 1775, Barrie returned with his mother to live with her relatives in Preston, Lancashire. As a post-captain, he saw service off North America during the War of 1812 and, in the years following, as a naval commissioner in Canada. Promoted to rear-admiral in 1837, Barrie was made a knight commander in the Royal Guelphic Order as well as the Order of the Bath.

Sir Francis Laforey was born in Virginia to a prominent naval family. His father, John Laforey, was a government official in Antigua, and he went on to achieve promotion to full admiral, as well as elevation to a baronetcy; Laforey has his own entry in this volume.

Although a few North American-born Royal Navy officers such as Barrie and Laforey had little personal connection to their places of birth, several others had much stronger ties to the New World. Generally, they were members of prominent families who had resided in the American colonies for generations, but were forced to flee their homes during the American Revolution because of their Loyalist sympathies. While many Loyalists did stay behind and eventually assimilated into the larger population, roughly 50,000 left the American colonies to live in exile in other parts of the British Empire. While most of them moved to Canada or in some cases to British-held islands in the Caribbean, a few thousand possessed the necessary wealth to seek exile in Britain itself. Life in the British Isles was not easy for these Loyalists, since their prospects were limited and they were generally viewed as outsiders. This contingent of Loyalists ultimately produced several high-ranking, American-born Royal Navy officers.

Although their family fortunes were typically lost or confiscated by US authorities, many of these Loyalist exiles had the connections and influence to obtain quality educations for their sons – a useful step in laying the groundwork for a successful career in that adopted land. One such example was Sir John Wentworth Loring of Massachusetts (1775–1852), who descended from a prominent New England family. The grandson of a Royal Navy commodore and son of the British commissary of prisoners during the American Revolution, Loring grew up in Reading, England. In 1789 he joined the service as a midshipman under the patronage of his uncle, fellow Massachusetts

native Captain John Loring. Loring went on to a distinguished career as a frigate captain, known best for his work in *Niobe* (40), before serving as lieutenant-governor of the Royal Naval Academy at Portsmouth from 1819 to 1837.

Sir Benjamin Hallowell of Massachusetts (1761–1834) and Sir Jahleel Brenton (1770–1834) of Rhode Island were also sons of New England. Jahleel Brenton was highly regarded for his service as flag captain of *Caesar* (80) under Lord Saumarez, as well as for his decisive victory over a French squadron off Naples in 1810, in which he was seriously wounded. He eventually reached the rank of vice-admiral and was created a baronet in 1812.

Hallowell, Ralph Miller and William Gordon Rutherfurd were three captains who were close to Nelson, and have separate entries in this volume. Despite their American roots, Loring, Hallowell, Brenton, Miller, and Rutherfurd spent little, if any, time in their native land following the Revolutionary War.

However, Sir Isaac Coffin (1759–1839) of Massachusetts was a unique case. Although he became a prominent British admiral, he maintained close ties to New England his entire life. Descended from a prominent Boston Brahmin family, Coffin enjoyed a distinguished Royal Navy career, serving in both operational and administrative positions. He was a close friend of both Lord Nelson and King William IV and served as a Member of Parliament. Coffin also spent a great deal of time in his native Massachusetts, particularly around Nantucket. He opened a school there and was awarded an honorary degree by Harvard University in 1826. However, this close association with New England came at a cost, and in the early 1830s he was dismissed as a possible candidate for elevation to the peerage on account of his close American ties.

Overall, the service and experiences of North Americans in Nelson's Navy present a fascinating yet little-explored chapter of British maritime history. Whether they were pressed men, volunteers, or professional naval officers, these thousands of North Americans made a real and lasting contribution to the Royal Navy and helped to secure its ultimate victory over Bonaparte. It is to be hoped that future research will uncover more details about their origins, motivation, wartime experiences, and their fates as veterans following the conflict. As with every other seaman who served in the Royal Navy during this period, they deserve to be remembered, regardless of nationality.

Sean Heuvel

→ The Class of Captains ←

The names of some of the captains who served with Nelson lived on in the Royal Navy's *Captain* class frigates built in the United States of America during the Second World War. The Admiralty originally intended that these ships would be named after the captains who served with Lord Nelson at the Battle of Trafalgar. Only fifteen were so named; however, six others who had fought under Nelson at the Battles of Copenhagen and the Nile were included. The remaining fifty-seven were given names of captains who had fought at the Battles of Camperdown, Cape St Vincent, and the Saintes, or in the Seven Years War and earli-er eighteenth-century wars, and the seventeenth-century Dutch wars. The names of some are obscure, but officers who had distinguished themselves in the American Revolutionary War seem to have been avoided.

Only one name was dropped, this ship being renamed shortly before her commissioning. HMS *Cockburn* was to be named after Rear-Admiral

HMS *Byard*, a Captain class frigate, leaving the builder's yard in Hingham, Massachusetts, in 1943. She was named after Sir Thomas Byard, who commanded HMS *Bedford* at the Battle of Camperdown in 1797. In the Second World War *Byard* was the first Captain class frigate to destroy a U-boat, the *U-841*, on 17 October 1943.

George Cockburn, until the Admiralty's historical branch stepped in and said another name should be selected. Why? Because Cockburn commanded a naval brigade in 1813 which helped capture Washington, DC, and he had led a group of British officers who ate a meal meant for President Madison, looted some items, and then set light to his residence and office. It was the hurried repainting of this building to hide the scars of war which led to it being named the White House. Instead the would-be *Cockburn* was renamed after Captain Thomas Drury.

The *Captains* were acquired as part of the provisions of the Lend–Lease Act passed by the United States Congress and signed into law by President Franklin Roosevelt in 1941. The agreement stipulated that the United States would lease war material to Britain, and with the end of hostilities, the said material would be returned.

In June 1941, as part of the Lend–Lease agreement, the Admiralty formally submitted a request to the United States Navy for 100 American-built escort destroyers for open ocean anti-submarine warfare, and between 1942 and 1944, 78 *Captains,* of which 32 were of the American *Evarts* class and 46 *Buckley* class, were built for the Royal Navy. All, except for those lost during the war, and one used as a test ship, were returned by 1947. This last, HMS *Hotham,* was returned in 1956.

The concept for the type of ship known by the Americans as a destroyer escort (DEs) was based upon the Royal Navy's requirement for an ocean escort and the United States Navy's requirement for a cheap mass-produced small-destroyer type of warship. In 1940 the United States Navy's Bureau of Ships adopted many of the design features of the Royal Navy's escort destroyers, especially the *Hunt* class, into what would become the *Evart* and *Buckley* class DEs. Besides these two, the United States built four other classes of DEs. The total number of all classes completed made the largest number (498) of a single type of surface warship ever built.

The *Captains* were actually two separate classes: the *Evarts* had diesel-electric drive engines, whilst the *Buckleys* had steam-turbine electric drive engines. Both types of power plants drove twin propellers and had twin rudders, making them highly manoeuvrable.

The *Evarts* and *Buckleys* were very similar in appearance. Both were flush-decked, all-welded, steel hulls constructed in prefabricated sections whose 'deckline flowed in a graceful sheer from foc'sle to midships'. This feature gave them considerably more freeboard at the bow than their British counterparts and, unlike their Royal Navy counterparts, the *Captains* 'had a long continuous superstructure from B to X gun'. To accommodate the steam-turbine electric drive, the *Buckleys* were 306ft in length, approximately 16ft longer than the *Evarts* design. This length required a two-foot broader beam as well as adding 200 tons to the *Buckleys'* displacement.

Both classes had similar sensor and weapons fit. They had US-designed radars, British navigational aids, high-frequency direction-finding equipment and sonars. As submarine killers, they possessed an extensive weapons suite: four depth charge throwers, two on each quarter, and two depth charge rails fitted on the stern. They carried 160–200 depth charges. The forward-firing Hedgehog anti-submarine mortar was also fitted.

However, their main gun armament was inadequate. Originally, it was intended that these ships would carry the excellent US-manufactured dual purpose 5in/38-calibre guns, in two single mounts located in the 'A' and 'Y' positions. Unfortunately, these weapons were in very short supply. Instead, both classes carried three US-manufactured 3in/50-calibre guns, in single mounts ('A', 'B', and 'X' positions) and an array of 20mm Oerlikon and some 40mm Bofors guns. The 3in gun lacked the hitting power to penetrate a U-boat's rounded pressure hull. The US-manufactured optical fire-control equipment for the 3in guns added to this inadequacy. They proved near to useless against attacking aircraft.

As these ships were being built, the Royal Navy sent their perspective crews to America on transatlantic ocean liners such as RMS *Queen Mary* and *Queen Elizabeth* from Liverpool to New York. Others were ferried by Royal Canadian Navy escort ships transiting back to Canada. Once in America, the crews began training on the equipment that was unique to these American ships, especially the engineers who had to train on the diesel-electric or steam-electric power plants.

Once these ships arrived in the UK, they were further modified to bring them closer to Royal Navy standards: more AA weaponry (for those ships operating as command ships), depth charges and life rafts, and 'messing arrangements to be brought to RN standards (the end of the unpopular cafeteria system), heads to be brought to RN standards (the end of the embarrassing troughs)'.

Other changes made to ships caused consternation when surviving units were returned to the US Navy: steel internal doors and cabin furniture had been removed and replaced with wooden ones, fireproof curtains, upholstery and bedding covers had been replaced with 'pretty chintz material'. The final complaint levelled against the British was that every ship was plastered with layers of non-fireproof paint.

The role that the *Captains* played during the Battle of the Atlantic was that of long-range anti-submarine escort. Most of them were organised into their own escort groups, comprising up to eight ships; usually four *Evarts* to four *Buckleys*: the *Buckleys* were faster and took less time to rejoin a convoy after hunting a U-boat.

In their primary role as convoy escorts and/or members of specialised hunter-killer groups, the *Captains* succeeded in sinking thirty-four U-boats and damaging many more. Thirteen U-boats were sunk during the first eight months of 1944, with most of the sinkings occurring in the Western Approaches to the British Isles and the English Channel.

Because of the robustness of their design, the *Captains* took on other roles that were not intended for ASW ships. For Operation Neptune, the invasion of France, several of the class were converted to headquarters ships and others to Coastal Forces Control Frigates (CFCFs) which were responsible for sinking at least twenty E-boats and damaging many more.

Despite the successes of the class, there were numerous losses. Of the seventy-eight ships, seven were sunk and eight written off as constructive total losses, approximately one-fifth of the class. Some fell victim to the German T–5 *Zaunkönig* ('Wren') acoustic torpedo that would home in on the sound of a ship's propeller. Others were lost defending the English Channel against attempts by German U-boats to interdict Allied shipping sailing to Northern France. Over 700 men lost their lives and hundreds more were wounded in these sinkings.

That was the price of the *Captain* class doing their job. However, the kill ratio of submarines to escorts was less significant in the brutal mathematics of the Battle of the Atlantic than the thousands of merchant ships, carrying the stuff needed to keep Britain alive and then to be used as a platform for the liberation of Europe, which arrived safely in British ports. In the proud tradition of dedication and heroism of Nelson's Band of Brothers, the *Captain* class acquired battle honours for the Arctic, Atlantic, Biscay, English Channel, Normandy, North Foreland and Walcheren.

On 17 April 2005, a memorial was dedicated at Britain's National Memorial Arboretum to the *Captain* class and to those killed. Nelson would have been pleased.

JOHN RODGAARD

Acknowledgements

This volume, *Nelson's Band of Brothers*, extends the work undertaken by the late Colin White and his team and published by Chatham Publishing as *The Trafalgar Captains* in 2005.

This editor is indebted to John Curtis, Randy Mafit and Richard Venn for their research into the Band of Brothers, and also to the many members of the 1805 Club who submitted survey forms and photographs. All this material is in the archive of the 1805 Club and I gratefully acknowledge the efforts of others on which *Nelson's Band of Brothers* is built, and the club's generous granting to me of unlimited access to this archive.

I would also like to draw to the reader's attention to Rif Winfield's *British Warships in the Age of Sail 1793–1817*, Patrick Marioné's *Complete Navy List 1793–1815*, and Pam and Derek Ayshford's *Ayshford Trafalgar Roll*. Each of these works represents decades of painstaking research, preparation and presentation of information and each is an indispensable yardstick by which all others must be judged. Without them this volume could not have been completed, and I and the naval history community in general owe Pam and Derek Ayshford, Patrick Marioné and Rif Winfield a huge debt of gratitude.

Also, I should like to mention the late Michael Philips for his database *Ships of the Old Navy*, now hosted on the *Age of Nelson* website, and Cy Harrison for his developing website *Threedecks* and I should like to thank them both for their unique contribution to the record of naval history.

I am particularly grateful to many other kind individuals who have unstintingly offered their expertise and advice to the project of this new *Nelson's Band of Brothers*, and especially Sim Comfort, Anthony Cross, John Curtis, Mark Eddon, Ray Eddy, Michael Nash, Patrick Marioné, Bob O'Hara, Rob Powell, Matthew Prince, Peter Warwick, Mark West, and the executors of the literary estate of Colin White. I would like to pay special thanks to Peter Turner, a recent member of the 1805 Club, who as well as being a contributor has assisted me as researcher and copy-reader at every stage of preparing this volume.

The contributors who have undertaken original research on their subjects and who have entered into a dialogue with their editor also deserve special thanks. This has been an international effort which has drawn in students and sages from Britain, Canada, Germany, Gibraltar, Malta, Spain, Sweden, and the USA. The contributors' names are listed in the notes which follow these acknowledgements, and I would like to record my warmest thanks to each and every one of them.

A special thanks to the overseas contributors, including Liam Gauci of the Malta Maritime Museum and to the estate of Edward Parslow for access to documents deposited there.

Thank you too to the vicars, vergers, wardens, parish councillors and parishioners of the churches throughout Britain and abroad who have enabled the images in this volume to be gathered, especially Val Little, Theresa Bowen, Christine Morgan, Alan Weedon, Jim Butterworth and Alexandra Aslett; the Revd Paul Owen at St Leonard's Church, Seaford; the Dean and Chapter of St Paul's, London; the Friends of the Canongate Kirkyard, Edinburgh; Ranjit Rai and Ravi Katari in India and the Reverend Krubha, St Mary's Church, Fort George, Chennai; Susan Landreth and Zane Pearson and the Rector and Wardens of St James' Church, King Street, Sydney, NSW; John-Dominic Curran and the Revd Martyn Davies of St Nicholas' Church, St Nicholas, Glamorgan; and to the householders and landowners, who have given permission for access to their churches and property for photography and the reproduction of images in this volume.

No work could be complete without the interest, energy and enthusiasm of a first-class publishing and editorial team, and I should like to thank Julian Mannering, Kate Baker, David Rose, Donald Sommerville and Stephanie Rudgard-Redsell.

However, all errors of commission and omission are mine and mine alone.

PETER HORE

Contributors

James Norwich Arbuthnot MP a descendant of James V of Scotland through his mother, Margaret Jean Duff; **Elizabeth Baker** former WRNS, and a member of the Nelson Society; **Tony Beales** IT consultant, company director and descendant of Charles Mansfield; **Tito Benady** Gibraltarian, retired London reinsurance underwriter, historian of the Rock, and FRHS; **Leslie H Bennett** born in England, broker and underwriter in California, biographer of Henry Blackwood; **Judy Collingwood** descended from Cuthbert Collingwood's youngest brother, John, international secretary, archivist and historian; **Sim Comfort** ex-USN, researcher, author and publisher of the age of fighting sail; **Robert Covert** third great-grandson of Francis Laforey, ex-US Army, longest serving CEO of an independent hospital in Michigan; **Anthony Cross** owner of Warwick Leadlay Gallery, with over 35 years' experience in his twin subjects – Nelson and Greenwich; **Henry Digby** a descendant of Henry Digby, an international banker who has researched the family archives with his father; **Bryan Elson** a retired captain RCN, whose books include a biography of Benjamin Hallowell; **Lars Ericson Wolke** professor of military history in Stockholm and in Åbo, Finland, who has written more than thirty books on the history of the Baltic; **Kenneth Flemming** former engineer in the RN, Tesco manager and wholesale food distributor, a founder member, life member and vice-president of the 1805 Club, and editor of the *Kedge Anchor*; **Charles Alan Fremantle** ex-RN, the last of a continuous line of Fremantles who served in the Royal Navy since 1777 and family historian with access to the comprehensive family archive loaned by his cousin Lord Cottesloe to the Buckinghamshire County Council; **Liam Gauci** author and since 2007 curator of the Malta Maritime Museum; **Agustín Guimerá** Canary-islander, who organised the bicentenary of the British attack on Tenerife in 1997, and research fellow at the Spanish National Research Council; **John R Gwyther** retired civil engineer, painter, and expert on the archipelago of La Maddalena, one of Nelson's favoured anchorages; **Christer Hägg** formerly of the Royal Swedish Navy, helicopter test pilot, former naval attaché in Washington DC, flag captain and chief of staff in the Swedish Fleet, and marine artist; **Sean Heuvel** author, who teaches Leadership and American Studies at Christopher Newport University, Newport News, Virginia, and is researching North Americans who served in the Royal Navy during the wars with France; **Peter Hore** a retired captain RN, obituarist and author or editor of a dozen books on naval strategy, naval history and biography; **Gillian Knight** school teacher with degrees from Birmingham and the Open University, whose interest in the Georgian Navy was sparked by reading the novels of Patrick O'Brian; **Martin Mosse** Oxford graduate, expert in operational research, and descendant of Robert Mosse who fell at the Battle of Copenhagen; **Bob O'Hara** ex-RN, ex-GCHQ, and professional researcher at The National Archives at Kew; **John Pilfold** the present namesake of John Pilfold; **Rob Powell** photographer, usually to be found chasing interesting subjects along the Thames, who has enjoyed visiting some of England's loveliest villages and churches to record the graves and monuments of Nelson's Band of Brothers; **Philip Robinson** with degrees from the Universities of London and Oxford, he retired in 2007 as the first vice-chancellor of the University of Chichester, his interest is in how ordinary people coped in extraordinary times; **John Robson** mining geologist and later a librarian, his two lifelong interests, maps and Captain James Cook, combined in 2000 when his book, *Captain Cook's World*, was published: he is now map librarian at the University of Waikato in Hamilton, New Zealand; **John Rodgaard** a retired captain USN, intelligence officer, author, North American secretary of the 1805 Club and a senior officer with the Naval Order of the United States; **Hilary L Rubinstein** graduate of the University of Keele and Simmons College, Boston, USA, and doctor of the Australian National University, and biographer of Philip Durham; **Eric de Saumarez** 7th Baron de Saumarez descended from Admiral James de Saumarez and from Philip Broke, lives within pistol-shot of Admiral James's home on Guernsey; **Nick Slope** naval historian and archaeologist, former chairman of the Nelson Society, Honorary Secretary of the Anglo-Israel Archaeological Society, his most recent excavation is on Nelson's Island, Aboukir Bay, Egypt; **Susan K Smith** graduated with a history degree from the University of California at Berkeley. She has written a biography of Nelson and published articles in the *Mariner's Mirror* and the *Trafalgar Chronicle*. **Genevieve St George** New Zealander whose love is history, has sailed the Pacific after Cook, a member of the Nelson Society, a friend of the National Maritime Museum and an angel for the Painted Hall Restoration; **Joe Stone** an independent researcher at Kew, who is reading history at Hull and hoping to continue historical research when he has graduated; **Stephen Tregidgo** worked in the educational services industry until retirement and has been interested in Nelson and the Georgian navy since childhood. He joined the 1805 Club in 2005 and is currently organising a review of memorial and grave sites which have been conserved by the club; **Thomas Richard Troubridge** 7th Baronet Troubridge, spent much of his early life in Malta and Ceylon where his father served in the RN. He joined Price Waterhouse in 1977 where he has had a variety of roles most recently spending four months a year in China and south-east Asia;

Peter Turner member of the SNR and 1805 Club, former consulting engineer, a cartoonist and creator of the AB&OS cartoon strip, who sails through naval history in his armchair; **Peter Warwick** chairman of the 1805 Club. A former investment analyst, he now organises major historical and commemorative events, and is an author and lecturer in naval and maritime history; **Mark West** a Chancery barrister specialising in real property and trust law, deputy judge, and chairman of the Forlorn Hope, a group which organises tours of Peninsular War sites. His articles for the *Trafalgar Chronicle* cover litigation after the Battles of the Nile and Trafalgar and the life of Robert Redmill; **Colin White** author, Nelson expert, chairman of the Official Nelson Celebrations Committee, Director of the Royal Naval Museum, Vice-President of the Navy Records Society and Chairman of the 1805 Club. Colin died in 2008; **Stephen Wood** was a museum curator for twenty-nine years, at the National Army Museum, London and the National War Museum of Scotland. He is a writer on British and French naval and military history as well as on arms and armour; **Jann Markus Witt** author with degrees from Kiel, Germany, the historian of the Deutscher Marinebund, and curator of the Marine-Ehrenmal at Laboe, and lecturer in naval history at the Marineschule, Mürwik; **Toby Young** journalist and educationalist, co-founder of the West London Free School. His mother was the producer, artist and writer Sasha Moorsom.

✦ Sources ✦

Specific sources are listed under each name. In general each entry has been checked for information against the standard works of reference such as William James's *The Naval History of Great Britain*, Laird Clowes's *The Royal Navy*, Marshall's *Royal Naval Biography*, Nicolas's *Dispatches and Letters of Lord Nelson*, O'Byrne's *Naval Biographical Dictionary*, etc, all of which are available online. They have also been checked against contemporary newspaper accounts accessed through The British Newspaper Archive and *The Times* Digital Archive, the Complete Navy List of the Napoleonic Wars 1793–1815 and the Ayshford Complete Trafalgar Roll. Other sources and their abbreviations are:

ADM: Admiralty files in The National Archives at Kew
BBA: the British Biographical Archive, series I and
    II, microfiche set and its companion, the British
    Biographical Index, 1989
Boase, Frederick, *Modern English Biography*, reprint,
    6 vols, Bristol, Thoemmes Press, 2000
Brenton, Captain Edward Pelham, *The Naval History*
    of Great Britain..., 2nd ed, 2 vols, London, Henry
    Colburn, 1837
Campbell, Dr John and John Kent, *The Naval History*
    of Great Britain..., 4th ed, 8 vols, London, 1818
Charnock, John, *Biographia Navalis...*, 6 vols, London,
    R. Faulder, 1794-8
DNB: the *Oxford Dictionary of National Biography*
    (accessed electronically)
Gent Mag: *The Gentleman's Magazine and Historical*
    Chronicle, which under this or like titles ran from
    1731 to 1922
James, William, *The Naval History of Great Britain...*,
    7th ed, 6 vols, London, Richard Bentley, 1898
NC: the *Naval Chronicle*, a British periodical published
    six-monthly in forty volumes between January
    1799 and December 1818, including biographies,
    histories, news, essays, and ballads
NMM: the National Maritime Museum at Greenwich
PROB: Probate files (wills) in the National Archives at
    Kew
Trafalgar Chronicle: yearbook of the 1805 Club

Ball: BBA, I, 60 : 405–416; II, 1275 : 56; DNB; NC vol xxii, p 520; PROB 11/1512; Nicolas see index. See also Lavery (1998). This entry draws also upon papers deposited at the Malta Maritime Museum archives by Mr Edward Parslow
Baytun: BBA, I, 82 : 137–139; II, 1290 : 264; DNB; Marshall, vol ii, p 543, 859, 871; Trafalgar Roll, p 191; ADM 9/1/88; PROB 11/1939
Berry: BBA, I, 101 : 310–348; II, 1303 : 67; Campbell, vol viii, p 352; DNB; Gent Mag (1831), i, p 270; Marshall, vol ii, p 774; Naval Chronicle, vol xv, p 177; Trafalgar Roll, p 266; ADM 6/90/42; ADM 107/11/244; PROB 11/1782
Bertie: DNB; Gent Mag (1825), ii, p 177; Marshall, vol i, p 380; Naval Chronicle, vol xxxvi, p 1;

ADM 107/7/43; PROB 11/1701. See also Ryan (1968) and Voelcker (2008)
Birchall: ADM 6/91/7. The *Bath Chronicle and Weekly Gazette* followed Birchall's career closely, eg 27 June 1793 and 10 November 1796
Blackwood: BBA, I, 114 : 107–114; II, 1313 : 60-62; DNB; Marshall, vol ii, p 642, 802; O'Byrne, p 86; NC, vol. xxxi, p 436; Trafalgar Roll, p 275; PRO ADM 9/1/108; ADM 107/11/174; PROB 11/1811; Nicolas see index. See also Bennett (2005) and Crawford (1999)
Bligh: BBA, I, 118 : 291–312; II, 1315 : 322–324; DNB; ADM 107/6/355; PROB 11/1603. See also DNB entry of Peter Heywood (1772–1831), Alexander (2003); Dening (1992); Mackaness (1951); and Witt (2014)
Brisbane: BBA, I, 148 : 53; DNB; Marshall, vol iii, p 400; ADM 6/91/137; ADM 107/14/83; PROB 11/1731; James, vol VI, p 470. His death and funeral in Sydney was reported in the *Australian* on 23 December 1826
Brodie: ADM 6/185/238; ADM 6/96/9–11; ADM 1/1530/59; ADM 51/1425. His death was reported in the *Morning Post*, 13 May 1811
Bullen: BBA, I, 167 : 372–377; Boase, vol i, col 468; DNB; Gent Mag (1853), ii, p 309; Marshall, vol iv, p 590; viii, p 444; O'Byrne, vol i, p 141; vol ii, p 144 n; Trafalgar Roll, p 39; ADM 9/2/230; PROB 11/2178. See also Dugan (1965)
Capel: BBA, I, 197 : 34–36; Boase, vol i, col 539; DNB; Gent Mag (1853), i, p 540; Marshall, vol iii, p 195; O'Byrne, vol i, p 167; Trafalgar Roll, p 285; ADM 6/95/42, ADM 107/21/135–137, PROB 11/2168. Clayton and Craig (2004); Tracy (2005); Wareham (2012)
Carnegie: BBA, I, 201 : 374–390, 1221 : 185–189; DNB; Gent Mag (1831), ii, p 79; Marshall, vol i, p 198; NC, vol xv, p 441; Ralfe, vol ii, p 400; PROB 11/1789
Clay: BBA, I, 237 : 131–132; II, 1388 : 208; Marshall, vol iv, p 697; O'Byrne, vol i, p 198; ADM 6/92/18; ADM 107/16/45; PROB 11/2032
Codrington: BBA, I, 245 : 92–131; Boase, vol i, col 665; DNB; Marshall, vol ii, p 635, 872; O'Byrne, vol i, p 207; Ralfe, vol iii, p 196; iv, p 489; Trafalgar Roll, p 213; ADM 6/91/151; ADM 107/14/87; PROB 11/2132. See also Codrington (1873)
Collingwood: BBA, I, 251 : 149–288; II, 1396 : 293–297; Campbell, vol viii, p 302; DNB; NC, vol xv, p 353; xxiii, p 350, 379; Ralfe, vol ii, p 336; Trafalgar Roll, p 27; ADM/36/6692; ADM 107/6; PROB 11/1511. See also Hore (2010), Hughes (1957); Warner (1968)
Conn: Trafalgar Roll, p 69; ADM 6/90/57; ADM 107/11/101; PROB 11/1523; the Kentish Gazette 29 June 1810. See also Knight (2005); Sugden (2012); Warwick (2005); White (2005)
Cooke: Campbell, vol vii, p 471; DNB; NC, vol

xvii, p 353; Trafalgar Roll, p 201; ADM 106/3028; ADM 107/7/77; PROB 11/1438

Cumby: Marshall, vol iv, p 966; PRO ADM 6/92/15; ADM 107/16/21; PROB 11/1895. See also Cordingley (2003)

Cuming: Marshall, vol ii, p 847; ADM 107/7/175; PROB 11/1690

Cuthbert: ADM 6/92/122; ADM 107/17/73; ADM 9/2/88; PROB 11/1639; Nicolas iii 61

Darby: BBA, I, 303 : 147; Marshall, vol i, p 268; ADM 6/87/262; ADM 51/ 1262; ADM 107/9/99; PROB 11/1691; Nicolas see index. See also Cordingly (2003)

Devonshire: Marshall, vol. iii, p 411; vi, p 180; O'Byrne, p 202; ADM 6/94/66, ADM 107/19/74PROB 11/1909

Digby: BBA, I, 327 : 7–13; Charnock, vol vi, p 119; DNB; Naval Atalantis, vol i, p 92; NC, vol xi, p 89; Ralfe, vol i, p 189; PROB 11/1556

Duff: Campbell, vol vii, p 478; Marshall, vol xii, p 383; NC, vol xv, p 264; O'Byrne, vol i, p 310, vol ii, p 333; PROB 11/1454

Dundas: BBA, I, 351 : 140; Marshall, vol iii, p 149; Trafalgar Roll, p 294; ADM 6/90/74; ADM 107/11/142; PROB 11/1944

Durham: BBA, I, 354 : 92–105; DNB; Marshall, vol ii, p 450, 867; O'Byrne, vol i, p 318; Ralfe, vol iii, p 38; Trafalgar Roll, p 134; *Edinburgh Magazine*, vol 12, 1799, p 319; *Morning Post*, 23 August 1844; *Hogg's Weekly Instructor*, 11 April 1846, p 99; *The Scotsman*, 20, 27 September 1817, *The Times*, 3 June 1839, *United Service Journal*, May 1844, p 104; Largo Kirk Session Records, 5 April 1790, 12 April 1795. See also Noah (1905)

Fancourt: Marshall, vol i, p 348; ADM 107/6/81; PROB 11/1713

Foley: BBA, I, 413 : 431–436; II, 1478 : 239; DNB; Marshall, vol i, p 363; O'Byrne, vol i, p 367 n; ADM 6/86/42–43; ADM 107/7/42; PROB 11/1811. See also Kennedy (1951); Tracy (1996); and Witt (2005)

Fremantle: BBA, I, 430 : 242; II, 1485 : 320; DNB; O'Byrne, vol i, p 380 n; vol ii, p 422; Trafalgar Roll, p 59; PROB 11/1630. See also Duffy (2005); Fremantle and Glover (2012); Nicolson (2005); Parry (1971); Pocock (2004); Smith (2007); and Wynne (1952). The editor and author are grateful for access to the Fremantle family archives for other references in this entry

Gould: BBA, I, 471 : 209–210; Marshall, vol i, p 339; O'Byrne, vol i, p 417; Ralfe, vol ii, p 483 ADM 107/7/126: Nicolas vol ii, p 464. See also Knight (2005); Lavery (1998); and White (2005)

Graves: BBA, I, 478 : 290–304; DNB; Gent Mag (1814), ii, p 87; NC, vol viii, p 353, 463

Grindall: Trafalgar Roll, p 78; ADM 107/6/201; PROB 11/1631. See also Elliot and Pickersgill (1980)

Hallowell: BBA, I, 505 : 371–377; Campbell, vol viii, p 381; United Service J., 1834, iii, p 374; 1835, i, p 95; DNB; Gent Mag (1834), ii, p 537; Marshall,

vol ii, p 465; Ralfe, vol iii, p 60; ADM 9/1/71; PROB 11/1836. See also Elson (2009)

Hamond: BBA, I, 510 : 343, 511 : 152–156; Boase, vol i, col 1310; DNB; Gent Mag (1863), ii, p 235; Marshall, vol iii, p 170; O'Byrne, vol i, p 455; PROB 11/2054)

Hardy: BBA, I, 516 : 73–91; DNB; Gent Mag (1839), ii, p 650; Marshall, vol iii, p 153; Trafalgar Roll, p 11; ADM 9/2/86; PROB 11/1918; Dorset History Centre D/ASH/B/Z4 and D/RGB; National Maritime Museum AGC/32 and PAR/150. See also Broadley and Bartelot (1906); and Orde (2008)

Hargood: DNB; Marshall, vol i, p 399; ii, p 865; O'Byrne, vol i, p 463 n; ADM 6/88/107; PROB 11/1921. See also Dugan (1966)

Harvey: BBA, I, 524 : 67–73; II, 1532 : 282; DNB; Gent Mag (1830), i, p 365; Marshall, vol i, p 273; Ralfe, vol ii, p 432. See also Adkin (2004); Adkins and Adkins (2007); Allen and Hore (2005); Knight (2005); Messenger (2003); Morris (2007); Whipple (1978); White (2005)

Hatherill: ADM 6/91/51; ADM 51/1350; ADM 107/14/4); PROB 11/1418; NMM CRK/16/1–20. See also Pope (1972)

Hennah: Marshall, vol iv, p 966; Trafalgar Roll, p 123; ADM 1/1914/176 and ADM 1/1941/127 (captain's letters); ADM 6/90/149; ADM 107/11/48; ADM 9/2/323; PROB 11/1810

Hood: BBA, I, 568 : 69–78; Campbell, vol viii, p 386; DNB; Gent Mag (1815), i, p 66, p 566; (1816), i, p 68; NC, vol xvii, p 1; O'Byrne, vol i, p 533; Ralfe, vol iv, p 55. See also Duffy (2005); Hood (1941); Kennedy (1976); MacKenzie (2012)

Hope: BBA, I, 570 : 424–426; II 1555 : 318; DNB; Gent Mag (1831), i, p 639; Marshall, vol ii, p 507; NC, vol xviii, p 269; Ralfe, vol iii, p 122; Nicolas, vol iii, p 465; PROB 11/1786

Inman: Campbell, vol viii, p 293; NC, vol xxv, p 1, ADM 107/8/42, PROB 11/1510

King: BBA, I, 648 : 123–125; DNB; Gentleman's Magazine, Sir Francis Laforey Obituary, October 1835 p 427–8; Marshall, vol i, p 160, vol ii, p 545; O'Byrne, vol i, p 613 n; Ralfe, vol iii, p 126; Trafalgar Roll, p 159; PROB 11/1836

Laforey: BBA, I, 657 : 407; DNB; Marshall, vol ii, p 446; Trafalgar Roll, p 113; PROB 11/1849; US Navy Department Library, British Admiralty Prize Case Books vol i, 1794–1796. See also Heathcote (2005); Martin (1898); Pocock (2005); Taylor (2012)

Lapenotiere: Marshall, vol x, p 384; Trafalgar Roll, p 309; ADM 6/92/170; ADM 107/17/90. See also Allen and Hore (2005); Hough (1973); Portlock (1789)

Lawford: Marshall, vol ii, p 496; ADM 107/6/350; PROB 11/1976

Louis: Campbell, vol viii, p 138; DNB; NC, vol xv, p 177; xvi 209, 214; xviii, p 34; O'Byrne, vol i, p 674 n. See also Louis (1951)

Mansfield: Trafalgar Roll, p 143 ADM 51/945 ADM 51/1185. See also Davis (1811); Mahan (1913)

Martin: Marshall, vol vi, p 290; ADM 51/4531/47; PROB 11/1676.

Miller: DNB; NC, vol ii, p 295, p 500–501, p 580–3; Nicolas, vol i, p 324, vol ii, p 377 and vol vii, p cliv; ADM 6/185/237; ADM 6/89/63; PROB 11/1331. See also Mahan (1918); Buckland (1999); Wynn (1952)

M'Kinley: BBA, I, 722 : 364 : 368; Boase, vol ii, col 637; Marshall, vol iii, p 441; O'Byrne, vol i, p 703; ADM 9/2/178; PROB 11/2147

Moorsom: BBA, I, 784 : 380–381, 784 : 386; Gent Mag (1835), ii, p 321; Marshall, vol i, p 410; Ralfe, vol iii, p 33; ADM 9/1/59; ADM 107/9/105; NMM AGC/M/5

Morris: DNB; Gent Mag (1830), i, p 467; Marshall, vol ii, p 488

Mosse: NC, vol v, p 352–353; ADM 6/87/229, ADM 107/6/77 PROB 11/1363/90; Essex Institute, American Vessels captured by the British during the revolution and war of 1812. See also Manwaring and Dobrée (1935); Millard (1897); Mosse (1955), and the Mosse family papers

Murray: DNB; NC, vol xviii, p 179; ADM 107/7/76; PROB 11/1618. See also Millard (1897); Aldridge (2001)

Nelson: BBA, I, 809 : 208–446, 810 : 1–129, 1234 : 193; II, 667 : 63–65; Campbell, vol viii, p 1; DNB; NC vol iii, p 157; xiv, p 386, 797; xv, p 37, 38, 222; Ralfe, vol ii, p 141; ADM 106/3028/720; ADM 107/6/386. See also Knight (2006); Oman (1947); Sugden (2004 and 2012); etc

Pellew: BBA, I, 863 : 139–140; DNB; Marshall, vol ii, p 454; O'Byrne, vol i, p 892 n; Ralfe, vol iii, p 55; Trafalgar Roll, p 150

Peyton: Nicolas vii p cxliv; PROB 11/1502. See also Lavery (1998) and the Peyton family papers courtesy of descendant Mr Kester Armstrong

Pilfold: DNB; Gent Mag (1835), i, p 322; Marshall, vol iv, p 963; Trafalgar Roll, p 232; ADM 9/2/322; ADM 6/93/173; ADM 51/1573; ADM 52/3557; ADM 107/18/136. See also Hawkins (1998) and the Pilfold family archives

Prowse: DNB; Gent Mag (1826), i, p 46; Marshall, vol ii, p 779; Ralfe, vol iv, p 112; Trafalgar Roll, p 303; ADM 51/1595; ADM 107/45; ADM 107/8/196; PROB 11/1711; *Dublin Journal*, 17 December 1805

Quilliam: Marshall, vol iv, p 962; Trafalgar Roll, p 12; ADM 107/22/161–163; PROB 11/1764); Trafalgar Chronicle (2002); archives of the Manx National Heritage

Redmill: Trafalgar Roll, p 248; ADM 6/23/206; ADM 6/23/391; ADM 9/2/28; NMM, AGC/B/19; NMM, LOG/N/P/2; *The Times*, 8 June 1786; *Caledonian Mercury*, 10 June 1786; *The Times*, 8 November 1786

Retalick: Nicolas, iii p 104, 114–123, iv p 415, vii p clxv; ADM 6/92/199; ADM 107/17/14; ADM 6/351/14

Riou: BBA, I, 932 : 87–88; Campbell, vol vii, p 281; DNB; NC, vol v, p 482; ADM 6/88/175;

ADM 107/8/87; PROB 11/1356. See also Kennedy (2001); Nagle (1988); Tracy (1996)

Rose: Nicolas, iv 305–308, 314, 436, 439, 463, 476, 500; ADM 9/2/150; ADM 107/7/153; PROB 11/1648

Rotherham: BBA, I, 950 : 23–28; DNB; Gent Mag (1830), ii, p 56; Marshall, vol iii, p 298; NC, vol xiv, p 469; Trafalgar Roll, p 29; ADM 9/2/142; NMM, LBK/38. See also Cordingley (2003)

Rowley: BBA, I, 952 : 214–215; Marshall, vol iv, p 683; NC, vol xxvii, p 228; O'Byrne, vol i, p 1012; ADM 6/92/74; ADM 6/185/237; ADM 107/16/77; PROB 11/2036

Rutherford Trafalgar Roll, p 223. ADM 6/92/204, ADM 9/2/20, ADM 107/17/98 PROB 11/1608. See also Clayton and Craig (2004);

Saumarez: BBA, I, 969 : 153–208, 969 : 220–223; Campbell, vol viii, p 394; DNB; Marshall, vol i, p 174; ii, p 864; NC, vol vi, p 85; O'Byrne, vol i, p 1029 n; Ralfe, vol ii, p 373; ADM 107/6/332. See also Anson (1748); Ekins (1824); Lavery (1998); Ross (1838); Shayer (2006); Voelcker (2008); Wilson (2006) and the de Saumarez archives at the Suffolk Record Office and on Guernsey

Stockham: BBA, I, 1044 : 342; O'Byrne, vol i, p 1123; Trafalgar Roll, p 241; ADM 6/352/35; ADM 6/352/35; PROB 11/1560; NMM, BGY/S/5. See also Clayton and Craig (2004)

Sutton: Marshall, vol ii, p 831. Nicolas see index; PROB 11/1808

Thompson: BBA, I, 1078 : 50; DNB; Gent Mag (1828), i, p 563; Marshall, vol i, p 390; ii, p 865; NC, vol xiv, p 1; O'Byrne, vol i, p 1175 n; Ralfe, vol iii, p 344, See also Nicolas

Troubridge: BBA, I, 1096 : 180–197; Campbell, vol viii, p 156; DNB; NC, vol xxiii, p 1; xxxviii, p 356; O'Byrne, vol i, p 1204 n; Ralfe, vol iv, p 397.

Tyler: DNB; Gent Mag (1835), ii, p 649; Marshall, vol i, p 372; O'Byrne, vol i, p 1218 n; Trafalgar Roll, p 87; ADM 107/7/100; PROB 11/1854). See also White (2005)

Upton: ADM 6/91/120; ADM 107/13/1; PROB 11/1664. See also Hardy (1811); Pitt (1851)

Walker: BBA, I, 1124 : 93–96; DNB; Gent Mag (1831), ii, p 270; Marshall, vol ii, p 848, 882; O'Byrne, vol i, p 1239 n; Ralfe, vol iv, p 155.

Watson: Marshall, vol ix, p 3; NC, vol iv, p 240; ADM 9/2/335

Westcott: DNB; NC, vol xii, p 453; ADM 107/6/349; PROB 11/1323

Whitter: ADM 6/92/239; ADM 37/1862; ADM 107/17/104; *Royal Cornwall Gazette*, 11 June 1808. See also Bond (1823)

Yelland: Marshall, vol ix, p 32; ADM 9/2/339; PROB 11/1736). See also Millard (1897)

Young: BBA, I, 1211 : 421–424; Marshall, vol vi, p 403; vii, p 432; O'Byrne, vol i, p 1338; Trafalgar Roll, p 312; ADM 6/91/274; ADM 9/4/1074; ADM 107/15/18; PROB 11/2053

✦ Bibliography ✦

Adkin, Mark, and Clive Farmer, *The Trafalgar Companion: The Complete Guide to History's Most Famous Sea Battle and the Life of Admiral Lord Nelson* (London: Aurum Press, 2005)

Adkins, Roy, and Lesley Adkins, *The War for All the Oceans: From Nelson at the Nile to Napoleon at Waterloo* (New York: Viking, 2007)

Adkins, Roy, *Trafalgar: The Biography of a Battle* (London: Little, Brown, 2004)

Aldridge, Barry, *'My Dear Murray …': Admiral Sir George Murray, KCB and the Ship Hotel, Chichester* (Privately published, 2001)

Alexander, Caroline, *The Bounty: The True Story of the Mutiny of the Bounty* (New York: Viking, 2003)

Allen, Derek, and Peter Hore, *News of Nelson* (Brussels: Seff Editions, 2005)

__, *American Vessels Captured By the British during the Revolution and War of 1812: The Records of the Vice-Admiralty Court at Halifax, Nova Scotia* (Salem, Massachusetts: The Essex Institute, 1911)

Anson, George, eds Richard Walter, Glyndwr Williams, and Benjamin Robins, *A Voyage Round the World* (London: Oxford University Press, 1974)

Ayshford, Pam, and Derek Ayshford, *The Ayshford Complete Trafalgar Roll* (Brussels, Belgium: SEFF, 2004)

Bennett, Leslie H, *Nelson's Eyes: The Life and Correspondence of Vice Admiral Sir Henry Blackwood KCB* (Brussels: Seff, 2005)

'Bicentenary of Trafalgar', *Mariner's Mirror*, 91 (2005)

Bienkowski, Lee, *Admirals in the Age of Nelson* (Annapolis, Md: Naval Institute Press, 2003)

Bond, Thomas, *Topographical and Historical Sketches of the Boroughs of East and West Looe* (London: J Nichols and Son, 1823)

Broadley, Alexander Meyrick, and R G Bartelot, *The Three Dorset Captains at Trafalgar* (London: J Murray, 1906)

Buckland, Kirstie, Ludovic Kennedy, and Ralph Willett Miller, *The Miller Papers* (Shelton: 1805 Club, 1999)

Byrn, John D, *Naval Courts Martial, 1793–1815* (Farnham, Surrey, England: Ashgate for the Navy Records Society, 2009)

Campbell, John, *The Naval History of Britain Including the History and Lives of the British Admirals* (London: John Stockdale, 1813)

Clayton, Tim, and Phil Craig, *Trafalgar: The Men, the Battle, the Storm* (London: Hodder & Stoughton, 2004)

Clowes, W Laird, Clements R Markham, A T Mahan, Herbert Wrigley Wilson, Theodore Roosevelt, and L. G. Carr Laughton, *The Royal Navy* (London: S Low, Marston and Co, 1897), p. Accessed via the internet

Codrington, Edward, *Memoir of the Life of Admiral Sir Edward Codrington, Edited and Abridged By Lady Bourchier* (London: Longmans, Green, 1873)

Corbett, Julian Stafford, *The Campaign of Trafalgar* (London: Longmans, Green, 1910)

Cordingly, David, *Billy Ruffian* (London: Bloomsbury, 2003)

Crawford, Abraham, and Tom Pocock, *Reminiscences of a Naval Officer: A Quarterdeck View of the War against Napoleon* (London: Chatham Publishing, 1999)

Davidson, James D G, *Admiral Lord St Vincent – Saint or Tyrant?* (Barnsley: Pen & Sword Maritime, 2006)

Davis, Joshua, *A Narrative Of Joshua Davis, An American Citizen, Who Was Pressed And Served On Board Six Ships Of The British Navy … The Whole Being An Interesting And Faithful Narrative Of The Discipline, Various Practices And Treatment Of Pressed Seamen In The British Navy, And Containing Information That Never Was Before Presented To The American People* (Boston: B True, 1811)

Dening, Greg, *Mr Bligh's Bad Language: Passion, Power, and Theatre on the Bounty* (Cambridge: Cambridge University Press, 1992)

Desbriére, Edouard, and Constance Eastwick, *The Naval Campaign of 1805* (Oxford: Clarendon Press, 1933)

__, 'Sir Samuel Hood 1762–1814', in *British Admirals of the Napoleonic Wars: the Contemporaries of Nelson* (London: Chatham Publishing, 2005)

Duffy, Michael, *Touch and Take: The Battle of Trafalgar, 21 October 1805* (Shelton, Notts: The 1805 Club, 2005)

Dugan, James, *The Great Mutiny* (New York: Putnam, 1965)

Edwards, Brian, 'Formative Years 1803 to 1805: A Perspective of the Royal Marines in the Navy of John Jervis, Earl St Vincent and Horatio, Lord Nelson', *Royal Marines Historical Society*, Special Publication 31 (2005)

Ekins, Rear-Admiral Sir Charles, *Naval Battles, From 1744 to the Peace in 1814, Critically Reviewed and Illustrated* (London: Baldwin, Cradock, and Joy, 1824)

Elliott, John, and Richard Pickersgill, *Captain Cook's Second Voyage: Journals of Lieutenants Elliott and Richard Pickersgill* (London: Caliban Books, 1980)

Elson, Bryan, *Nelson's Yankee Captain: The Life of Boston Loyalist Sir Benjamin Hallowell* (Halifax, NS: Formac Publishing Co., 2008)

Feldbæk, Ole, *The Battle of Copenhagen 1801* (Barnsley: Leo Cooper, 2002)

Fitchett, W. H, *Nelson and His Captains: Sketches of Famous Seamen* (London: John Murray, 1911)

Fraser, Edward, *The Enemy at Trafalgar* (London: Chatham Publishing, 2004)

Fraser, Edward, *The Sailor Whom Nelson Led: Their Doings Described by Themselves* (London: Metheun & Co, 1913)

Fremantle, John, and Gareth Glover, *Wellington's Voice* (London: Frontline Books, 2012)

Gardiner, Robert, *The Campaign of Trafalgar, 1803–1805* (London: Chatham Publishing, in association with the National Maritime Museum, 1997)

Hardy, Charles, *Register of Ships Employed in the Service of the Honourable the United East India Company from 1760 to 1810* (London: Black Parry and Kingsbury, 1811)

Hawkins, Desmond, *Pilfold: The Life and Times of Captain John Pilfold* (Horsham: Horsham Museum Society, 1998)

Heathcote, T A, *Nelson's Trafalgar Captains and Their Battles* (Barnsley: Pen & Sword Maritime, 2005)

Hood, Dorothy, *The Admirals Hood* (London: Hutchinson, 1941)

Hore, Peter, 'Every Dog Shall Do His Duty: The Biography of Collingwood's Dog "Bounce"', *Trafalgar Chronicle*, (2010)

__, *The Habit of Victory: The Story of the Royal Navy, 1545 To 1945* (London: Sidgwick & Jackson, 2005)

Hough, Richard, *Captain Bligh and Mr Christian: The Men and the Mutiny* (New York: E P Dutton, 1973)

Hughes, Edward, *The Private Correspondence of Admiral Lord Collingwood* (London: Navy Records Society, 1957)

James, William, and Frederick Chamier, *The Naval History of Great Britain* (London: R Bentley, 1837). Accessed via the internet

Kennedy, Ludovic, *Nelson's Band of Brothers* (London: Odhams Press Limited, 1951)

Knight, Roger, *The Pursuit of Victory: The Life and Achievement of Horatio Nelson* (London: Allen Lane, 2006)

Lavery, Brian, *Nelson and the Nile: The War against Napoleon* (Annapolis, Md: Naval Institute Press, 1998)

Le Fevre, Peter, and Richard Harding, *British Admirals of the Napoleonic Wars: The Contemporaries of Nelson* (London: Chatham Publishing, 2005)

Louis, Henry Brackenbury, *One of Nelson's Band of Brothers: Admiral Sir Thomas Louis Bt* (Malta: St Edward's College, 1951)

Mackaness, George, *The Life of Vice-Admiral William Bligh RN FRS* (Sydney: Angus & Robertson, 1951)

Mackenzie, Alexander, *History of the Mackenzies, With Genealogies of the Principal Families of the Name* (Rare Books Club, 2012)

Mackenzie, Robert Holden, *The Trafalgar Roll: The Ships and Their Officers* (London: Chatham Publishing, 2004)

Mahan, A T, *The Major Operations of the Navies in the War of American Independence* (London: Sampson Low, 1913)

Mahan, A T, *The Influence of Sea Power upon History, 1660–1783* (Boston: Little, Brown, 1918)

__, *The Influence of Sea Power Upon the French Revolution and Empire, 1793–1812* (Boston: Little, Brown, 1892)

__, *The Major Operations of the Navies in the War of American Independence* (New York: Greenwood Press, 1969)

Manwaring, G E, and Bonamy Dobrée, *The Floating Republic: An Account of the Mutinies at Spithead and the Nore in 1797* (Edinburgh: Pelican, 1935)

Martin, Thomas Byam, and R Vesey Hamilton, *Letters and Papers of Admiral of the Fleet Sir Thos. Byam Martin, GCB* (London: Navy Records Society, 1898)

McGrigor, Mary, *Defiant but Dismasted at Trafalgar* (Barnsley: Leo Cooper, 2004)

Messenger, Charles, *Unbroken Service* (London: MDA Communications, 2003)

Millard, W S, *The Battle of Copenhagen: Being the Experiences of a Midshipman On Board HMS Monarch, Told By Himself* (Maidstone: W S Vivish, 1897)

Morris, Richard Sidney, *Merchants, Medicine and Trafalgar: The History of the Harvey Family* (Loughton, Essex: Loughton & District Historical Society, 2007)

Mosse, Rev Charles H, *Mosse Family Notes* (Unpublished, 1955)

Murray, Alexander, and Philip Charles Henderson Calderwood Durham, *Memoir Of The Naval Life And Services Of Admiral Sir Philip C H C Durham, GCB, Chevalier De L'ordre Du Merite Militaire De France* (London: Murray, 1846)

Nagle, Jacob, and ed John C Dann, *The Nagle Journal, A Diary Of The Life Of Jacob Nagle, Sailor, From The Year 1775 To 1841* (New York: Grove Press, 1988)

Nicolson, Adam, *Men of Honour: Trafalgar and the Making of the English Hero* (London: Harper Collins, 2005)

Noah, Mordecai, *Travels In England, France, Spain, and the Barbary States, in the Years 1813–14 and 15* (New York: Kirk and Mercein, 1819)

Oman, Carola, *Nelson* (London: Hodder and Stoughton, 1947)

Orde, Denis A, *In the Shadow of Nelson: The Life of Admiral Lord Collingwood* (Barnsley, England: Pen & Sword Maritime, 2008)

Parry, Ann, *The Admirals Fremantle* (London: Chatto and Windus, 1971)

Pitt, William, *The Cabin Boy: Being The Memoirs Of An Officer In The Civil Department Of The HM Navy, Well Known By The Name Of Billy Pitt* (London: Whittaker & Company, 1851)

Pocock, Tom, *Stopping Napoleon: War and Intrigue in the Mediterranean* (London: John Murray, 2004)

Pope, Dudley, *The Great Gamble: Nelson at Copenhagen* (London: Weidenfeld & Nicolson, 1972)

Portlock, Nathaniel, *A Voyage Round The World; But More Particularly To The North-West Coast Of America: Performed In 1785, 1786, 1787, And 1788, In The King George And Queen Charlotte, Captains Portlock And Dixon* (London: John Stockdale, Piccadilly; and George Goulding, Covent Garden, 1789)

Ross, Sir John, *Memoirs and Correspondence of Admiral Lord De Saumarez, Vol I* (Project Gutenberg, 1838)

Rubinstein, Hilary L, *Trafalgar Captain: Durham of the Defiance, the Man Who Refused to Miss Trafalgar* (Stroud: Tempus, 2005)

Ryan, A N, *The Saumarez Papers: Selections from the Baltic Correspondence of Vice-Admiral Sir James Saumarez 1808–1812* (London: Navy Records Society, 1968)

Shayer, David, *James Saumarez: The Life and Achievements of Admiral Lord De Saumarez of Guernsey* (St Peter Port: La Société Guernesiaise, 2006)

Smith, Jane, *The Nelson Monument, Portsdown Hill: A Seamark Re-Discovered* (Portsmouth: The Nelson Society, 2007)

Sugden, John, *Nelson: Dream of Glory* (London: Jonathan Cape, 2004)

__, *Nelson: The Sword of Albion* (London: Pimlico, 2012)

Taylor, Stephen, *Commander, The Life and Exploits of [Edward Pellew] Britain's Greatest Frigate Captain* (London: Faber & Faber, 2012)

Tracy, Nicholas, *Nelson's Battles: The Triumph of British Seapower* (Barnsley: Seaforth, 1996)

__, *Who's Who in Nelson's Navy* (London: Chatham Publishing, 2005)

__, *Trafalgar: An Eyewitness History* (London: Penguin Classics, 2005)

Voelcker, Tim, *Admiral Saumarez Versus Napoleon* (Woodbridge: Boydell Press, 2008)

Wareham, Tom, *Frigate Commander* (Barnsley: Leo Cooper, 2004)

Warner, Oliver, *The Life and Letters of Vice-Admiral Lord Collingwood* (Oxford: Oxford University Press, 1968)

Warwick, Peter, *Voices From the Battle of Trafalgar* (Newton Abbot [England]: David & Charles, 2005)

Whipple, A B C, *Fighting Sail* (Alexandria, Va: Time-Life Books, 1978)

White, Colin, *Nelson the Admiral* (Stroud: History Press, 2010)

__, *Nelson: The New Letters* (Woodbridge: Boydell Press, 2005)

__, *The Trafalgar Captains* (Annapolis, Md: The Naval Institute Press, 2005)

Wilson, Anthony M, *The Happy Warrior: A Life of James Saumarez of Guernsey* (Universal Publishing Solutions Online, 2006)

Winfield, Rif, *British Warships of the Age of Sail, 1793–1817* (London: Chatham Publishing, 2005)

Witt, Jann M, *Die BOUNTY War Sein Schicksal: Das Abenteuerliche Leben Des William Bligh* (Darmstadt: Gebundene Ausgabe, 2014)

__, *Horatio Nelson: Triumph Und Tragik Eines Seehelden; Sein Leben Und Seine Zeit; 1758–1805* (Hamburg: Koehler, 2005)

Wynne, Elizabeth, Eugenia Wynne, and Anne Fremantle, *The Wynne Diaries, 1789–1820: Passages Selected and Edited by Anne Fremantle* (London: Oxford University Press, 1952)

Picture Credits

Index

Index of Ships

All ships are British unless otherwise indicated.

Abbreviations:
Dan = Danish
Dut = Dutch
Fr = French
It = Italian
Port = Portuguese
Rus = Russian
Sp = Spanish
Swed = Swedish
US = American